The Prehistory of Language

STUDIES IN THE EVOLUTION OF LANGUAGE

General Editors
Kathleen R. Gibson, *University of Texas at Houston,*
and James R. Hurford, *University of Edinburgh*

PUBLISHED

The Origins of Vowel Systems
Bart de Boer

The Transition to Language
Edited by Alison Wray

Language Evolution
Edited by Morten H. Christiansen and Simon Kirby

Language Origins
Evolutionary Perspectives
Edited by Maggie Tallerman

The Talking Ape
How Language Evolved
Robbins Burling

Self-Organization in the Evolution of Speech
Pierre-Yves Oudeyer
translated by James R. Hurford

Why we Talk
The Evolutionary Origins of Human Communication
Jean-Louis Dessalles
translated by James Grieve

The Origins of Meaning
Language in the Light of Evolution 1
James R. Hurford

The Genesis of Grammar
Bernd Heine and Tania Kuteva

The Origin of Speech
Peter F. MacNeilage

The Prehistory of Language
Edited by Rudolf Botha and Chris Knight

The Cradle of Language
Edited by Rudolf Botha and Chris Knight

Language Complexity as an Evolving Variable
Edited by Geoffrey Sampson, David Gil, and Peter Trudgill

[For a list of books in preparation for the series, see p. 349]

The Prehistory of Language

Edited by
Rudolf Botha
Chris Knight

OXFORD
UNIVERSITY PRESS

OXFORD

UNIVERSITY PRESS

Great Clarendon Street, Oxford OX2 6DP

Oxford University Press is a department of the University of Oxford.
It furthers the University's objective of excellence in research, scholarship,
and education by publishing worldwide in

Oxford New York

Auckland Cape Town Dar es Salaam Hong Kong Karachi
Kuala Lumpur Madrid Melbourne Mexico City Nairobi
New Delhi Shanghai Taipei Toronto

With offices in

Argentina Austria Brazil Chile Czech Republic France Greece
Guatemala Hungary Italy Japan Poland Portugal Singapore
South Korea Switzerland Thailand Turkey Ukraine Vietnam

Oxford is a registered trade mark of Oxford University Press
in the UK and in certain other countries

Published in the United States
by Oxford University Press Inc., New York

British Library Cataloguing in Publication Data
Data available

Library of Congress Cataloging in Publication Data
Data available

Typeset by SPI Publisher Services, Pondicherry, India
Printed in Great Britain
on acid-free paper by
MPG Books Group, Bodmin and King's Lynn

ISBN 978–0–19–954587–2 (Hbk.)
       978–0–19–954588–9 (Pbk.)

3 5 7 9 10 8 6 4 2

Contents

Preface and acknowledgements

Together with its companion volume—*The Cradle of Language*—this book grew out of a conference held in Stellenbosch, South Africa, in November 2006. The organizers deliberately held the event in the part of the world where modern language is now believed to have evolved. In addition to prominent linguists, psychologists, cognitive scientists, and specialists in artificial intelligence, the conference featured some of the world's leading archeologists, historical linguists, primatologists, and social anthropologists, in many cases bringing specialist knowledge of distinctively African data and perspectives.

Shortly after the conference, we decided to publish not only the contributions from invited speakers but papers selected from the refreshingly wide range of disciplines represented at the event. Chapters dealing more specifically with the African origins of language and culture appear in *The Cradle of Language*. The present volume offers state-of-the-art discussions of more general aspects of language evolution. Both reflect the authors' extensive additional work on their original papers.

The Cradle of Language Conference was organized by Rudolf Botha. It was sponsored by the University of Stellenbosch and the Netherlands Institute for Advanced Study in the Humanities and Social Sciences. We gratefully acknowledge generous financial support from the University of Stellenbosch, the Ernest Oppenheimer Memorial Trust, and South Africa's National Research Foundation; we also warmly thank Connie Park for her dedicated work in compiling, reformatting, and editing the manuscripts.

Chris Knight, London
Rudolf Botha, Stellenbosch

March 2008

List of figures

List of tables

List of abbreviations

ACC	Accusative
AF	Agent Focus
AP	Adverb Phrase
BNC	British National Corpus
C	Complementizer
CP	Complementizer Phrase
D	Determiner
DP	Determiner Phrase
FLB	Language faculty broadly construed
FLN	Language faculty narrowly construed
HPP	Head Preference Principle
LMP	Late Merge Principle
Nom	Nominative
NP	Noun Phrase
OED	Oxford English Dictionary
P	Preposition
PP	Preposition Phrase
Pat	Patient
PF	Perfect
PHON	Mapping to Sensory Motor interface
Pres	Present
S	Sentence
SEM	Mapping to system of thought
SIP	Specifier Incorporation Principle
Spec	Specifier
T	Tense
3P	Third person
TP	Tense Phrase
TOP	Topic marker

uF   Uninterpretable feature
UG   Universal Grammar
V   Verb
v   Little v, or light verb
vP   Light VP
VP   Verb Phrase

Notes on the contributors

Rudolf Botha is Emeritus Professor of General Linguistics at the University of Stellenbosch and Honorary Professor of Linguistics at Utrecht University. In 2001–2 and 2005–6 he was a fellow-in-residence at the Netherlands Institute for Advanced Study. His research includes work on the conceptual foundations of linguistic theories, morphological theory and word formation, and the evolution of language. He is the author of twelve books, including *Unravelling the Evolution of Language* (Elsevier, 2003). He was the organizer of the Cradle of Language Conference held in November 2006 in Stellenbosch, South Africa.

Frederick L. Coolidge, PhD, is a professor of psychology in the Department of Psychology, University of Colorado at Colorado Springs. He conducts research in behavior genetics, personality and cognitive assessment, and the evolution of human cognition. Contact: Psychology Department, PO Box 7150, University of Colorado, Colorado Springs, CO 80933-7150. Email: fcoolidg@uccs.edu.

Ian Cross teaches at the University of Cambridge, where he is a fellow of Wolfson College. He has published widely in the field of music cognition, including two co-edited books. His principal research focus is on music as a biocultural phenomenon, involving collaboration with psychologists, anthropologists, archeologists, and neuroscientists.

Bart de Boer did his PhD in artificial intelligence at the Vrije Universiteit Brussel under the supervision of Luc Steels. He has worked as a postdoctoral researcher for Patricia Kuhl at the University of Washington, and as an assistant professor at the artificial intelligence department of the Rijksuniversiteit Groningen. He is currently working as a researcher on the evolution of speech at the Amsterdam Center for Language and Communication of the Universiteit van Amsterdam under Paul Boersma.

ROBIN DUNBAR graduated from the University of Oxford with a BA in Philosophy and Psychology, and then did a PhD on primate behavioral ecology at the University of Liverpool. He held research fellowships at the Universities of Cambridge and Liverpool, and teaching posts at the University of Stockholm (Sweden), University College London and Liverpool University. He is now Professor of Evolutionary Anthropology and Director of the Institute of Cognitive and Evolutionary Anthropology at the University of Oxford. He is co-director of the British Academy Centenary Research Project (Lucy to Language: The Archaeology of the Social Brain).

WILLIAM D. HOPKINS received a BA in Psychology from the University of Wisconsin at Madison in 1983. He holds an MA (1986) and a PhD (1990) in Psychology from Georgia State University, Atlanta, Georgia. He was Associate Professor of Psychology, Berry College, Rome, Georgia from 1994 to 2006 and has been Associate Professor of Psychology, Agnes Scott College, Atlanta, Georgia since 2006. He has research scientist affiliations at the Language Research Center, Georgia State University, Atlanta, Georgia; Yerkes National Primate Research Center, Emory University, Atlanta, Georgia; and the Great Ape Trust of Iowa.

CHRIS KNIGHT is Professor of Anthropology at the University of East London. He is best known for his first book, *Blood Relations: Menstruation and the Origins of Culture*. His recent research has focussed on the evolutionary emergence of language.

KEVIN LALAND is Professor in Biology at the University of St Andrews. His work on niche construction and gene-culture co-evolution is complemented by experimental studies of social learning, innovation, diffusion, and tradition in fish, birds, and primates.

DAVID A. LEAVENS took a BSc in Anthropology (Honors) from the University of California, Riverside, in 1990; an MA in Anthropology from Southern Illinois University at Carbondale, Illinois in 1993; and a PhD in Biopsychology from University of Georgia, Athens, Georgia in 2001. Since 2000 he has been Lecturer/Senior Lecturer in Psychology at the University of Sussex.

JOHN MITANI received an AB in Anthropology from the University of California, Berkeley, and a PhD in Anthropology from the University of California, Davis. He conducted postdoctoral research at the Rockefeller University, and is currently a professor in the Department of Anthropology, University of Michigan. Mitani conducts field research on the social behavior and vocal communication of apes. He currently directs a long-term project investigating the behavior of chimpanzees at Ngogo, Kibale National Park, Uganda. The Ngogo chimpanzee community generates considerable interest because of its unusually large size, with over 140 individuals.

STEVEN MITHEN is Professor of Early Prehistory and Dean of Science at the University of Reading, UK. Before moving to Reading in 1992, he studied and taught at the Universities of Sheffield, York, and Cambridge. He undertakes archeological excavations in western Scotland and southern Jordan exploring the character of late Pleistocene and early Holocene hunter-gatherer communities, and the transition to the Neolithic and farming economies. Other research interests include the use of computation methods in archeology and the evolution of the human mind, language, and music.

JOHN ODLING-SMEE is the co-author with Kevin Laland and Marc Feldman of a book on niche construction, published by PUP in 2003. He is currently Lecturer in Human Sciences at Mansfield College and the School of Anthropology at the University of Oxford.

SIMONE PIKA holds an MA in Biology and wrote her PhD at the MPI for Evolutionary Anthropology, Leipzig, Germany in collaboration with the Department of Ethology, University of Münster, Germany. She did her first postdoctoral fellowship at the University of Alberta, Canada, and her second postdoctoral fellowship at the University of St Andrews, Scotland. Her research interest centers on the evolutionary roots of language by pin-pointing similarities and differences in signal use in humans, non-human primates, birds, and elephants in captivity and the wild and investigating the underlying processes of social cognition.

TIMOTHY P. RACINE holds a BA in Psychology (Honors)(1998), an MA in Psychology (2000), and a PhD in Psychology (2005) from Simon Fraser

University, Burnaby, British Columbia. He was Assistant Professor in Psychology at the University of Manitoba from 2005 to 2007. Since 2007 he has been Assistant Professor in Psychology at Simon Fraser University, Burnaby, Canada.

Sonia Ragir is a professor of Anthropology, College of Staten Island, CUNY, and a research associate at the American Museum of Natural History, New York City. She has been teaching human evolution and animal play and communication at the City University of New York since 1968. Her publications focus on the emergence of language and culture in human evolution and include the negotiation of shared meaning in social play and in emerging Sign Languages as models for the origin of language.

Eric Reuland was born in 1944 in Rotterdam. He studied Slavic Languages and General Linguistics at Groningen University, where he also completed his PhD, and worked as Assistant and Associate Professor in the Department of General Linguistics. In 1992 he was appointed Professor of Linguistics at Utrecht University. From 1995 to 2004 he was Director of the Utrecht Institute of Linguistics OTS and from 1995 to 2002 he also served as Director of the National Graduate School of Linguistics LOT. His main research interest—as reflected in a range of publications and dissertations supervised—is the interface between the syntactic and the interpretive systems, and more generally the way the language system relates to other cognitive systems.

Sue Savage-Rumbaugh is a research scientist at the Great Ape Trust of Iowa, Des Moines. She built a unique colony of language-competent apes, whose comprehension of spoken English has been generally accepted after years of debate in the scientific community. Her desire to understand why cross-fostered apes learned to comprehend and communicate with language led her to investigate the systematicity of their social interactions in general and to look at play from the perspective of a communicative discourse.

Luc Steels is a professor in the Computer Science Department of the University of Brussels (VUB) and Director of the Sony Computer Science Laboratory in Paris. Together with several generations of students he has been exploring how various aspects of language, from sound and meaning to lexicon and grammar, can emerge in populations of artificial embodied agents.

MAGGIE TALLERMAN is Professor of Linguistics at the University of Newcastle upon Tyne. She has spent her professional life in north-east England, teaching first at Durham and then at Newcastle. Her current research interests fall into two quite distinct categories: the origins and evolution of language, particularly syntax, morphology, and the mental lexicon; and the syntax and morphosyntax of Brythonic Celtic, particularly modern Welsh. She is the author of *Understanding Syntax* (Hodder Arnold, 2nd edn 2005), editor of *Language Origins: Perspectives on Evolution* (OUP, 2005), co-author of *The Syntax of Welsh* (CUP, 2007, with Robert Borsley and David Willis), and is currently producing the *OUP Handbook of Language Evolution* (with Kathleen Gibson).

ELLY VAN GELDEREN is a syntactician interested in language change. Her current work shows how regular syntactic change (grammaticalization) can be accounted for by (Minimalist) Economy Principles that help a child acquire a language and analyze it in a different way from previous generations. She is a professor in the English Department at Arizona State University and the author of fifty articles/chapters and six books, the most recent ones being *Grammaticalization as Economy* (2004) and *A History of the English Language* (2006).

WENDY K. WILKINS (PhD, UCLA, 1977) is currently the Provost and Vice President for Academic Affairs and Professor of Linguistics at the University of North Texas. She has also served as Professor of Linguistics and Cognitive Science at Michigan State University, from 1998 through 2007, and Dean of the College of Arts and Letters at MSU, from 1998 until 2005. She was Professor and Associate Dean of Liberal Arts and Sciences at Arizona State University (1994–8), and also held other administrative positions at ASU (1988–94). She was a visiting faculty member in Linguistics at the University of Washington (1986–8) and the University of Massachusetts (1977–8). In Mexico she held professorial and research positions at several institutions (1978–86), including El Colegio de México, El Museo Nacional de Antropología e Historia, Universidad Nacional Autónoma de México, and Universidad Autónoma Metropolitana Unidad Ixtapalapa.

GHOFUR ELIOT WOODRUFF hails from New Zealand, where he earned his Masters degree in Music at the University of Canterbury. He is currently working towards a PhD at the University of Cambridge, exploring ecological theories of communication in music with Ian Cross.

THOMAS WYNN, PhD, is Professor of Anthropology in the Department of Anthropology, University of Colorado at Colorado Springs. His research focusses upon cognitive and Paleolithic archeology. Contact: Anthropology Department, PO Box 7150, University of Colorado, Colorado Springs, CO 80933-7150. Email: twynn@uccs.edu.

1 Introduction: rewards and challenges of multi-perspectival work on the evolution of language and speech

RUDOLF BOTHA

The chapters in this volume on the prehistory of language are meant to serve two general purposes. First, they are representative of work of substance currently being done in an area where quality is not consistently dissociated from quantity. Which, of course, is not to say that the accounts offered in these chapters are therefore without limitations. The point, rather, is that in presenting work by scholars of repute, these chapters give a good idea of the depth of understanding that can be achieved at present.

Second, collectively, the chapters provide a striking illustration of how such understanding is achieved: by the adoption of a diversity of perspectives and approaches. Thus, in attempting to account for facets of the evolution of language and speech, these chapters represent a variety of perspectives: social, cultural, archeological, paleoanthropological, musicological, anatomical, neurobiological, primatological, and linguistic, to mention only some. The authors, moreover, adopt a variety of approaches for unraveling the evolution of language and speech, including ones involving comparison, correlation, simulation, and theoretical analysis. Since various of the perspectives and approaches at issue are associated with different disciplines, the chapters in this volume also clarify the sense in which present-day work on the evolution of language and speech can be said to be "multidisciplinary."

Taken individually, then, what are these chapters about? In what follows, I identify the main perspective—often there are ancillary ones as well— from which each chapter elucidates the one or more facets on which it focusses. And I indicate how the chapter relates in terms of perspective to chapters that precede or follow it. In outlining each chapter's central argument, I am forced by limitations of space to abstract away from specifics.

As a consequence, I am unable to show just how richly varied most of the chapters are in what they claim about the evolution of language or speech, in how they argue for their claims, and in how they engage with relevant literature. Readers will discover this for themselves, and to their delight, I believe.

In Chapter 2, Robin Dunbar, characterizing himself as an "evolutionary biologist," takes up the general questions "Why did language evolve?," "When did language evolve?" and "Why do only humans have language?" He argues that language evolved primarily not to facilitate the exchange of factual information but rather to serve social bonds by providing a substitute for social grooming, which he considers to be the main mechanism that our fellow primates use for bonding social relations. This hypothesis allows him to account for unrelated facts about brain size, group size, grooming patterns in primates, how we use language, what we talk about, conversation group sizes, and so on. From this hypothesis, moreover, follows naturally why, among the primates, only humans are likely to have evolved language: no other species evolved group sizes large enough to require more than grooming for social bonding. Addressing the question of when language evolved, Dunbar hypothesizes that this happened relatively late, probably with the appearance of anatomically modern humans about 200,000 years ago. And he argues that language evolved out of non-verbal forms of music-like vocalization, so-called chorusing, which served for the purpose of social bonding from about the appearance of archaic humans approximately 500,000 years ago. Among the perspectives offered by Dunbar on the evolution of language, the social one is clearly the central one.

In Chapter 3, Luc Steels provides another social perspective on the evolution of language, his main hypothesis being that sociality is a crucial prerequisite for the emergence of language. He argues in essence that human language, being symbol-based, can easily be used to cheat at the linguistic level by pretending that something is called or expressed in one way whereas you know that it is not, and at the factual level by lying. Steels assumes that, for language to be able to develop, individuals should (i) be willing to adopt linguistic conventions and categorizations introduced by others; (ii) align their conceptual and linguistic inventories as much as possible to those of others, and (iii) use language in an honest way, being maximally cooperative in doing all of this. If this sociality assumption is not adopted, language-like communication does not get off the ground or is much less successful. This is argued by Steels on the basis of results of agent-based language games developed by him and his colleagues. The argument is consonant with a scenario—discussed by Chris Knight in Chapter 17 of the companion volume *The Cradle of Language* (henceforth *The Cradle*)—in terms of which a "social revolution" begun in Africa enabled early hominins to lift themselves out of a Darwinian world into a social and cultural one.

Two other chapters link up with Dunbar's in positing an evolutionary link between language and music: the first by Steven Mithen, the second by Ian Cross and Eliot Woodruff. Mithen in Chapter 4 argues, to begin with, that we should return to ideas about the relationship between language and music advocated by scholars such as Rousseau, Darwin, and Jespersen. Next, Mithen further articulates the view that language and music co-evolved, a view which he ties in with recent arguments to the effect that protolanguage was holistic. According to Mithen, the proposal of a music-like protolanguage enables us not only to explain certain continuities between human speech and primate vocal communication but also to explain the seeming alacrity with which newborn infants respond to language and music alike, and the significant overlaps of the respective brain regions recruited for language and music. In addition, he cites reasons of different kinds for assuming that protolanguage used holistic phrases, not compositional ones. And he discusses a number of reasons why so-called hominin holistic phrase communication would have had a degree of musicality. In interweaving various strands of evidence in support of his views, Mithen gives an illustration of the extent to which work on language evolution has become in his view an interdisciplinary endeavor.

The idea that language and music may have co-evolved is entertained also in Chapter 5, with Cross and Woodruff proposing that language and music constitute complementary components of what they refer to as the "human communicative toolkit." Drawing on ethnomusical, cognitive, and neuroscientific evidence, they suggest that music is a communicative medium with features that are optimally adapted for the management of situations of social uncertainty. They propose that music achieves this by presenting the characteristics of an honest signal, while underspecifying goals in a way that permits individuals to interact even while holding personal interpretations of goals and meanings that may actually be in conflict. In support of their proposal, Cross and Woodruff adduce a theory of meaning in music: on this theory, the experience of music is accounted for in specific ways by reference to principles that are said to underlie both animal communication in general and human communicative interaction in particular. Exploring the implications of this theory for the evolution of language, Cross and Woodruff argue that, as complementary components of the "modern human communicative toolkit," music and language are best thought of as having co-evolved from a precursor communicative system that embodied features of both.

The perspective on the evolution of language provided in Chapter 6 by John Odling-Smee and Kevin Laland is partly similar to those of earlier chapters in assigning a central role to social and cultural factors. Their main objective, though, is not to comment on what the evolution of language might have involved by way of specifics but rather to provide an alternative evolutionary framework within which that evolution can be explored. This framework is based on two reciprocal causal processes that feature in evolution: natural selection and niche construction, the latter being used by organisms to choose, regulate, construct, and destroy their environments. To Odling-Smee and Laland, cultural niche construction is particularly pertinent, since in their view the need for better ways of transmitting information is crucial to the cultural niche in which language may have evolved. More specifically, they suggest that language may have co-evolved with human cultural niche construction, with language serving as a means of facilitating and advancing the social transmission of life-skills to young hominids, particularly in our own species.

Sonia Ragir and Sue Savage-Rumbaugh, in Chapter 7, develop yet another social perspective on the evolution of language, the one afforded by social play. Social play and language use, they maintain, are similar in a number of ways. In both cases, participants negotiate hierarchically ordered moves and exchanges that can be modified and rearranged through repetitive actions and shared goals into normative, rule-governed behavior. Such similarities, they propose, make social play a "proper model" for understanding the emergence of language. Support for this comes, they claim, from data which on their analysis show that social play is indeed a "profoundly normative and, thus, self-organising communicative activity." They rely for evidence on a fine-grained analysis of a period of social play among apes in an outdoor enclosure at the Language Research Center, Georgia State University—thereby adding to their chapter a primatological perspective on the evolution of language.

Chapters 8 and 9 present in some detail two further primatological perspectives on the evolution of language. Thus in the former chapter, David Leavens, Timothy Racine, and William Hopkins review evidence, accumulated over the last hundred years or so, for deixis in great apes. Some of this evidence suggests that great apes easily develop deictic repertoires in the complete absence of any explicit attempt to train them. Leavens, Racine, and Hopkins accordingly conclude that deixis—in the sense of the ability to direct the attention of another to a specific locus—is a capacity shared by great apes and humans. And assuming that deixis in great apes cannot ultimately derive from bipedalism or other adaptations, they conclude that our hominin ancestors were pre-adapted for joint attention, which makes deixis a component of the faculty of language in the broad sense of Hauser, Chomsky, and Fitch (2002).

In their review of the evidence for deixis in great apes, Leavens, Racine, and Hopkins refer to a particular deictic gesture which has been called the "directed scratch" by Simone Pika and John Mitani. In Chapter 9, Pika and Mitani give a description of how this gesture is used referentially by chimpanzees in the wild. It involves one chimpanzee male making a relatively loud and exaggerated scratching movement on a part of its body such that the movement can be seen and heard by his grooming partner. This gesture is shown by Pika and Mitani to be used communicatively to indicate a precise spot on the body and to request future action, namely grooming. The directed scratch appears to Pika and Mitani to be similar in form and in function to homesigns—the signs used communicatively by deaf children who have not been exposed to a manual sign language. Pika and Mitani hold that, like homesigns, directed scratches involve a form of reference and are therefore able to specify a distinct action—a property which, in turn, qualifies them as "characterizing signs." Pika and Mitani accordingly conclude that directed scratches may constitute the first step towards symbolic gestures. In addition, they consider their findings to be consistent with the hypothesis that certain gestures of a sort still used today by our closest living relatives may have been crucial in providing the modality within which the precursors of symbolic communication evolved.

In Chapter 10—the first that looks at the evolution of language from a linguistic perspective—Maggie Tallerman investigates the origins of some basic features of the human lexicon. She proposes that a word-based lexicon evolved by a process of building on ancient conceptual categories that were probably shared by all primates. This process, she argues, furthermore involved the use of the hierarchical structure that was already in place in primate cognition. In terms of Tallerman's proposal, a cognitive continuity is established between early humans—possibly *Homo ergaster*—and pre-human primates. That continuity is manifested, on her account, in other ways as well: she argues that the learning of categories is aided by labels both in humans and in non-human primates, and she argues that word-learning is aided by a set of innate learning biases. In support of her various hypotheses, Tallerman draws evidence from psycholinguistic studies, from work on category-specific brain defects, and from the study of pre-linguistic infants and non-human primates—making her chapter one of those that are richly textured from an evidentiary point of view.

In the next two chapters, aspects of the evolution of syntax are considered from the perspective of syntactic theory and diachronic change. Thus, subscribing to Noam Chomsky's Minimalist Program, Eric Reuland argues in Chapter 11 that it is "too simplistic" to view language as primarily a symbolic system used for communication. This view, he maintains, leads to an interpretation of the archeological record that is "too naïve." Central to Reuland's argument is the assumption that natural language is a computational system by which linguistic form and semantic interpretation are mapped systematically on to each other. The mapping is based on an inventory of lexical items and a combinatory system that includes the process known as "recursion" which, roughly, has the capacity to form infinitely long sentences by embedding phrases within phrases. The introduction of this process, Reuland argues, altered the nature of linguistic signs, severing the direct connection between form and interpretation. This gave rise to desymbolization, which he considers to be the "most characteristic" property of language. If his view is correct, evidence of symbolic activity by itself would not be a proper diagnostic of the presence of language, Reuland concludes.

Elly van Gelderen in Chapter 12 argues explicitly that Chomsky's biolinguistic approach has much to contribute to the study of language evolution, a view implicit to Reuland's chapter. To develop her argument, she pursues the question of what historical syntax can reveal about the "shape of original language"—with the question couched now in terms of this biolinguistic framework. Her position, in essence, is that the emergence of syntax followed the path followed by diachronic language change, a path also taken by children in acquiring language. She provides for two steps along this path, the first being the organizing of the thematic layer of language through Merge, a syntactic principle by which two expressions are combined into a composite one. Grammaticalization, she argues, is the other step that is responsible for markings in the grammatical layer. As typical examples of grammaticalization, she cites instances where prepositions take on the function of case markers, verbs that of auxiliaries and affixes, and pronouns that of agreement morphemes. These diachronic changes, van Gelderen maintains, occurred in early language too and continue to occur in contemporary languages. And, she argues, they can be captured in terms of cognitive economy of syntactic derivation, as provided for in the Minimalist Program.

Noting that recursion is considered to be the hallmark of modern language, Frederick Coolidge and Thomas Wynn address in Chapter 13 two fundamental questions about its evolutionary emergence: "What is the relationship of recursion to modern language and thinking?" and "What might be the mechanism or subspecies of recursion that bestows its advantages to cognition?" In addressing these questions, they cite empirical evidence which in their opinion shows that recursion requires not only greater working memory capacity but also greater phonological storage capacity. And they propose that recursion arose as a function of an increase in phonological storage capacity and/or working memory capacity. In their view, these capacities were enhanced by a genetic neural mutation that occurred sometime between 150,000 and 30,000 years ago. That change made possible longer recursive and canonical utterances and a consequent increase in the complexity and information content of sentences. Considering the question of how enhanced working memory, by way of recursion, may have enabled modern thinking, Coolidge and Wynn speculate that it (i) may have given the speaker the ability to "hold in mind" a greater number of options, giving him more behavioral flexibility and even creativity; (ii) may have aided the rapid evolution of culture through "thought experiments"; and (iii) may have been required for fully symbolic thought, as reflected in therianthropic art such as the *Löwenmensch* of Hohlenstein-Stadel and Hohle Fels cave.

In Chapter 14, Bart de Boer investigates the effect of the lowering of the larynx in humans, providing an articulatory/acoustic perspective on the evolution of speech. For his investigation, he uses Mermelstein's model of the geometry of the human male vocal tract, a model in which the contours correspond to the actions of the muscles involved in speech. In the experiment run by de Boer with this model, the area of the acoustic space that is accessible by a model of the male vocal tract—a space similar to the maximum vowel space—was compared with the accessible area of the female vocal tract. Since these vocal tracts differ not only with respect to the position of the larynx (lower for the male), he included in the comparison an artificial model on which the larynx has a female shape but is located in the male position. On de Boer's interpretation of the simulation results, the female vocal tract is better than the male tract for producing distinctive speech sounds. All in all, this indicates to de Boer that there is an evolutionary advantage to a vocal tract that has a pharyngeal and an oral cavity of equal length, as in the case of the female tract. He accordingly concludes that a different evolutionary explanation for the lower position of the male larynx needs to be found, the theory of size exaggeration as proposed by Tecumseh Fitch and his colleagues being a likely candidate.

In Chapter 15, the final one, Wendy Wilkins sets out a strategy for investigating the evolutionary biology of language. Central here is the following thesis: In order to understand the emergence of linguistic capacity as an innovation in the hominid line, it is necessary to work backwards from language-relevant anatomy. The assumption is that each piece of the anatomical mosaic will have a different evolutionary story, and that each story will be more or less evident in ancestral species, depending on the availability of biological evidence in the fossil record. Wilkins illustrates the use of this strategy by discussing the evolution of Broca's area and the parietal-occipital-temporal junction (POT) plus Wernicke's area, areas of the brain taken by Wilkins to be "necessary, if not sufficient, for language." In the view of Wilkins and her research associate Jenny Wakefield, the complex comprising Broca's area and the POT was evolutionarily shaped to improve the neurological control of the hand and thumb, and became available for exaptation after the divergence of the hominid and pongid lineages. This position, Wilkins argues, gains further support from recent work on primate neuroanatomy. She argues, too, that certain evidence from primate neuroanatomy indicates that there is a particular aspect of conceptual structure which is specific to humans and, moreover, specific to language—these properties making this a candidate for inclusion in the faculty of language narrowly construed (FLN).

As the chapters in this volume demonstrate, multi-perspectival work on the evolution of language and speech has generated a wealth of ideas about what may have been involved in the relevant processes. Multi-perspectivalism, thus, clearly has its rewards. But it also brings with it new challenges for the future, most notably the challenges that are raised by the need to integrate ideas which, on the face of it, seem hard to reconcile in unifying and internally coherent theories of the evolution of language and speech. To illustrate what challenges of this sort are about, I sketch below three instances drawn from chapters in this volume. This is not meant to detract in any way from the merit of these chapters, all rated highly in peer reviews. The concern here is with something else altogether: namely, a fundamental question that arises in multi-perspectival work on the evolution of language and speech, the question of how to deal with the divergence of ideas.

Consider as the first instance two of the notions of language that feature in this volume:

(1) Language is open-ended and fluid, particular languages lacking any clear or definite underlying system (Steels, Chapter 3).

(2) Language is a computational system that embodies a systematic mapping between form and interpretation (Reuland, Chapter 11).

How, if at all, can these two notions of language be reconciled in a coherent, unifying theory of language evolution? On what basis can their relative merit be appraised? Is there sufficient agreement about the conditions that a conception of language should meet? (Botha, *The Cradle*: ch. 5). Or, to consider one more alternative, are Steels and Reuland actually concerned with the evolution of two different entities related terminologically only— by being called "language?" Incidentally, the notions of language indicated above are but two from among a large number that have been adopted in work on the evolution of language (Botha 2003: 13–15).

As a second instance, here are two of our contributors' ideas about the primary function for which language emerged:

(3) Language evolved primarily as a substitute for social grooming (Dunbar, Chapter 2).

(4) Language evolved as a means of facilitating and advancing the social transmission of life-skills to young hominids, particularly in our own species (Odling-Smee and Laland, Chapter 6).

How can these two ideas—intriguing as they are—be made to cohere within an inclusive framework? For instance, could they be subsumed under a more general, unifying conception? And how do they relate to other ideas about what the primary function of language might have been—for instance, to aid thinking or to express thought? More generally, as for the merit of an idea about the primary function of emerging language—on what basis is it to be judged? Could the nature of that basis be other than empirical? This question arises if Fitch, Hauser, and Chomsky (2005: 185) are correct in believing that "from an empirical perspective, there are not and probably never will be data capable of discriminating among the many plausible speculations that have been offered for the original function(s) of language." It also arises if "primary" and "original" are to mean the same thing. These are some of the questions that are bound to arise in attempts at knitting together the two ideas stated above within a coherent, unifying theory of the evolution of language.

The third instance is to do with similarities between language and some other phenomenon that are claimed to be evolutionarily significant. Again, the specimen claims below are drawn from the present volume:

(5) Similarities between modern language and music indicate that language and music have a shared, music-like, precursor (e.g. Mithen, Chapter 4).

(6) Similarities between language and social play indicate that social play is a "proper model" for understanding the emergence of language (Ragir and Savage-Rumbaugh, Chapter 7).

How would these two interesting ideas fit together, if at all, in a unifying theory of language evolution? What is to be the basis for judging that the similarities between language and a given phenomenon, say music, possess lesser or greater evolutionary significance than do the similarities between language and a given other phenomenon, say social play?

These three pairs of seemingly divergent ideas—and many more such pairs, triples, and so on are to hand in the literature—give some indication of the challenges that will have to be faced in future research aimed at incorporating into unifying theories the ideas thrown up by multi-perspectival work on the evolution of language and speech.

A first step in constructing such theories will be to subject truly incompatible ideas to comparative appraisal across disciplinary or sub-disciplinary boundaries. This will require some consensus among the participating disciplines or subdisciplines about the principles on which individual comparative appraisals are to be based. A second step will be to obtain clarity across disciplinary boundaries about what theoretical unification involves. Transcending these boundaries may well be the most daunting challenge to be faced in future work on the evolution of language and speech.

2 Why only humans have language

ROBIN DUNBAR

2.1 Introduction

Language is a problem from an evolutionary point of view: our efforts to explain its origins and distribution are inevitably confounded by the fact that only one species actually has it. I decline to debate the old chestnut about whether bees or whales have language, since I do not believe it is especially relevant to the nature of human language and its origins. The bald fact is that no species other than our own has evolved a communication system of such sophistication and complexity. It is this that we have to explain, not whether any other species exhibit precursors for this capacity (which I am quite content to agree they do). The issue is not whether animals share some of these properties with us in some degree (something that, as an evolutionary biologist, I sincerely hope is not in doubt), but whether they exhibit the full-blown phenomenon as we find it in humans. On that score, the answer is surely no. And there is little more we can usefully say on the topic. The more interesting question then is: *Why* do only humans have language?

I want to do three things in this chapter. First, I will briefly summarize the reasons why language might have evolved, and what we are to make of these. I will then consider what this has to tell us about why only the hominin lineage evolved the capacity for language. Finally, I will revisit the analyses that I did with Leslie Aiello (Aiello and Dunbar 1993) on the timing of language evolution in the hominin fossil record using new estimates for all the equations involved in order to explore the sequence by which language might have evolved, and the transitional states involved.

2.2 Why did language evolve?

The reason why we have the capacity for language has rarely troubled those disciplines such as linguistics, anthropology, and psychology that have been interested in language (or speech). If they have given it more than a passing thought, they have invariably assumed that language evolved to allow us to exchange technical information—explaining how to make tools, coordinating hunting (perhaps even gathering?), giving instructions on how to get from A to B, maybe even providing the occasional erudite disquisition on the nature of the universe during moments of relaxation around the camp fire of an evening. We might refer to these collectively as instrumental theories of language function. The role of grammar as a mechanism for encoding information lends obvious support to this claim since grammatical structure is obviously essential for the transmission of any such information.

However, herein lies the real issue: Language is extremely good at allowing us to convey information, but that fact does not of itself specify what kinds of information are involved. If we could show that the structure of grammar was specifically designed to facilitate the exchange of instrumental information, that would be strong evidence in favor of the hypothesis. However, any such analysis would be unable to specify what kinds of information grammar is best adapted for. This is because knowledge about the social world in which we live is just as complex in information-processing terms as instrumental knowledge about the physical world. Moreover, the social world is characterized by being unusually dynamic: The physical world changes, but it does so on a slow and predictable scale, whereas the social world is in constant flux and its changes can seem to be almost random. If language is about exchange of information, then it is just as likely to have evolved to allow us to navigate our way around our very complex social world.

Three separate hypotheses for the social functions of language have been offered. Miller (1999) proposed what he termed the Scheherazade effect: Language evolved to enable us to advertise our value as a prospective mate and, once mated, to service that relationship by maintaining the mate's continued interest. An alternative was offered by Deacon (1997), who pointed out that humans are somewhat peculiar in having pairbonded mating arrangements embedded within large multi-male/multi-female social groups where one or both sexes might be away for significant periods of time (even if only during the day); to minimize the risk of mate-theft, he suggested, it was necessary to have social contracts that identified particular individuals as "spoken for" (and thus beyond what one might think of as the "copulatory pale"). Social contracts, he argued, require language, and since, following Lovejoy (1981), he held that monogamy was an early-evolved trait, he assumed that language must have evolved early. The third possibility, proposed by Dunbar (1993, 1996), is that language evolved to service social bonds in a more generic sense by providing a substitute for social grooming, the main mechanism that our fellow primates use for bonding social relationships (Dunbar 1991; Lehmann et al. 2007). For humans, as with all primates, effectively bonded social groups are essential for successful survival and reproduction, and since grooming has a natural limit on the size of group that can be bonded by it, language was necessary to break through this glass ceiling and allow larger groups to evolve.

The alternative, more conventional view is, of course, that language evolved to facilitate the exchange of useful factual information. On this instrumentalist view, the fact that humans use language for idle chit-chat is not, of course, in doubt. What is at issue is whether this kind of conversational exchange is the reason why language evolved, or merely a by-product of having language for some more useful purpose—something we do because we have the ability to use language's information-carrying capacity for any number of other purposes when we have nothing better to do. In their view, the social use of language is merely a frivolous emergent property of the real purpose for which language evolved. This, of course, is a perfectly reasonable view, but merely asserting something to be true does not constitute a test, never mind evidence. In such cases, it is often helpful to reverse the logic and see if one can argue the converse case—that the instrumental uses are in fact parasitic on the social functions of language. Doing so gives us two contradictory hypotheses to test between, and that always provides heuristic power.

The difficulty at this point is finding satisfactory ways of testing these kinds of hypotheses. Because behavior does not fossilize, testing an evolutionary—or, indeed, any historical—hypothesis is always somewhat challenging, since we invariably lack the relevant kinds of historical evidence. However, testing between alternative hypotheses in these cases has the added problem that alternative functional hypotheses often make the same generic predictions: They are both, after all, intended to explain why the phenomenon exists. Thus, predicting that language evolved to allow information-exchange, for example, is not especially helpful because both social and instrumental hypotheses make the same assumption. What is required is a different approach.

In fact, there are two well-established approaches to this kind of hypothesis-testing. One is the comparative method exploited so successfully by Darwin in most of his major works: As he pointed out in the *Origin*, the method rests on being able to fill in so many of the individual jigsaw pieces that any alternative hypothesis is simply implausible. The other is known as the method of critical tests and was developed by Isaac Newton: Here, one tests between competing hypotheses directly by forcing them into competition such that the empirical data can only support one hypothesis at the expense of all the others. Its merit as a methodology is that it allows one to test simultaneously between several alternative hypotheses in a context where only one of them can be true. To do this, it is usually necessary to search among the details of the assumptions and mechanisms that underpin each hypothesis in order to find points where the assumptions on which the hypotheses rest necessarily make contradictory predictions. In many cases, this will be about ancillary aspects of the system into which the phenomenon is embedded. Examples where this methodology has been used in the study of behavior can be found in van Schaik and Dunbar (1990), Dunbar et al. (2002), and Calhim et al. (2006). We can apply both methods to the question of language evolution.

Darwin's comparative method consists in adducing a range of different kinds of integrated evidence and argument that shows how one explanation provides a more comprehensive explanation at several different levels for the phenomenon of interest. This is the method I used in my original publications on this topic (see Dunbar 1993, 1996, 1998). I sought to demonstrate: (1) that there was a problem (bonding unusually large social groups) which required a more efficient mechanism than social grooming (the conventional primate mechanism for doing this, and hence the baseline from which we have to start); (2) that language met this requirement very nicely because it allows us to cut through some of the constraints on grooming; and (3) that the evidence confirmed the derivative prediction that conversation time would be devoted disproportionately to social topics (Dunbar 1993; Dunbar et al. 1997).

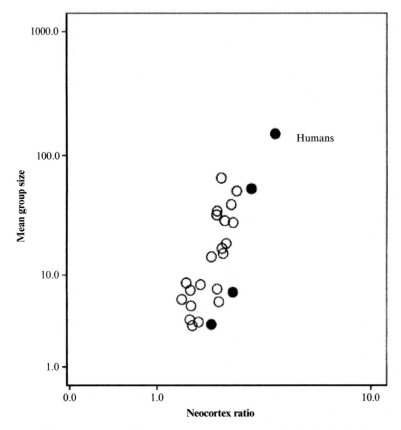

FIG. 2.1. Mean group size plotted against neocortex ratio for individual primate genera (one species per genus). The value for modern humans (upper right) is based on the value obtained for human social networks (Hill and Dunbar 2003). Hominoids (solid circles) are distinguished from monkeys (open circles).

The basis of this argument is that, in primates, there is a cognitive limit to the size of social groups that a species can maintain (the social brain hypothesis: Dunbar 1992, 1998; Barton and Dunbar 1997), that primates bond these groups by social grooming, and that the amount of social grooming a species does is more or less linearly related to group size (Dunbar 1991; Lehmann et al. 2007). Extrapolating across these relationships for modern humans predicts a group size of about 150 (Figure 2.1), which is large by primate standards (about three times larger than the average group size for chimpanzees and baboons, for example). We have

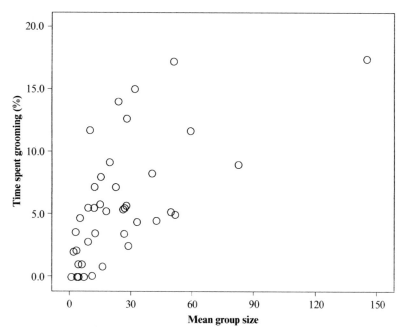

FIG. 2.2. Mean time devoted to social grooming by individual primate species, plotted against mean group size. Redrawn from Lehmann et al. (2007).

been able to show that groups of 150 are characteristic of a wide range of contemporary and historical human societies (Dunbar 1993; Zhou et al. 2005), and seem to represent the number of individuals we know as persons (i.e. those with whom we hold a personal relationship). The predicted grooming time for these "natural" groupings of about 150 individuals is 36.6% using the new equation from Lehmann et al. (2007) (Figure 2.2), which is double the highest average time spent grooming (17.4%) for any primate species. This is a little lower than the original estimate given in Dunbar (1993), but does not change the substantive argument.

The absolute upper limit on grooming time for any individual primate group (as opposed to average for a species) is 20% of total day time and does not seem to be the result of any endogenous limit set by the animal's biology, but rather is an exogenously determined limit set by the competing demands of other core activities (foraging, resting, etc.). In effect, this limit at 20% creates a glass ceiling on social group size at about eighty individuals, and effectively prevents further increases in group size when these are required by novel ecological conditions. The glass ceiling can only be broken through when some more efficient way is found to use time for social bonding.

This is not a trivial problem: anthropoid primates (including humans) live in deeply bonded societies whose coherence has to be maintained through time by some form of social interaction (Dunbar and Shultz 2007), and there appears to be a very explicit limit on the amount of time that primates can devote to this kind of activity. We cannot argue that this does not apply to humans or their immediate ancestors unless we also want to claim that humans do not behave like other primates (even though they obviously do when it comes to the cognitive constraints on group size). In other words, if we try to dodge the problem, we end up having to make radically different claims about the nature of human behavior and cognition that are necessarily ad hoc. Rather, what we need to ask at this juncture is whether hominins found some way of effectively circumventing this problem. My suggestion (Dunbar 1993) was that language allowed hominins to break through the glass ceiling precisely because it enabled them to use their time more efficiently for social bonding (Dunbar 1993). Table 2.1 summarizes some of the many ways that language might do this.

Two of the more important constraints on conventional primate bonding are that grooming is very much a one-on-one activity (as, of course, it still is with us). (Note that, in primates, social or allo-grooming is not a purely hygienic activity: Although it does serve to clean the fur and skin, grooming in monkeys and apes has much more in common with massage and other forms of affiliative physical contact in humans like cuddling, petting, stroking, etc.: Dunbar 1991, 1996.) That language is more efficient in social bonding terms is indicated by the fact that humans from a wide range of contemporary societies actually spend an average of exactly 20% of their day engaged in social interactions (Dunbar 1998). Indeed, the difference between this observed value (20%) and the required social time predicted by the primate grooming equation ($\sim$37%) suggests that language is in fact about twice as efficient as grooming as a bonding mechanism.

If language really does serve a social bonding function, then we should expect the way it is used in everyday conversations to reflect this: They should mainly be social in character, and not instrumental. This does not mean that conversations cannot be about technical topics or involve

TABLE 2.1. *The advantages of language over social grooming as a mechanism for bonding social groups*

Benefits of language	Constraints of grooming
Exchange information about state of network	What monkeys do not see, they do not know about
Multi-task (walk and talk, eat and talk)	Grooming can only be done on its own
Identify group members (dialects and shared knowledge as social badges)	Inferences only about personal relationships
Reinforce group membership	Reinforce dyad membership
Police freeriders	Punishment of freeriders only by withholding grooming
Manage reputations in respect of all kinds of relationship	Inferences in respect only of grooming reliability
Talk to several individuals at the same time	Grooming is a strictly one-on-one activity

instruction: The original argument was couched in terms of whether instrumental functions are a prior property and social functions an emergent property or whether the converse is true (social functions are prior, and instrumental ones emergent), not in terms of whether only one of these functions was true. Hence, the way language is used in everyday conversations should provide us with some light on this. In practice, several studies of conversation content in both post-industrial and traditional societies show that social topics predominate in normal, freely forming, everyday conversations, accounting for about 65% of total conversation time (Dunbar et al. 1997).

So far, then, this argument has taken a number of otherwise unrelated facts (brain size, group size, grooming patterns in primates, how we use language, what we talk about, conversation group sizes) and shown how they constitute a coherent set that can be explained by the suggestion that language allowed hominins to cut through the constraint that grooming time placed on social group size. Instrumental or instructional uses for language can be viewed as a natural emergent property once social language is in place: Once you can talk about something, you can talk about anything.

The more general claim of a social role for vocal (as distinct from purely verbal) communication has received significant support from two recent studies of animal communication. McComb and Semple (2005) have shown that, in primates, vocal repertoire size correlates with social group size (and with time spent grooming). This suggests that, as social group has increased, there has been selection pressure to increase the role of vocal exchanges as a means of supplementing grooming, and that this has been reflected in the generation of a corresponding level of vocal complexity. Similarly, Freeberg (2006) showed that, in naturally occurring flocks of chickadees (a small American finch), the uncertainty (and hence complexity) of vocal calls was greater in larger flocks than in smaller ones. Freeberg was able to confirm this with an experimental manipulation of captive birds. It is not, of course, clear exactly what role vocal exchanges play in either of these cases, but the substantive issue is, I think, that increasing group size seems to require more sophisticated vocal communication. Indeed, it is noteworthy that primate species like gelada (*Theropithecus gelada*), that both live in very large (if loose) social groups and devote a great deal of time to social grooming (they hold the primate record for most time spent grooming), also use complex vocal exchanges ("chorusing") to maintain contact with their core social partners while they are feeding (a form of grooming-at-a-distance) and as prompts and reminders during grooming bouts (personal observation). Taken together, these studies give added grounds for seeing language as a natural outgrowth of that pressure (and not, incidentally, as being derivative of a gestural phase, as some have argued).

Can we use the critical tests methodology to unpack language evolution? The answer is yes, though the success of the method rests on being able to identify key traits that discriminate unequivocally between alternative hypotheses (the critical tests). These are traits in which the prediction made by one hypothesis contrasts with those made by all the others. Table 2.2 lists a number of traits characteristic of language and the predictions for these made by each of four hypotheses for the function of language that I outlined above—the classic instrumental hypothesis and the three alternative social ones. The critical tests are indicated by the asterisked predictions: These are exclusively true of only one of the four

TABLE 2.2. *Critical tests analysis of hypotheses for language evolution. The body of the table gives the predictions that each of the four main hypotheses proposed to date would make in respect of the individual traits in the left-hand column. The observed condition is listed in the right-hand column*

	Instrumental hypothesis	Social Hypotheses ⟶			Observed findings
		Scheherazade	Contracts	Gossip	
Sex difference in use	*M > F	M = F	M = F	*M < F	M < F
Mates talk more than other dyads	no	*yes	no	no	no
Frequency of daily use	low	high	low	high	high
Context specificity	high	high	high	*low	low
Night-time use	no	yes	?no	yes	yes
First appearance in fossil record	early	?early	early	*late	late
Task-oriented	*yes	no	no	no	no
Used mainly in social contexts	no	no	yes	yes	yes
Main topics of conversation	*tasks	*mating	*contracts	*social	social
Number of tests [or critical tests*] confirmed	1 [0/3]	5 [0/2]	3 [0/1]	9 [4/4]	

* Critical tests that unequivocally differentiate one hypothesis from all the others; number of critical tests confirmed (and number of tests available) is given in parentheses at foot of table for each hypothesis.

hypotheses. The right-hand column gives the observed findings. We can count both the overall number of hits and misses that each hypothesis achieves and the numbers of critical tests that each hypothesis correctly predicts. Although by no means comprehensive, the evidence from how language is used and when it is likely to have evolved all points unequivocally to the gossip hypothesis, with none of the other hypotheses receiving significant support. It would be desirable to have a better balance of traits across the four hypotheses, but, as a tentative first step in this direction, this approach offers a promising way forwards.

In sum, I used the comparative method to build a comprehensive account aimed at showing that a single principle (language evolved so as to facilitate social bonding) can explain a large array of features by which we differ from other apes and monkeys. This makes comprehensive sense of a number of otherwise unrelated facts. The critical tests analysis allowed us to pitch this hypothesis more formally against its competitors in such a way as to force them into competition. The gossip hypothesis received unequivocal support: It was the only hypothesis whose predictions were confirmed on all nine tests, and the only one to pass all its critical tests.

We are left with one minor point to resolve, namely the relationship between the three social hypotheses. Ostensibly, the gossip hypothesis receives overwhelming support, and we could take this as conclusive evidence to dismiss the Scheherazade and contract hypotheses. While there is some support for both the other two hypotheses, each encounters difficulties over claims of priority. The Scheherazade hypothesis facilitates reproductive bonding, but why should bonding suddenly become so problematic when many other species manage perfectly well without language and the need to keep one's mate entertained? Miller (1999) explicitly argued that the Scheherazade effect was a consequence of sexual selection, and I am certain he is right. But it is another matter to claim that language evolved explicitly for this purpose. Sexual selection is an especially powerful mechanism for exploiting phenomena that already exist, and it can as easily be argued that, once language is in place for more general reasons, then sexual selection is very likely to exploit it. Indeed, the Scheherazade effect looks like a very plausible additional mechanism to Deacon's social contract hypothesis for enforcing reproductive pairbonding. It might thus have arisen off the back of either the gossip hypothesis or the social contract hypothesis. The social contract hypothesis faces somewhat similar difficulties. Why were social contracts so essential for maintaining pair-bonded relationships? After all, a small African bird, the little bee eater, also has pairbonds set within a larger multi-male/multi-female community and faces exactly the kinds of problems that Deacon identified, yet manages without language (Emlen 1984).

In the end, however, the bottom line for both hypotheses is that they leave the group bonding problem unresolved. This simply cannot be ducked, and neither hypothesis offers any mechanism for this crucial process. Indeed, Deacon's argument about social contracts only becomes an issue once there are large groups, so we have to solve the problem of how to bond large groups before "marriage" contracts become an issue. In contrast, the gossip hypothesis offers a single mechanism that not only resolves the bonding problem, but also encompasses the other two hypotheses as emergent properties.

2.3 When did language evolve?

That hominins at some point broke through this glass ceiling suggests that the selection pressure to evolve larger groups must have been quite intense. Since we know that the upper limit on (average species) group size in primates is about 50 and anatomically modern humans have an equivalent figure of 150, there has to be some transition between these two limits during the course of human evolution. There are really just two possibilities. One is that group size underwent a dramatic step change from ~50 to ~150 all at one go, and that language came in as some kind of macro-mutation at the same time. The other is that group size is tightly constrained by brain size, and that, during the course of hominin evolution, group size changed steadily between these limits in close step with the changes in brain size.

Given that, in primates as a whole, group size seems to be tightly constrained by brain size (Dunbar and Shultz 2007), it would seem at best odd to insist that hominins had completely sidestepped the constraints under which all our primate cousins labor. The first option would thus seem implausible. One would have to argue that hominin group sizes had initially been limited by brain size (while hominins were still more or less conventional apes), broke free from this (while they were evolving on the long road to hominization), and then suddenly returned to being constrained again as they became fully modern. The short answer is that it doesn't really make sense to suppose that hominins at any stage in their long history were any different from other primates. Hence, we really have to conclude that the second option is much the more likely. Hominin group sizes tracked hominin brain size, just as they do in all other anthropoid primates.

Figure 2.3 plots the pattern of brain size change over the course of hominin evolution, based on new estimates of cranial volume for fossil hominins taken from de Miguel and Heneberg (2001). To obtain these values, I first calculated a mean value from all the estimates given for cranial volume for each of the 199 fossil hominin specimens in the de Miguel and Heneberg sample, provided the specimen was considered adult and brain size was based on a direct estimate (i.e. anything labeled as a "preliminary value" was ignored). I then calculated an average cranial volume for each local population (defined as all the crania from the same site that occur within the same 50,000-year time period). Finally, I used the equation given in Table 2.3 to convert these cranial volumes to brain volumes. Figure 2.3 can be interpreted as a long, slow, but fairly steady, increase in brain size over time, culminating in a dramatic acceleration in the closing stages (the last 500,000 years). However, pooling all individuals in this way somewhat belies the irregularities in the underlying pattern: Differentiating between species suggests there were two moderately dramatic phase changes (one with the appearance of *Homo erectus* ~2.0 MYA, the other with the appearance of archaic humans ~0.7 MYA), both of which coincide with periods of major climatic instability. Variance analysis suggests three major clusterings in the data: the australopithecines, an *erectus* group (possibly including the habilines), and a *sapiens* group (including both archaic and AMH). The data for the *erectus* group on its own suggest a distinct sigmoid pattern through time with a steep rise in brain size to ~1.5 MYA, after which it remains stable till ~0.5 MYA, and finally a final steep increase (most of which seems to be associated with Asian *erectus* populations). In fact, a cubic equation provides the best fit to the *erectus* data ($r^2 = 0.458$, $F_{3,17} = 4.78$, $p = 0.014$).

I used these brain data to estimate mean group size by interpolating first into the regression equation for neocortex ratio for primates (from Aiello and Dunbar 1993) and then into the equation relating mean species group size to neocortex ratio in hominoids from Figure 2.1 (see Table 2.3). These group sizes were then interpolated into the new Lehmann et al.

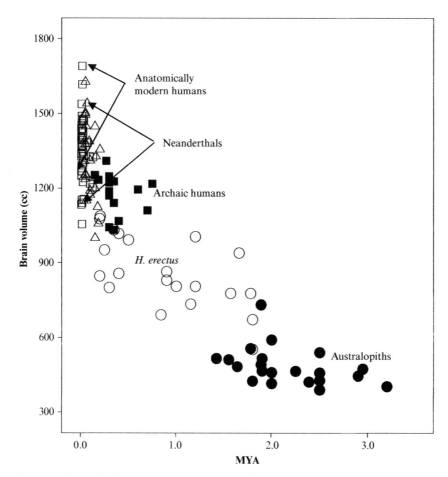

FIG. 2.3. Mean brain size for individual fossil hominin populations. A population is defined as all crania from a specific site within a 50,000-year time window. Brain volume estimates are based on de Miguel and Heneberg (2001). The populations are grouped into five main taxonomic groupings: australopiths, solid circles; *Homo ergaster/erectus* populations, open circles; archaic humans [*H. heidelbergensis* and allies], solid squares; Neanderthals, triangles; anatomically modern humans (to 10 KYA), open squares.

(2007) equation relating grooming to social group size in African primates. In extrapolating grooming time requirements to hominins, I followed Lehmann et al. (2007) and used a restricted grooming time equation derived from the primate data for group sizes less than forty. Lehmann

TABLE 2.3. *Equations used in calculations of group size, grooming time, and intentionality*

Variable	Equation	r^2	F	df	P
Brain size (cc)[a]	$\log_{10}$(brain vol., cc) $= 3.015 + 0.986$ $\log_{10}$(cranial vol., cc)	0.995		1,34	<0.001
Neocortex ratio[b]	$\log_{10}$(neocort ratio) $=$ $-0.618 + 0.200^*$ $\log_{10}$(brain vol., mm^3)	0.857		1,24	<0.001
Group size[c]	ln(group size) $=$ $-3.307 + 5.924^*$ln (neocortex ratio)	0.953	40.22	1,2	0.024
Grooming time (%)[d]	Groom $= 1.382 +$ 0.234^*(group size)	0.318	13.97	1,30	0.001
Frontal lobe volume (cc)[e]	FLV $= -7.133 + 0.372^*$ (brain vol., mm^3)	0.999	3733.31	1,4	<0.001
Intentionality[f]	Intentionality level $=$ $1.011 + 0.00734^*$FLV	0.988	83.63	1,1	0.069

a) From Martin (1989)
b) From Aiello and Dunbar (1993)
c) Figure 2.3
d) Recalculated from Lehmann et al. (2007), for groups of less than 40
e) Data source:
f) From Figure 2.5

et al. (2007; see also Dunbar 1991) argued that larger groups are forced to compromise on grooming time by the demands on other activity budget components, and we want to know how much time an individual *ought* to devote to social interaction in order to bond its social group independently of any constraints from other ecological factors.

The resulting estimates of required grooming time for individual fossil hominin taxa are given in Figure 2.4. These calculations yield slightly lower values than my original (Dunbar 1993) estimates: the original grooming equation yielded a grooming time requirement of 40.8% for anatomically modern humans, while the new equation gives 35.9%. However, the pattern remains the same: the australopithecines are well within the

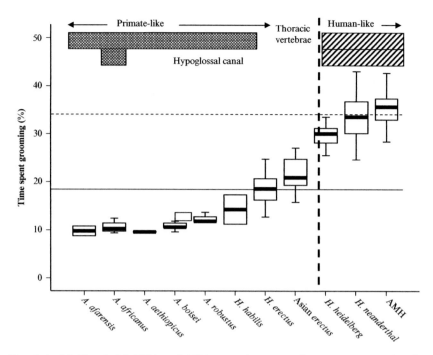

FIG. 2.4. Median (with 50% and 95% ranges) percent time spent grooming for fossil hominin taxa. Grooming time is estimated by successively interpolating cranial volumes for individual populations (from Fig. 2.3) into the equations for brain volume, neocortex ratio, group size, and then grooming time for primates, using the equations given in Table 2.3 (following Aiello and Dunbar 1993). Super-imposed on this graph is the approximate distribution of primate-like (stippled bars) and modern human-like (solid bars) thoracic vertebrae (from MacLarnon and Hewitt 1999) and hypoglossal canals (from Kay et al. 1998). The vertical dashed line demarcates the time period at which all three datasets suggest the capacity for speech might have evolved.

upper limits for primate grooming time (20%), the *erectus* group exhibit levels that hover comfortably around the 20% limit, and it is not really until the appearance of archaic humans that the grooming time significantly exceeds the 20% limit, rising rapidly to ~37% in anatomically moderns.

These results suggest that the capacity for some form of language-like communication had to be in place by 500,000 years ago, but probably not a lot before. This is in close agreement with such anatomical evidence as there is (mapped on to Figure 2.4). The data on the relative size of the thoracic vertebral canal (indicative of the ability to manage the close breath control needed for speech) indicate that this was modern in form (i.e. much larger for body size than expected for the primate average) in the earliest available archaic humans (i.e. by ∼500 KYA), but still primate-like in *Homo ergaster* as late as 1.5 MYA in Africa (with a fossil gap spanning the intervening period) (MacLarnon and Hewitt 1999). The equivalent data for the hypoglossal canal (which should reflect motor control over the tongue and the vocal space) fit quite well with this, with relatively large, modern human-like canals after 500 KYA, and more primate-like ones prior to about 2 MYA (Kay et al. 1998; Jungers et al. 2003). Although the hypoglossal canal data have been hotly disputed (albeit not always on the basis of sound reasoning or common sense), the broad consensus from these three very different sources of evidence seems to point to a significant moment in the evolution of language that coincides with the appearance of archaic humans sometime around 0.5 MYA.

There is, however, an issue here as to what we are seeing at this point: Is it language or "speech" (i.e. the capacity to formulate complex vocalizations, but not yet ones that have grammatical structure)? One possibility is that true language (i.e. vocalizations with consistent, information-bearing syntax) appeared later and was preceded by a period of vocal exchange that was more emotion-bound and less information-bound— perhaps some form of communal "singing" not unlike the kinds of contact call exchanges found among gelada baboons. Gelada contact calls differ in a number of important ways from those found in other baboons (and more generally other primates, with the possible exception of callitrichids and bonobos). These rather moan-like calls are far more variable in form than the distinctly grunt-like contact calls of *Papio* baboons, are more intensely imbued with emotional overtones, are used in a much wider range of circumstances than baboon contact calls, and are used in very distinctive chorusing exchanges.

This form of chorusing (which, to my knowledge, is all but unique among the primates) can occur at two levels. Individuals often engage in dyadic exchanges with their principal grooming partners while feeding (and hence unable to groom). Second, in some cases, once initiated these exchanges can spread through the harem (the one-male reproductive unit) and create an intense group chorus, especially when the group is feeding. Both kinds of exchanges probably allow members of the unit to maintain spatial contact with each other (and especially their primary coalition partners) without the need to be continuously breaking off from feeding to monitor the surroundings. This may be especially important in the large herds of 200-300 animals that gelada habitually form, because animals can easily become separated from each other. In this respect, it may be no accident that units avoid calling when neighbors are calling (personal observation), suggesting that they may be trying to avoid interference with neighboring units.

One possibility, then, is that language evolved via an intermediate musical phase similar to chorusing of this kind. Unfortunately, the anatomical evidence per se cannot differentiate between singing and language, since the same control over breathing and the vocal apparatus is needed for both. Thus, the 0.5 MYA rubicon may mark the appearance of some form of intensely music-like exchanges, with full grammatical language (i.e. language as we know it today) emerging only later—perhaps with the appearance of anatomically modern humans at around 200 KYA. Alternatively, and in the absence of any real evidence, fully grammatical language may have arrived all of a piece early (i.e. at 0.5 MYA) without an intervening "musical" phase. The substantive issue hanging in the balance here, of course, is whether the Neanderthals had archaic-like "singing" (if language evolved via an intermediate musical phase at ~0.5 MYA) or full-blown language (if language is unrelated to music and evolved early in a single event). We have no way of distinguishing between these two possibilities at this point, although the genetic data for "grammar genes" (Enard et al. 2002)—insofar as they actually tell us anything at all about language or grammar!—would tend to support the first (i.e. language evolved late and is unique to modern humans and their immediate ancestors).

There is, however, a further reason for emphasizing an intervening musical phase before full language, and this is the fact that language itself does not provide the psycho-pharmacological mechanism that makes grooming do the job it does for primates (i.e. the production of endorphins that seems to create the sense of bonding in dyads who groom regularly). Moreover, if, as I have argued, full language appears late (i.e. with anatomically modern humans), there is a bonding gap between what can be done with grooming and the point at which language kicks in as a substitute. If this gap was filled by a form of chorusing, the endorphin-producing capacities of music (and especially song and dance) would provide a natural bridge (Dunbar 2006, 2007). Otherwise, we have a problem about how hominin societies are bonded during the intervening period.

2.4 Why do only humans have language?

If we accept the argument as I have laid it out above, then it naturally follows that, at least among the primates, only humans are likely to have evolved language: No one else has evolved group sizes large enough to require more than grooming for social bonding. However, language also depends on cognitive abilities that may likewise be unique to humans—the capacity to understand another individual's mind state, otherwise known as theory of mind or mentalizing. Theory of mind is crucial to language because engaging in conversation with someone requires the speaker to pay close attention to the listener in order to be sure that the message is getting across (so as to try rephrasing if it is not), while the listener has to pay close attention to the speaker in order to determine just what it is that the speaker is intending to mean. As effective as language is for transmitting information, the reality is that both speaker and listener have to work quite hard to follow the ins and outs of a conversation. Without theory of mind to allow us to reconstruct the mental state of the speaker in particular, conversation would be very stilted, would be limited to simple factual exchanges, and would certainly lack the richness of modern human exchanges.

Theory of mind can be expressed as one level in a reflexive series of levels of intentionality (the capacity to use mental state verbs like *I think, I believe, I suppose,* etc.). In the sequence "I *think* that you *believe* that I *suppose* that we *understand* that Jane *wants*...", conventional theory of mind equates with second order intentionality ("I *think* that you *believe* [something is the case]"), a level that normal human children achieve at age 4–5 years. We have shown in a number of studies that the upper limit for normal adults is fifth order (Kinderman et al. 1998; Stiller and Dunbar 2007), with the intermediate levels being achieved progressively between the ages of 6 and 13 years (Henzi et al. 2007).

The fact that normal human adults have a limit at fifth order intentionality has a number of implications for us. First, it may impose a limit on the number of people we can hold in a conversation. Henzi et al. (2007) showed that the size of children's play groups (the number of individuals that a child actively played with at any given moment) correlates with their performance on intentionality tasks. It seems likely, then, that it will also limit the number of minds that the speaker (or listener) can engage with in a conversation. Conversation groups have a rather strict upper limit on their size (one speaker plus three listeners: Dunbar et al. 1997). Given that *social* conversations will often involve talking about an absent third party, this would suggest that the number of mind states that someone typically has to work with is five. Interestingly, Shakespeare sets this limit on the number of speaking parts in any one scene in his plays (Stiller et al. 2004): This obliges the audience to work at fifth order (because they have to *believe* that ...)—and Shakespeare himself, of course, to work at sixth order since he has to intend that his audience believes, etc. More importantly, perhaps, in this context, it is this ability for an audience to handle the mind states of four individuals on the stage that really makes it possible for a playwright (or any other storyteller) to write an intellectually and emotionally demanding drama: The audience has to *suppose* that Iago *intends* that Othello *believes* that Desdemona *loves* Cassio and that Cassio also *loves* her. Anything less than this, and the drama loses its bite: Why should Othello care if Desdemona has fantasies about Cassio? He only has reason to be bothered *if* he believes that Cassio reciprocates her interest, since then there is a serious risk that Desdemona might run away with someone else. Likewise, if we remove Iago from the drama, the play becomes a mere torrid account of an everyday love triangle, and would be over in just one scene. The play achieves its dramatic heights because Iago plays his insidious part in working on Othello's mind, thereby creating the uncertainty and dramatic tension (will Othello believe him, or will he trust his own judgment?) on which the play's success hangs.

Dunbar (2003) noted that there is an apparent relationship across the primates on mentalizing skills, with humans having their limit at fifth order intentionality, great apes at about second order (albeit only just), and monkeys in general being limited to first order. This scale seems to be linearly related to the absolute volume of these species' respective frontal lobes (Figure 2.5). While we probably shouldn't place too much weight on this finding without more extensive data, the fact that this relationship appears to be strictly linear (when we would expect a random selection of data to be more scattered) and that the various ape and monkey species cluster tightly together gives sufficient confidence to allow the relationship to be used to estimate intentionality capacity in fossil hominins across

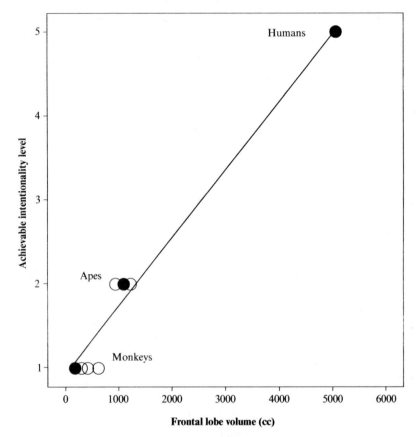

FIG. 2.5. Maximum achievable level of intentionality for humans, great apes, and monkeys, plotted against frontal lobe volume. Intentionality is known only for humans (5th order) and chimpanzees (just about 2nd order), and is presumptive for monkeys at 1st order; frontal lobe volumes are estimated from total neocortex volume for all monkey species except rhesus macaque. Great apes include chimpanzee, gorilla, and orangutan; monkeys include rhesus macaque, baboon, mangabey, and patas monkey.

time. Again, we should note that this is not the kind of extrapolation beyond the data range that so often arouses suspicion: Rather, our extrapolations are firmly grounded at either end of the distribution in what apes and modern humans, respectively, can do; all we are doing is filling in the gaps that must once have been occupied by real individuals. Our question is much more one of where the break-points are in this sequence.

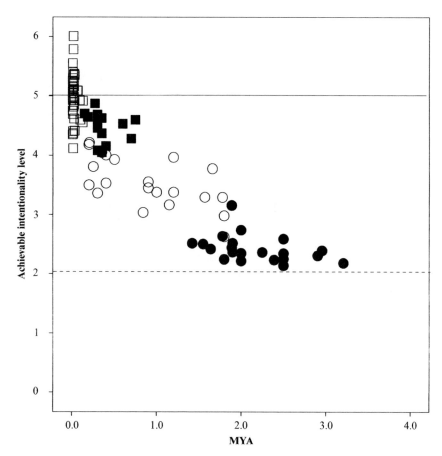

FIG. 2.6. Predicted maximum achievable level of intentionality for individual hominin populations. Values are estimated from cranial volume (from Fig. 2.3) by successive interpolation through the equation for frontal lobe volume for primates and the regression equation given for Fig. 2.5. Australopiths: solid circles; *H. erectus*, open circles; archaic humans, solid squares; anatomically modern humans (to 10 KYA), open squares.

Figure 2.6 plots interpolated intentionality capacities for the same set of fossil hominins shown in Figure 2.3, using a regression equation to derive frontal lobe volume from total brain size (based on primate data) and a best-fit equation from the three real datapoints in Figure 2.5 to relate intentionality capacity to frontal lobe volume. Figure 2.6 indicates that the australopiths would have remained well within the generic ape capacity at second order intentionality, with *Homo erectus* broadly being able to cope with third order. Fourth order could not have been achieved prior to the arrival of archaic humans, but, equally, none of them would have been able to aspire to fifth order, which these data suggest could only have been achieved by anatomically modern humans.[1]

These results indicate that, while *erectus* may have been able to conceive quite sophisticated (by primate standards) mental descriptions of their physical and social worlds, these would nonetheless have been quite limited (by our standards) in the number of individuals they could have maintained as a coherent interacting group. Furthermore, if intentionality capacity also reflects non-social propositional recursiveness (and the two are correlated: Stiller and Dunbar 2007; Stylianou 2007), then *erectus* would have been limited to quite simple propositions ("[I believe that]: [this is [the house]]"). That would certainly give some significant improvement over apes in terms of their ability to construct both their social and physical worlds in their mind's eye, but it would still significantly limit the complexity of the propositions they could deal with, as well as the social world they could manipulate. Archaic humans would, of course, be better off: they could have aspired to one level higher ("[I believe that]: [this is [the house that [Jack built]]]"), which clearly makes a very significant difference to the level of complexity they could deal with, but it is still significantly less than the level of complexity of which anatomically modern humans are capable ("[I believe that]: [this is the house [that Jack built [which is made of straw]]]").

We might be able to use these results to give further insight into when language might have evolved. It has been suggested that language helps us to manage thought (rather than the other way around). This is not to say that language makes thought possible, but rather that language helps us manage more complex propositional sequences. That being so, we can ask: At what level of recursion does language become essential? In other words, if, as some claim, we cannot manage recursion (or the complex analysis of the world that this makes possible) without language, then when does language become crucial—given that apes seem to be able

---

[1] Note that I have not included Neanderthals in this analysis: There are good reasons to believe that their brains may have been organized sufficiently differently to ours (due to the size of their defining "occipital bun") that they had significantly smaller frontal lobes than mere total brain size would imply. We are currently working on how to resolve this, and until we do I prefer to reserve judgment on Neanderthal cognitive capacities.

to cope quite adequately with second order recursion without language? Could we manage a third or fourth order intentional mental world without language? This is a strictly empirical question, but I would hazard the guess that, while third order is definitely possible without language, fourth order might be more debatable. If language is essential for fourth order recursion, then perhaps archaic humans did have fully grammatical language as we would understand it today (i.e. language with full recursive grammar allowing multiply-embedded phrase structures) rather than a simple language consisting of single words like nouns or verbs (or pigeon-like languages that consist only of simple noun+verb statements). If so, then we may be confident that Neanderthals had language in this fully modern sense too. If not, then language must have evolved with anatomically modern humans (in which case, neither archaic humans nor Neanderthals had it).

It is not obvious how we can test this directly, especially since cases where individuals can achieve the higher orders of intentionality without also having language in some form are probably all but non-existent. However, normal adults do vary somewhat in their competencies on intentionality tasks (Stiller and Dunbar 2007) and may lose the higher order competencies during the clinical phases of such conditions as bipolar disorder (Kerr et al. 2003) and schizophrenia (Swarbrick 2000). Similarly, children exhibit a natural developmental sequence from second order at aged 4–5 years through to fifth order sometime before adulthood, and this might provide us with a natural experiment. Henzi et al. (2007) found that, while there is considerable individual variation, children have typically mastered third order intentionality by about 6 years of age, fourth order by about age 9, and fifth order by age 11. Asking how well children cope with embedded reasoning tasks as they master successive levels of intentionality during development might give us some insights into the constraints that the capacity for thinking reflexively in this way might have. Such a study has yet to be done.

3 Is sociality a crucial prerequisite for the emergence of language?

Luc Steels

3.1 Introduction

Research into the origins of language can either be carried out from an empirical or from a theoretical angle. From an empirical angle one seeks data about early symbolic culture and about precursors of language-like communication or complex meaning in animals. Many of the chapters in this volume report progress in this area. From a theoretical angle, one seeks to define the cognitive mechanisms and social interactions that are necessary and sufficient for the emergence and cultural evolution of language-like communication systems. Once we know what these mechanisms and interaction patterns need to be, we can go back to the linguistic, biological, and archeological record for evidence of when and how such mechanisms might have emerged in human evolution. The present chapter falls within this domain of theoretical research. A theoretical approach need not be purely speculative—far from it. Just as in theoretical physics or theoretical biology, we can use mathematical analysis, computer simulation, and possibly physical experimentation (with robots, for example) to test the consequences of particular hypotheses. Theoretical modeling is in principle neutral. Opposing hypotheses can be tried out and compared and their coherence and validity tested. Thus one can investigate a strong nativist position just as easily as a cultural or social one.

The work reported here has been funded and carried out by the Sony Computer Science Laboratories in Paris. I have profited enormously from many discussions with Chris Knight to help pin down and clarify the social prerequisites for language. Martin Loetzsch, Frederic Kaplan, Emily Wang, and other members of Sony CSL Paris and the VUB AI Lab in Brussels played major roles in the experiments discussed here.

This chapter reports theoretical research exploring the hypothesis that language evolved in a cultural fashion as a complex adaptive system. Individuals either use routine solutions to solve communication problems or invent new conventions to repair failed communicative attempts, using their available cognitive and physiological capabilities. Different form–meaning pairs then start to compete for dominance in usage, allowing more complex forms of language to outcompete simpler forms if they lead to more successful communication with less effort or allow greater expressive power. The first part of the chapter explains this hypothesis in more detail, outlining how we have been using agent-based modeling with language games to explore it.

Much research into the origins of communication takes a Darwinian point of view, in the sense that it tries to show how communication and communication systems may emerge despite the fact that individuals are entirely driven by their selfish genes. No strategy of communication can be evolutionarily stable unless cheating and exploitation by others can be avoided. Animal signaling systems have solved this problem by being analog, unconscious, mostly genetically determined, and costly (Maynard-Smith and Harper 2003). However, symbol-based communication systems, such as human languages, are discrete, under conscious control, conventionally established, and not costly. This makes them much more powerful because it is easy to adapt them to deal with new situations and to express complex compositional meanings, which is difficult to do in a purely analog, costly medium. But it makes it also easy to cheat, both at the linguistic level (by pretending that something is called or expressed in one way whereas you know that it is not) and at the factual level (by lying).

Our agent-based models of language games are beginning to show how symbol-based communication systems with properties similar to human natural languages can arise and be culturally transmitted. But a crucial assumption we had to make in all these models so far is that the agents are "ultrasocial" instead of Darwinian. Sociality here means that agents are programed to cooperate fully in order to make their verbal interactions a success. They are not only set up to adopt linguistic conventions and categorizations introduced by others; they are also programed to align without hesitation their conceptual and linguistic inventories as much as possible to those of others. Speakers must be willing to adopt the perspective of listeners and try to imagine the impact of their communication on others. Moreover, agents are programed to play the language game in an honest fashion. They use conventions and conceptualizations that they take to be common in the group and give honest feedback to indicate whether the attempt at communication was successful.

Ultrasociality hence appears to be a necessary prerequisite to originating and sustaining symbolic cultural communication from the perspective of these models. This has led to criticism from biologists, who argue that it is an unrealistic assumption; on the other hand, it has led to endorsement from anthropologists, who believe that ultrasociality is precisely a unique trait of our species. A central problem in anthropology is therefore to explain how early hominins were able to lift themselves out of a Darwinian world into a cooperative social and cultural world. A scenario based on a "social revolution" that began in Africa and balanced the power relations between men and women is in this respect a very likely candidate (Knight 2008, *The Cradle*: ch. 15). It is also highly plausible that symbolic culture is a necessary factor for the further stimulation and development of sociality, creating a kind of circular causality, where language reinforces sociality and sociality enables language (Richerson and Boyd 1997).

In this chapter I do not propose a theory to explain how sociality may have arisen or how it gets reinforced by an existing language system. Instead, I examine the extent to which ultrasociality is indeed a crucial prerequisite. Is it the case that if the sociality assumption is not adopted at the linguistic level, communication systems do not get off the ground at all? Is sociality not only a sufficient but also a necessary condition for the emergence and transmission of complex symbol-based communication? And how strict does sociality have to be? Is it possible that some form of linguistic cheating can be tolerated? And how can an existing communication system reinforce sociality once it has emerged? Before delving into these issues, I first summarize our main hypothesis for the cultural evolution of language (section 3.2), give an example of the language game experiments we have been carrying out (section 3.3), and then turn to the sociality question itself (section 3.4).

3.2 Language as a complex adaptive system

Debates on the origins of language are traditionally divided between those emphasizing genetic evolution (both of the language faculty and of the conceptual repertoire that can be used for the meaning of language expressions) versus those that emphasize cultural evolution. An intermediate position assigns an important role to genetic assimilation, arguing that culturally evolved systems could have become genetically engrained. Within the cultural evolution scenario, there are still many possibilities. Our research group has been exploring the theory that language has evolved and continues to evolve as a complex adaptive system. What exactly do we mean by this?

3.2.1 *System versus systematicity*

Work on Emergent Grammar (Hopper 1987) and Construction Grammar (Croft 2001), as well as observations of real language use in natural dialog (Pickering and Garrod 2004), shows that there is no clear-cut static "system" uniformly known and used by all speakers of a language community. Instead, there is huge variation as all elements of a language undergo constant change through the individual actions of language users. New sounds get into a language or existing sounds get modulated. New words pop up or old words acquire new meanings. New grammatical constructions arise and existing words or constructions are coerced into new uses. New concepts and conceptualizations arise. All of this can happen in the course of a single dialog. Most inventions or variations do not survive beyond their short-term context, but some of them do and when these adoptions are added layer upon layer they lead to long-term observable language change. Almost all these inventions are made by adults. For example, new words in the lexicon, such as words for new technological devices like mobile phones or new forms of social and economical organization, are clearly introduced by adults and they then propagate. Data show clearly that the same is true for syntactic change (Francis and Michaelis 2002) and for phonetic change (Labov 1986).

Of course there is systematicity in language use, both in terms of the ideolectal habits of a single speaker and at the communal level, otherwise understanding across individuals would be impossible and language evolution could not be cumulative. But the great strength of human language is precisely its open-ended, fluid character, so that it can adapt extremely quickly to cope with the never-ending stream of possible novel meanings that need to be expressed. This highly dynamic view of language contrasts with that usually adopted in structuralist linguistics and particularly generative grammar, which takes the stance that there is a clear, definite system underlying a particular language like English—so much so that it is possible to capture it in a formal calculus such as generative grammar—and that there is a static core shared by all languages, which is so stable that it has become innate (Chomsky 1995).

Taking language fluidity seriously has a number of important consequences with respect to possible scenarios for the evolution of language. It implies that the decisive moment in the origins of human language cannot have been some mutation or series of mutations that suddenly gave rise to an innate universal grammar, as some authors have argued (Pinker and Jackendoff 2005; Bickerton 1984). Typological evidence shows convincingly that not even linguistic categories (such as noun, dative, agent, etc.)—let alone all possible patterns of usage—are universal and uniform across a language community (Haspelmath 2007) or can be pressed into an innately fixed enumerable set. If no universal grammar exists as a blueprint for all languages, then such a grammar cannot be innate and cannot genetically evolve. Taking fluidity seriously also implies that an "iterated learning" framework (Boyd and Richerson 1985; Kirby and Hurford 2002) must be questioned. According to this model, children acquire "the" language system from their parents, possibly with some error or generalization, and then use this to generate input data for the next generation of child learners. This approach assumes that there is a clear communal system to be learned and that all innovation and change happens during the narrow window of child language acquisition. But empirical data shows that language innovation is only driven by those who have already mastered enough systematicity and influence in the community so that their innovations have a chance to start spreading (Croft 2000). As Mufwene (2002) has put it: Language users are not in the business of learning a system but of communicating, and they use all possible resources to achieve that goal. This is particularly obvious in creole formation, where you can see how resources of different languages are pulled together by adult speakers and streamlined to shape their communication systems.

3.2.2 Invention and repair strategies

If neither genetic evolution nor iterated grammar induction is the main source for the origins and spreading of linguistic structure, then what is it? We argue that it is the actions of individual speakers and hearers that collectively construct and adapt the pool of linguistic resources available to a language community within the context of their situated verbal exchanges. The principal motivation is to succeed in communicating while maximizing expressive power—speakers want to be understood and hearers want to understand. Both have to minimize effort in order to manage the task at all and in order to be as efficient as possible. Language users are viewed as problem solvers. If solutions exist to handle a communicative task they will use them, but if not they will stretch or expand their inventories. It follows that a "theory of language" should identify the various repair strategies that speakers and hearers use in order to invent or creatively reuse bits of language through communication.

An example of a repair strategy is the following. Suppose that a speaker wants to express some category, such as a color or size or shape, for discriminating an object from another one in a shared situation. If the speaker does not have a word for this, he may decide to invent a new one or recruit an existing word and slightly expand its meaning. When the hearer then hears the word he will initially be puzzled because he does not know the word or finds its usage unexpected. However, if the hearer can reconstruct the meaning by reference to the shared context or from additional feedback, he can then expand his own inventory with the new word–meaning association. This shows that new linguistic material can get into an individual's inventory in two ways: either by his inventing it as speaker, or by his adopting it as hearer. Here is another example. Consider the sentence "John sneezed a napkin off the table" (Goldberg 2006). In this case the verb "sneeze," which is normally intransitive (i.e. it does not take a direct object), is nevertheless used transitively by the speaker within a cause-movement construction. In order for the hearer to make sense of this utterance, he has to coerce "sneeze" into a transitive verb as well. This is an example of syntactic recategorization, widely known to be one of the key driving forces in grammaticalization (Traugott and Heine 1991). Grammaticalization occurs when these novel syntactic usage patterns have been sufficiently conventionalized that they are no longer seen as odd.

Repair strategies are partly generic—relying on speakers' and hearers' abilities at problem solving and analogy making—and partly specific to a language. For example, in English you can say "I bike home" based on the repair strategy that you can turn the noun expressing the instrument of an action into a verb (another more recent example is "I emailed him a picture"). However, you cannot say "I subwayed home last night" or "I train home today" (which you can in Dutch—as in "Ik trein naar huis vandaag"). Clearly there are limits to the recategorization of instruments as verbs in any particular language. And so there is a two-level system: an inventory of form–meaning pairs (constructions) which are routinely used, and an inventory of repair strategies which become active when some sort of problem occurs. Each individual keeps his own inventory at both levels. The communal system is nowhere represented but is emergent from the inventories (ideolects) of the individuals.

3.2.3 *Selectionism all the way*

If speakers and hearers continuously expand or change their linguistic inventories, then how can there ever be any systematicity? This is the problem of the "invisible hand." How can there be (relatively) global coherence without a central coordinator and without telepathy? The Complex Adaptive Systems hypothesis proposes that this is done by processes of selection: There is a source of variation with competition between variants, as a result of which some variants become positively selected. Genetic evolution by natural selection is one example of a selection process but many other examples are to be found in nature and in human behavior—as in the operation of the economy. In language, we get selection at different levels (for similar arguments, see Croft 2000; Mufwene 2002; Oudeyer and Kaplan 2007).

First of all, even within a single individual, there is a struggle between different ways of saying or interpreting something. Different words or grammatical constructions may be competing to express the same meaning (synonymy); alternatively, different meanings may be competing for the same expression (polysemy). There is a winner-take-all situation because the speaker can only say one thing and the hearer must in the end adopt one hypothesis and test whether it makes sense. Second, there is a struggle between preferred conventions within the population as a whole. Thus there was a struggle between different words for "mobile phone" which was won in the US by the term "cell phone" and in Britain by the word "mobile." Language users still understand both alternatives but now tend to prefer just one. The individual and communal selection systems are coupled in the sense that individuals will prefer constructions that are known and used by others in order to increase their own communicative success. Hence, a word or grammatical construction that is becoming more frequent in the population will gain even more popularity, similarly to the way certain opinions become dominant. Note that the communal selection processes are a side effect of the individual selection processes. In other words, the strategies of the agents must be such that even if they have only local knowledge and even if they act in their own interest (which is to achieve communicative success) they still arrive collectively at effective solutions.

In parallel to the individual and communal language level, we find a struggle between competing repair strategies at both the individual and communal levels. For example, suppose a combination of predicates (such as "big" and "blue" and "box") needs to be expressed. If a word is missing for one of these predicates, the speaker has two possible strategies: Either a new word is invented for the total combination (holistic coding) or a new word is invented only for the part for which no word yet exists (compositional coding). Depending on the environment and the selection pressure, one or other strategy will win. Compositional coding will win if the frequency of use of the parts of meaning exceeds that of the holistic unit. Moreover, speaker and hearer should understand each other's novel sentences because knowing the meaning of the parts should enhance communicative success. Holistic coding will win if meanings do not recur very often as parts of other meanings, if specific combinations occur often enough, and/or if applying multiple rules is more costly than applying a single one (de Beule and Bergen 2006). Here is another example. A case grammar can be built using morphological affixes (as in Latin or German), particles (as in Japanese), or word order and prepositions (as in English). Clearly once a particular strategy is adopted, language users will tend to solve all problems related to event–object expression in the same way, even though there may be remnants of earlier dominant strategies in current language use. Hence English once had a system of Latin-like morphological affixes for marking case; this was replaced by a system based on word order and prepositions. Remnants of the older system are still seen in the use of pronouns ("he" versus "him"). Similarly, the older system of building past tense by modulating the verb stem (as in "is" vs. "was" or "came" vs. "come") has been replaced by a strategy in which the past tense is built by using "-ed" (as in "walk" vs. "walked"). But again we see remnants of the older system even though it is no longer productive.

3.2.4 *Transitions in language complexity*

The competition between alternative repair strategies and the invention and recruitment of new strategies to handle new types of problems gradually pushes the complexity of language from holistic words to multi-word utterances and from there towards patterns and grammatical constructions (Steels 2005). This must have happened in the past with the emergence of the first prehistoric languages but it will happen every time a language community for one reason or another loses a sufficiently powerful communication system, for example because speakers are brought together from different language communities in stress situations (as in creole formation, see Mufwene 2001) or because speakers are impaired (as in the Nicaragua case). Thus, a case grammar may start to develop when the need is felt to express the roles of objects in events. If a purely lexical language without case expression were used, confusion (and hence communicative failure) might arise—as in "John gives Mary the book" versus "Mary gives John the book." In the first instance the expression of event–object relations can be handled with ad hoc patterns (for example, one in which the giver in a giving action always comes before the verb), but as more situations must be expressed, a more general solution needs to be found, which involves strategies that introduce new syntactic categories (nominative, accusative, etc.) and new semantic categories (agent, patient, etc.) as well as case markings of the syntactic categories (through prepositions, word order, affixes, etc.).

Summarizing, the Complex Adaptive Systems approach to language emergence and language dynamics proposes that language systems remain fluid as they are continuously adapted by their users. The communal language and its systematicity are forever an emergent outcome of the repair actions and consolidation strategies of speakers and hearers. An explanation for the origins of language from this point of view consists therefore of a definition of the general cognitive architecture and interaction patterns that support these various selection processes, an examination of repair strategies and an understanding of their effect on emergent languages—and an investigation of how new strategies, including strategies that increase the complexity of a language, can arise and become widespread.

The Complex Adaptive Systems hypothesis is of course only one of the many possible hypotheses on how language may have evolved. The genetic evolution scenario (Pinker and Jackendoff 2005) is another one, and several others are discussed in the present volume. These other hypotheses are also coherent and equally deserve further testing by theoretical investigations, but in our own work we focus on the Complex Adaptive Systems hypothesis.

3.3 Language game experiments

I now summarize the framework of language games that we have been using for studying and validating this selectionist approach (Steels 1995). The framework is in many respects similar to theoretical frameworks used in economics and sociology to study opinion dynamics, social dynamics, the spreading of cultural artifacts, and so forth (see e.g. Axelrod 2005). They involve the definition of an agent and an interaction pattern (a game) which exercises and influences the internal structures of the agents but has a collective effect. It is possible to study such systems through mathematical analysis (see e.g. Baronchelli et al. 2006), but in our group we focus on agent-based simulations. We define exhaustively in computational terms the cognitive architecture of an agent, which includes generic facilities for symbolic processing, such as unifying and merging feature structures (Steels and de Beule 2006), as well as procedures for detecting failures and executing repairs, and scripts for interacting with other agents. Agents start their activity without any prior linguistic or conceptual inventory and must gradually build this up as part of their language games. Agents take turns playing speaker and hearer, so that they each develop the competence to speak as well as that to understand, and all of them have equal rights to invent new bits of language or decide whether to reuse material introduced by someone else.

An agent can exist as a software object with the interaction pattern simulated on a computer; alternatively, we can use physically embodied agents (robots) operating in a real world environment in order to address questions such as how internally represented meanings are transduced into language, how meanings arise grounded in the real world experiences of the agents, and how different perspectives on the scene influence the emergence of language. The robotic agents now come equipped with a vision system, pattern recognition, and machine learning for categorizing the world, and motor behaviors for creating a joint attention frame and for pointing. The cognitive architecture is implemented on computers running on board the robots.

Here is one example of such an experiment, described in more detail in Steels and Loetzsch (2008). We call it the perspective reversal experiment because it examines how far spatial language can emerge in order to express sentences such as "the ball is to the left of the box," or "the ball rolls from my left to your right." This requires not only the emergence of spatial categories such as "left" and "right" but also potentially markers of the perspective from which description is made, such as "my" in "my left." Of course the robots do not come up with English words but will say things like "badibo mo wabodo" which we as observers need to analyze in retrospect as if we were studying an unfamiliar foreign language.

The perspective reversal experiment uses physical robotic "agents" (the Sony ERS7 AIBO), which roam around freely in an unconstrained indoor environment containing balls and boxes. The robots have no direct way of communicating except through visual or auditory means and they have no way to read or set each other's internal states. Even though we, as experimenters, can track the complete internal state of each robot based on wireless communication between the robot and a base station, there is no central control, neither of the physical behavior nor of the cognitive operations that a robot performs. The robots are completely autonomous. In other words, once the experiment starts, the situation becomes similar to observational experiments with animals. Moreover, although the experiment employs only two robot bodies, it is relatively straightforward (and is routinely done) to carry out experiments with a much larger population of agents: The state of an agent (its perceptual, conceptual, and linguistic inventory at a particular point in time) is after all a software state, and so it can be "downloaded" into a specific robot body before interaction starts and "uploaded" to another robot body at the end of an interaction. So we can have as many agents as we wish even with a small number of robots.

The language game used in the perspective reversal experiment is a description game. The speaker describes to the hearer what is novel about the present scene compared to the previous one. It works in the following manner. Two robots walk around randomly. As soon as one detects the ball, it comes to a stop and searches for the other robot, which also looks for the ball and stops when it sees it. Then the human experimenter pushes the ball with a stick so that it rolls a short distance, for example from the left of one robot to its right. This movement is tracked and analyzed by both robots and each uses the resulting perception as the basis for playing a language game, in which one of the two (acting as the "speaker") describes the ball-moving event to the other (the "hearer").

To do this, the speaker must first conceptualize the event in terms of categories like "left" and "right" that distinguish the latest event from the previous one, for example, that the ball rolled "away from the speaker and to the right," as opposed to "towards the speaker," or, "away from the speaker but to the left" as opposed to "away from the speaker but to the right." The available categories are perceptually grounded in the sense that they are processes operating over the sensory data. They are built up by the agents stimulated by the need to conceptualize a scene and aligned during the consolidation phase based on the outcome of a language game. Agents can perform perspective reversal. This means that the speaker is able to perceive the position of the hearer and then geometrically transform the scene to make a good guess about what the hearer is seeing. He can then use this transformed sensory image to conceptualize the scene from the viewpoint of the hearer or to reconstruct how the hearer might interpret what he is about to say. The hearer can also use perspective reversal by perceiving the position of the speaker and geometrically transforming his own view of the scene in order to reconstruct that of the speaker. The hearer can then use this transformed view to extract the speaker's world model and use that to interpret a sentence which would not make sense otherwise.

Next the speaker transduces this conceptualization using whatever linguistic resources in his inventory express it best and have been most successful in the past, and transmits the resulting utterance as an acoustic signal to the hearer. The hearer parses the utterance to reconstruct its possible meanings and applies them to the current scene.

The game is a success if, according to the hearer, one of the meanings not only fits with the current scene as it is perceived by him but is also distinctive with respect to the previous scene. For example, if a ball was to the left of the box in the previous scene and in the current scene it is still to the left, then a description "the ball is to the left of the box" is not considered to be appropriate, even though it fits with the scene, because it does not describe a novel property of the current scene. The hearer then signals success or failure and both agents use this feedback to update their internal states. Note that there is no human intervention involved. The robot agent playing the role of hearer autonomously decides whether the game was a success or not.

Neither a prior language nor a prior set of perceptually grounded categories (properties, relations, prototypes, etc.) is programed into the agents. Indeed, the purpose of the experiment is to see what kinds of categories and linguistic constructions will emerge given specific repair strategies and, more specifically, whether the emergent languages involve perspective marking and grammatical constructions to express them. Agents therefore need their cognitive machinery not only for playing the game and utilizing their available conceptual and linguistic inventories, but also for expanding these inventories by creating (as speaker) or adopting (as hearer) new categories, new words, and new grammatical constructions as the need for them arises.

Figure 3.1 shows the results of the experiments. The top graphs show the outcome of an experiment, in which both agents have exactly the same sensory experience. This is done by sending the sensory image of the speaker by wireless to the hearer. We see that the agents quickly arrive at very high communicative success, implying that a shared lexicon and ontology has evolved. The bottom graphs show the normal case in which each agent uses his own sensory experience, which is always different from that of the other. For example, one robot could be looking at the ball from the opposite side to another robot, so that what is "left of the ball" for one is in fact "right of the ball" for the other. Agents use perspective reversal if they believe that this will result in a more reliable communication, but in this experiment they do not express it yet (another experiment where they do express perspective is discussed shortly). We see that agents nevertheless reach an above chance degree of success despite the severe challenges posed by real world interactions, perceptual processes, and embodied communication.

When we study the communication systems that emerge in these experiments, we see that they have the kind of properties Hockett (1960) identified as characteristic for human language. These include "arbitrariness" (there is no specific reason why something is labeled in a particular way apart from convention); "productivity" (the capacity to say or understand things that have never been said before); and "displacement" (the robots implicitly talk about what is novel with respect to a situation which is no longer the current one). The basic selection processes discussed earlier are at work here, with different words competing for the same meaning

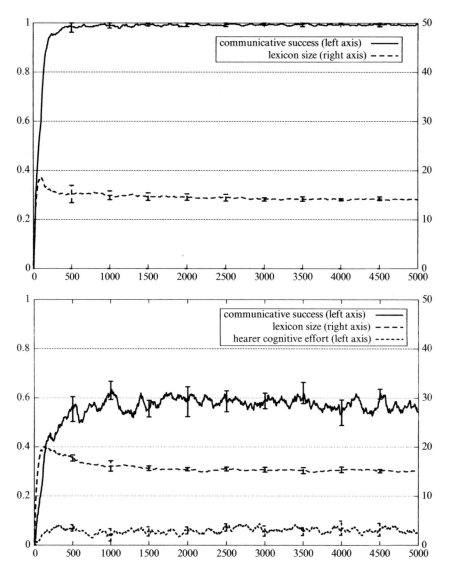

Fig. 3.1. Results from 5 different experimental runs of 5,000 language games in a population of 10 embodied agents. Top: Robots use the same sensory experiences to build a world model and play the language game. We see that a communication system gets quickly off the ground. The top line shows communicative success, which reaches 100% quickly. The bottom line shows the average size of the lexicon of all agents. The lexicon gradually becomes optimal. Bottom: Robots now each use their own sensory experience. They may also use egocentric perspective transformation as part of the process of conceptualizing what to say. Success is close to 50% and the lexicon is stable. The bottom line shows cognitive effort, which is quite high because agents continuously check both their own and the other agent's perspective in order to speak or interpret an utterance.

and different meanings competing for the same word. But synonymy and homonymy are progressively dampened.

We have been experimenting successfully with many other robots, including humanoid robots, other kinds of environments, and other types of language games, thus steadily covering more and more features of language, such as expression of event–object structure, polysemy, etc. All these experiments have the same underlying structure: We set up an interaction pattern among agents by giving them specific scripts, we create an environment in which these interaction patterns make sense, and then we endow the agents with repair strategies for fixing problems in their communication as well as for consolidating their inventories after a game.

3.4 The sociality assumption

We now turn to the issue of sociality. Sociality is not a simple parameter that can be switched on or off but is a design principle that has to be embedded in all aspects of the cognitive architecture and the interaction scripts of the agents. In this section I highlight three specific examples of experiments that shed more light on how far sociality is a crucial prerequisite.

3.4.1 *Joint attention*

Joint attention means (i) that speaker and hearer have a sufficiently shared context so that the possible meanings of an utterance are highly constrained, (ii) that they are engaged in a shared cooperative activity so that both can gauge whether their communication was successful or not, and (iii) that they have the means to correct miscommunication by additional dialog or by motor behaviors such as pointing. The necessity of each of these aspects can be established firmly through language game experiments: If the set of meanings is not constrained then the search space of possible meanings becomes so large that listeners cannot make educated guesses about the meaning of unknown words or constructions, and consequently a shared language system will not get off the ground. When agents do not get feedback about the success or failure of the game or have no way to correct their miscommunication they can still use cross-situational learning, comparing different situations to see what is common and thus induce possible meanings. Cross-situational learning is much more inefficient and hence leads to less communicative success.

Joint attention arises at many levels in the animal world, for example in animals that are hunting together. But studies, particularly of non-human primates, have shown that animal forms of joint attention are much weaker compared to even very young human infants (Tomasello et al. 2005). It is usually argued that in a Darwinian world, strong forms of joint attention put individuals at risk of exploitation and hence are not evolutionarily stable strategies. For example, if others can easily detect through body posture and eye gaze in which direction you are looking, they glean information about your intention and can take advantage of the situation for themselves.

We have carried out an experiment to test the importance of joint attention through language games on the AIBO robot (see Steels and Kaplan 2001 for details). The language game was in this case a naming game, in which one robot learned words for objects in its environment, a red ball, a toy robot called Poo-chi, and a small puppet called Smiley, from a human experimenter. The robot sees many views of the same object from different perspectives and cannot know whether one view is connected to the same object or not, so he has to learn how different views are clustered. Two conditions were examined (Figure 3.2, left): (a) the experimenter interacts strongly with the robot, showing objects expressly to enable better joint attention, naming the objects, and giving precise feedback as to whether the name used by the robot is correct; (b) the experimenter cites the name of the object when he believes the robot is paying attention to it, but the experimenter has no absolutely clear idea what the robot sees as he moves around freely in the environment, and the experimenter does not give feedback. Condition (a) reflects a strong social engagement and condition (b) does not. Figure 3.2 (right) shows that the results of social learning (condition (a)) are significantly better than those involving a weaker form of interaction. Only the red ball gives condition (b) a result above 50%, which is largely due to the fact that the AIBO robot has been programmed to have a strong tendency to focus on red balls. Clearly, without strong joint attention, communicative success dives below chance, with the result that the evolution of communication does not get off the ground.

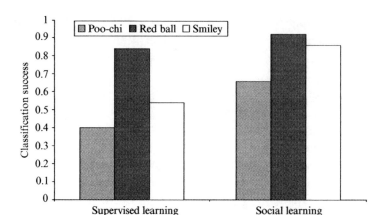

Fɪɢ. 3.2. Graph showing the success rate at which the object was named correctly.

3.4.2 *Perspective reversal*

Another aspect of sociality is the ability to adopt the perspective of the other, which is often seen as one of the key capacities making up a "theory of mind" ability. An extensive literature exists showing that the capacity for theory of mind is much weaker in animals, including non-human primates, compared to human subjects. This is partly due to the level of intelligence of animals, but also to how much we expose our internal states to others through language, emotional gesturing, etc. so that they can reconstruct our intentions and desires (Deacon 1997).

The importance of perspective reversal for bootstrapping a successful communication system can easily be demonstrated within the context of the perspective reversal experiment briefly discussed earlier. When speakers are not able to adopt the perspective of the listener or vice versa, situations are unavoidable where communication will fail. Thus suppose a speaker and a hearer stand facing each other with a block in between them and a ball on each side of the block. If the speaker says "the ball left of the block" this will generate communicative failure, because left for the speaker is right for the hearer. Hence the listener will point to the wrong block and the speaker will correct, causing both speaker and hearer to lose confidence in the words for left and right. We see this in another experiment (Figure 3.3 top) in which agents are not given the power of perspective reversal. They produce similar situations to the one shown in Figure 3.1 (top and bottom). Clearly no communication system is getting

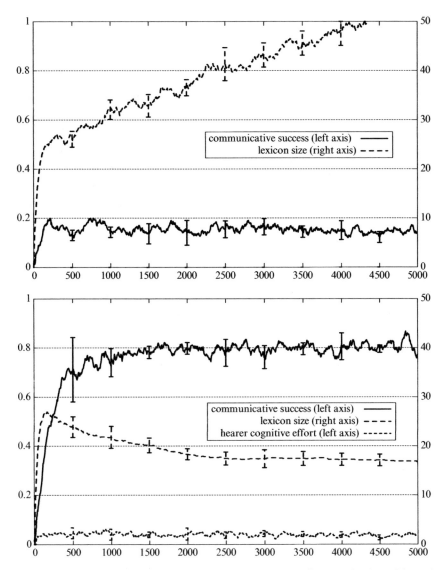

FIG. 3.3. The top graph shows communicative success (bottom line) and lexical coherence (top line) for an experiment in which the agents are unable to carry out perspective reversal but nevertheless have to describe situations in which the spatial relations between objects depend on the point of view on the scene. No success is achieved and the lexicon keeps on growing further and further without reaching coherence. The bottom graph shows the same measures but now for an experiment in which agents do mark perspective. Performance has augmented significantly with respect to Figure 3.1 (bottom), where agents do not mark perspective. Cognitive effort is also slightly lower.

off the ground. Both communicative success and lexical coherence remain very low.

Figure 3.1 (bottom) has already shown that agents are capable of handling their communicative problems better if they use perspective reversal. Each time they check which perspective makes sense. When the speaker describes what is novel about a scene he tests whether a description from the hearer's perspective would have a higher chance of communicative success than one from his own perspective. Similarly, the hearer checks whether an interpretation of the scene from the speaker's perspective makes more sense than one from his own perspective and picks an arbitrary solution if both are equally plausible. This strategy leads to a successful system but agents can be more cooperative by marking explicitly from which perspective they are describing the scene. The result of this strategy is shown in Figure 3.3 (bottom). We see that communicative success is higher and agents reach a minimal stable lexicon. The cognitive effort is also slightly lower.

This example demonstrates that the motivation for speakers to express certain aspects of meaning—in this case perspective—is a desire to be sufficiently clear and helpful to the listener that communicative success is more likely and effort is minimized. The listener is also expected to make all possible effort to understand the speaker, but given the enormity of the problem, he can use any help he can get. So a cooperative attitude is really the driving force towards the lexicalization and grammaticalization processes that shape complex language.

3.4.3 *The reciprocal naming game*

A third experiment examines more directly how strictly the sociality assumption needs to hold with respect to telling the truth in communication (see Wang and Steels 2008 for more details). It is based on the reciprocal naming game, which combines two games: a signaling game originally introduced by Crawford and Sobel (1982) and a naming game (Steels 2005). The signaling game is a classic cooperate or defect game. It involves two agents, S (signaler) and R (receiver), where S is better informed than R about the environment and may potentially give misleading information. R carries out an action based on the message transmitted by S. Because S may try to deceive, R must decide on the basis of trust in S to believe him. Just as in the prisoner's dilemma game, it can be shown that a tit-for-tat strategy can lead a group to be successful in the signaling game, if agents keep selfish behavior in check by punishing cheaters and by rewarding cooperation (Trivers 1971). The reciprocal naming game experiment uses this strategy as a base line. Agents keep a record of the cooperative behavior of other individuals and act accordingly in a cooperative or non-cooperative way.

However, instead of supplying a fixed convention in advance, the reciprocal naming game adds the difficulty that agents must self-organize their communication system from scratch. We will use the same lateral inhibition dynamics as used earlier on in the perspective reversal experiment, and indeed in all the experiments we have carried out. The critical question is whether a lexicon will still emerge even if the agents have the opportunity to cheat, which unavoidably leads to confusion in lexicon formation. It is much harder for an agent to learn the convention in the group because it receives contractory feedback.

I refer to the original chapter for details of the implementation, but just point to two major conclusions. The first one (see Figure 3.4) shows that if agents use a tit-for-tat policy in the signaling game coupled to the standard naming game lateral inhibition dynamics, a communication system will indeed get off the ground in co-evolution with the trust relations between the agents. So sociality can develop alongside language and both can mutually enforce each other. On the other hand if they have no way to punish defectors then communicative success hovers around chance (Figure 3.4 top).

We also examined the effect of having free-riders in the population, which are agents which will never cooperate. As long as the number of free-riders is small, a successful communication system can still bootstrap; however, when free-riders are in the majority, it is in an agent's best interest to follow the same strategy of non-cooperation and hence the communication system will collapse. The impact of an emergent communication system on the maintenance of sociality is not so obvious. A lexicon is fairly stable because it is not easy for one agent to enforce a new global consensus once it exists. Moreover, when an opponent cheats once with a word, the other player will disbelieve the message in the next round and hence will be proof against future cheating. It is in the interest of both cooperation and deception to use the agreed naming conventions.

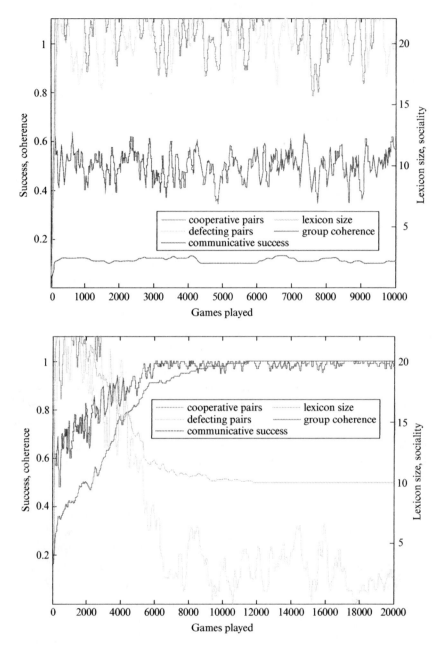

Fig. 3.4. Reciprocal naming game in a population of 10 agents self-organizing a lexicon of names for 10 objects. Top: Agents do not use a tit-for-tat strategy. They are unable to detect or punish cheaters. Communicative success (middle line) remains around 50%. Bottom: Agents use tit-for-tat to establish and maintain social cooperation. A lexicon now self-organizes easily and agents reach 100% communicative success.

3.5 Conclusions

Agent-based modeling is progressively showing us what kind of cognitive architecture and interaction patterns agents need in order to self-organize communication systems with human language-like properties, such as arbitrariness (i.e. conventionality), productivity, displacement, etc. But these experiments also show that there is a very important prerequisite, namely that agents have to behave socially. Sociality is reflected both in the cognitive processes and in the interaction patterns (language games) of the agents. Ultrasociality, that is sociality beyond immediate kin, implies that there is a risk of exploitation and apparently animal communication systems are not prepared to take this risk. But human languages do, and as a consequence they are richer and adapt faster compared to animal communication systems. It is a deep puzzle how this kind of ultrasociality could have arisen through Darwinian evolution, a puzzle not addressed in this chapter (but for thoughtful discussions and hypotheses see Knight 2008, *The Cradle*: ch. 15; Richerson and Boyd 1997). One thing is sure: that sociality is a crucial prerequisite for language and that language in turn must have helped maintain sociality in our species. I have described three experiments which substantiate the necessity of social cooperation; other experiments in the same vein can be imagined.

4 Holistic communication and the co-evolution of language and music: resurrecting an old idea

STEVEN MITHEN

4.1 Introduction

In his 1895 book, *Progress in Language*, Otto Jespersen, one of the greatest language scholars of the nineteenth and twentieth centuries, proposed that "language began with half-musical analysed expressions for individual beings and events" (Jespersen 1983 [1895]: 365). He was not the first to associate the evolution of language with music; Jean Jacques Rousseau's 1781 *Essai sur l'origine des langues* was a reflection on both music and language (see Thomas 1995). It was partly as a reaction to such writings that the Parisian Société de Linguistique imposed their infamous 1866 ban on discussions about the origin of language. That ban was largely effective for more than a century, but as from the 1990s it was thoroughly over-ridden with the start (Bickerton 1990; Pinker and Bloom 1990) of what has become an avalanche of discussions, conferences, and publications about how language evolved (e.g. Dunbar 1996; Hurford et al. 1998; Carstairs-McCarthy 1999; Knight et al. 2000; Wray 2002; Christiansen and Kirby 2003; Tallerman 2005; Cangelosi et al. 2006). Within this remarkable body of work, however, the insights of Rousseau and Jespersen that language and music are likely to have co-evolved appear to have been largely forgotten, or at least ignored. There have, of course, been exceptions, notably in 1973 when John Blacking argued that there had once been a "nonverbal, pre-linguistic, musical mode of thought and action," although his work has also not been drawn upon by those writing about the evolution of language. This neglect of music is, perhaps, one reason why progress on this issue has been less forthcoming than one might have hoped.

In this chapter I wish to return to the view that language and music co-evolved and to relate this to recent arguments that protolanguage was holistic rather than compositional in nature (Wray 1998, 2000; Arbib 2003, 2005). I will argue that musicality is indeed a key to understanding how language evolved: in essence, we can speak together because we once sang together. Note that I am using the term musicality rather than music as, whereas the latter is a cultural construct, the former simply refers to variations in pitch, rhythm, tone, and timbre of the voice and the equivalent with regard to movements of the body.

4.2 Music and language

Language—whether spoken or gestural—has a degree of musicality, the extent of which varies according to the specific language being spoken and the context in which it is being used. By definition, tonal languages rely on variations of pitch to a greater extent than non-tonal languages; yet even the latter makes extensive use of prosody to either define or simply nuance the meaning of utterances. The use of variations in pitch, rhythm, tone, and timbre is particularly striking when one is listening to accomplished orators—the likes of Hitler, Luther King, and Churchill. The musical qualities of their orations are evidently playing a key role in their effectiveness. But perhaps the most familiar and significant example of the musicality of language is that used when speaking to infants, known as "infant directed speech" (IDS) or more popularly as "motherese" (an inappropriate term as male siblings, relations, friends, and fathers also modify their spoken language when addressing infants).

The key characteristics of IDS are the extended articulation of vowels, heightened pitch, and exaggerated pitch contours. Research by Fernald (e.g. 1989, 1991, 1992) and others (e.g. Papousek et al. 1991; Monnot 1999) has shown that these are not simply used to facilitate the acquisition of language by infants; the musicality of speech has its own function in terms of its emotional impact on the infant.

The issue of emotion is important—and is also neglected in recent studies of language evolution. Indeed, paleoanthropology in general has neglected to address the emotional lives of human ancestors, perhaps not unreasonably as there is no evident methodology for how to do so. But even casual observations of great apes indicate that their social behavior cannot be understood without reference to their emotional states and how these are manipulated by vocalizations and physical actions such as grooming among chimpanzees, sex among bonobos, and chest-beating among gorillas. As the same is unquestionably the case for modern humans—as our own life experiences will testify—the absence of reference to the emotional lives of extinct hominins appears to be a serious omission. Such neglect has partly arisen because studies of protolanguage have focussed on the existence or otherwise of words and grammar (e.g. Bickerton 1995, 2000; Jackendoff 1999, 2002) rather than the musicality of communication by which emotion is expressed and often induced in others.

Looking beyond the musicality of language among modern humans, further significant similarities can be found between music and language that suggest an evolutionary association. Both music and language are combinatorial and hierarchical systems of communication and expression; both can be described as forming families within which patterns of descent, blending, and development can be reconstructed; both language and music have three modes of expression: the voice, the body, and as writing.

There are also important differences. Whereas language excels at communicating information, music excels at expressing emotion. Music is non-symbolic in the sense that there are no shared meanings of a semantic nature for sequences of sounds within one "music community" as there are for words within a speech community. Cross (1999, 2001) has stressed the significance of this by invoking the notion of "floating intentionality" for music: everyone can agree to share the experience of a piece of music without needing to agree to share a meaning that one of more individuals may wish to impose on the music. Music also lacks a grammar of the type found in language. A musical style does, of course, have rules and these can be referred to as its grammar if one wishes to do so (e.g. Lerdahl and Jackendoff 1983); but as such, this is a quite different type of grammar to that found in language, which serves to add a secondary level of semantic meaning to utterances, above and beyond the meaning of each individual word. Musical grammars do not do this; indeed they cannot because musical pitches (the equivalent of words) simply lack any shared semantic meanings to be built upon by a musical grammar.

4.3 Possible evolutionary relationships between music and language

The musicality of language, and the similarities and the differences between music and language, are open to three evolutionary interpretations (Figure 4.1, Brown 2000).

1. One of these systems of communication and expression might be largely derivative of the other. This is how Pinker (1997) thinks of music as a recent cultural invention occurring after the biological evolution of language and hence of no evolutionary significance. The converse argument could be made: that language is a relatively recent spin-off from an ancient form of musical communication and expression.

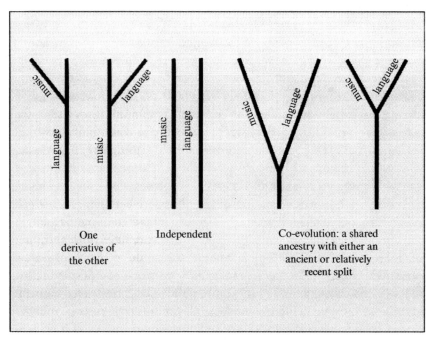

FIG. 4.1. Possible evolutionary relationships between language and music, after Brown (2000)

2. The second evolutionary interpretation is one that stresses the differences rather than the similarities and proposes that language and music have completely independent evolutionary histories, with their overlaps being a consequence of recent cultural history. This is the implicit position of the majority of studies on language origins from the last two decades (e.g. Bickerton 2000) that have found no need to make any reference to musicality.

3. Third, music and language might have evolved from a single form of ancient communication and expression that had elements of both systems but cannot be adequately characterized as primarily one or the other. This is Brown's (2000) view, resurrecting the ideas of Jespersen and Rousseau; he adopts the term "musilanguage" for this ancient system that, at some time in human evolution, bifurcated into the two (overlapping) communication systems that we now refer to as music and language.

Two key lines of evidence suggest that Brown is correct—although the term "musilanguage" is problematic as it leaves his theory open to a criticism of teleology. One line of evidence comes from studies of non-human primates. Many studies have now documented continuities in behavior, perception, cognition, and neurophysiology between human speech and primate vocal communication (Seyfarth 2004). As such, it appears incontestable that human language evolved from a communication system that had strong similarities to that used by primates, and especially the chimpanzee today. This rejects the arguments for discontinuity between primate vocalizations and human speech forwarded primarily by linguists (e.g. Bickerton 1990; Arbib 2005).

This is not, however, to minimize the difference between primate calls and human speech. A fundamental difference is that the former are holistic utterances—they are not constituted by words combined with grammatical rules (see Mitani 1996 for a review) as are the majority of human utterances, which are henceforth referred to as being compositional. Primate holistic calls are limited in number and used in restricted contexts, the classic examples being the predator alarm calls of vervets (Struhsaker 1967; Cheney and Seyfarth 1990) and the pant hoots of chimpanzees (Mitani 1996; Mitani and Gros-Louis 1995). We should also note, however, that primate holistic vocalizations also have a significant degree of musicality. Indeed, they are rather more like human musical phrases, which are also holistic in character, than spoken utterances. Richman (1987) has described the rhythmic chattering of geladas, while the "duetting" of gibbons has been extensively studied (e.g. Mitani 1985; Geissmann 2000). More generally, the variations of pitch, rhythm, tone, and timbre of primate vocalizations—that is, their musicality—play an essential role in their use for manipulating the emotional states and behavior of other individuals.

A second line of evidence to support the existence of a "musilanguage" form of communication comes from newborn infants, who appear to arrive in the world as eager to respond to music as they are to acquire language. Trevarthen (1999: 174) described babies as being "born with a musical wisdom and appetite." In this regard, it would seem unlikely that music could be a spin-off from language acquisition, while the musicality of IDS appears to be an intuitive recognition that language and music are significantly entwined together. Indeed, they are inseparable within the infant experience of, and response to, the world (Trehub 2003).

A potential third line of evidence is the manner in which music and language are constituted in the brain (Peretz and Zatorre 2003). This remains little understood, however, with the existing evidence being open to various interpretations. On the one hand, there appears to be substantial evidence from studies of those suffering from brain damage or congenital conditions that music and language have significant degrees of independence in the brain, even a double disassociation. Hence some individuals who suffer from aphasia appear to have intact musical abilities (e.g. Luria et al. 1965; Mendez 2001; Metz-Lutz and Dahl 1984; Miller 1989), while conversely those suffering from amusia appear to have intact linguistic abilities (e.g. Wilson and Pressing 1999; Peretz 1993; Peretz et al. 2002)—although the evidence for this is more questionable than the former. On the other hand, brain scanning has indicated that there are significant overlaps in which brain regions are recruited for music and language (e.g. Patel 2003; Maess et al. 2001; Parsons 2003). The immense difficulty we face is that there have been a limited number of studies and the methodological challenges facing each study and its interpretation are immense. Any individual brain is the product of both an evolutionary and a development history, and the degrees of brain plasticity are increasingly recognized as substantial. In general, our ability to draw evolutionary implications from neuroscience remains problematic.

4.4 An early or late bifurcation?

In light of the evidence from primate vocalizations, babies, and IDS, the third possibility—a shared evolutionary history—is the most persuasive scenario suggested by Brown (2000). This provides us with two options: an early or a late bifurcation into the two systems that we now call music and language. The key question is when did the holistic utterances that had been used by our hominin ancestors become segmented to create words and eventually compositional language? "Segmentation" is the term that Wray (1998, 2000) introduced for the process by which individual elements of holistic phrases came to have an independent meaning from the rest of the phrase; Arbib (2005) used "fractionation" for the same process. An alternative scenario is that holistic phrases did not become segmented but were merely supplemented and then overwhelmed by the use of words and grammatical rules, resulting in a communication system dominated by compositional language but which still made the occasional use of holistic phrases.

One possibility is that this transition from holistic phrases to compositional language occurred relatively early in human evolution, say at the origin of the genus *Homo* sometime before two million years ago, or even much earlier at the time of the common human/chimpanzee ancestor. This scenario is effectively the same as the independent evolution interpretation for music and language. It is the one implicitly adopted by Bickerton (1990, 1995, 2000), who argues for a protolanguage constituted by words without grammar, or by Jackendoff (1999, 2000), who proposed the presence of a protogrammar using rules such as "agent-first."

An alternative possibility is that the bifurcation of a holistic "musilanguage" into the two (overlapping) communication systems that we call language and music occurred relatively late in human evolution, say at the origin of modern humans at sometime after 200,000 years ago. This proposition has had relatively little consideration in the evolution of language literature but has been implicitly promoted by the linguist Alison Wray in her seminal 1998 article entitled "Protolanguage as a holistic system for social interaction." Wray had not appreciated the musicality aspects of a holistic protolanguage and hence the significance of her own work for the origin of not only language but also music. Her article was the first (to my knowledge) to argue that large-brained hominins, such as the Neanderthals, were communicating by holistic phrases rather than a protolanguage with words and limited (if any) grammar, or even fully modern compositional language.

Wray's was a radical proposition—and one of the most important in our studies of language evolution for at least the past two decades. It is one that is, I believe, essentially correct for six reasons.

4.5 Six reasons for the use of holistic phrases rather than a compositional protolanguage by pre-modern humans

1. *This is the most parsimonious interpretation.* The behavior of pre-modern humans as evident from the archeological record can be explained by reference to the use of holistic phrases; as this is a simpler and more ancient form of communication than compositional language, it is the most parsimonious interpretation to accept. There is no reason to think that the tool-making skills of pre-modern humans, such as those required to manufacture Acheulian or Levallois tools (Pelegrin 1993), required compositional language for their transmission or acquisition. Even among modern humans skill acquisition is dominated by observation and trial and error, with minimal, if any, instruction. Indeed, all attempts to infer language abilities from stone tools have been unpersuasive (e.g. Dibble 1989; Toth and Schick 1993): While this may reflect the absence of an appropriate methodology, it is more likely because compositional language was simply not required for stone tool manufacture and hence there are no linguistic implications to be discovered. Similarly, big game hunting, as was evidently undertaken by species such as *Homo heidelbergensis* and *Homo neanderthalensis* (e.g. Thieme 1997; Roberts and Parfitt 1999), does not appear to require compositional language in light of the coordinated hunting of social carnivores and chimpanzees (e.g. Stanford 1999).

2. *Sociality requires communication but not compositional language.* Early *Homo* most likely lived in communities with intensified sociality as compared to those of living primates today (Dunbar 2004). As Dunbar has argued, such sociality is likely to have created selective pressure for enhanced communication—the basis for his theory of the "gossip" origins of language (Aiello and Dunbar 1993; Dunbar 1996). But as Wray (1998) explained, even among modern humans with compositional language, communication about the social world often takes the form of formulaic

utterances—our modern equivalent of holistic phrases. In fact, one might even argue that there is an inverse relationship between the extent of social knowledge about individuals and the need for novel utterances. The latter are more significant when meeting and needing to find out about individuals that one does not know—i.e. for talking with strangers. In this regard the widely accepted social intimacy of early hominin communities appears to preclude the need for compositional language.

3. *The cultural stability of pre-modern humans.* One of the most striking features of the archeological record before the origin of modern humans is the extent of cultural stability. Acheulian handaxes remain as the most elaborate component of Paleolithic technology for more than a million years (Wynn 1995); the Neanderthals were manufacturing essentially the same types of artifacts when they appear in the fossil record at c. 250,000 years ago as they were immediately prior to their extinction after 50,000 years ago (Mellars 1996; Stringer and Gamble 1993) (notwithstanding the issue of the Chatelperronian—most likely a consequence of Neanderthals imitating the technology of modern humans; Mellars et al. 2007). This cultural stability is present at a coarse level of analysis; there is variation and change in the archeological record with hominins responding to raw material availability, resource distributions, and climate change (e.g. Ashton and McNabb 1994; Turq 1992). But what we see are minor variations around a limited number of behavioral themes. This degree of cultural stability is incompatible with a presence of compositional language, even if this is no more complex than the protolanguage of Bickerton or of Jackendoff with a small number of protogrammatical rules. Compositional language is the motor for cultural change: The possibility of creating an infinite number of new utterances would lead to the possibility of creating new types of tools as knowledge about tool effectiveness and manufacturing methods is exchanged. And there should be no doubt that hominins would have benefited from some cultural innovation. The skeletal remains of the Neanderthals, for instance, indicate that they were a marginal population teetering on the edge of demographic survival with high frequency of injuries and illness (Trinkaus 1995). If there was ever a population that could have benefited from the invention of sewing needles, bows and arrows, and stone architecture it was the Neanderthals. The fact they did not, along with the overall pattern of Neanderthal and other hominin cultural stability can only be explained by their use of a communication system that is reliant on a fixed number of holistic phrases.

4. *The absence of symbolic artifacts.* It is, of course, impossible to be absolutely confident that the stone artifacts, discarded bones, and other debris left by pre-modern hominins were entirely devoid of symbolic meanings. Among modern humans, natural landscape features (e.g. trees and hills) and unmodified objects (e.g. stones and shells) can have complex symbolic meanings. This might also be the case for pre-modern humans. Nevertheless the absence of any modified objects that are likely to have symbolic meanings prior to the Blombos finds from 70,000 years ago (Henshilwood et al. 2002), or indeed the intense use of red ochre in the African MSA as from c. 165,000 years ago (Marean et al. 2007; Knight et al. 1995), appears to make this unlikely. There are, of course, numerous objects that are claimed to have symbolic meanings, such as the Berekhat Ram "figurine" (d'Errico and Nowell 2000) and various pieces of scratched bone and stone (Mania and Mania 1988; Bednarik 1995). I remain unpersuaded by any of these as examples of symbolic behavior (Mithen 1996a, 2000). The absence of such symbolism would be unlikely if hominins were using either a proto- or a fully modern language in which words were acting as discrete symbols: I find it inconceivable that hominins could think and act by using verbal symbols but did not use visual symbols.

5. *A protolanguage which was compositional in nature would have been unstable.* If the bifurcation of an original musilanguage form of communication into two systems of language and music occurred relatively early in human evolution, then we would have had at least one and perhaps several million years of hominins using a protolanguage of the type that Bickerton and Jackendoff promote—words with limited (if any) grammar. In light of various studies within computational linguistics by Kirby (2000, 2001, 2003) and others (e.g. Batali 2002), this appears unfeasible. These have shown that grammatical structure is an emergent property of the cultural transmission of protolanguage from one generation to the next. Hence once a Bickertonian-like protolanguage had appeared, this would have rapidly developed into fully compositional language. So if, as Bickerton argues, *Homo erectus* had possessed a protolanguage with words, it is inconceivable that this did not evolve into fully modern compositional language for at least another 1.8 million years.

6. *If it was not the appearance of compositional language, what else was the cause of the cultural changes associated with the appearance of modern humans?* Although the specific chronology and geography of modern

human origins in Africa may still be debated, the fact that modern humans were behaviorally and cognitively quite different to other hominins is incontestable. Their rapid dispersal across the globe, cultural elaboration, manufacture of composite tools, invention of agriculture, and development of state societies are quite unlike anything achieved by other species of *Homo*. The origin of fully modern compositional language and the resulting impact on cognition and behavior appears as the only viable interpretation for such a dramatic change in hominin lifestyles—indeed there is simply nothing else on offer at the paleoanthropological table. As such, and in light of the instability of a proto-compositional language, this implies that hominins used a holistic-based form of communication up until the origin of modern humans soon after 200,000 years ago.

4.6 Six reasons why hominin holistic phrase communication would have a degree of musicality

The six reasons I have presented above argue that the communication systems of pre-modern hominins were holistic in nature: compositional language, either in a proto- or modern form, is simply incompatible with the character of the archeological record. I now want to take this argument a step further and propose that those hominin holistic communication systems would have had a significant degree of musicality in terms of making use of variations in pitch, rhythm, tone, and timbre. Once again, I will provide six arguments for why this is likely to have been the case.

1. *The evidence from anatomy.* There has been an enormous effort to reconstruct the vocal and aural tracts of human ancestors and relatives, an extraordinarily challenging task in light of the absence of soft tissues (e.g. Lieberman 1979; Houghton 1993; MacLarnon and Hewitt 1995; Aiello 1996; Clegg 2001). Interpretations of hyoid bones have played a prominent part in the debates, especially regarding the similarities between the Neanderthal and modern human vocal tracts (Arensburg et al. 1989, 1990; Lieberman 1990). At the risk of over-simplification, all that is necessary to note is that from an early stage in human evolution, hominins appear able to make a wide diversity of sounds and hence had the capacity for a degree of musicality in their communications, one significantly greater than that present in chimpanzees. The reduction of dental size in *Homo* and the

descent of the larynx arising from bipedalism are changes that appear to have been by-products of selection pressures unrelated to communication (Aiello 1996), whereas other changes, such as to the structure of the inner ear (Martinez et al. 2004), may have been specifically selected for enhanced vocalizations. This anatomical evidence does not, of course, necessarily mean that hominins were making extensive use of variations in pitch, rhythm, tone, and timbre. It simply indicates that the capacity was present to do so. A similar circumstantial argument can be made for an enhanced use of gesture, body language, and dance by the evolution of a bipedal anatomy. Indeed, it is interesting to note that the specific anatomical features we have for bipedalism appear to be beyond those necessary for walking alone (Bramble and Lieberman 2004). While endurance running has been evoked as an explanation, such anatomical features would have also facilitated dancing and could even have been selected specifically for such displays.

2. *Singing and dancing for social bonding.* Cooperation between individuals would have been a critical factor throughout human evolution, especially after people began to engage in carcass scavenging and big game hunting. A widespread manner in which modern humans develop the necessary levels of social bonding and trust to enable such cooperation is by singing and dancing together (Blacking 1973; McNeill 1995; Dunbar 2004). Quite why this is so effective remains unclear: It is most likely related to the generation of various neurotransmitters arising from physical activity and the creation of shared brain states within a group of individuals (Freeman 2000; Benzon 2001; Dunbar 2004). There is no direct evidence (that I know of) for singing and dancing by pre-modern humans; indeed the evidence for this would be no more than empty spaces (e.g. see Gamble 2007: fig. 6.1), although the curious structures at Bilzingsleben could feasibly have related to performance (Gamble 1999: 153–172; Mithen 2005: 173–175).

3. *The need to be emotional.* To have been effective, "rational" decision makers, our ancestors would have had to have been emotional beings (Damasio 1994; LeDoux 1996; Oatley and Jenkins 1996). Emotions of happiness, sadness, disgust, and anger are evident among non-human primates (de Waal 1982; Goodall 1986), and are widely accepted as being universal among all humans (Ekman 2003). As such, they can be confidently attributed to our human ancestors. I suspect that more complex emotions

such as shame, guilt, and embarrassment would have also been present in light of the arguments for social complexity and the role of such emotions in social relationships (Frank 1988). Hominins would have needed to feel and express emotions and induce emotions in others, for the success of both their social interactions and their own internal decision-making processes. Among modern humans and non-human primates, the pre-eminent manner in which emotion is expressed and induced within others is by using vocalizations with particular pitch sequences and rhythms, and their equivalence in gesture and body movement.

4. *Looking after infants.* The presence of musicality in the verbal and gestural communications made to infants by adults (and older siblings) was noted above. These play a key role in the emotional arousal of the infants and are universally found among modern humans. So it would appear likely that such musicality was also present in the communications made to infant hominins. Recent studies have argued that as from two million years ago, there was an increase in the period of infant dependency, eventually forming a discrete life-history period that we refer to as childhood (Thompson et al. 2003). This largely arose from the interaction of bipedalism—requiring a relatively narrow pelvis—and the increases in body and brain size, resulting in the need to give birth to effectively immature infants. These would have required substantial care-giving, creating various demands on nursing mothers (Key and Aiello 1999). As Dissanayake (2000) and Falk (2004) have argued, one consequence is likely to have been the use of musicality in communications with such infants, possibly even singing, for precisely the same reasons that these are used by parents today.

5. *Display for mate attraction.* Charles Darwin proposed that "it is probable that the progenitors of man, either the males or females or both sexes, before acquiring the power of expressing mutual love in articulate language, endeavoured to charm each other with musical notes and rhythm" (Darwin 1871: 880). Miller (2000) extended such arguments to propose that the human capacity for making music was a product of sexual selection during human evolution. While we lack any direct evidence for this, it is likely that mate competition was important in human evolution, especially after the reduction in sexual dimorphism and prior to the evolution of male–female pair-bonding (the date of which remains unclear) (Key and Aiello 1999). Singing and dancing are key forms of social and

sexual display in modern humans and it would seem unlikely that this was absent in pre-modern humans.

6. *Mimicry of the natural world*. Traditional societies make extensive use of mimicry of animals and birds in their communications (e.g. Marshall 1976; Donald 1991; Berlin 2005). This was once drawn upon in theories of language origins, but has recently been largely ignored as the social rather than natural world has been seen as providing the key selective pressures. It appears inherently likely—although once again cannot be proven— that hominins also used imitations of birds and animals. Moreover, their dispersal into Eurasia after two million years ago and exploitation of temperate and tropical environments with new types of animals and birds may have resulted in selective pressures for such mimicry. As such, this would have added a further element of musicality into their communications.

4.7 Talking with strangers: the transition from Hmmmmm to compositional language

I have so far argued that (1) pre-modern communication would have been based on holistic phrases, and (2) such holistic phrases would have had a significant degree of musicality. Whereas Brown (2004) used the term "musilanguage" to refer to this type of communication system, my preference has been to use "Hmmmmm," partly to avoid any accusations of teleology (Mithen 2005). Hmmmmm stands for *H*olistic, *m*anipulative, *m*ulti-*m*odal, *m*usicality, and *m*imetic, which I believe were the key features for this general type of communication system, one that no doubt varied between hominin species and communities. The essence of this would have been a relatively fixed set of holistic phrases with complex semantic meanings, used for recurrent situations and events, in conjunction with body language and moderated by variations in pitch, melody, and rhythm to nuance their meaning and emotional content. As I have explained above, it is this type of communication system that is compatible with the variation and patterning in the archeological record and consistent with what we know about primate vocalization and modern human language. The latter is, of course, radically different, being based on words and grammar resulting in the possibility of an infinite set of utterances, in dramatic contrast to a fixed set of holistic phrases.

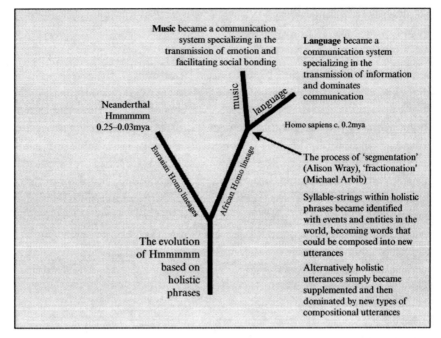

Fig. 4.2. The bifurcation of Hmmmmm in the African lineage of *Homo*, leading to the emergence of compositional language, music, and cognitive fluidity

According to this proposal, language and music as relatively independent systems of communication and expression emerged from the form of Hmmmmm used by the immediate ancestor of modern humans in Africa, sometimes referred to as *Homo helmei*—or indeed from the earliest form of *Homo sapiens* itself (Figure 4.2). Compositional utterances using words and grammar would have come to dominate the use of holistic phrases, with these arising either independently or from the segmentation of holistic phrases in the manner proposed by Wray. This transition from holistic phrases to compositional language would have occurred during the early part of the African Middle Stone Age. It would appear to have been significantly complete by 70,000 years ago in light of the engraved ochre and shell beads from this date at Blombos Cave, which are generally taken to be a reflection of the presence of compositional language (Henshilwood et al. 2002, 2004)—although this remains to be fully demonstrated.

I have two suggestions for how the selective pressures that resulted in the transition from holistic to compositional language may have arisen: the need for enhanced learnability and an increased degree of social and economic fragmentation. Both of these concern an increase in the need to communicate with people for whom one has limited social knowledge—which I characterize as "talking with strangers."

By learnability, I mean a communication system with two characteristics: first, a communication system that can be relatively easily acquired as a "second" language, in the manner that we are able to acquire a language today which is used by people outside of our own social group and about whom we have limited knowledge; second, a communication system for which novel utterances can be created and learned. Holistic protolanguages would have had low degrees of learnability because they required high degrees of knowledge about those to whom one is communicating, i.e. the other members of one's own social group. Such knowledge would include their social relationships, life history experiences, personality traits and daily activities, and would have been acquired implicitly, simply by observation within a socially intimate group. In such holistic protolanguage using groups, there is a limited need for novel utterances (and often for any utterances at all). Indeed, an answer to the question of why the Neanderthals lacked compositional language is simply that they did not have very much to talk about. While holistic protolanguages are sufficient for such socially intimate groups, they are not conducive to being learned by an outsider to the community as a second language owing to such an outsider's lack of social knowledge of the community.

If Hmmmmm did indeed lack the characteristics of learnability, then problems would have arisen within Middle Stone Age groups if communication was increasingly required with "strangers." This may have arisen from an increased degree of contact between social groups with different forms of Hmmmmm, and more substantially if there was movement of people between such groups, perhaps for marriage. Such contacts and movements would have created the selective pressures for methods of communication that could be acquired and learned without reliance on the degrees of social intimacy necessary for holistic communication. Moreover, there would simply have been more to communicate about because each participant in a communicative act would have been less able to predict the behavior and thoughts of the other.

One possible indicator for increased contact and movement of people between groups is when raw materials are found at distances from their sources beyond those that one would expect from direct raw material procurement. Such movements of raw materials would need to indicate more than simply an increase in exchange between social groups and intermittent contact between "strangers." As has been recognized in recent times, exchange between hunter-gatherers can occur as "silent trade," in which goods are left at one location by one party and then taken by another, who leaves something in return, without requiring any verbal exchange (Woodburn 1980). Selective pressures for compositional language would have only arisen when there was a substantial need to communicate with strangers who had a different form of holistic protolanguage, and consequently I stress the actual movement of people between groups.

My second proposal for how the selective pressures for compositional language may have arisen, that of increased social and economic fragmentation, is simply a variant of this initial proposal. If there was an increased degree of social differentiation and economic specialization within a group, then its members would, in effect, become more like "strangers" to each other. In other words, they would have lesser degrees of knowledge about each other's day-to-day activities and experiences. In this context, holistic protolanguage becomes less effective and pressures for more learnable communication systems within a social group would have arisen.

Both of these proposals—the movement of people and increased social/economic specialisation—have archeological correlates that appear to be significant features of the African Middle Stone Age. McBrearty and Brooks (2000) describe how raw materials in eastern Africa have been found at distances greater than 300km from their source, the distance suggesting that they result from long-distance exchange rather than deliberate collecting forays. McBrearty and Brooks also provide an array of evidence for increasing economic and technological specialization during the MSA, such as mining, fishing, bead manufacture, and bone tool manufacture and use (see also Henshilwood and Sealy 1997; Henshilwood et al. 2004). This evidence implies increasing differentiation in persons' activities and spatial location during the day and hence social fragmentation creating selective pressure for compositional language rather than holistic phrases.

4.8 The cognitive impact of compositional language

The "talking with strangers" scenario provides the selection pressures for the emergence of compositional language, as the use of holistic phrases would have no longer provided a sufficient communication system to compete with those individuals using words and grammar and hence capable of novel utterances. Once some words and grammatical rules had appeared, the transition to a predominantly compositional language may have been rapid in light of the seemingly emergent grammatical properties of such communication systems once they are passed through the bottlenecks of intergenerational cultural transmission.

By this process compositional language would have emerged as the principal communication system for the transmission of information. But such language is relatively poor at other tasks which had been core features of the Hmmmmm communication system, notably the expression of emotion and social bonding. Hence a second specialized communication system would have emerged from what amounted to a bifurcation of Hmmmmm—that which we now call music. These two systems overlap in their characteristics and in some communities are far more entwined than in the modern-day west (e.g. the Mbendjele pygmies of the Congo, as described by Lewis in *The Cradle*).

The cognitive impact of compositional language would have been immense: the transition from a domain-specific to a cognitively fluid mentality, as I have argued elsewhere (Mithen 1996b, 2005). Carruthers (2002, 2006) has supported such arguments by his more detailed and philosophically informed research into mental structures, concluding that the sentences we form within our minds play the key role in what he calls intermodular integration—effectively the same as cognitive fluidity. It is from this that the capacity for analogy and metaphor arose in the human mind, these providing the basis for art, science, and religion, and the production of objects such as incised ochre and bead necklaces as found at Blombos cave.

4.9 Summary

The last two decades have seen significant advances in our understanding of the evolution of language. One of the most important developments has been enhanced interdisciplinary dialog, as epitomized at the Cradle of Language conference. Nevertheless, understanding how language evolved and its impacts on cognition, behavior, and culture remains one of the most demanding and important challenges facing paleoanthropology.

This field will no doubt move forward by new discoveries in the fossil and archeological record, new developments in our understanding of the brain, and new theoretical insights. But we must not forget the insights of some of the older ideas that may have lacked any empirical support when originally forwarded and spent some time out of fashion. The idea that language and music co-evolved is one such idea, one that should return to play a key role in our studies. While the particular arguments and scenarios I have presented in this contribution may require some revision or even be entirely incorrect, my key argument is simply that the musicality of language may be one of the most important clues as to its evolutionary history.

5 Music as a communicative medium

IAN CROSS AND GHOFUR ELIOT WOODRUFF

5.1 Introduction

Like language, music appears to be a universal human capacity; all cultures of which we have knowledge engage in something which, from a western perspective, seems to be music (Blacking 1995), and all members of each culture are expected to be able to engage with music in culturally appropriate ways (Cross 2006). Like language, music is an interactive and participatory medium (Small 1998) that appears to constitute a communicative system (Miell et al. 2005), but one that is often understood as communicating only emotion (Juslin and Sloboda 2001). This immediately raises a significant question: Why should an apparently specialized medium for the communication of emotion have arisen in the human species? After all, language and gesture provide extremely potent media for the communication of emotion, yet we as a species have access to a third medium—music—which would appear to be quite redundant.

However, the notion that the function of music is wholly and solely to communicate emotion is called into question by much recent ethnomusicological research, which suggests that although many of the uses of music will indeed impinge on the affective states of those engaged with it, music fulfills a wide range of functions in different societies, in entertainment, ritual, healing, and the maintenance of social and natural order (see e.g. Feld and Fox 1994; Titon 1996; Nettl 2005). These considerations shift attention away from the question of *why* we have music towards the examination of *how* it is that music can fulfill such a wide range of functions, and *what*—if anything—renders it distinct from language as a communicative medium (for language also appears capable of fulfilling the functions that have been attributed here to music).

Music performs a huge array of functions across different cultures, but one very generic feature that they all appear to share is the management of social relationships, particularly in situations of social uncertainty. Such situations include, but are not limited to:

- significant life transitions for individuals, and for individuals as part of a wider community, such as adolescence to adulthood, childhood to adolescence, life to death (Blacking 1976, on the *domba* initiation ceremonies of Venda girls at menarche; Feld 1982, on the Kaluli *gisalo* funerary ceremony)

- circumstances where the integrity or stability of a community is per-ceived to be threatened or is felt to require reaffirmation (Slobin 1993, particularly on the social dynamics of the *klezmer* revival)

- the affirmation—or even encouragement—of propitious relationships between the social order and that which sustains it, for example, the natural environment construed as an agentive and hence prospectively social force (Turnbull 1965, on the Mbuti pygmies' use of song to mediate their relationships to their forest environment)

- the management of inter-group relationships, e.g. by constituting a mutually accessible framework for non-conflictual between-group interactions (Clendinnen 2005, on early music and dance encounters between British sailors and Australian aboriginal inhabitants; Marrett 2005, on the system of ceremonial reciprocity developed at Wadeye in Northern Australia), or by serving as a mechanism for consolidating within-group bonds so as to enhance the likelihood of success in inter-group encounters (Richards 2007, on the use of music by West African child militias)

- those involved in the formation of individual, and collective, within-group identity (MacDonald et al. 2002, on music's roles in creating and projecting identities in contemporary western cultures)

- instances of personal crisis (Sloboda et al. 2001, on the use of music for the regulation or self-regulation of affect)

- the hazards and uncertainties of the most universal of human experi-ences, that of caregiver–infant interaction (Trevarthen 1999/2000).

Of course, language also plays a significant role in such situations of social uncertainty, enabling the sharing of intentions and intentionality and articulating and sustaining the contexts of social relationships. But language possesses at least one capacity that music does not share: that of expressing and communicating propositions and propositional attitudes. At the limit, language is capable of articulating—or of being interpreted as articulating—simple and complex propositions that may bear specific and unambiguous meanings. Music, whatever else its powers, is incapable of so doing; as Blacking (1995: 237) observed, "Not only can the 'same' patterns of sound have different meanings in different societies; they can also have different meanings within the same society because of different social contexts." In this chapter we shall be suggesting that music's inability to express unambiguous meaning underwrites its powers to manage situations of social uncertainty and exploring a framework for understanding how music appears able to sustain such polyvalent significance.

5.2 Language and music in situations of social uncertainty

Humans are an intensely and complexly social species (Foley 1995; Dunbar 1996). For such a species, communication is at a premium; any individual's likelihood of survival and reproduction will depend not only on their individual capacity to deal with their physical environment in terms of threats and resources, but also on the optimization of their capacities to engage with conspecifics (Shennan 2002). Hence from an evolutionary perspective, at first glance language, with its capacity to denote resource location, disseminate resource availability, broadcast perception of danger, enhance transmission of behavior, share intentions and intentionality, and sustain social relationships, appears to offer all that might be required in terms of an effective communicative medium.

But the use of language, with its potential for specificity and singularity of meaning, may also pose problems. When social situations are on the edge—encounters with strangers, changes in social affiliations, disputed courses of action—the fact that language can be interpreted as unambiguously denoting individual feelings, attitudes, and intentions can tip situations over into conflict, between groups or within groups. In situations of social uncertainty language may become inefficacious or even dysfunctional. However, as we have noted, it is in just these types of situation that music appears most likely to manifest itself. Why should music appear to be the preferred medium of communication—or at least, of interaction—in such contexts? To address this question it is first necessary to explore what might be the requirements on a communicative system optimally adapted to manage social uncertainty.

From an ethological perspective it can be argued that such a system should either be, *or be interpreted as*, capable of only honest signalling (revealing to the receiver qualities of the signaller that are relevant to the communicative situation: Számadó and Szathmáry 2006). In other words, the process of producing signals would have to incorporate features of which the interpretative scope would necessarily be constrained by an unambiguous fit between signal characteristics (acoustical and motoric) and the costly and hard-to-fake motivational-intentional and bodily states inferable as underlying signal production. The sense of an honest signal would be further enhanced were it to be rooted in mechanisms which increased the likelihood that participants interacting in this communicative medium would experience each other's states and intentions as mutually manifest. At the same time, it would be necessary that the interpretative scope of the communicative system should be broad enough so as not to require precise alignment between the motivations and intentional states of participants. In other words, the signals produced should be polysemic or ambiguous, capable of multiple interpretations. While some of these requirements appear to be contradictory (how can a signal be honest yet polysemic?), it will be argued here that music provides an example of a communicative medium that conforms to all these requirements.

5.3 Music as "honest signal"

The idea that music constitutes an "honest signal"—or at least, a "natural sign"—is embedded in much thinking about music. The widespread and longstanding view (traceable back to classical Greek thought) that music is primarily a communicator of emotion has already been alluded to, and is not unique to western conceptions of music (see e.g. Basso 1985). Thinking about music from an evolutionary perspective, Darwin (1872/1998) was happy to adopt the "remarks" of "Mr Litchfield" (one of his correspondents, who had "long attended to the subject of music") in suggesting that music mirrors or captures the relationships between affective state and sound that are found across a wide range of species, embodying in the musical signal clues as to the emotional state of its producer. As he puts it (1872/1998: 94), "A great part of the emotional effect of a song depends on the character of the action by which the sounds are produced", that "character" being contingent on the emotional state of the music's producer (though Darwin is careful to note that "this leaves unexplained the more subtle and more specific effect that we might call the *musical* expression of the song" [italics in original]). Hence music, as an expression of emotion, constitutes an "honest signal" in revealing to a listener qualities of the music's producer that are necessarily concomitant on the nature of the signal.

Music certainly appears to be experienced as having consistent, though very broad, emotional significance for listeners, a fact that has been exploited in numerous experiments exploring the behavioral, cognitive, and neural underpinnings of affective states and using music to elicit generically different affective states as a highly effective Mood Induction Procedure (e.g. Albersnagel 1988). Music is also a ubiquitous facet of the experience of film and other media such as computer games, being employed to manipulate the emotional responses of audiences to the unfolding cinematic narrative or game situation (Gorbman 1987; Kassabian 2001). It is notable that music tends to be used in Mood Induction Procedures (MIPs) simply on the grounds that it works, and works more effectively than other methods (such as the linguistic and bio-graphically based Velten MIP); rarely is any compelling rationale advanced in the Mood Induction literature for why music might have such powers. Equally, the affective powers of music in cinema and multimedia have rarely been subjected to exploration and explanation (amongst the few exceptions being the work of Boltz 2001, 2004 and Cohen 2001). However, recent theories of animal vocal communication might afford some clues as to music's efficacy in influencing the affective states of listeners.

In a recent review of animal communication systems, Seyfarth and Cheney (2003) conclude that most, if not all, non-human animal commu-nication is achieved almost contingently, as signallers are unaware of the means whereby their vocalizations effect their consequences. Yet a substan-tial literature (see e.g. Owren and Rendall 2001) suggests that there are at least some consistent correspondences between signal structure and signal outcome in animal communication. These consistencies form the focus of Owings and Morton's (1998) approach, which aims to remove some of the contingency from animal acoustic interaction by dispensing with the notion of information transfer and adopting a pragmatic approach, suggesting that animals, in producing vocal and other sounds, are generally seeking to manage their physical and social environments rather than to transmit information. At the same time, other animals—conspecifics and members of other species—are seeking to assess the import of the signals emitted by others. This "management-assessment" framework is largely governed by relationships between the acoustical characteristics of the signals produced and the biological consequences that can be inferred from the acoustical features of the signal.

Processes operating over evolutionary timescales act to integrate sensitivities to those relationships into the sensory and behavioral repertoires of animals. These sensitivities can then be brought to bear in the inferences made in assessment of prospective biological consequences associated with the signal characteristics as well as in the use of signals with particular features to manage the social or physical environment. A simple example would be the case of a small animal seeking to defend a territory in an environment where little visual information is available, who might produce signals at as low a frequency as can be achieved to broadcast an impression of large size. Were this to be achievable at a lower cost to the sound producer than the cost likely to be incurred by engaging in physical combat, then the use of such signals—and the capacity to produce ever lower-frequency signals—would afford a strong evolutionary payoff (in terms of survival and reproduction) for those members of the species more capable of producing low-frequency signals consistently at a low cost to themselves, who would then be likely to come to dominate the species' genotype. At the same time there would also be selection for those members of the species most capable of correctly inferring likely size (and hence, likelihood that the sound producer constitutes a real and prospective threat, capable of inflicting physical damage) from the sounds produced by conspecifics. Hence processes of both management and assessment would work together to generate an evolutionarily stable strategy, referred to by Owings and Morton as Expressive Size Symbolism.

These correspondences of sound structure and biological significance are not limited to the frequency domain: Owings and Morton note that, as well as frequency, other acoustical parameters of the sound signal, including bandwidth and intensity, tend to co-vary with the prospective significance of biological situations. Evolutionary processes act to inscribe in the genomes of many species predispositions towards particular motivational states according to different features of the acoustical signals they encounter and produce in the form of what Owings and Morton term a "motivational-structural" code. These authors are thus postulating a close relationship between the motivational states of organisms (governed by affective systems) and the global structural characteristics of acoustic signals.

It would be surprising if such motivational-structural principles did not account for significant aspects of the human response to sound, given the extent to which we share appetitive, reproductive, sensory, and limbic systems with many other species; the dynamics of at least the latter two are likely to have been profoundly shaped by the history of our predecessor species' interaction with the regularities of the environments they encountered and successfully navigated. Hence a close relationship can be postulated between the motivational states of listeners and the global structural characteristics of musical sound. Indeed, while the now substantial experimental literature on affective responses to music (for a review, see Juslin and Sloboda 2001) finds very few consistencies in listeners' response, those few that can be found seem to relate *either* to whether or not the music employed is personally selected by, and hence is meaningful to, the participants, *or* to global structural characteristics of the music (Evers and Suhr 2000; Husain et al. 2002). Moreover, the idea that music may incorporate features that can be interpreted in motivational-structural terms is supported by findings that music has consistent effects on animal behaviors that are interpretable as a consequence of the capacity of its global structural characteristics to "modify physiological arousal levels" (Rickard et al. 2005: 252).

One can think of motivational-structural principles as constituting a locus for natural meaning in music, endowing music with the potential to be employed and interpreted as an honest signal. Nevertheless, experimental evidence (e.g. Blood and Zatorre 2001) suggests that listeners' affective responses to music are also mediated by other factors, notably prior personal engagement with a particular piece or genre. This account of the operation of motivational-structural processes has parallels in the work of Pavlov, who noted that even when a stimulus–response relationship could be classified as *unconditioned* or *innate*, it could be overridden by conditioning. Hence the actuation of motivational-structural principles in listeners' responses to music does not mean that the significance for listeners of any music that activates these principles is fixed. While roughly consistent motivational states may be elicited by a piece of music in listeners, this condition is not sufficient unambiguously to endow the piece with a specific meaning. However, the operation of motivational-structural processes is likely to set limits on the range of possible significances that may be abstracted by listeners from a given musical stimulus; motivational-structural principles hold the experience of meaning in music on a leash.

5.4 The human dimensions of musicality

Motivational-structural principles are best thought of as contributing only one aspect or dimension of music's capacity to signify; other factors that endow it with a sense of communicable meaning must be adduced, such as prior personal associations. Responses to music are evidently motivated by a history of personal engagement (Davies 1978), yet this history is not wholly individual and personal; it is mediated by, and rooted in, culture. Responses to, and indeed, capacities for, music are the result of active participation in, and engagement with, the dynamics and specificities of particular cultural contexts and processes, as well as of individual life histories. They are shaped by the conceptions and uses of music that exist within a specific cultural framework (Nettl 2005), by the contingencies of cultural formation and change (Feld 1996), by enculturative, formal, and personal learning processes (Deliège and Sloboda 1996), and by associations of music with episodes in and aspects of an individual's life history (MacDonald et al. 2002).

The consequences of these participatory and culturally specific factors and processes can be thought of as providing the substrate for a culturally enactive dimension to musical meaning, co-existing with the motivational-structural dimension. In contrast to the principled nature of the latter dimension, the operations of the culturally enactive dimension in attributing meaning to music may appear intensely arbitrary. They are evidenced, for example, in the use of music as cultural emblem (as in the use of different pieces of music by the followers of different football clubs); or in the categorical distinctions that might be drawn within a culture between music and other phenomena—often religious or liminal—that, from the perspective of another culture, might appear to be musical; or in the existence of constraints on the types of musical behaviors held to be appropriate for different age-groups in certain societies.

We can now postulate two dimensions in the experience of meaning in music, one which relates to aspects of our experience of the world that are conditioned by our biological heritage and that may have some cross-species generality—the **motivational-structural** dimension—and one which derives from the particularities of the cultural contexts in which we develop and come to play a part—the **culturally enactive** dimension. Both dimensions would be simultaneously operational in the experience of music, yielding a *sense* of an honest signal but allowing meanings in music to appear fluid and contestable (within personally and culturally defined limits). This distinction between the biological and the cultural in articulating the dimensions of musical experience appears neatly to conform to the venerable nature–nurture dichotomy. However, there are aspects of the experience of musical meaning that call such a simple dichotomous account into question.

Even in the absence of cultural knowledge we can experience the sound of the music of another culture *as* music; when we encounter the sounds of Japanese Noh theatre, or of Banda initiation music from Central Africa performed in hocket (each member of the group playing alternate single notes) on *ongo* (bark trumpets), we are likely to try to bring to bear on that experience the cognitive resources appropriate to the experience of music within our own culture, with greater or lesser success. We may profoundly misinterpret the other culture's music, but we are likely to experience it as music. While motivational-structural principles may play a role in shaping such experiences, other factors would seem to be implicated. We seem to experience the music of another culture as music in ways that are different from those in terms of which we might experience other sets of sounds (such as the contingent sounds of the natural world) as music. In considering how we make sense of "other" musics, John Blacking suggested (1995: 238) "[that] there must be supra-cultural cognitive resonance, and that there must be levels at which different composers, listeners and musical systems use the 'same' musical modes of thought." It can be suggested that the locus of such "supra-cultural cognitive resonances" is to be found in the similarities in the ways in which music embodies, and is the result of, particularly *human* modes of interaction across cultures, deriving from a generic human "capacity for culture."

Recent explorations of the human capacity for culture have focussed on the nature of "theory of mind" (see Gopnik 1999): the ways in which animals may attribute mental states to others. It appears that only humans can be conceived of as possessing a full-blown "theory of mind": As Call and Tomasello (2005: 261) note, even our nearest primate relatives, chimpanzees, "have the cognitive skills to recall, represent, categorize and reason about the behavior and perception of others, but not about their intentional or mental states." In a recent paper Tomasello et al. (2005: 680) have proposed that the human capacity for culture is rooted in a capacity for, and motivation towards, "shared intentionality," which "refers to collaborative interactions in which participants have a shared goal (shared commitment) and co-ordinated [and mutually understood] action roles for pursuing that shared goal."

In the context of such a capacity, human communication systems would have to be understood as motivated (at least in part) by a need to make inferences about others' states of mind and intentions as well as about the physical and biological contexts of any communicative act. Thus human communicative signals must be understood as conditioned as much by the need to establish a common cognitive context for the act of communication as they are by the need to communicate information (see e.g. Sperber and Wilson 1995). This particular aspect of human communicative systems can be understood as underlying a dimension of musical meaning that enables Blacking's "supra-cultural cognitive resonances" in the experience of music, and can be referred to as music's socio-intentional dimension.

This dimension would be oriented towards attributions and interpretations of human agency and intentionality in engagement with music (see also Watt and Ash 1998). It would be rooted in performative actions and sound structures that could be interpreted as affording cues about shared intentionality that direct attention in interaction. These actions and sound structures could be interpreted as declarative or imperative, concerned with the direction of another's attention to an object or event distinct from the individuals involved in the interaction. They may construe as disclosural or dissimulative, evoking a sense that they denote distinct and different communicative intentions. These interpretations are likely to arise because music typically exhibits structural characteristics that are directly analogous to features manifested in speech and that are of significance in establishing the *pragmatic* contexts of utterances (Wilson and Wharton 2006). Prosodic characteristics of speech such as intonation, rhythm, and stress help partition the discourse into meaningful articulatory units. These units serve not only to reinforce syntactic and semantic structures but also to signal the communicative intentions of the speaker. These intentions may be manifest even in situations where propositional content is absent, such as when listening to a foreign speaker convey a message without understanding precisely what is being said. Moreover, such features are realized not only in the acoustic domain but also through physical gestures (Kendon 2004; Krahmer and Swerts 2007).

The socio-intentional dimension of music can be thought of as fundamentally pragmatic in relying on gestural and acoustical cues to impart a sense of communicative intent. It is likely to relate not so much to *what* unfolds musically as to *how* the music unfolds, comprising as it does experiential correlates of the music's temporal structure and being bound up with processes of expectation and anticipation (see e.g. Huron 2006) or inhering in features of the musical surface such as melodic contour. The operation of this dimension of musical meaning is unproblematically evident in contexts in which music involves interactive participation. Here, music can be thought of as exhibiting features similar to those of linguistic dialog, being exemplified in specific contoural and accentual structures (Palmer and Hutchins 2006), call and response patterns, or antecedent-consequent phrase structures. The socio-intentional domain would also be present even in contexts that involve apparently passive listening to recorded music. In such contexts it would be experienced in terms of traces of human behavior, embodying cues as to human action or intention (or to the body-imagistic schemas that may underlie human action and inter-action) in ways that have the semantic openness to afford the experience of joint action, joint attention, and joint intention.

The three dimensions of musical meaning postulated above—the motivational-structural, culturally enactive, and socio-intentional—are all likely to be co-present in any experience of music or engagement in musical behavior. Music is a medium that rests on semantic indeterminacy, which has elsewhere been referred to as "floating intentionality" (Cross 2003). Engagement with music thus affords access to multiple and simultaneously available layers of meaning, allowing participants in a musical behavior to interpret the significance of the music individually and independently while collectively affording to participants a sense that the music embodies an honest signal. Hence music can be viewed as embodying the characteristics of the medium optimally adapted for the management of social uncertainty outlined earlier, though one feature attributed to that medium, that of being rooted in mechanisms that increase the likelihood of participants experiencing each other's states and intentions as mutually manifest, remains to be properly addressed for the case of music.

Across cultures, music is typically experienced as structured regularly in time, even when the events of the musical surface do not exhibit overt temporal regularities. Engagement with music typically involves the entrainment of action and attention to a commonly inferred, more-or-less regular and periodic pulse (Drake and Bertrand 2001). Participants in a musical activity will regulate the temporal alignment of their musical behaviors by engaging in continual processes of mutual adjustment of the timing of actions and sounds; even those who appear engaged in "passive listening" to music will be modulating their attention according to the ways that the flow of the music affords scope for a regular pulse to be abstracted (Jones and Boltz 1989). The ability of interacting humans to produce and to entrain to a more-or-less regular auditory stimulus through processes of mutual adjustment of period and phase (Repp 2006) seems to underpin not only musical behaviors but a variety of human communicative acts; recent work has shown that temporal entrainment is implicated in a variety of communicative situations and is manifested in a variety of forms, from eye movements (Richardson et al. 2006) to postural changes (Shockley et al. 2003). However, only in music will entrainment be consistently and continuously oriented around a regular pulse (Bispham 2006).

In the context of collective musical behaviors, processes of entrainment are likely to endow the communal activity with a powerful sense of joint and coordinated action, allowing the emergence of a sense that aims are shared and enhancing the likelihood that participants will experience each other's states and intentions as mutually manifest. Hence entrainment processes in music provide a potent means of promoting a sense of joint affiliation that helps maintain the collective integrity of a musical act even though music's floating intentionality affords each participant the possibility of interpreting its significance quite differently. Music's semantic indeterminacy (rooted in the simultaneous availability of at least three dimensions of musical meaning), together with its affiliative powers (rooted in processes of entrainment and in its exploitation of motivational-structural principles), render it effective as a communicative medium that is optimized for the management of situations of social uncertainty.

5.5 Language and music as communicative systems; similarities and differences

This framework for understanding music suggests that it can be clearly differentiated from language as a mode of communicative behavior. In contrast to the fluidity and instability of meaning that are imputed to music in this chapter, language has tended to be identified as a communicative medium that bears explicit meaning, being capable of expressing semantically decomposable propositions (see e.g. Hockett 1960; Montague 1974). Yet language can also possess many of the capacities of music; language can, self-evidently, be employed in the management of social relations. And language is often quite as ambiguous as music is here claimed to be, from the vaporous mendacity of the corporate mission statement to the significatively freighted elusiveness of poetry (where it also exhibits many of the temporal regularities that underlie entrainment processes in music). We argue that language and music should properly be distinguished as tending towards opposite poles on a continuum of capacity for *specificity* of meaning (Cross 2005), and that there are common frameworks applicable to the understanding of at least some meaning processes in both language and music.

We see those frameworks as most pertinent to understanding the parallels between pragmatic aspects of language in discourse and the socio-intentional dimension of the experience of music. The idea that musical meaning has a socio-intentional dimension is predicated in part on the notion that performers utilize melodic and other musical structures as a means of making manifest communicative intentions or attitudinal stances, and that listeners interpret these intentions and stances. These structures can be thought of as having a discourse function similar to prosodic structures in speech: They provide contextual and narrative cues within an interactive framework. This similarity can be seen to arise from a common origin in the human voice. The mechanisms underlying vocal production lend themselves to certain prosodic forms with communicative affordances that are equally suited to both music and language.

The proposition that music and language are related in this way is supported by the work of Ohala and Gussenhoven on the discourse functions of prosodic structures in language. They outline three biological speech codes—of frequency, effort, and production—to explain the widespread appearance of similar prosodic structures across cultures (Gussenhoven 2002, 2005; Ohala 1984, 1994).

The frequency code is so named owing to the recruitment of the frequency dimension in the communication of basic social and power relations. The code was adapted by Ohala from Morton's original formulation of motivational structures (Morton 1977), and posits that similar principles underlying animal communication are evident within the prosody of human speech. Operating on the principle that low sounds convey large size, a speaker might utilize the lower range of their voice in conversation to convey those attitudes that have a natural correlation with large size, such as confidence, dominance, or aggression. Conversely the higher register may be used to express submission, subordination, and absence of threat. Gender identity and gender roles may also be expressed through the dimension of frequency, insofar as gender role is relevant to a given community.[1] Finally, the higher vocal register is sometimes used to convey uncertainty, which is said to underscore the questioning effect of rising terminals often present in interrogatives (Bolinger 1978). Hence, in addition to our species-specific capacity for language and propositional meaning, we communicate certain attitudinal and affective states through tone of voice.

The effort code correlates the energy expended in the production of speech with a number of states naturally associated with speaker effort (Gussenhoven 2005). Wider prosodic contours require more effort to produce and can be interpreted as conveying enthusiasm, obligingness, authority, and insistence. Conversely, a lack of commitment, enthusiasm, or interest may be signaled by narrow contours associated with less effort. The prosodic function of *focus*, in which a word is highlighted by way of raised pitch (House 2006; Sperber and Wilson 1995) is also attributed to the perception of speaker effort through this code. A third code, the production code, derives from the acoustic relationship between frequency and subglottal breath pressure (Gussenhoven 2005; see Titze 1994 for a

---

[1] The effects of the frequency code are relative to an individual's voice range; it is not suggested that all higher-pitched voices sound submissive and that all lower voices are aggressive.

detailed discussion of the physiological mechanics involved). Subglottal pressure is highest at the beginning of an utterance and drops gradually as breath is exhaled, resulting in a progressive lowering of pitch known as declination (Ladd 1984; Wennerstrom 2001). Hence a natural, biological process links the beginnings of utterances with higher pitch and the endings with lower pitch. The production code serves to partition speech into meaningful articulatory units by exploiting this natural association: High phrase beginnings signify new topics and low phrase endings signify closure. Conversely, low phrase beginnings and high phrase endings signify continuation.

In spite of their roots in Morton's original formulation of motivational-structural principles, Ohala's and Gussenhoven's codes can be conceived as operating, both in language and in music, not in motivational-structural but in socio-intentional terms. From this perspective, musical contours are no longer construed as autonomous auditory events whose sole purpose is to elicit an esthetic end-state. By varying the width of intervals in a melodic contour, performers can exploit the effects of the effort code to convey affective states and attitudinal stances. Wider intervals might be used to make a performer's enthusiasm or assertiveness manifest, whilst narrower intervals might convey more subdued emotions or even a lack of interest. Declarative and dissimulative intentions might equally be revealed through wide and narrow intervals respectively. Peaked contours might serve to highlight ostensively certain features of a musical utterance, a function analogous to that of focus in speech prosody. In terms of the production code, ascending and descending contours can be used in performance to partition the musical discourse by providing articulatory cues at phrase boundaries. A descending terminal contour may signify closure in music by invoking the association between declination and phrase endings. Conversely, an ascending terminal contour might signal continuation. While the effects of the production code in music are still being explored empirically, there is telling anecdotal evidence that performers exploit this code. For instance, the pervasiveness of the arch contour in western folk song (Huron 1996) could be accounted for in terms of the efficacy of the descending terminal to indicate closure. Evidence from neuroscience suggests that the perception of phrase boundaries in music elicits similar neural responses to those of speech (Knösche et al. 2005).

The role of the frequency code in music perception has received some empirical attention (Huron et al. 2006) although much remains to be explored. That the frequency code has been implicated in the human communicative system would suggest that a sensitivity to socially relevant vocal meaning is part of our evolutionary heritage; sound at a basic social level does not constitute a *tabula rasa* on which meaning is freely inscribed as it has been endowed with social significance through evolutionary processes. However, it is not suggested that music's interpretation is bound to these codes. The cross-cultural variability of musical forms and meanings (referred to above as rooted in music's culturally enactive dimension) is in accord with Gussenhoven's (2005) claim that culturally specific encoding can and does override the communicative functions implicit in his proposed linguistic codes.

Music and speech share other features that govern their production and perceptual form. They are bound by the temporal constraints of working memory on the integration of serial event structure in perception and production. These limitations are overcome, in part, by employing hierarchical structures to coordinate the production and perception of simultaneous organizational levels. Hierarchical structures optimize transmission and perception by enabling several levels to be accessed simultaneously, such structures being evident in the prosodic domain of speech in the grouping of hierarchically related levels of foot, word, and intonational phrase (Yallop and Clark 1990). Music has been interpreted as exhibiting similar types of hierarchical groupings; Lerdahl and Jackendoff (1983: 314–332) note that parallel types of formalisms appear applicable to the prosodic domain of language and to the time-span domain of tonal music. That language and music overcome the same temporal-acoustic limitations using hierarchical modes of transmission suggests that common communicative operations are in evidence.

Metric structures also provide a temporal framework that facilitates social interaction through entrainment. The metric hierarchy of music takes the form of the interaction of isochronous beats at different temporal levels; in language, the timing of syllables or the alternation of stressed and unstressed syllables (Auer et al. 1999). Although language is less intuitively associated with such metric processes than is music, this distinction is one of degree rather than kind. That isochronous beat structures in music provide a predictive framework with which listeners align their attention is well established (Jones and Boltz 1989). With respect to entrainment, the metric structures of music must be sufficiently quantized to facilitate the predictive mechanisms necessary for performers to engage physically with music—to play along with each other in real time. Although laboratory experiments have established a similar claim for language—that rhythmic structures serve to align speakers' and listeners' attention (Dilley and McAuley 2007 in revision; Pitt and Samuel 1990)—it remains unclear whether everyday speech exhibits isochrony to the degree required for physical entrainment. Speakers of English exhibit periods of isochrony, both within an individual's utterance and sustained from speaker to speaker (Couper-Kuhlen 1993). However, such isochrony is rarely sustained or quantized to the same degree as music. Whilst studies have suggested that listeners and speakers entrain gross and fine motor movements to speech (Condon 1986; Wilson and Wilson 2005), this appears intermittent and is far removed from the sustained participatory engagement between individuals afforded by music. This highlights an important difference between the social function of language and music: Music, like language, uses entrainment to coordinate interaction, but in music this serves a primary function and hence its cues for interaction are more strongly evident.

5.6 Music and language in evolution

Language and music appear to share more significant features as communicative systems than differentiate them. We are arguing that what appears to distinguish them most clearly is their efficacy in different social contexts (see also Cross 2006); both language and music are instrumental in achieving social goals, but language organizes social action while music organizes sociality. Language has the capacity to express unambiguous, semantically decomposable propositions; music lacks this capacity, displaying a consistent ambiguity. Nevertheless, both language and music exemplify *symbolic* behaviors, most evident in music in the culturally enactive dimension. Both music and language rely on codes that relate the structures of the sounds that they employ to physical—biological—causes, but music embodies features that are shared with other systems of animal communication in the form of motivational-structural principles, whereas language's prosodic codes are best conceived of as bound by processes specific to human communication and located in the socio-intentional domain. Both music and language exhibit periodicity, but language's periodicities tend towards the intermittent and, in interaction, afford reciprocity of engagement, whereas music's periodicities enable collective synchronous engagement.

Language seems closest to music when it has a phatic function (as in the exchange of conventional phrases of greeting used as a preliminary to establish social relationships). Music, in our view, exemplifies and emphasizes the phatic dimension of social interaction, constituting a foundational medium for "phatic communion" (Malinowski 1974). This could be taken to suggest that music preceded language in the evolution of human communicative systems (as Mithen's (2005) reliance on Wray's (1998) theory of holistic protolanguage would imply). Moreover, music, in the present view, incorporates features of non-human animal communication systems in the form of the motivational-structural dimension, suggesting a degree of evolutionary continuity that does not appear so evident for language.

However, the fact that music exploits the motivational-structural dimension does not necessarily mean that "music" should be conceived of as more ancient than language. Were music's efficacy to be located solely in the motivational-structural dimension, there would indeed be every reason to conceive of it as evolutionarily prior to language. However, music, as discussed here, relies not only on the motivational-structural dimension but also on the socio-intentional and culturally enactive dimensions—in addition to the capacity for entrainment—for its efficacy. Moreover, it has been postulated that aspects of language rely, just as do aspects of music, on the motivational-structural code (as in Ohala's original proposal for the frequency code), although, as noted above, it is more appropriate to conceive of the operation of the frequency code in speech as situated within the socio-intentional domain. Hence the fact that there are apparent continuities between aspects of musical experience in the contemporary world and aspects of animal communicative systems does not necessarily mean that "music" preceded language in evolutionary terms. We would argue that music and language are complementary aspects of the modern human communicative toolkit, each functioning to achieve ends in respect of which the other may be less efficacious; they are best thought of as having co-evolved, most probably appearing as discretely identifiable suites of behavior with modern *Homo sapiens* though likely to have emerged from precursor communicative systems that embodied features of both.

Unambiguous evidence for music appears early in the modern human archeological record in Europe in the form of the Geissenklosterle pipe, dating from about 38 kya (Conard and Bolus 2003) and the remarkable series of pipes from Isturitz, extending from the Aurignacian to the Magdalenian (d'Errico et al. 2003). All these musical artifacts are extremely sophisticated, exhibiting many features of historic wind instruments; they are highly unlikely to be the earliest manifestations of human musicality, and it is to be expected that earlier periods may yet yield archeological evidence for musical behaviors. Moreover, the prevalence of music in native American and Australian societies in forms that are not directly relatable to recent historic Eurasian or African musics is a potent indicator that modern humans brought musicality with them out of Africa. This is not to suggest that musicality emerged, fully fledged, with modern humans. While there is no archeological evidence that Neanderthals possessed a faculty for musicality (the much-touted Divje Babe "flute" has been securely shown to be the result of carnivore activity, see e.g. d'Errico and Villa 1997), there is equally no evidence that they did not. However, the paucity of evidence for Neanderthal symbolic behaviors could be taken to suggest that music may have played a less significant—or less effective—role for Neanderthals than it does for modern humans.

Music has a potent proximate function in the management of social relationships in situations of social uncertainty. This suggests that the possession of a capacity for musicality can be interpreted as having played a significant role in the evolutionary processes that resulted in the emergence of modern humans, in facilitating our extraordinary social and cognitive flexibility, and as continuing to play that role in consolidating and sustaining those flexibilities (Cross 2005). However, to propose that music is likely to have had adaptive value in human evolution leaves unaddressed the question of how and why a capacity for something like musicality arose in the first place. It can be suggested that a faculty for music emerges as an exaptive consequence of progressive altriciality in the later hominin lineage as a means of co-opting and regulating the exploratory value of childhood modes of thought and behavior into the adult repertoire (Cross 2003, 2005).

5.7 Conclusions, and known unknowns

The view of music presented here is, as far as we can judge, consonant with the available evidence from cognitive, neuroscientific, cross-specific,

and ethnographic sources. Nevertheless, many aspects either remain unresolved or require further exploration. The instantiation of motivational-
structural principles in our responses to music is hinted at by the results
of studies of musical affect (Husain et al. 2002; Huron et al. 2006), but
requires to be evaluated more broadly, and, indeed, cross-culturally. The
same issue arises in respect of the socio-intentional domain; while empirical research suggests that forms of human interaction are encoded in
musical structure (e.g. Watt and Ash 1998) and many theories of music's
meanings implicitly or explicitly make such a claim (e.g. Cook 1998; Cox
2001), more substantive experimental research is required. Indeed, such
research will need to take account of Gussenhoven's formulations and
should help elucidate relationships between aspects of prosodic structure
in language and their analogs in music.

A further area that urgently requires more research is that of the potential species-specificity of the human entrainment capacity. At present,
there is no good evidence that non-human mammalian species can either
exhibit spontaneous capacities to entrain that are comparable to human
capacities (which involve intentional alignment of periodic behaviors by
means of both period and phase correction) or are motivated so to do
(Bispham 2006; though see Fitch 2006a). Until reliable data are available, the notion that entrainment is a significant and species-specific—
but species-general—feature of human communicative interaction must
remain hypothetical, though highly probable. Moreover, the nature of
interactive temporal coupling in language remains sparsely explored; further exploration is required to shed light on the communicative affordances offered by entrainment in linguistic interaction.

It has been proposed that the faculty of language is uniquely differentiated from other human communicative modes by processes of recursion (Hauser et al. 2002), though this proposal has been challenged by
researchers who claim that recursion is evident in a range of human
behaviors and cognitive processes (e.g. Arbib 2005). While many theories
of music rest on the premise that it embodies recursion—or, at least, hier-
archicality (most comprehensively, Lerdahl and Jackendoff 1983)—there
is a paucity of empirical evidence for this contention. Moreover, theories
of music that have addressed the issue of recursion have generally done so
in respect of a limited range of possible musics, generally confining themselves to western tonal music of the common-practice period from c. 1600

to 1900 (though see Hughes 1991). Cross-cultural studies are required in order to fill this lacuna (Stevens 2004).

While archeology has yielded rich data concerning the early appearance of musicality in the modern human record, much remains unexplored. In particular, no early artifacts that can be unambiguously identified as musical have been found outside Eurasia (Morley 2003), though significant Neolithic finds have been made in China (Zhang et al. 1999). It is possible that no such artifacts exist to be discovered outside Eurasia, but this seems highly unlikely given the current universality of musical behaviors across cultures. It might be the case that such artifacts existed but have not survived in the archeological record, but it seems more likely that such artifacts indeed exist but remain either to be discovered or to be identified. Increased interest in, and greatest sophistication concerning, possible archeological traces of early musicality (see e.g. d'Errico et al. 2003) make it likely that much more will be learned about the emergence of musicality in the future.

Finally, there exists a significant empirical obstacle to our understanding of the relationships between language and music. While a vast body of comparative data exists for languages across cultures, in terms both of structure and of use, no similar body of data exists for music, which severely limits their comparability as communicative media. Although significant research has been undertaken that has elucidated many of the cognitive and neuroscientific underpinnings of human musicality, at present bodies of theory and batteries of tools that have broad applicability in identifying common characteristics across musical cultures, and that are widely accepted, do not yet exist. In the 1960s and 1970s, the American ethnomusicologist Alan Lomax embarked on the Cantometrics project (Lomax et al. 1978), which was intended to provide just such comparative data in respect of music. Had this been successful, it would have provided secure bases for identifying commonalities and divergences in music across cultures, and for mapping the distribution of musical practices across geographical space and historical—and prehistorical—time. However, Lomax's methods and findings were severely criticized (see e.g. Feld and Fox 1994) and have never received broad acceptance. Nevertheless, new statistical techniques have recently been applied to Lomax's coded data which have already yielded suggestive hypotheses (Leroi and Swire 2006) about the relationships between geographical distributions of cross-cultural musical types and historical and evolutionary processes. Having said this, several of the criticisms raised in respect of the original project remain. Were the bases for these criticisms successfully to be addressed, we would be able to trace the relationships between language and music, and the evolution of human systems of communication, with a much greater degree of certainty.

6 Cultural niche construction: evolution's cradle of language

JOHN ODLING-SMEE AND KEVIN N. LALAND

6.1 Introduction

Standard evolutionary theory is highly successful, based as it is on solid mathematical foundations and a rich empirical tradition, constantly renewed by exchanges of hypotheses and data among diverse researchers. Yet, despite its successes, it does not provide a satisfactory basis for understanding human evolution. Primarily, this is because standard evolutionary theory's assumptions limit what it can explain. Significantly, it largely neglects the role of niche-construction in evolution (Odling-Smee et al. 2003). As a result, it has inadvertently erected conceptual barriers that make it difficult to integrate evolutionary biology with several neighboring disciplines, including developmental biology, ecosystem-level ecology and the human sciences (Lewontin 1983; Odling-Smee et al. 2003; Laland et al. in press).

Here we describe how niche construction can usefully be regarded as a process which, combined with established evolutionary processes, improves understanding of human evolution. By integrating human niche construction with gene-culture co-evolutionary theory (Cavalli-Sforza and Feldman 1981; Laland et al. 2000; Richerson and Boyd 2005), we develop an evolutionary framework to explore the evolution of language.

6.2 Niche construction

Standard evolutionary theory is summarized in Figure 6.1a. Sources of natural selection in environments (E) provide the context in which diverse

We are grateful to Derek Bickerton, Eörs Szathmáry and Tecumseh Fitch, for their helpful comments, and constructive criticisms of an earlier draft.

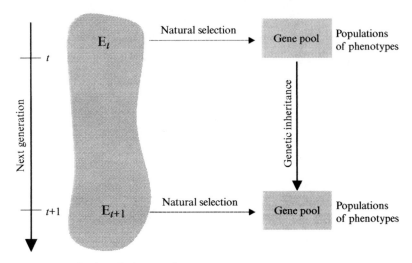

FIG. 6.1a. Standard evolutionary theory

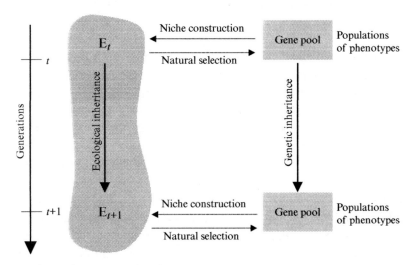

FIG. 6.1b. Niche construction theory

organisms compete to survive and reproduce, influencing which genes are passed on to the next generation. The adaptations of organisms are assumed to be consequences of autonomous natural selection moulding organisms to fit pre-established environmental templates. These templates are dynamic because processes that are independent of organisms frequently change the worlds to which organisms adapt. However, the changes that organisms bring about in their own worlds are seldom thought to have evolutionary significance, and are rarely viewed as evolutionary processes.

One problem with this view is that it discourages consideration of the feedback in evolution caused by the modification of environments by organisms. Organisms, through their metabolisms, behavior, and choices, partly create and destroy their selective environments. In doing so they transform some of the natural selection pressures that feed back to themselves and other organisms (Lewontin 1983; Jones et al. 1994, 1997; Wright and Jones 2006), selecting for different genotypes from those that would have been selected in the absence of niche construction (Laland et al. 1996, 1999). It follows that the adaptations of organisms cannot be exclusively consequences of organisms responding to *autonomous* natural selection: Sometimes they must be consequences of niche-constructing organisms responding to selection previously transformed by their own activities, or those of their ancestors (Odling-Smee et al. 2003).

Lewontin (1983) summarized these points by two pairs of differential equations, the first pair representing standard evolutionary theory:

(1) a. $dO/dt = f(O,E)$,
    b. $dE/dt = g(E)$.

In equation (1a), evolutionary change in organisms, dO/dt, depends on both organisms states, O, and environment states, E. In equation (1b), however, environmental change during time, dE/dt, depends only on environmental variables (E), not the actions of organisms. Lewontin complained that is not how evolution works, suggesting that a more accurate depiction is:

(2) a. $dO/dt = f(O,E)$,
    b. $dE/dt = g(O,E)$.

Equation (2a) is the same as (1a), but equation (2b) now allows environmental change to also be dependent on the environment modifying acts of active organisms, O.

Lewontin's position is close to ours (Odling-Smee et al. 2003), so we will use it to describe niche construction. The first step is to characterize a niche, which for our purposes can be conceived of as the set of natural selection pressures to which an evolving population is exposed (Odling-Smee et al. 2003).

(3) $N(t) = h(O,E)$

In equation (3), $N(t)$ represents the niche of a population of organisms O at time t, where the dynamics of $N(t)$ are explicitly driven by both selection arising from independent environmental variables in E, and by the environment-modifying activities of niche-constructing organisms O. Here $N(t)$ is an evolutionary as well as an ecological niche. Everything in equation (3) is evolving: The population, O, is evolving, as usual; O's selective environment, E, is in part co-evolving as a consequence of O's genetically "informed" or possibly "brain-informed" niche-constructing activities; finally the niche relationship itself, $N(t)$, is evolving as a function of O's and E's interactions.

6.2.1 *Example*

For illustration, consider the example of earthworm niche construction. (Numerous other examples, from all kingdoms of life, can be found in Odling-Smee et al. 2003.) Earthworm activities were originally studied by Darwin (1881), who showed that earthworms are terrific niche constructors. By burrowing, dragging organic material into the soil and mixing it with inorganic material, and by their casting, which serves as the basis for microbial activity, earthworms dramatically change both the structure and chemistry of soils. Soils that contain earthworms, compared with those that do not, demonstrate enhanced plant yield, less surface litter, more topsoil, more organic carbon, nitrogen, and polysaccharides, better porosity, aeration, and drainage, and enhanced invertebrate and plant diversity (Satchell 1983; Lee 1985; Meysman et al. 2006; Barot et al. 2007). Earthworms live in partly self-constructed worlds: Some selection on contemporary earthworms has been transformed by the prior niche-constructing activities of prior generations of earthworms.

Turner (2000) compared some physiological characteristics of earthworms with other animals, making a surprising discovery: Earthworms are equipped with the "wrong" kidneys. Different kinds of kidneys are typically found in different animals, depending on where they live. Animals living in fresh water are in danger of being flooded by excess water, so fresh water kidneys have to excrete surplus water. Animals living in the sea are in danger of being killed by excess salts, so marine kidneys have to get rid of salts. Animals living on land are in danger of drying up, so terrestrial kidneys must prevent desiccation by retaining water. The crucial point is that earthworms, obviously terrestrial animals, are equipped with very nearly typical freshwater kidneys. What seems to have happened is that earthworms have retained the freshwater physiology of their earlier aquatic ancestors, even though they have lived on land for 50 million years. The solution to this paradox is that earthworms solve their water- and salt-balance problems by niche construction. Earthworms produce well-aggregated soils with weakened matric potentials (a weakened ability for the soil to hold on to water), which makes it easier for them to draw water into their bodies. All of this earthworm activity, however, highlights a problem with the standard concept of adaptation. In this case it is the soil that is doing the changing, not the worm, to match the demands of the worm's freshwater physiology (Turner 2000). The adaptive fit between organisms and their environments is not just a matter of selection shaping traits in responsive organisms, but also of active organisms modifying environments by niche construction, often to suit themselves.

6.3 Limitations of standard evolutionary theory

Biologists are familiar with niche construction (Odling-Smee et al. 2003). Special cases of niche construction have been incorporated in mathematical models that are broadly compatible with standard evolutionary theory, for example, in models of frequency- and density-dependent selection (Futuyma 1998), habitat selection (Hanski and Singer 2001), maternal inheritance (Kirkpatrick and Lande 1989), extended phenotypes (Dawkins 1982), and co-evolution (Thompson 1994). The fact that organisms can, and frequently do, alter their environments is also well known to ecologists, who often describe niche construction as "ecosystem engineering" (Jones et al. 1994, 1997; Meysman et al. 2006; Stinchcombe and Schmitt 2006). Yet in spite of these approaches, the full significance of niche construction is unappreciated. What has been missing is the explicit recognition that niche construction is a distinct, co-directing causal process in evolution in its own right, rather than a mere product of selection (Odling-Smee et al. 2003; Laland and Sterelny 2006). Why has such a seemingly obvious process been marginalized by biologists for so long?

The answer probably lies in a seldom reconsidered foundation assumption of standard evolutionary theory concerning the role of environments in evolution. Godfrey-Smith (1996) drew attention to it by describing standard evolutionary theory as an "externalist" theory. It is externalist because it uses the external environment as its fundamental explanatory reference device (Odling-Smee 1988), explaining the internal properties of organisms, their adaptations, exclusively in terms of sources of natural selection in external environments.

But living organisms are not just "passive" physical objects (Waddington 1969; Lewontin 1983)—they are active, as well as reactive, and unlike non-living objects, they can, indeed must, "push back." To stay alive organisms *must* gain resources from their external environments by non-random, fuel-consuming work, and they must dump detritus. Non-random work also requires organisms to "know" what they are doing, both structurally and functionally, at least to some extent. Therefore, and again unlike passive abiotic objects, organisms must be "informed" by meaningful information, and minimally by whatever "semantic information" is carried by their genes. It means that organisms are bound to impose some non-random changes on their environments through their work (Odling-Smee et al. 2003).

We can now pin down the reference device problem bequeathed by standard evolutionary theory. One of the "causal arrows" in one of Lewontin's equations (equation (2b)) is pointing in the "wrong" direction, from organisms to environments (the state of environments is caused in part by the prior state of organisms). This "causal arrow" is incompatible with the externalist assumption of standard evolutionary theory, making it difficult to describe any change in natural selection that is caused by prior niche construction as a cause of evolution. Instead, the standard theory is repeatedly forced by its own assumptions to "write off" all observed instances of niche construction as nothing more than the phenotypic, or extended phenotypic (Dawkins 1982), consequences of previous natural selection. Standard evolutionary theory can recognize niche construction as a product of evolution, but it cannot recognize it as a cause.

6.4 Niche construction theory

The solution adopted by niche construction theory was to change evolution's explanatory reference device. Instead of describing the evolution of organisms relative to external environments, Odling-Smee et al. (2003) describe evolution relative to organism–environment relationships, or "niches", as in equation (3). Niches incorporate "two-way" interactions between organisms and their environments (Chase and Leibold 2003; Odling-Smee et al. 2003). This change of reference device renders evolution an "interactionist" theory (Godfrey-Smith 1996).

Niches work because they are theoretically "neutral." The niche relationship between niche-constructing organisms and their naturally selecting environments does not impose any kind of bias, either in favor of natural selection or in favor of niche construction. Instead it allows natural selection and niche construction to be modeled as *reciprocal* causal processes in evolution. This simple revision allows niche construction to be fully recognized as a cause of evolutionary change.

Figure 6.1b (on p. 100) illustrates the resulting scheme. Here, the evolution of organisms explicitly depends on both natural selection and niche construction. Inheritance has two major components, genes and "ecological inheritance." The latter comprises the legacy of modified selection pressures resulting from habitats and resources chosen and modified by ancestral niche construction (Odling-Smee et al. 2003). Hence, the selective environments encountered by organisms are partly determined by independent sources of natural selection, for instance, by climate, or physical and chemical events, and partly by what informed organisms do, or previously did, to their own and each other's environments, by niche construction.

We end up with two major causal processes in evolution instead of one, natural selection and niche construction, and two major inheritance systems, genetic and ecological inheritance.

6.4.1 *Modeling niche construction*

It is also possible to model niche construction formally, as a causal process in evolution. Mathematical models can be built that capture the modification of sources of selection in environments by prior niche construction, the subsequent selection of organisms in the face of transformed selective environments, and the modified adaptations of organisms that evolve.

We will briefly describe the logic, but not the maths, that underpinned our models (Laland et al. 1996, 1999, 2001). We used two-locus population genetic theory and focussed on a single population, and two genetic loci only, labelled **E** and **A**. We assumed that: (i) the population's capacity for niche construction is influenced by the frequency of alleles at the first, or E locus; (ii) the amount of some resource, **R**, in the population's environment, depends either wholly or in part on the niche-constructing activities of past and present generations of organisms in the population; and (iii) the amount of this resource, **R**, subsequently influences the pattern and strength of selection acting on alleles at the second, or **A** locus, in the same population. The resource **R** could be any environmental resource or condition modified by niche construction. For instance, it could be a food item, an abiotic resource such as water, a chemical element, or an artifact such as a nest, burrow, or mound. Changes in **R** may also depend on independent agents in the population's environment, including abiotic agents. The basic model can be generalized because the two genetic loci, the **A** locus and the E locus, do not always have to be in the same population, but could be, for instance, in two co-evolving populations.

The results obtained from our models (Odling-Smee et al. 2003) and others (Schwilk and Ackerly 2001; Ihara and Feldman 2004; Borenstein et al. 2006; Hui, Li, and Yue 2004; Silver and Di Paolo 2006), all indicate that adding niche construction to natural selection makes a difference. Niche construction can modify environments to generate modified selection that can override independent sources of selection, driving populations down alternative evolutionary trajectories to new equilibria. Niche construction can initiate new evolutionary episodes. It can influence the amount of genetic variation carried by populations. It can generate unusual evolutionary dynamics, such as time-lags and momentum effects. Niche-constructing traits can even drive themselves to fixation. There are two important general conclusions from this body of theory: Niche construction is both tractable to theoretical analyses and evolutionarily consequential. Adding niche construction to evolutionary theory changes our understanding of how evolution works.

6.5 Social niche construction

There is one kind of niche construction that we have not yet explicitly considered, "social niche construction." The social niche is the subset of natural selection pressures in an evolutionary niche that stem from interactions with other organisms in their social groups. It constitutes the resources (e.g. food), services (e.g. grooming), and other outputs (e.g. threats) provided by organisms for each other. It also includes all the ways in which individual organisms can actively defend themselves, compete with, form alliances with, cooperate, exploit, or manipulate, other organisms, and by doing so modify some of the natural selection pressures they encounter in their niche (Laland et al. in press). Below we argue that social niche construction probably played a major role in the evolution of human societies and the evolution of language.

Consider an infra-human example. Flack et al. (2006) showed how the stability of the social niche of pigtailed macaques (*Macaca nemestrina*) depends on the monkeys having sufficient time and security to engage in certain social interactions. For example, individual macaques require sufficient time and security to groom, play, and sit in close contact with each other, to "construct" their social groups. However, primate societies are prone to being destabilized by conflicts between individuals, for example, over access to food or mates. Flack and colleagues describe how, in pigtailed macaques, stable social networks depend on "policing" by a small number of high-status males who prevent conflicts from escalating, either by actively intervening and terminating them, or just by their physical presence. When this "policing" was experimentally disabled by the "policers" being physically removed from their group, the macaque "social niche" was destabilized, and social disorder increased. Without "police" the social group broke up into small cliques, with high levels of conflict. Conversely, when the "policing" was operational, the macaques built larger social networks characterized by greater partner diversity and increased cooperation. Flack and colleagues suggested that, in pigtailed macaques, "policing" significantly alters the construction of the social resource networks that make group living advantageous.

The macaque example illustrates two general, if self-apparent, points about social groups. First, it implies that, for some species, living in functioning social groups is advantageous because it increases the fitness of individual members of the group. There are both benefits and costs of belonging to a group, the former including better anti-predator defenses or more efficient foraging, and the latter including increased competition and risk of pathogen transfer (Krause and Ruxton 2002). Secondly, the active formation and maintenance of a social group depends critically on the members of a group being able to communicate with each other. Flack and colleagues show how, in pigtailed macaques, policing is only possible because the status of individual macaques can be signaled to other group members through a "status communication network." For instance, the status of subordinate animals is constantly signaled to the "policers" with "silent bare teeth" displays.

Group living therefore appears to depend on two kinds of niche construction. One refers primarily to the consequences of group living, constructing a social context for existence, with benefits such as safety in numbers or social foraging. It concerns how the construction of social niches by social organisms modifies conventional sources of natural selection in their environments, to the potential fitness advantage of most members of their groups, and broadly corresponds to the kinds of niche construction we have previously described (Odling-Smee et al. 2003). One difference is that it may involve "group niche construction," that is it may demand shared fitness goals and some cooperation from multiple members of a group.

The other kind of niche construction is more relevant here. It concerns the construction of communication links and networks in social groups, without which adaptive group living is probably impossible. We call it *communicative niche construction*. In general, communicative niche construction depends on the ability of organisms to convey meaningful information to and from each other through their bodies (e.g. Gray and McKinnon 2007), products, or activities (e.g. Heyes and Galef 1996; Heyes and Huber 2000; Odling-Smee 2006).

Communication among organisms is obviously an extremely general phenomenon. It ranges from quorum-sensing in bacteria to human language (Krause and Ruxton 2002). The communication can be crude, it can be indirect, and it needs not be restricted to conspecifics, nor be social. For instance, many animals deceive predators in other species by sending "dishonest" signals to them, for instance by mimicry or camouflage (Maynard-Smith and Harper 2003). Many parasites, including micro-organisms, manipulate their hosts to their own advantage, and often to the disadvantage of their host, by transferring "hostile messages" to them (Krause and Ruxton 2002). For example, viruses can insert "hostile messages" in their hosts' genomes, and thereby change the phenotypic expression of their hosts, to the virus's advantage (Combes 2001). Animal parasites can do the same. A brood-parasite can transmit a "hostile signal" to its host's brain. A vivid example is a parasitic cuckoo chick, which evokes a feeding response from its foster parent by emitting rapid begging calls, equivalent to the collective calls of the entire brood of the host bird that the cuckoo chick has just killed (Davies et al. 1998). In primates and other large-brained organisms, communicative niche construction typically depends on animals sending "messages" to and from each other's brains, in ways that involve a degree of learning and cognition (Fragaszy and Perry 2003).

Animal communication has been studied for decades without being called "niche construction" (Thorpe 1958; Maynard-Smith and Harper 2003), so why call it "niche construction" now? Partly, to emphasize that all organisms are active components of each other's environments, and that between-organism communication typically induces phenotypic changes among the communicators. Organisms are therefore likely to modify one or more of the natural selection pressures in their own and in each other's environments by communicating.

But communication among individuals is not sufficient to account for how communicative niche construction can have evolutionary consequences for populations, as well as developmental consequences for individuals. For that to be possible the consequences of communicative niche construction must scale-up from the individual level to a population level by accumulating in a population's environment and by being transmitted across multiple generations through an inheritance system. When individual organisms communicate with each other, they usually belong to the same generation or adjacent generations. No organism lives long enough to modify selection for multiple successive generations of their populations, merely by communicating. So how can communicative niche construction affect evolution?

The answer is that although individual organisms do not live long, their niche-constructed products, be they termite mounds, beaver dams, or the organization of social groups and the communication networks on which that organization depends, can last much longer. The organization of animal societies, and their communication networks, can be transmitted across multiple generations of a population as an ecological inheritance (Figure 6.1b on p. 100). Thus, it is possible for communicative niche construction to modify one or more natural selection pressures in populations of social organisms repeatedly and consistently, and thereby to affect their evolution in a directional manner. If that happens, communication fully qualifies as another kind of niche construction.

An example is provided by a Namibian species of termite (*Macrotermes michaelseni*). Here, individual termites live for only three or four months, but the average age of their mounds, and of the persisting communication systems their mounds embody, has been estimated at 1,200 years (Turner 2007). That corresponds to many generations of termites, more than enough for termite populations to evolve in response to termite-modified environments. The persistence of primate social organizations, and their dependence on inherited communication networks, may be less easy to pin down, because they are less concrete. A possible exception is our own artifact-producing human ancestors, whose artifacts can tell us something about past human social organizations. However, in primates too, the transgenerational organization of social groups, including human social groups, should correlate with a transgenerational capacity for communicative niche construction.

6.6 The evolution of communicative niche construction

Now we can turn to a question raised by Számadó and Szathmáry (2006): "What selective scenario was responsible for the emergence of language?" We will couple that to a question of our own: "To what extent was that selective scenario itself a product of niche construction?" Initially, we will consider both these questions relative to the evolution of communicative niche construction in general, before focussing on human language.

Two preliminary points apply to all forms of communicative niche construction. First, communication can only *directly* modify biotic sources of natural selection, by acting on whatever semantic information is carried by other organisms. It cannot act directly on any source of selection that does not itself carry and express semantic information. This distinction occurs because other organisms, unlike abiota, contain two different kinds of resources, material and informational resources, and both can affect the fitness of a focal niche-constructing organism. Another organism in its environment may act as a physical resource, such as a food item, for a niche-constructing organism. Alternatively, the genome or brain of another organism may act as a "bank" of potentially useful semantic information for the niche-constructing organism. In the latter case, any niche-constructing organism capable of communicating with another organism could potentially change it, copy it, or manipulate it in a way that subsequently changed the phenotypic expression of either itself or the other organism, and thereby affect its own fitness. If an individual organism is unable to communicate with another organism, however, then effectively the other organism's informational resources do not exist. This builds on Lewontin's (1983) point that organisms largely "define" their own environments.

Second, the recognition that other organisms carry both material and informational resources may eventually require an extension of our previous models. Hitherto, for simplicity, our treatment of the resource R, modified by niche construction, was restricted to physical energy and material resources. However, where the resource comprises other organisms in an environment, it may sometimes usefully be conceptualized as composed of two distinct components, a physical energy and matter component, labeled R_p, and a semantic information component, labeled R_i.

The fitness of organisms, as measured by their capacity to survive and reproduce, depends directly on their ability to gain physical energy and material resources from their environments (R_p); to defend themselves from physical threats in their environments; and to dump physical detritus back in their environments. But in addition, these related abilities depend on organisms being physically adapted in their niches, and organisms cannot be adapted without being sufficiently informed, *a priori*, by relevant semantic information (R_i).

Thus physical resources (R_p) have a fitness value for organisms that is directly measurable in terms of survival and reproduction. Semantic information (R_i), however, has only an indirect fitness value, potentially measurable in terms of how much the prior possession of R_i by developing organisms reduces their subsequent uncertainty about how to acquire and maintain fitness through the adaptive control of R_p. The relationship between R_i and R_p is complicated. R_i will only confer a direct fitness cost, because the acquisition, storage, and use of semantic information always costs organisms some expenditure of physical resources. Calculating the value of any net fitness benefit of R_i will require both the calculation of the prior costs of the information expressed in the adaptations of organisms, measured in R_p, versus whatever fitness benefits, again measured in R_p, the organisms subsequently gain, because now they carry informed adaptations (Odling-Smee et al. 2003; Bergstrom and Lachman 2004).

We can now consider the nature of the selective environments that may have favored communication among social animals living in groups. Any organism that invests in communication must be forced to "cash in" the cost of whatever semantic information is involved in its communications, with net gains or overriding benefits, in the form of extra energy and material resources, as a consequence of its communications. We use this general expectation to generate a shortlist of possible selection pressures favoring the evolution of communicative niche construction in social animals.

First, we would expect natural selection to favor individuals that minimize the *a priori* costs and maximize the *a posteriori* benefits of their communications, relative to their competitors. Second, we would expect selection for organisms that invest more in social niche construction, including more effective social communication networks, provided their greater investments subsequently pay off in terms of (i) increased net group benefits, with (ii) increased net individual benefits to members of the group, in particular (iii), by enhancing the personal benefits to the communicator, irrespective of whether their communications also enhance benefits for other members of their group.

The third of these predictions opens the door to "cheats," who reap group benefits from the cooperative behavior of other group members but fail to pay their share of the costs. Trivers (1971) described different ways of cheating. Conventional cheats are the so-called "free-riders" who fail to pay any of the fitness costs involved in gaining group benefits (Hammerstein 2003). An example is an animal that never risks giving an alarm call, but who benefits from the alarm calls of others. But it is also possible for cheats to operate in more subtle ways (Trivers 1971), for instance, by never quite pulling their weight in paying the costs of cooperation, or always exploiting more than their "fair share" of the benefits. Accordingly, we would expect (iv) selection for the detection, punishment, policing, and expulsion of cheats, in social groups. We would also expect (v) selection for "better" cheats, especially for more subtle cheats, for instance, cheats that take advantage of the communication networks in their social groups to enhance the benefits of their cheating, while concealing it from others. Indeed, we would expect (vi) a continuous "arms race," or struggle for social status, or social power, in any social animals that live in groups (Dawes et al. 2007).

6.7 Human cultural niche construction

These proposed sources of natural selection favoring communicative niche construction still fail to account for the evolution of human language.

Why? Why is human language unique in comparison with other animals' communication systems, and what extra sources of selection are needed to explain its evolution? We suspect it will not be possible to advance our understanding of the origins of language without taking into account the exceptional potency of human cultural processes in general, and of human cultural niche construction in particular.

Countless organisms choose and partly construct suitable environments for themselves, often in response to environmental challenges created by ancestral niche construction, and often precipitating further evolutionary episodes when they do so (Odling-Smee et al. 2003). Unlike almost all other species, however, humans can respond to ancestrally niche-constructed environments in two ways (Figure 6.2): either through further, and usually cultural, niche construction (route 1), or through further genetic evolution (route 2).

The first way (route 1) comprises an adaptive cultural response to a change in the environment that was previously induced by earlier cultural niche construction. Suppose humans change their environment by polluting it, the polluted environment could subsequently stimulate the invention and spread of a new technology to counteract the contamination. If this happens, route 1 comprises a culturally induced change in an environment that favors an effective cultural response, with no impact

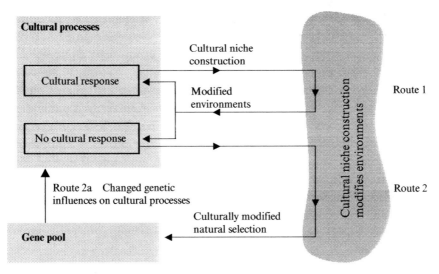

Fig. 6.2. Alternative responses to feedback from cultural niche construction

on human genetics. Theoretical analyses suggest that cultural responses to self-imposed modified selection typically occur more rapidly than genetic responses, and often render genetic responses unnecessary (Laland et al. 2001; Odling-Smee et al. 2003). This makes route 1 the more likely human response to any new adaptive challenge.

The second way (route 2) applies when human cultural processes fail to provide an effective response to an environmental change, such that culturally modified environments give rise to modified natural selection pressures, subsequently changing gene frequencies. Darwin originally emphasized the gradualistic character of evolution, and for many years evolutionary biologists followed suit. More recently biologists have been able to measure rates of response to selection in animals and plants, and have discovered that selection often operates much faster than hitherto conceived (Dwyer et al. 1990; Grant and Grant 1995; Kingsolver et al. 2001). Kingsolver and colleagues (2001) reviewed 63 studies that measured the strength of natural selection in 62 species, and found that the median selection gradient was 0.16, enough to cause a quantitative trait to change by one standard deviation in just 25 generations (c. 500 years for humans). That suggests that significant human evolution could occur in a few hundred years or less, and opens the possibility that humans could have evolved solutions to many self-imposed problems over the last few millenia. It also emphasizes the likely importance of route 2 in human evolution, and provides a rationale for applying the theory of gene-culture co-evolution to human evolution (Cavalli-Sforza and Feldman 1981; Boyd and Richerson 1985; Laland et al. 2000; Richerson and Boyd 2005).

Several examples of genetic responses to human cultural niche construction exist (Odling-Smee et al. 2003). One is provided by the agricultural practices of a population of Kwa-speaking yam cultivators in West Africa (Durham 1991). These people cut clearings in forests to grow crops, with a cascade of consequences. The clearings increased the amount of standing water, which provided better breeding grounds for mosquitoes and increased the prevalence of malaria. That, in turn, modified natural selection to favor the sickle-cell S allele because, in the heterozygous condition, the S allele confers protection against malaria. Here culture did not damp out natural selection, but rather induced it. Other candidate genes, in other populations, may also have been favored by culturally modified natural selection, because they also provide resistance to malaria, including G6PD, TNFSF5, and alleles coding for hemoglobin C and Duffy blood groups (Balter 2005). In addition, there is evidence of genes being selected because they confer resistance to other diseases, including AIDS and smallpox (CCR5), and hypertension (AGT, CYP3A) (Balter 2005). Indeed, recent statistical analyses of the human genome have revealed nearly two thousand human genes that show signals of strong and recent selection, many of which are expressed in the immune system and brain (Wang et al. 2006; Voight et al. 2006). Wang et al. (2006) write: "Given that most of these selective events likely occurred in the last 10,000–40,000 years...it is tempting to speculate that gene-culture interactions directly or indirectly shaped our genomic architecture."

These data suggest that evolutionary events induced by human cultural niche construction could sometimes have fed back to affect the biological capability for cultural processes. Route 2a (Figure 6.2) represents genetic endowments, predispositions, and aptitudes that could have influenced what humans learn, how they behave, how they communicate, and in general, their capacities for expressing culture. A candidate example is the expensive-tissue hypothesis of Aiello and Wheeler (1995). These authors noted that reductions in hominid gut size correlate to increases in relative brain size. They suggested that the cultural practices of hunting and scavenging led to better diets, including increased meat consumption, making the large guts associated with herbivorous diets unnecessary, and allowing more energy to be invested in brain tissue. Enlarged neocortices and increased cognitive capacities may then have allowed hominids to express more cultural innovations, such as the cultural practice of cooking, which subsequently permitted a further reduction in gut size and another increase in brain size (Wrangham et al. 1999). Deacon (1997: 323, fig. 11.1) invokes a similar feedback loop, which he labels "Baldwinian selection," as a possible explanation for the evolution of human language. The Baldwin effect refers to a selective process in which an initially learned trait subsequently becomes unlearned, a special case of the selective feedback represented by route 2a.

6.8 The evolution of language

Can the niche construction approach offer an alternative basis for understanding the evolution of language? We believe so, but are not experts on human language, and are not qualified to spell out precisely how. Also, we are aware of a concern, expressed by students of human language, that it is all too easy to construct plausible stories about the origins of language because there are so few well-established facts to constrain them (Számadó and Szathmáry 2006).

One approach we endorse, from Számadó and Szathmáry (2006), describes four criteria for determining the validity of competing theories:

1. The theory must account for the honesty of early language.
2. The concepts proposed by the theory should be grounded in reality.
3. The theory should explain the power of generalization, which is unique to human language.
4. The theory should account for the uniqueness of human language.

To these, we add a fifth criterion:

5. The source of selection should exhibit the appropriate level of environmental variation.

Our reasoning here is based on theoretical explorations of the adaptive value of cultural transmission (Boyd and Richerson 1985; Aoki and Feldman 1987; Feldman et al. 1996). We treat human language as a component of human culture, and highlight two well-established features of language. First, notwithstanding the role of evolved structure in language acquisition, human language is learned, and learned socially. Second, at least relative to communication systems in other species, human languages change rapidly, not just through changes in gene frequencies, but at an entirely different level, a cultural or linguistic level (Deacon 1997). Given that non-human primate communication is largely unlearned (Janik and Slater 1997), and probably changing at rates little different from other biologically evolved characters, we can ask "What was language needed for?" that required it to be socially learned and rapidly changing. Theoretical analyses suggest that cultural transmission is favored in variable, but not too variable, kinds of environments.

In an environment that is changing comparatively slowly, or that exhibits relatively little spatial heterogeneity, populations are able to evolve appropriate behavior through natural selection, and learning is of little value. At the other extreme, in rapidly changing or highly variable environments asocial learning pays, provided the environment retains some semblance of predictability. Social learning is favored at intermediate rates of change, as individuals can acquire relevant information without bearing the costs of asocial learning, but with greater phenotypic flexibility than unlearned adaptations. Within this window of environmental variability, vertical transmission of information (social learning from parents) is thought to be an adaptation to slower rates of change than horizontal transmission (social learning among unrelated individuals of the same cohort), with oblique transmission (offspring learning from non-parent adults) somewhere in-between.

Herein lies an important point. If other primates do not learn their calls, this implies that the content over which they communicate must be relatively stable. Conversely, humans have socially learned communication, which implies that the selection pressures favoring language must have been changing, and changing at a rate that evolved forms of communication could not track.

Let us now turn to consideration of the context of language evolution, in the light of these criteria and from the niche-construction perspective. Here we will assume that something like modern language first appeared at some point between 1 million and 50,000 years ago, and that it did so in a member of our genus. This is not to suggest that as rich a phenomenon as language suddenly appeared in its full-blown modern state. Clearly language is not the product of a point mutation, even allowing for adaptive restructuring by developmental systems. We prefer a gradualistic account for the emergence of language, which potentially explains the transition from non-human primate-like communication systems.

From a comparative perspective, we can see that extant apes species, such as chimpanzees, orangutans, and bonobos, are extremely reliant on social learning, often including sophisticated forms of social learning such as imitation (Whiten et al. 1996; Whiten 1998; Whiten et al. 1999; van Schaik et al. 2003). Young chimpanzees and orangutans acquire a variety of foraging skills (as well as other cultural traits such as grooming techniques, social signals, and courtship displays) from adult members of their local community. These apes exhibit extensive tool-using repertoires, and show behavioral traditions that exhibit considerable inter-population variation (Whiten et al. 1999; van Schaik et al. 2003). The richness of extant ape culture suggests that the constancy of Oldowan and Acheulian stone tool traditions may be misleading. Members of our genus are likely to have constructed richer and geographically more diverse cultural repertoires than extant apes, including both stone and non-stone tool-using traditions, and local, population-specific, learned and socially transmitted foraging repertoires. We encourage researchers studying human language to take account of this culturally constructed context for language evolution.

We end this section with a sketch designed to illustrate the kind of reasoning that the niche-construction perspective encourages. Számadó and Szathmáry's first criterion, that the theory must account for the honesty of early language, seems to us likely to be important. The reasoning here is that, given the low production costs of speech or gesturing, dishonest signaling could easily evolve unless language emerged in a context in which it did not pay to cheat, because of shared interests among communicators. This suggests that communication among kin may have been an important early factor, since honest, low-cost signals can evolve quite easily among relatives (Johnstone and Grafen 1992). We are also attracted by the points, emphasized by Deacon (1997) and Fitch (2004, 2005), that children learn language at an early age, long before any application of language during adulthood, and that children selectively hear some structures and ignore others, and so generate selection for language structure that is "child friendly."

Humans transmit more learned information across generations than any other species (Laland et al. 2000). Conversely, animals typically depend primarily on horizontal transmissions based on simple forms of social learning (Galef 1988; Laland et al. 1993). A comparative perspective thus implies that the earliest forms of social transmission were probably horizontal, and that the lineage leading to *Homo sapiens* has been selected for increasing reliance on vertical and oblique cultural transmission. The theoretical analyses of the evolution of culture, described above, imply that a shift towards increased transgenerational cultural transmission reflects a greater constancy in the environment over time. Such a shift is difficult to reconcile with culture being favored by variation in an autonomous external environment because there is no evidence to suggest that environments have become more constant over the last few million years, but rather the opposite, and if they had, other protocultural species would also be expected to show more transgenerational transmission than they do. Richerson and Boyd (2005) have suggested that independent (e.g. climatic) sources of environmental variation are the primary selection pressures favoring the human capacity for cultural transmission, but these vary on entirely the wrong scale.

To us, a more compelling hypothesis is that our ancestors constructed the environmental conditions that favored hominid reliance on culture

(Odling-Smee et al. 2003), building niches in which it paid them to transmit more information to their offspring (Laland et al. 2000). The more an organism controls and regulates its environment, and the environment of its offspring, the greater should be the advantage of transmitting cultural information across generations. For example, by tracking the movements of migrating or dispersing prey, populations of hominids increase the chances that a specific food source will be available in their environments, that the same tools used for hunting will be needed, and that the skin, bones, and other materials from these animals will be at hand to use in the manufacture of additional tools. Such activities create the kind of stable social environment in which related technologies, such as food preparation or skin processing methods, would be advantageous from one generation to the next, with methods repeatedly socially transmitted across generations. Once started, cultural niche construction may become an autocatalytic process, with greater culturally generated environmental regulation leading to increasing homogeneity of the social environment as experienced by old and young, favoring further transgenerational cultural transmission.

The emergence of language can be viewed in the same way. Non-human apes exhibit largely unlearned vocalizations, but also some gestural communication, with some evidence for semanticity in their signals (Janik and Slater 1997; Zuberbühler 2005). A shift from unlearned to learned vocalization suggests an increase in the rate of change of the source of selection for primate communication. An explanation for this in terms of a changing independent external environment (e.g. fluctuating climate) is not particularly credible, for several reasons. First, once again, the scale of climatic change is too slow. Second, an external source of selection ought equally to have favored learned communication in other primates. Third, the requirement for increasing rates of change in the external selective environment for language contradicts the requirement for increasing stability in the external selective environment for culture.

Conversely, if we regard the source of selection for language to be a feature of the self-constructed environment, such problems are alleviated. For instance, what features of the self-constructed ape environment change rapidly, and vary geographically? From a comparative perspective, the most obvious answer is their ape "cultural" practices, particularly their tool use and material "culture." One characteristic of human culture, particularly recently, and most evident in technology, is its cumulative nature, with an increase in the complexity or efficiency of cultural elements with time; but such "ratcheting" is largely absent from non-human ape culture (Tomasello 1994). A second feature is exponential growth in cultural complexity and diversity with time (Ghirlanda and Enquist 2007). So, at some stage in the last 1 million years, our potent-niche-constructing ancestors may have generated cultural variants—tools, foraging techniques, social signals, courtship rituals, self-medicative treatments—at such a rate that they could not communicate about their world without constantly evolving better ways of communicating. If each new tool, foraging technique, display, or treatment has to be learned, and if, as the comparative evidence suggests, cultural variants such as tool use are typically learned by young apes from their mothers and older siblings (Whiten et al. 1999), then conceivably human language may have co-evolved with human cultural niche construction as a means of facilitating and enhancing socially transmitted life-skill acquisition in young hominids, particularly in our own species, where cumulative cultural change is evident. Moreover, with each new means of exploiting the local environment with increased efficiency, we should see a potential increase in the environment's carrying capacity. Other theoretical analyses have found that even costly forms of communication can spread if the increment in absolute fitness (more children) outweighs the cost in relative fitness (Bryson et al. in preparation).

We suspect that the selective scenario for language begins here, but it is also likely to have been amplified in various other ways. First, population-level diversity in material culture creates the opportunity for trade. Other animals trade niche-constructed resources for services, or services for services; humans trade niche-constructed resources. With trade comes negotiation, and further selection for effective communication. Second, culturally transmitted population-specific diversity in a spatially variable environment creates a premium on recognizing and learning from locals, who have useful local knowledge, rather than outsiders. Theoretical analyses suggest that conformity is favored in such circumstances, with several important consequences, including the evolution of ethnic markers, cooperation within groups, and conflict between groups (Boyd and Richerson 1985; Richerson and Boyd 2005), all potentially favoring enhanced communicative skills. Third, cooperation, in turn, allows the possibility of cheating over cooperative endeavors. At least in humans, subtle cheats might operate by gaining control of communication networks, ensuring that the messages that were sent maximized their returns. Conceivably, this form of cheating might select for more competent, skillful communicators.

Such a selective scenario has the advantage that it explains the uniqueness of human language. Human language is unique (amongst extant species) because humans uniquely exhibit the potent cultural niche construction necessary to construct a sufficiently diverse, generative, and changeable world that demands talking about.

We end by reiterating our ignorance of the human language literature. We are not really qualified to comment on the evolution of human language. Our main objective is to offer an alternative evolutionary framework, based on two reciprocal causal processes in evolution, natural selection and niche construction, particularly cultural niche construction, instead of natural selection only (Laland and Sterelny 2006). Our hope is that this alternative framework may prove fruitful to those who do know about language, and can come up with more plausible and better-supported accounts than the above, and some testable predictions. In this respect we are encouraged that some language scholars have already started to use niche construction theory (Bickerton in press; Clark 2005), as well as related ideas (Deacon 1997).

7 Playing with meaning: normative function and structure in play

SONIA RAGIR AND SUE SAVAGE-RUMBAUGH

7.1 Social play and language

This chapter explores the potential of social play to generate shared fields of reference and simple rules in the co-construction of intentional actions and routines in which players demonstrate mutual awareness through structured signals, monitoring the attention of others, and cooperative engagement with an object. As we shall see, co-constructed actions negotiate the means to mutually acceptable ends, and rules emerge that redirect the flow into familiar kinds of games. Repetition, with variation, creates rules that govern and bind a flexible repertory of basic motor skills, social responses, and communicative behavior. The response of a player redefines and/or limits another's intent; thus, the shared semantic understandings of objects, actions, and/or gestures that signal, query, or motivate the next move emerge as a function of this interaction. Co-constructed intentions are inherently shared, and salient gestures, sounds, and "incipient acts" evoke the meaning of moves that have been played into existence. Because play actions, movements, and gestures are often without their "real world" consequences or instrumental functions, these salient acts can become free to "stand for" or re-present their meaning in non-play contexts. In social play as in language, participants negotiate hierarchically ordered moves and exchanges that can be modified and rearranged through repetitive actions and shared goals into normative, rule-governed behavior. We propose that these dialogic structural and normative functions make social play a proper model for understanding the emergence of language, as a negotiated, self-organizing system rather than a system of communication limited to modern human societies (Ragir 2002; Savage-Rumbaugh et al. 1998).

Burghardt (2005) summarized five criteria that identify play: (1) a limited immediate function; (2) an endogenous component in which the activity appears to be spontaneous, voluntary, intentional, pleasurable, rewarding, or reinforcing, and done for its own sake (autoletic); (3) structural or temporal differences from ethotypic behavior; (4) the repetition of salient actions and themes within and across play bouts; and (5) finally, a relaxed behavioral field relatively free of stress. Although play appears to serve multiple extrinsic functions, these five criteria effectively distinguish most forms of play including social, object, and locomotor play in all animal species.

Play and ritual contain similar routinizing, emancipating, and decontextualizing properties (Givón 1998; Haiman 1994). However, play offers more creative freedom and consequently may be more likely to generate novel forms, structures, and meaning than rituals, which remain relatively fixed due to their important functions in the group. Even the signals of the communicative repertory may be transformed during play from an attempt to inform or influence the behaviors of others to a representation of that intention. While being about a social world, play, like ritual and language, is sensitive to its own constraints on form and meaning and as a result, is a self-organized negotiated communicative system (Putnam 1988). The idea that social play is fundamental to a negotiated and, thus, normative reinterpretation of experience and to the emergence of language in human evolution has been set forth many times (Bateson 1950; Bjorklund and Green 1992; Bruner 1976; Donald 1991; Knight 2000); this view has been overshadowed for many years by claims that the human capacity for symbolic representation and a compositional semantics was exapted from functional social rituals such as group "chorusing," long-term reciprocity, and/or other affiliative behaviors (Deacon 1997; Dunbar 1996; Merker 2000; cf. Knight 2000).

Peaks of play activity coincide with periods of central nervous system maturation—proliferation of information-specific neural networks that, we are positing, serve as substrates upon which the emergence of shared systems of communicative signals depend (Adams 1997; Adams and Cox 2002; Byers 1998). We will argue here that the semantic compositionality that appears so unique to language is manifest in the form and flow of social play. Participants in play co-construct meaning in a social context in real time, and simple rules appear to guide hierarchically embedded patterns of action. Rather than learning to read the minds of others, participants negotiate normative interpretations of experience in social play and assume that others will behave according to the expected norms (Elman et al. 1996; Flack et al. 2004). Playful interactions manifest a normative structure, communicative intent, and a sense of fair play (Bekoff 2001; Dugatkin and Bekoff 2003). Moreover, we suggest that without early developmental opportunities to acquire these co-constructed patterns of behavior through play, the kind of neural substrate that supports a rapid, automatic access to public systems of normative behavior such as agonistic and mating displays, communication (Burghardt 2005), and even language may be adversely affected.

The key point to be made about the repertoire of social play is that complexly coordinated units of movement/gesture become automatic in the participants as they mature. Because the goals of these joint activities are co-constructed, there is little need to assume that individuals are self-conscious of their own intentions, much less those of other players. The meaning of an action, gesture, and/or gaze emerges as the product of an interaction between players rather than as the intent of a single individual and is, therefore, mutual. As will be shown later in the chapter, the repetitive choreography of play, the action-based tickling, hiding, chasing, harmless-biting, -wrestling, -slapping, etc. become tokens of types of acts. In the illustration of ape play described below, the participants level the playing field and moderate the intensity of play through self-handicapping, the exchange of actor–recipient roles, and a constant signaling of the next move through gaze, posture, incipient acts, and gesture. The rules or "syntax" of an ongoing intentional activity need not be innate; instead they are "negotiated" into existence through a process of conjoined action with others in what has been referred to as a dynamic dance (King and Shanker 2003).

During play, ape and human children re-present and recombine the elements of sensory-motor and social repertories in infinitely varied ways. Acts that are reiterated and rarely subdivided stand out in the flow of events; they become automated, effortless, and create the basic locomotor/gestural lexicon used to negotiate and explore the possibilities of a game. Salient or incipient acts come to represent or signal familiar moves or exchanges. The more formalized and abstracted representational signals or systems of communication emerge as a result of reiteration and historical continuity only in well-established communities. We suggest that these processes have not been previously understood because relatively little attention has been paid to (1) play's striking resemblance to other more formal representational systems (Bak 1996; Bateson 1973; Donald 1991; Renyolds 1981); (2) the involvement of play in stimulating neural connections that pattern rapid sequences of complex communicative skills (Bekoff and Allen 1998; Edelman 1987; Kirby 1999: Siviy 1998); and (3) the coincidence of play and a critical period of rapid learning in all young mammals (Byers 1998; Fairbanks 2000; Miller and Byers 1998).

Systemic functional linguists (Benson and Greaves 2005; Thibault 2005; Taylor 1997) argued that the compositional form and meaning of language discourse was fundamentally co-constructed. Taylor (1997) characterized normative meta-discourse in spontaneous conversation as a matter of negotiation about matters of fact and meaning between the parties concerned. The repetition within a discourse reflected on and negotiated its normative function. Taylor (1997: 15) argued that the concepts of right and wrong, correct and incorrect are of the very essence of engaging and maintaining conversational discourse between participants. Similarly in play, signals that requested another's permission to take a turn or continue, and penalties for breaking these rules such as light slaps, lunges, and dispersal, re-enforced the rules of engagement. In the discussion that follows, we attempt to demonstrate that social play is profoundly normative and, thus, a self-organizing communicative activity. This will be done through a detailed analysis of thirty seconds of roughly twenty minutes of social play that took place in a large outdoor enclosure at the Language Research Center (LRC), Georgia State University (LRC Video Archive P08/29/1989, Great Ape Trust of Iowa).

7.2 Parameters of play in the social group

As a demonstration of the communicative, syntactic, and normative functions of play, we focussed on the game between an adult, female bonobo, Matata, about twenty years of age, and a juvenile, common chimpanzee, Panzee, four years of age. Savage-Rumbaugh, who cared for, observed, and played with the LRC colony daily between 1980 and 2007, introduced two novel objects into the outdoor yard to promote social play—a red PVC climbing-apparatus or "jungle-gym" and a fiberglass pool with several inches of water at the bottom. Matata was born and raised in the rainforests of the Congo Basin, Zaire, until she was six years old and, upon capture, was sent to the Yerkes Primate Facility in Georgia. Panzee was born at Yerkes and co-raised with Matata's daughter Panbanisha at the LRC. On the day of filming, Matata, three of her offspring, Panzee, and an adolescent orangutan socialized together in the outdoor yard. Matata was the oldest and most socially experienced ape in the group. For the analysis presented here, we examined the fifth of twelve play bouts between Matata and the juveniles that occurred on and around the jungle-gym.

We summarized some very general social norms that were typical of this group and appeared to be integral to negotiating the game. These rules appear to be generally true of primate social groups and not specific to either captivity or the unique capabilities of this ape colony.

We looked at the initial event in the play sequence frame-by-frame to help us determine how to code the episode. In the initial move (0–3 seconds), Panzee peered through the fallen jungle-gym at Matata, held it with both hands, lifted it a couple of inches, and immediately let it down; an "incipient act" that signaled her intent to push the jungle-gym up and toward Matata. In an earlier bout, Panzee pushed the fallen apparatus toward Matata without signaling intent or receiving permission, and Matata appeared to interpret this earlier move, perhaps correctly, as an aggressive display and chased her away (Rule 2: see Table 7.1).

Panzee both indicated her intent and appeared to wait for approval before proceeding. Although Matata was off-camera when Panzee signaled, it became clear that Matata understood and approved because she helped to guide the jungle-gym as Panzee pushed it upright and steadied it as Panzee climbed to the top. Moving the jungle-gym upright required a substantial physical tension between Panzee's push and Matata's steadying guidance. Toward the end of the video, Panzee and Panbanisha (a four-year-old bonobo) attempted to lift and then climb the apparatus without Matata's help, and to their surprise and discomfort it fell over. Regardless of how a player went into the play bout, consecutive co-constructed moves frequently produced quite different goals than those originally intended by any particular player. What actually happened in an ongoing negotiation reflected the shared intent as realized by the players, and the simultaneous coding of conjoined actions was the only way to accurately reveal those intentions. Matata gave Panzee permission to erect and climb the jungle-gym; she appeared not only to respond cooperatively to Panzee's focussed

TABLE 7.1. *General social rules guide ape play interactions*

Rule Number	Rule
1	Adults define and constrain play roles when playing with youngsters.[†]
2	When the status of individuals is not equal, the lower ranking individual must seek and receive permission for each new play action directed toward the dominant individual. If a subordinate player fails to seek and obtain permission, the bout ends and/or becomes aggressive.
(a)	In the play bout, intent is indicated and permission sought through small or uncompleted movements that anticipate the intended action, gestures, and/or some kind of eye contact.
(b)	Juveniles, but not infants, need to seek the permission of adults during play before engaging in behavior that might be interpreted as potentially aggressive.
3	Unequal partners must give each other license to proceed with play moves. The irony is that while there can be novel actions in play, there can be no surprise actions—unless an indication of a "surprise" was signaled as part of the prior communiqué.
4	Various structurally well-defined games, such as "tag," "king of the mountain," "hide and seek," "follow the leader," chasing or groping with eyes covered, and simulated elements of functional repertories are repeated throughout an episode in a multitude of variations; thus, the rules of these familiar games are understood by participants and observers alike. Infants often sit on the side or hang above and observe, or they may play along as subordinates to other players who take the active complementary roles.
5	All the intentional actions in a play exchange are conjoined so that each action is only made possible by the support of others. The form and intention of one participant's act makes co-action by the other participant possible and vice versa.

[†] Indeed, the play between the LRC juveniles without the significant influence of a dominant adult is noticeably simpler in structure; a video taken one year later shows Panzee and Panbanisha at five years old playing a relatively symmetrical game in which they chase and displace each other from a tire-swing with little communicative subtlety.

gaze and incipient action, but she reshaped Panzee's actions through her co-action. This complementary role revealed not only Matata's intention to engage Panzee's immediate query to set up the jungle-gym, but also a mutual desire for play. The normative content of the game was negotiated, while the participants and specific content varied noticeably from one bout to the next.

7.3 Methods of analysis

We observed and coded these play exchanges using a focal-subject event recorder designed specifically for the coding and analysis of behavioral interaction through time. We coded actions as conjoined **moves** that directed an exchange toward some immediate intentional goal. The *Sub-Trak Coding Software* created a time-ordered transcript of activity for each subject that included individual acts in conjoined behavioral moves, the intent or apparent goal of each move, and communicative gestures or eye-contact (Takach and Lindtvedt 2005; Ragir et al. 2005). The identification of token acts with actors tended to de-emphasize the co-constructed nature of the moves; however, we modified the coding fields to reflect simultane-ous, overlapping, and/or alternating actions by coding the simultaneous activity of both participants on a single time-marked line of code (cf. Table 7.1). We then reviewed the record to identify, if possible, the proximate goals of every move and the communicative acts that signaled their begin-ning and/or end.

   Using the social parameters listed above as a guide to the configuration, the role of each participant was coded in each conjoined move (Table 7.1). We revealed the form and content of the play bout through the physi-cal and temporal constraints of co-action, the signaling of intended co-action, and the acceptance and/or rejection of a signaled intent through the negotiation of the direction and culmination of each conjoined move. Our focus on the co-construction of moves rather than individual acts revealed the negotiated nature of intent between the players and the emergence of shared goals. Emphasizing the rules of engagement pointed us toward an understanding of adult/juvenile play exchanges from several earlier studies (Douglas 2006; Lindtvedt et al. 2005; Ragir et al. 2005).

   At this level of description, inter-observer reliability rarely became an issue; the negotiations that directed and redirected moves resulted in a shared immediate goal, changed goals, or terminated the bout. Armed with some understanding of the normative rules of social exchange in the colony (Table 7.1) and focussed on co-actions as opposed to individual actions and reactions, it became relatively easy to recognize and describe these rapid, complexly coordinated, yet inherently simple conjoined moves. When Panzee lunged somewhat aggressively, Matata responded with a big play face. By responding playfully to the ambiguity of Panzee's communication, Matata successfully redirected the move and continued the game. Thus, we assumed that Matata had agreed to let Panzee climb the jungle-gym, or sit at its summit, or lunge at her head, etc., as long as she continued to hold the tower and reacted playfully.

If play was co-constructed, the dyadic moves rather than discrete turns of individuals were the unit of analysis. In a sense, the moves of an exchange that constituted the play discourse were interpreted as semantic phrases, and the slight pauses that marked points of negotiation also served to signal changes in the direction of the "flow" of co-actions. Since both parties participated in creating the flow, the issue of whether or not a player correctly interpreted another's behavior *a priori* need not arise. We thus approached this game as a contextually embedded discourse in which the whole exchange was a process of "negotiation, explicitly an establishing and/or exercising of authority, an invocation of rights, and an imposition of constraints between parties about [how the game] and, indeed, how life should be played" (Taylor 1997: 12).

7.3.1 *Observations and analysis*

In the joint action described below, the two actors coordinated the stable, upright position of a red, PVC, climbing-apparatus (the jungle-gym) on the soft, woodchip ground cover so that one and/or the other participant might climb; Matata clearly understood the properties of the object and substrate. Panzee lifted and Matata modulated the direction and speed of the motion and held the jungle-gym stable when upright, and Panzee's glance and quick lift and release of the object marked the beginning of the co-action. Panzee moved smoothly from erecting to climbing, without pausing to check if Matata would permit her to climb. No second query was necessary, since Matata held the jungle-gym upright as a signal for Panzee to climb. There were two physically and temporally ordered parts to the conjoined moves—lifting the jungle-gym into position and climbing it—and the participants had to understand both parts in order to perform such a complex sequence of synchronous complementary actions. This dynamic co-construction of intentions was also characteristic of the other moves in the game. The frame-by-frame analysis of the conjoined moves of all participants revealed the rules and the negotiated normative content of this episode of social play.

Table 7.2 includes the context embedded descriptors for all moves. While there is not room here to analyze every move, the normative rules in Table 7.1 did appear compatible with all of the exchanges. Moreover, signaling of intent and co-constructed action characterized each move.

Let us take Exchange IV @ 8–12 seconds.

Here we find that Panzee **looks up** to signal her intent to climb, Matata **supports** the structure with her foot just as Panzee's weight would have tipped it over if she had not done so. Matata "pretends" to stop Panzee from **climbing** by **tapping** on her hands as she **reaches** for the top to pull herself up. Panzee **moves** each hand **away** just as Matata touches it. Were Matata really trying to keep Panzee off the top, she would lunge, as she has done in the past, to displace her. After her hand is tapped three times, Panzee **crouches** low and exaggerates her gaze toward Matata, as one last query, before she **swings** fully to the top. Following this **eye contact**, Matata very firmly **supports** the structure with both hands and one foot so that Panzee may **swing** to the top instead of climb, and Matata allows Panzee to **pause** and **sit** when she reaches the top.

In Exchange VI/23–29 seconds:

After Panzee successfully negotiated her climb to the top, she re-**challenges** Matata by **rocking** the jungle-gym once **softly** and then, after a **pause**, makes **eye contact** with Matata. Matata looks back, and Panzee vigorously **rocks** the jungle-gym twice. Then, Matata invites Panzee to **come to** her. Matata's free arm **stretches up and out** toward Panzee, while Panzee **crouches** very low bringing her face to the level of Matata's. They **gaze at** each other, and Panzee **swings** toward Matata, but **leaps off** the apparatus rather than jumping into Matata's arms. Matata with a wide **play-face reaches** around her back, but does not touch or grab; rather her **cupped hand follows** Panzee down to the ground—a **gesture** more typical of carrying or guiding than restraining.

(Savage-Rumbaugh, LRC Video, Outdoors, 8/29/89)

Back on the ground Panzee fled, and Matata dropped the jungle-gym to the ground instead of holding it up, thus bringing the second variation and this play bout to an end. The exchange above was the culmination

TABLE 7.2. *A simplified time-marked description of conjoined moves*

Time in seconds	Move	Matata's action	Panzee's action
0–1 Exchange I	1. Attention bid	Off camera	Look at MT
	1. Elaborate	Off camera	Lift jungle-gym
2–3.2	2. Erect JG	Guide JG	Push JG erect
3.2–5	3. Sustain and Climb JG	Stabilize JG	Climb JG to top
4.9 Exchange II	1. Attend/consent	Mutual gaze	Mutual gaze
	1. Elaborate	One foot on 1st rung	Stand bipedal
5–6.9	2. MT Challenge	Starts to climb up	Grab ceiling chain-link
	2. Elaborate	Climbs toward top	Steady JG from ceiling
6	3. Displace	Grabs at PZ	Arches away MT
6.8	4. Displace	Grabs PZ at waist	Leaps off JG
	4. Disengage	Lets go of PZ	Holds JG
	4. Elaborate	Steps off and steadies JG	Looks at MT and holds JG
6.9–7 Exchange III	1. Confront	Eye-contact/hold JG	Eye-contact/hold JG
	2.	Chase/grab PZ	Retreat MT
	2.	Hold/steady JG	Hold JG
	3. Redirect attention	Mutual gaze	Mutual gaze
	4. Disengage/pause	Look away PZ	Look away MT
8–12 Exchange IV	1. Challenge/climb JG	Mutual gaze	Mutual gaze
	2. Synchronous	Step up 1st rung to steady	Step up 1st rung to climb

(*cont.*)

TABLE 7.2. (Continued)

Time in seconds	Move	Matata's action	Panzee's action
	3. Elaborate	Braces JG w/on foot up	Look up/Climb
8.5	4. Challenge	Slaps PZ hand hold	Reaches for top rung
9	5. Comply	(poor visibility)	Withdraw and crouch
9.5	6. Challenge	Slaps PZ hand hold	Reaches for top rung
10	7. Comply	(poor visibility)	Withdraw hand
10.5	8. Challenge	Slaps PZ hand hold	Reaches for new hold
11	9. Comply	(poor visibility)	Withdraws hand
12–15 Exchange V	1. Request/Permit	Eye-contact/gesture w/ palm up	Crouches/peers thru JG at MT
14	2. Sustain/Climb	One hand follows PZ w/out contact	Climb to top of JG and sit
15–29 Exchange VI	1. Co-attend	Mutal gaze/pause	Mutual gaze/pause
17	2. Disengage/	Look away PZ	Look at MT
20–21	3. Attention bid	Continue	Look away and rock JG
	4. Respond	Eye-contact PZ	Eye-contact MT
	4. Respond	Stare PZ	Stops rocking
21–22.5	6. Pause/joint-rocking	Looks to camera	Follow MT gaze
23	6. Attend		Look at MT
23.5	7. Attention bid	Looks back to PZ	Rocks back very vigorously

24	Synchrony-eye contact	Pulls back as arch reaches the tipping pt.	Moves toward MT as she pulls
24.5	Synchrony-eye contact	Releases pull on JG	Pulls back from MT
25	Synchrony	Eye-contact at end of arc	Eye-contact at end of arc
25.5	Synchrony/eye-contact	Pulls back on JG	Shifts forward to MT
27	9. Offer/engage	Mutual gaze	Mutual gaze
27.2	9. Offer/comply	One hand release JG	One hand release JG
27.4	9. Continue	Raise free hand/arm wide open/play face	Crouch/lean to MT
27.5–29	10. Continue/disengage	Free arm follows the path of PZ's descent/ hand cupped up/play face	Leap off JG
29–31 Exchange VII		Stare/Chase PZ/holds JG	Stare/hold JG/backs away from MT
30		Topple JG	PZ crouches behind JG
30.4		Tug up on falling JG/hop/stamp on one foot	PZ flees up fence
31		Climbs on fallen JG and sits	Off camera

of a successful negotiation, as evidenced by the orderly sequence of many moves, the cooperation between players, and their play-faces and pants. In bouts described above, the negotiated moves/intentions are signaled by incipient acts ("lift and release" and a single "tentative rock") that represented a request, invitation, or intention to initiate the signaled activity. No moves were identical: In the first instance, Matata climbed up to displace Panzee from her seat at the top, and in the second she tapped Panzee's hands to detain her climb to the top of the jungle-gym (see Table 7.2). Unlike Panzee when Matata climbed to the top, she focussed her gaze and stood bipedal but did not pause to seek permission. Panzee, nonetheless, aware of Matata's intent, held the rungs of the jungle-gym with her feet and the ceiling chain-link with both hands while Matata climbed. Panzee facilitated Matata's challenge; if Panzee had not delayed her leap away and/or neglected to grab the chain-link ceiling, the apparatus would have toppled under Matata's weight. Communicative exchanges guided the timing and direction of the players' moves through several variations of conjoined actions, and a well-formed game emerged from this negotiation.

Much of the interpersonal synchronization of play occurred very rapidly (in less than one thirtieth of a second), and its rhythm was fundamental to maintaining the flow of keep-away, chase/flee, attack/retreat, climb/steady, and the rocking of the apparatus without interrupting or spoiling the fun. The need for rapid co-coordination appeared to establish the communicative salience of these gestures. Thus, rocking the jungle-gym required close attention to the synchronized pulls/releases and the carefully timed reversals of tension that kept the jungle-gym from toppling over. They accomplished this synchronization by means of continuous eye contact as well as the mutual tactile sensations of movement and balance from the apparatus on the soft substrate.

The roles of each participant were discrete and contrasting (lift/stabilize, chase/flee, climb up/keep off, attack/defend, pull/release) and the actor/reactor roles were frequently reversed. Repeated moves varied in timing, intensity, and context; these alterations and repeats elaborated the normative interpretation of the play exchanges for participants and observers. The ways in which past moves anticipated the next move and influenced the performance of subsequent instances of "similar moves" demonstrated the sensitivity of the moves to each other. The use of incipient acts from co-constructed moves to signal intent demonstrated the trajectory toward a public representation of intent that might be lifted out of play and reconstructed in non-play contexts. Such schematization and abstraction of familiar moves implied their communicative function, and the normative rules that govern a long and satisfying play bout reflected the underlying "grammar" of oft-repeated games.

Flirting with danger—the knowledge that an intentional or unintentional misstep or asynchrony in timing or intensity could elicit real threats and reprisals—appeared to be another source of pleasurable excitement in this game. Panzee challenged Matata's control over the jungle-gym by dragging or lifting it and by threatening its stability when sitting/ standing/rocking at the top. The reconstruction of this particular episode of jungle-gym play through an analysis of the dyadic moves and intentions gave us access to a meta-dialog. Panzee's ostensible goal was to demand, threaten, cajole, or negotiate her way to the top of the jungle-gym. Thus, Matata's role was to sustain and guide Panzee's challenge, to re-challenge or transform threats into play, and to mentor her skill at negotiating her way to the top.

An underlying paradox existed in the necessity for the dominant player to support the inexperienced challenger in her climb to the top of the jungle-gym. Thus, the game required that Matata be an advocate, challenger, and witness to Panzee's success. Similar to the game of "Capture the Hill," this exchange required an audience, and someone to take exception to, compete for, and define the value of capturing the summit. The final episode (ten minutes after the events recorded in Table 7.2) re-emphasized real-world social relationships, which were unaffected by the challenges of the game, and Matata "captured the hill." Matata ended the game and ascended the erect jungle-gym by steadying it on a vertical roof-pole without the help of Panzee. At the top, she sat and stared down at Panzee and Panbanisha on the ground, who looked back and then away.

The players did not pretend to a status or roles different than their own in everyday life; however, many actions within the exchange involved self-handicapping and "communicative representations," as when Matata touched rather than hit Panzee's hands to keep her from climbing (Bateson 1973). The players' expressions of pleasure and the spontaneity, repetition, and variation in the exchange marked the activity as a "state of play" (Burghardt 2005). The formulation of rules and norms, rather than a rigid repetition, informed both participants and observers how to play the game and, ultimately, how to operate flexibly and effectively in the community.

7.4 Repetition and the negotiation of form and meaning

The social play described above consisted of a series of repetitions across hierarchically organized scales of observation and analysis. Repetition featured prominently at each level of analysis: the individual motor activity, the sequences of intentionally negotiated moves, and the multi-move co-constructed play bouts. The beginning and the end of a repeated move or sequence of moves bracketed the intentional information that constituted its semantic content. Salient moves repeated in novel combinations explored, modified, and elaborated their meaning (Benson and Greaves 2005; Givón 1998; Putman 1988; Ragir 1994; Thibault 2005). The reiteration of such elements bracketed content at each hierarchical level, resulting in greater efficiency and rhythmic consistency in the motor-coordination of individual acts, the synchrony and counterpoint of dyadic moves, and the co-construction of the intentionality of interactive moves. As in any other system of communication, meaningful units of play must be easy to perform and comprehensible to others (Kirby 1999). Repetition functions to streamline the coordination of co-joined actions, and to abstract complexly synchronized or alternating sequences to make them easier to identify, understand, and perform (Givón 1998; Ragir 1994).

Ultimately this multi-level negotiation between participants and objects, within a social and physical context produced a shared understanding of the rules, means, and ends for each phase of the game.

7.5 The neuro-developmental biology of play

The spontaneous emergence of language comprehension in two of the bonobos at LRC raised the possibility that the cognitive substrate supporting semantic compositionality was a function of cross-fostering apes in a rich ape/human social environment (Savage-Rumbaugh et al. 1993, 1998). In humans and apes, play peaks during post-natal periods of dendritic proliferation and pruning. Neuroscientists have argued that repetition generates semi-permanent, experience-dependent networks of information-specific cortical connections that occur as a result of activity-dependent learning during juvenile growth and maturation (Adams 1997; Adams and Cox 2002; Arbib 2005; Corballis 1992; Kaczmarek 2000; Morgan and Curran 1991; Robertson 1992). Thus, repeated conjoined moves, communicative gestures, and normative negotiations of social play influence the structuring of activity-dependent neural networks that become specialized for particular kinds of information and cognitive functioning.[1] Byers (1998) and Miller (Miller and Byers 1998) argued that play activity made a profound contribution to long-term, information-specific systems of neural connectivity and was the source of the neural specialization that underlay automated adult behavioral repertoires. Fairbanks (2000) suggested that the embedded structure, semantic compositionality, and normative rules embodied in social play might restructure the maturing neural substrate and adapt communicative understanding to particular social contexts and histories. Kortmulder (1998) proposed that the communicative and locomotor possibilities explored in a relaxed, flexible, creative behavioral field of play resulted in the automaticity of indivisible behavioral elements that groups exapted and renegotiated into relatively inflexible, functional repertoires and rituals for survival defense and reproduction. Calvin (1983), Deacon (1997), and Edelman (1987)[2] proposed that the construction of functional neural networks involved synaptic competition that resulted in the localization of cognitive function, including that of communication.

---

[1] Repetition has a similar streamlining and standardizing effect on autoletic activity as well. But it is rare that perceptual-motor autoletic play or "practice" become stylized or abstract; rather the form becomes more efficient, precisely sequenced, and automatic, and instead of representing content, it becomes coordinated into a goal-directed behavioral repertory.

[2] Edelman (1987) argued, in *Neuronal Darwinism*, that perceptual categorization, memory, affect, and motor capacities were linked in Hebbian neural networks to form value-laden cortical maps developed one upon the other in ordered hierarchies. These networks make highly idiosyncratic links between percept and meaning and remain available for modification throughout life. Dendrites and synapses proliferate and restructure themselves most rapidly during a critical post-natal period that begins at birth, peaks after weaning, and wanes before puberty. Synaptic growth modifies the established dendritic network throughout life, and synaptogenesis constrained by a cortical axonal and dendritic infrastructure relatively fixed in childhood can account for the continued ability to learn throughout adulthood.

Panskepp (1998) and Siviy (1998) among others (Vanderschuren et al. 1997) have focussed the evidence for a distinct topographical distribution of neurochemical activity during play that evokes feelings of pleasure. Siviy (1998) entertained two hypotheses regarding some delayed benefits of play: (1) that play actively engaged biochemical mechanisms associated with environmental stressors, and (2) more to the point, that through the release of opiates play stimulated the desire to explore, learn, and innovate (cf. Panskepp 1998). He argued that any behavior that involved the release of monoamines in as global a manner as play should be expected to alter the future sensitivity of the organism's response to stressful situations such as competition, innovation, and risk-taking. Play bathed the entire cortex in natural opiates (e.g. dopamine, serotonin, and norepinephrine); the effect of these neurotransmitters not only had the potential to reward and motivate play but also to synchronize excitation across cognitive and activity domains.

Kaczmarek (2000), Robertson (1992), and Morgan and Curran's (1991) work on the transcription of "immediate-early" genes (f-cos) at the site of synaptogenesis concluded that the widespread biochemical activation of the cortex during play was a critical link in the molecular machinery associated with learning and memory. Thus the pleasure associated with play stimulated synaptogenesis in the cortex and certain subcortical structures (e.g. thalamus and hippocampus), especially during relatively novel and/or risky activities. Siviy (1998) linked synaptogenesis and as a result learning to repeated stimulation of sensory-motor neural networks, the opiate bath, and the associated feelings of pleasure that accompany play. This global stimulation of the brain not only enhanced local connectivity within and between columnar networks but also increased novel dendritic and synaptic connections between cognitive domains that were previously unconnected.

By recruiting activity over many cortical and subcortical areas, intentional representations co-constructed in play activate parts of networks also involved in non-play interactions. Thus, meaningful patterns of information have a multiplicity of connections that were reactivated in both play and non-play contexts, and the formation of an information-specific network that facilitated the easy retrieval of significance or relevant pattern of response in either context (cf. Adams 1997). Brown (1998: 254) proposed that the sculpting action of juvenile play on neural patterning was similar to that of other fundamental super-organizers in nature;

i.e., that play functioned as an "attractor" and stabilized the form and meaning of socially shared behavioral repertoires automated in the developing brain of each participant (cf. Bak 1996).

7.6 Discussion

Instead of coding players' actions as fixed tokens of kinds of behavior that could be divorced from their function within the context, this analysis coded the meaningful events of play as conjoined moves in a negotiation within and about the play situation and experience—as in a conversation about the goal of the play exchange. Thus, we modeled our analysis of the complex and rapid flow of play between two apes on the analysis of language discourse (Benson and Greaves 2005; Taylor 1997) and meaningful gestures (Kendon 2004; Thibault 2005). Play was governed by a tendency to streamline and economize frequently repeated actions just as described in the dynamic simulation of language formation, in creolization, and in the emergence of signed communication from homesign to Sign Language among the Deaf (Kirby 1999; Ragir 2002). In other words, in social play as in other forms of social competition and cooperation, repetitive exchange allowed participants to abstract units that were rarely subdivided, whose virtually infinite combinations were governed by simple rules and motivated by the pleasure and anxiety of engaging in play. The unconscious systematization of exchanges in dynamic social activities inevitably resulted in recursive structures in social exchanges including language, music, and dance in human society (cf. Bak 1996; Sole and Goodwin 2000).

Social games differentiated functional roles and norms through spatial, temporal, and stylistic patterns of engagement such as offense or defense, in the look and feel of signals or identifying markers, as well as the explicit and implicit rules of play. The play episode, the nature of the players, and the immediate context bound the meaning of communicative gestures even more than the context of the sentence bound the meaning of a word. It is likely that the systematicity that emerges from playful repetition provides a semi-permanent neural substrate not only for rules of reiteration but also for the behavioral flexibility and semantic creativity of animal and human social groups. Representations of content and patterns of compositional semantics were negotiated in ongoing simulative play and generate well-formed, rule-like exchanges of information. Syntactic structures frequently appear in negotiated systems, whether or not the subunits out of which the expressions are built are individually meaningful, as in whale- and bird-song (Corballis 1992), and in the production of such presentations as agonistic or courtship rituals in animals, and human dance, music, sculpture, and the manufacture of stone tools.

Children and animals play for the pleasure it affords them; they are continually negotiating the ambiguity of form and content, notions of order, and the introduction of novel objects, subjects, and dyadic moves. The events reflected in this chapter illustrated a highly normative, hierarchically structured, social object play governed by a simple set of rules that produced moves and actions that had been observed to structure non-play activities in the colony as well. By playing with Matata and the Pan-acculturated humans inside the colony, the LRC juveniles became particularly adept at co-constructing norms, rules, and meanings that crossed species repertories. The game differentiated functional roles through spatial, temporal, and stylistic separations in the sequences of play, in the patterns of engagement, in the look and feel of identifying markers, as well as in explicit and implicit rules of play (Dugatkin and Bekoff 2003).

Play is one of many forms of negotiated, self-organizing, dynamic systems that emerge during ontogeny (Bruner 1976; Bjorklund and Green 1992). This fundamentally communicative activity dominates the developmental phase of performance-dependent neural and muscular specialization in animal and human young and participates in the structuring of neural networks, modularization of function, and cognitive specialization. Form and meaning are co-constructed in play, and they serve in public systems of representation and not simply as signs of emotional states over which the individual has no control. Ape social play and perhaps all social play is first and foremost a negotiation about what is possible, what is permitted, and how to do it effectively with others. The normative and reflexive qualities of social play suggest that play has not only a proximal autotelic function but also the distal effect of generating a neural substrate that support the shared fields of behavioral and social understanding necessary for complex communication.

Some linguists mistakenly attributed such semantic compositionality only to "human language" (Pinker 1994). Ape play, like language, was embedded in a larger context of social roles, and social history beyond that of the current game, and such embedding constrained acceptable ways of playing just as in spontaneous conversation. These games were profoundly normative and, therefore, an intentionally communicative activity. We propose that these dialogic structural and normative functions make social play a proper model for understanding the dynamic negotiation of language meaning, form, and syntax as an emergent, self-organized system of communication (Ragir 2002; Savage-Rumbaugh et al. 1998). Such a dynamic, epiphenomenal understanding of language formation has parsimony and biological conservatism on its side and might allow us to tell a more plausible evolutionary story.

Acknowledgements

The authors gratefully acknowledge help and advice given by Mr William Fields, Director of the Bonobo Facility at the Great Ape Trust of Iowa, whose support has been essential for the completion of this project. The research described in this paper was supported, in part, by the National Institutes of Health (NIH) grant NICHD06016 which provided funds for the original video and archival support for the collection from which this material was drawn, and the Templeton Foundation Forgiveness Study, of which this research effort was a central part as a sense of fairness and the capacity to forgive appear central to play. Dr Ragir received financial support from the Great Ape Trust, PSC/CUNY Research Foundation, and a College of Staten Island Presidential Fellowship. Finally, the authors owe an inestimable debt of gratitude to Ted Townsend whose most generous and enduring support of ape language has enabled these special Bonobos to continue to live together as a group in an environment designed solely for their needs. Only the perpetuation of such a human/ape community has made work such as this possible.

8 The ontogeny and phylogeny of non-verbal deixis

DAVID A. LEAVENS, TIMOTHY P. RACINE, AND WILLIAM D. HOPKINS

8.1 Introduction

It is widely reported that our nearest living relatives, the great apes, lack a "declarative" mode of communication. There are few reports of any ape, regardless of rearing history, explicitly informing another about a state of the world as an apparent end in itself; see e.g. Tomasello (2006). Historically, the term "declarative" has been used to classify a particular form of sentence or linguistic communication. However, the use of this concept to describe non-verbal communication stems from the introduction by Bates et al. (1975) of the term "proto-declarative" to describe pointing by human babies with the apparent goal of fostering a state of shared apprehension of distant events or objects with a communicative partner. But a declaration is a linguistic act; it is therefore not immediately clear if the term should be applied to non-verbal communicative behavior by either non-human primates or pre-verbal humans (Leavens 2004a; Leavens and Hopkins 1998; Racine 2005; Susswein and Racine 2008). And apes in captivity adopt numerous non-verbal deictic behaviors, including manual pointing. Although observations of manual pointing are limited almost entirely to captive great ape populations, recent studies indicate that other manifestations of non-verbal deixis, such as directed scratching (Pika and Mitani 2006), may be much more common in wild ape populations than heretofore appreciated. Although older children and perhaps some enculturated apes occasionally point to share experience as an end in itself,

We are grateful to Kim Bard, Jim Hurford, Jeremy Carpendale, Noah Susswein, the late George Butterworth, Fabia Franco, and many others for discussions of the issues raised here. We are also grateful to two reviewers, Christine Johnson and Simone Pika, with whose critical comments we were able to substantially improve this chapter.

here we argue that pointing, and other non-verbal deictic behaviors, serve fundamentally instrumental functions (Racine et al. 2008). As a result, we will further argue that the cognitive origins of non-verbal deictic acts are similar, regardless of the ostensible motivation of the signaler. To do so, we review research on deixis in the great apes, discuss the distinction between imperative and declarative communication in greater detail, and then consider the meaning of proto-declarative pointing. We conclude that epigenetically heritable caregiving environments of hominins, probably beginning in the Plio-Pleistocene, foster manual pointing in early infancy (Davidson 1997; Leavens, Hopkins, and Bard 2005) and implicate an interaction of hominoid cognitive capacities with hominin-unique features of early infancy. Hominins were, thus, pre-adapted for one aspect of the faculty of language in the broad sense: joint attention (Hauser et al. 2002).

8.2 Deictic great apes

In humans, pointing emerges at roughly the same age as the first single-word utterances, at approximately one year of age (e.g. Butterworth 2003). As a result, there is a dynamic interplay between pointing gestures and speech communication, beginning very early in the development of recognizable speech. Until recently, many researchers claimed that pointing was a uniquely human behavior, indexing uniquely human cognitive and anatomical adaptations for reference (e.g. Butterworth 2003; Donald 1991; Povinelli and Davis 1994). Although our nearest living relatives, the great apes, are capable of extending their index fingers independently, humans seem to be almost pre-adapted for pointing with the index finger; in a vertical arm posture, with the wrist relaxed, the resting state of the index finger is well above a plane defined by the rest of the fingers, in contrast to chimpanzees in which species the fingers at rest line up in a row (Povinelli and Davis 1994). In typical human development, human infants first respond to the pointing of others to near objects at approximately nine months of age. Then they begin to produce pointing gestures, themselves, at approximately one year of age. By the middle of the second year of life, they can follow others' pointing and gaze to more distant objects, even when those objects are not initially in their field of view (Adamson 1996; Butterworth 2003; Franco and Butterworth 1996). This capacity is referred to by developmental psychologists as "joint attention." Human infants, therefore, display remarkable skill in following into the focus of attention of their social partners, and later in intentionally capturing and redirecting the attention of their social partners to specific foci through deployment of deictic gestures, of which pointing is the paradigmatic example. Moreover, there have been published claims to the effect that pointing is not observed in any non-human animal (e.g. Butterworth and Grover 1988; Donald 1991; Petitto 1988). In consideration of these apparent ontogenetic and phylogenetic patterns, it was reasonable to suggest that non-verbal deixis, the ability to direct attention to a specific location, object, or event, reflected human species-unique cognitive adaptations for joint attention (e.g. Butterworth and Grover 1988; Corballis 1991; Donald 1991). Joint attention is widely and reasonably considered to be crucial for language acquisition (Baldwin and Moses 1996; Hauser et al. 2002; Tomasello 2003; Werner and Kaplan 1963). Thus, by the last decade of the twentieth century, a consensus was forming that both language and its ontogenetic precursors, joint attention and non-verbal deictic communication, evolved uniquely in the human lineage since the evolutionary split with chimpanzees, approximately 5-7 million years ago (cf. Hauser et al. 2002).

It therefore came as a surprise to many scientists that apes in captivity very frequently point, in the absence of any explicit training (e.g. Leavens and Hopkins 1999; Leavens, Hopkins, and Thomas 2004; Leavens, Russell, and Hopkins 2005). As perusal of Table 8.1 makes clear, pointing has been reported in captive apes by many different researchers over the last ninety years, although the first experimental study of pointing by apes was relatively recent (Call and Tomasello 1994). The gestures in Table 8.1 are described as "spontaneous" because these apes were not explicitly shaped to produce any particular kind of manual gesture, yet they chose to point manually, or displayed other deictic behavior. Although pointing and other deictic behaviors are common among captive apes, they have only rarely been reported in feral populations, living in their natural habitats (Inoue-Nakamura and Matsuzawa 1997; Pika and Mitani 2006; Veà and Sabater-Pi 1998).

It is also frequently, but incorrectly, claimed that apes never point amongst themselves. For example, Moll and Tomasello (2007: 643) wrote that "there has not been a single reliable documentation of any scientist in any part of the world of one ape pointing for another." Povinelli et al.

TABLE 8.1. *Reports of spontaneous deictic behaviors by apes. All behaviors are points with extended fingers (single or multiple), unless otherwise noted. Individual apes may be listed in multiple sources*

Species, study, experimental condition	Group[a]	N[b]	Comments
Orangutans (*Pongo pygmaeus*)			
Furness 1916	Unknown	1	
Miles 1990	L	1	
Gómez and Teixidor 1992 (cited in Gómez 1996)	Z	1	
Call and Tomasello 1994	L	1	
Gorillas (*Gorilla gorilla*)			
Patterson 1978	L	1	
Tanner 2004	Z	2	
Tanner, Patterson, and Byrne 2006[c]	Z,L	2+[d]	Touch self deictically
Bonobos (*Pan paniscus*)			
Savage-Rumbaugh, Wilkerson, and Bakeman 1977[c]	Z	3	
Savage-Rumbaugh 1984	L	1	
Savage-Rumbaugh 1986[c]	L	1	
Savage-Rumbaugh, Shanker, and Taylor 1998	L	1	
Veà and Sabater-Pi 1998[c]	W	1	
Chimpanzees (*Pan troglodytes*)			
Furness 1916	Unknown	1	
Kellogg and Kellogg 1933	H	1	Point to self
Yerkes 1943	C	1	Point to self
Hayes and Hayes 1954	L	1	
Gardner and Gardner 1971	L	1	
Rumbaugh 1977	L	1	
Terrace 1979	L	1	
Woodruff and Premack 1979	C	4	
Fouts, Hirsch, and Fouts 1982	L	1	
de Waal 1982[c]	Z	1+[d]	
Bard and Vauclair 1984[c]	C	1	Touch object
Tomasello, George, Kruger, Farrar, and Evans 1985[c]	Z	1	Point to self

(*cont.*)

Table 8.1. *(Continued)*

Species, study, experimental condition	Group[a]	N[b]	Comments
Savage-Rumbaugh 1986[c]	L	2	
Boysen and Berntson 1989	L	1	Touch object
Leavens, Hopkins, and Bard 1996	C	3	
Krause and Fouts 1997	L	2	
Inoue-Nakamura and Matsuzawa 1997[c]	W	1+[d]	Touch object?
Leavens and Hopkins 1998	C	53	
Menzel 1999	L	1	
Whiten 2000	L	1	
Bodamer and Gardner 2002	L	4	
Leavens, Hopkins, and Thomas 2004			
Visible food condition	C	25	
Hidden food condition	C	28	
Experiment 2	C	7	
Leavens and Hopkins 2005			
Near, small	C	9	
Near, big	C	8	
Far, small	C	6	
Far, big	C	8	
Leavens, Russell, and Hopkins 2005			
Predelivery: banana	C	22	
Predelivery: half-banana	C	20	
Predelivery: chow	C	24	
Postdelivery: chow	C	13	
Pika and Mitani 2006[c]	W	6+[d]	Deictic scratching[e]

Notes: [a]Groups: "W" refers to feral apes in their natural habitats; "Z" refers to zoo-housed apes, or apes raised in circumstances approximating zoo conditions; "C" refers to non-language-trained, laboratory chimpanzees and includes those captured from the wild as infants, those raised in peer groups, and those raised by their mothers in these captive settings; "H" refers to home-raised apes that have not received language-training; "L" refers to language-trained apes. [b]"*N*" refers to the number of apes reported to display pointing or other deictic behaviors in each source. [c]Deictic activity observed during communication between apes. [d]"+" used where only the minimum number of pointing individuals can be derived from published sources. [e]Pika and Mitani referred to this behavior as "directed scratching."

(2003:45) wrote that "there is no evidence that...chimpanzees use [index-finger pointing] (or any other kind of pointing gesture) with each other." In fact, pointing and other referential behaviors have been observed during communication between apes, both in the wild, as noted above (Inoue-Nakamura and Matsuzawa 1997; Pika and Mitani 2006; Veà and Sabater-Pi 1998) and in captivity (Bard and Vauclair 1984; Savage-Rumbaugh 1986; Savage-Rumbaugh et al. 1977; Tanner et al. 2006; Tomasello et al. 1985; de Waal 1982). Savage-Rumbaugh (1986), for example, reported thirty-seven pointing gestures between the chimpanzees Sherman and Austin in a single chapter, including several photographs of these events. Such observations contradict claims by Povinelli et al. (2003) and Tomasello (2006; Moll and Tomasello 2007) that apes never point amongst themselves. Nevertheless, the majority of reports in Table 8.1 involve communication between apes and humans.

Experimental studies of the manual gestures of captive apes have revealed that these are intentional signals. What we mean by this claim is that the pointing and other manual gestures of the great apes meet the same objective, publicly verifiable criteria that define the human developmental transition to intentional communication originally developed by Bates and her colleagues (1975; see also Bard 1992; Rolfe 1996; Sugarman 1984). For example, apes look back-and-forth between humans and unreachable food while gesturing (Figure 8.1); gaze alternation while gesturing is a widely used criterion for the human developmental transition to intentional communication (e.g. Bates et al. 1975; Tomasello 1995). Like human children (e.g. Golinkoff 1986), apes also persist in and elaborate their communication in the face of communicative failures (Cartmill and Byrne 2007; Leavens, Hostetter, Wesley, and Hopkins 2004; Leavens, Russell, and Hopkins 2005; Poss et al. 2006). Also like human children (e.g. Bakeman and Adamson 1986; O'Neill 1996), apes are sensitive to the visual orientation or attentional status of their communicative partners, switching communicative modalities depending upon whether or not a communicative partner is attentive (Bodamer and Gardner 2002; Hostetter et al. 2001; Krause and Fouts 1997; Leavens, Hostetter, Wesley, and Hopkins 2004; Liebal, Pika, Call, and Tomasello 2004; Liebal et al. 2006; Pika et al. 2003, 2005; Tomasello et al. 1994). Finally, apes do not point to unreachable food in the absence of an observer, hence these are manual gestures, not frustrated attempts to reach for the food (Leavens et al. 1996, 2004; Poss et al. 2006). By these operational criteria, the deictic

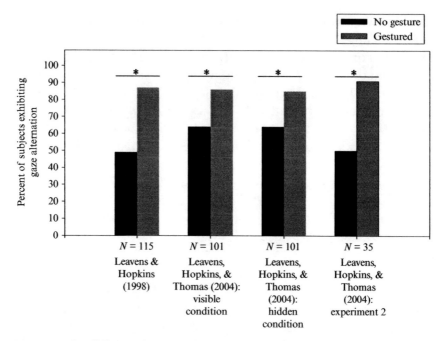

FIG. 8.1. The differential association of gaze alternation with manual gestures in captive populations of chimpanzees. Although about half of the chimpanzees who did not gesture alternated their gaze between unreachable food and an experimenter, a significantly higher proportion of chimpanzees who gestured also displayed gaze alternation. Asterisks signify that $p < .05$.

gestures of apes are intentionally communicative behaviors; at some risk of redundancy, we emphasize that these are the same criteria by which intentional communication is defined in human children.

It is now relatively uncontroversial that great apes in captivity commonly develop pointing and other deictic behaviors to control the behavior of their caregivers, usually in apparent requests for delivery of food and other desirable items. Elsewhere, we have articulated a theoretical interpretation of ape pointing that emphasizes the ecological similarities between infant humans and captive apes in fostering the development of these deictic behaviors. We interpret pointing, in which an animate being is manipulated to instrumental ends, as a tool-using strategy, what Bard and others have termed "social tool use" (e.g. Bard 1990; Leavens 2004a; Leavens et al. 1996; Leavens, Hopkins, and Bard 2005, 2008; Leavens, Russell, and Hopkins 2005). Due to physical constraints on free movement both human infants and apes in captivity face the Referential Problem Space, which is a series of related episodes in which the attainment of otherwise unreachable items depends upon the manipulation of an animate being (Leavens, Hopkins, and Bard 2005, 2008). Leavens et al. 1996 stated:

We find it difficult to conceive of a circumstance in which a wild ape is dependent on the capture and direction of another's attention to obtain an otherwise unattainable object that is distal to both of the interactants. In most imaginable circumstances, a feral ape can easily locomote to proximity with any desired food or object in its environment. The situation is dramatically different for the 12-month-old human infant, who is capable of establishing both an interest in a distal object and joint attention with an adult but is limited in locomotor capacity. It is precisely this circumstance that is encountered by captive, attention-directing apes, except that the barrier is not due to endogenous limitations on locomotion but to exogenous limitations (i.e., the cage mesh); thus, pointing is one solution to a specific problem requiring the use of another's agency (i.e., social tool use; Bard 1990). The particular situation that requires pointing as a solution may only be encountered by apes in captive situations.   (Leavens et al. 1996: 352)

Apes in the wild do, of course, frequently face circumstances in which they manipulate their social partners to relinquish items their social partners have in their possession (e.g. Bard 1992; Nishida and Turner 1996), and this fosters dyadic communication, but not communication about objects distant to both parties (but see Ueno 2006 and references therein). Leavens and his colleagues have repeatedly noted that, because both wild and captive apes are sampled from the same gene pool, differences between these groups in their pointing behavior cannot be attributed to genetic differences (Leavens 2004a; Leavens et al. 1996; Leavens, Hopkins, and Bard 2005, 2008; see Figure 8.2). Thus, pointing to request delivery of otherwise unreachable objects develops in both humans and captive apes as a gestural solution to a particular kind of problem frequently encountered by human infants and captive apes, but not wild apes. Recent observations of wild chimpanzees using a directed scratch to manipulate grooming partners into grooming specific parts of their bodies underscore the ease with which deictic communication arises in great apes, whenever the situation calls for it (Pika and Mitani 2006).

Tomasello (e.g. 1999, 2003) has termed the social shaping of such gestures "ontogenetic ritualization" and he allows (2003) that human pointing might emerge in this manner for some children. He argues, though,

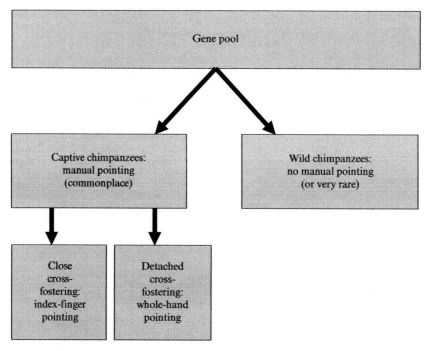

Fig. 8.2. Captive and wild apes are sampled from the same gene pool. Therefore, the different propensities of the different groups to point, and differences in pointing posture, are not genetic differences; chimpanzee pointing is a consequence of environmental influences on development.

that this is the exclusive manner in which they get off the ground in non-human primates, whereas in the human line the typical route is through a process of recognizing the intentionality of conspecifics (see also Tomasello and Carpenter 2005).

Thus, the idea is that apes, and some would claim the present authors, are behaviorists, whereas human infants are mentalists. There is considerable argument in the contemporary literature to the effect that although apes might point to request food, they do not point to change the states of knowledge of their social partners, and this is widely held to constitute a species difference in socio-cognitive abilities between humans and other apes (e.g. Carpenter et al. 1998; Povinelli et al. 2003; Tomasello 2006). This argument rests fundamentally upon the claim that human babies, as young as twelve months of age, *do*, in fact, point to change the knowledge states of their social partners. The following exegesis, in which we question the empirical and epistemological bases of this claim, represents a synthesis of an argument arrived at independently by Leavens, Hopkins, and their colleagues, on the one hand (e.g. Hopkins et al. 2007; Leavens 2004a; Leavens, Hopkins, and Bard 2005, 2008; Leavens, Russell, and Hopkins 2005), and Racine and colleagues on the other (e.g. Racine 2004, 2005; Racine and Carpendale 2007a, b, c; Susswein and Racine in press).

8.3 Declarative and imperative communication

Bates et al. (1975) described pre-linguistic communication by human infants in terms of a then popular functional characterization of language, Austin's (1962) Speech Act Theory (cited in Bates et al. 1975). According to Austin, every speech act has a locutionary, an illocutionary, and a perlocutionary aspect. The locutionary attribute of speech is, in effect, its propositional content. The illocutionary attribute of speech is the intention of the speaker. The perlocutionary attribute of a speech act is the effect upon the listener, intended or not. Bates and colleagues applied this scheme to the developmental sequence of communication in human infants. Young infants are in a "perlocutionary" stage, as their communicative actions have incidental social consequences, prior to the development of complex, goal-directed behavior. Somewhat older infants enter the "illocutionary" stage, in which babies' communicative intentions are manifest prior to their signaling and with the onset of the use of conventionalized signals. Finally, children begin to make propositions, displaying "locutionary" behavior near the end of the second year of life.

In pre-linguistic children these attributes are communicated via "performatives": non-linguistic vehicles for communication, including manual gestures and vocalizations. Bates et al. (1975) noted that although there were numerous categories of performatives, they focused upon two: imperative and declarative acts. In language, an imperative is a command or a request. Therefore, Bates and her colleagues referred to pre-linguistic requests or demands as "proto-imperatives." At the time of the original article, there had been a traditional consensus that declaratives were commitments to the truth-values of propositions. However, based on their interpretation of Parisi and Antinucci (1973, cited in Bates et al. 1975), Bates and her colleagues defined declaratives as a special kind of imperative, in which the speaker intends "for the listener to attend to or assume some piece of information" (p. 208). Thus, the "proto-declarative" is "a preverbal effort to direct the adult's attention to some event or object in the world" (p. 208). They go on to define "the imperative...as the use of the adult as the means to a desired object [and] the declarative [as] the use of an object (through pointing, showing, giving, etc.) as the means to obtaining adult attention" (p. 209). By "attention" the authors meant some kind of "adult response—laughter, comment, smiles and eye contact" (p. 216). Thus, in its original formulation, proto-declarative communication was defined as the instrumental use of communication about an object to elicit infant-directed responses from the caregiver (Moore and Corkum 1994). And parents know well that older children often use verbal means to direct attention in an identical manner ("Look at me/this, Dad") where the goal is not to share attention as a means in itself but rather for the parent to consider the child an object of attention, with presumably reinforcing effects for the child.

It is important to emphasize that, in this original formulation, both imperatives and declaratives are linguistic categories. Because of this, as Leavens and Hopkins (1998) noted, it is ambiguous whether any non-linguistic organism can, in principle, display "proto-imperatives," "imperatives," "proto-declaratives," or "declaratives." In this sense, imperatives are, formally, attempts to demand with language, and proto-imperatives are attempts to demand with performatives that are ontogenetically prior to (and necessary for) language. Similarly, declaratives are, formally, attempts to redirect attention with language, and proto-declaratives are attempts to redirect attention with performatives that are ontogenetically prior to (and necessary for) language. In these senses of the terms, therefore, no non-human organism could be reasonably asserted to display either (proto-)imperative or (proto-)declarative communication. In the canonical senses of these terms, imperatives and declaratives are confined in their applicability to linguistic organisms, or, in other words, humans and humans alone.

There are, however, less stringent uses of the terms in common use in the contemporary psychological literature, in which "imperatives" are simply demands or requests and "declaratives" are attempts to draw the attention of a social partner to some locus such that joint attention (the mutual contemplation of an external entity) is an end in itself (Baron-Cohen 1995; Povinelli et al. 2003; Tomasello 2006). Thus, researchers have characterized these two modes of communication as being, on the one hand, requests (imperatives), and, on the other hand, comments (declaratives) (e.g. Tomasello and Camaioni 1997). There are numerous claims to the effect that although imperative communication is widespread in the animal kingdom, the latter motivation to communicate declaratively about objects, events, agents, etc., is a uniquely human phenomenon that indexes uniquely human cognitive abilities (e.g. Baron-Cohen 1995, 1999; Povinelli et al. 2003; Tomasello 2006; Tomasello and Carpenter 2005; Tomasello et al. 2007).

The most recent formulations of imperative and declarative communication attempt to define these modes of communication by reference to underlying psychological processes, or mental states, which purportedly differentiate the two kinds of communication (e.g. Tomasello 2006; Tomasello et al. 2007). For example, Baron-Cohen (1989, 1995) characterized imperative communication as an attempt to influence the behavior of a social partner and declarative communication, even when displayed by young infants, as an attempt to influence the mind of a social partner. Thus, what makes an act proto-declarative from this perspective is the state of mind of the pointer *behind* the activity, rather than the activity itself. This contrasts sharply with the original formulation by Bates et al. (1975), in which it is clear that babies communicate declaratively to influence the behavior of their social partners ("laughter, comment, smiles and eye contact"; p. 216). We argue that these more recent mentalistic interpretations of declarative pointing are problematic for numerous epistemological, ontological, pragmatic, and empirical reasons, and that these concerns have implications for our understanding of the development, distribution, and evolution of a deictic capacity, and therefore the evolution of language. This way of thinking, we think, also helps to fuel the continuing debate over primate social cognition, in that it is tied up with a static and we would argue, largely Cartesian, view of meaning and mind (Johnson 2001; Leavens et al. 2008; Racine 2004; Racine and Carpendale 2007b; Susswein and Racine 2008, in press). Instead, we assume a distributed view of mind that puts causal factors—be they psychological, biological, or sociocultural—in their proper place, which in the case of joint attention necessarily is situated in a history of interaction between two or more subjects, some shared referent and some particular sociocultural and physical surround (Sinha 1999, 2005). In fact, joint attention is paradigmatically a distributed cognitive act.

8.4 The meaning of proto-declarative communication

It is common, but we think flawed practice in the contemporary psycho-logical and primatological literature to study the behavior of human babies or chimpanzees and then deduce the hidden psychological processes that "cause" that response pattern. This is really a manifestation of a long-standing problem that philosophers have worried about for quite some time, namely the so-called problem of other minds, which is how we come to believe that there are minds inhabiting the bodies that we find around us. We think that the epistemological weaknesses of this model of cognitive functioning that posits independent minds residing in sep-arate skulls, and "causing" the behavior of mental organisms, is brought into particularly clear focus when we study non-symbolic systems, like human infants and most apes. This model of mental causality introduces radical gaps between agents and then posits some sort of epistemological glue—mutual co-construction of others' mental states—with which to put agents together again (Zlatev et al. 2008). But as we have shown earlier, primates seem to understand the contours of their social worlds well enough to navigate them with little difficulty (and see Barrett and Henzi 2005; Johnson 2001; King 2004). Given this, it is seems odd to the present authors that activities involving proto-declarative pointing or other means of directing attention would pose insurmountable obstacles for great apes in general. But many researchers continue to conclude that there are telling differences in the joint attentional repertoires of primate species. We suspect that the problem of other minds might in fact be part of the problem.

The problem of other minds has an obvious relation to quarrels over the ontogeny or phylogeny of social cognition. For example, if one's theory of (social) knowledge is that individual minds must be aware of or even "represent" the intentional states of others in order to interact with them, then cognition seems to be a private, individual event with no intrinsic relation to the social, biological, physical, and cultural world in which it breathes life. On the other hand, if one conceives of knowledge of other minds as a property of the very interactional and historical circumstances within which individual minds arise, then one's approach to subjectivity and intersubjectivity is presumably quite different. Although we unapolo-getically lean heavily towards the latter conception, we believe that these seemingly incompatible views of mental life are in fact reconcilable when one realizes that they refer to quite different aspects of mind. In the first instance, individual psychological processes are the figure in the ground, but with the danger of being given far too much credit for the activities with which they are tied up. In the second manner of thinking, individual psychological processes run the risk of being given short shrift if any shrift at all. We believe there is some confusion afoot that must be cleared up before the social cognitive landscape can be fully appreciated.

Johnson (2001), in her juxtaposition of mental representational and distributed views of cognition, shows how a distributed account of cognition can be used to account for primate social cognition in general (see Susswein and Racine in press for a fuller discussion of Johnson's model of distributed cognition). Leavens and his colleagues (Racine et al. 2008) locate this sort of analysis in a consideration of what communication is, which they conclude to be an inherently distributed phenomenon that is illegitimate to locate in only one particular part of a communicative system, namely, individual brains. One can also broach these issues in terms of the meaning of activity in order to remind researchers that what we mean by, for example, proto-declarative pointing is logically not what might be said to be in the head of someone pointing (Racine and Carpendale 2007a, c; Racine et al. 2008; Susswein and Racine 2008). Because we have no objective, empirical access to the contents of others' heads, what we mean by the expression "proto-declarative pointing" must be defined with respect to its overt manifestation involving media physically distinct from the head. There is no direct measure of the hypothetical mental processes occurring when human children or great apes communicate. Furthermore, all of the evidence upon which we categorize the communicative acts of children and great apes as imperative or declarative in function constitutes publicly available, objectively measurable behavior. As a result, it is *a fortiori* incorrect to suggest that ontogenetic or phylogenetic discrepancies pivot around differences in, for example, representational capacities alone (e.g. Leavens 2002).

It is easier to see why this is so when one realizes that an extended index finger in and of itself means nothing. Furthermore, whether a tendon that exists in the human hand does or does not occur in other species does not change this (Povinelli and Davis 1994). What physically enables a given agent to point involves issues that are orthogonal to considerations of what is conveyed by the act of pointing (Racine et al. 2008; Susswein and Racine 2008). Therefore, putative selection pressures for a species-typical pointing gesture, although potentially important in a causal sense, are similarly irrelevant to defining a gesture's meaning (Butterworth 2003). An act of pointing means what it means by virtue of the fact that it is used in some particular interactional situation to do some specific work. Such a situation is necessarily social in that it requires another to observe the point. It is also biological, in that it requires particular evolved capacities; physical, in that it requires objects or states of affairs to which to refer; and cultural, in that members of different cultures direct attention in characteristic ways. More succinctly, this activity is tied up with what Wittgenstein (1958) called a "form of life."

While it is also the case that engaging in proto-imperative or proto-declarative communication requires particular psychological capacities, we argue that researchers are not referring to such processes when we call an act declarative. As contemporary research paradigms show (e.g. Liszkowski et al. 2004), it is the functional consequences of a point that define its meaning. When an infant is presented with an object to which to point, an experimenter responds by acknowledging the infant's gesture. If the infant is satisfied, the researcher considers the point declarative; if the infant persists, then the point is considered imperative. This makes it clear that what discriminates these actions is not the mental state of the infant; the meaning of the point is a function of the situation, distributed across the people present, contingencies between the behaviors, the specific physical context, and so on.

Now, of course infants do think about what is going on around them, be they human or non-human primates. Older human infants, perhaps because of the opportunity to exploit the representational medium *par excellence* of language, also acquire the ability to reflect on their activities offline. But the development of such second-order abilities do not make an act mean what it means (Racine and Carpendale 2007a, c). It is here that the distinction between causal and definitional issues in social developmental theory comes into focus (Racine 2004, Susswein and Racine 2008, in press). Classifying an act as imperative or declarative requires agreement on what counts as an instance of declarative communication. Although uses of terms can and do change, there simply must be a prior (logical) basis upon which a concept is defined before empirical investigations are possible (Bennett and Hacker 2003). The root mistake, we think, in current mentalistic and nativisitic explanations of social cognition is one of assuming that psychological or evolutionary processes, in and of themselves, *cause* the activity in question.[1] The communicative behaviors we see in human and non-human primates are embedded in social relationships. In the case of pointing, we find that apes in some socio-ecological circumstances (captive environments) point very frequently, whereas apes in other socio-ecological circumstances (wild environments) virtually never point (Leavens, Hopkins, and Bard 2005; Figure 8.2). Thus, the psychological and evolutionary prerequisites for pointing are possessed by all apes, but pointing arises in only some rearing contexts. This demonstrates that pointing, or pointing of a particular kind, such as proto-declarative pointing, cannot be solely attributable to individual psychological attributes or species' evolutionary history. Thus, logically, the meaning of pointing cannot be attributed to individual psychological processes causing the behavior.

8.5 Hidden assumptions

In addition to the above epistemological concerns, when it is said that animals do not communicate declaratively, there are a number of often implicit assumptions that make such claims either obviously invalid, *a priori*, or almost impossible to test, empirically (Leavens 2002, 2004a, b; Leavens, Hopkins, and Bard 2005).

8.5.1 *Hidden assumption #1: early rearing history of apes is irrelevant to the development of declarative communication*

One of the most significant unspoken assumptions is that the often impoverished circumstances of captivity, or the traumatic circumstances of entering captivity, have no deleterious influences on apes' motivations to engage with humans, or otherwise affect their sociocognitive development (e.g. Bard and Leavens in press; Leavens 1998, 2004a; Leavens et al. 2008).

---

[1] This criticism seems to apply to researchers of opposing theoretical orientations who argue about the ontogeny of joint attention (e.g., Carpenter, Nagell, and Tomasello 1998; Moore 1998) or its phylogeny (e.g., Tomasello, Call, and Hare 2003a, b; Povinelli and Vonk 2003). One must apparently agree on quite a bit to disagree (for a more detailed discussion of this point, see Racine et al. 2008).

Let us consider some of the more common ape rearing histories observed in captivity (see also Call and Tomasello 1996).

(i) *Orphaned from the wild, after witnessing their mothers being shot to death.* Many older apes were brought into captivity from the wild. Almost universally, as infants or juveniles, these apes witnessed their mothers being killed, were roughly captured and shoved into a box, then shipped under abysmal, sometimes lethal conditions to various facilities in the western world, including biomedical research, zoo, entertainment, and exotic pet industries. No researcher would study the communicative behavior of a group of human children who had experienced this kind of prolonged trauma and then attempt to generalize from that sample to the rest of the human species. Yet, when the subjects are apes, it seems that even very talented researchers develop a kind of "blind spot," proceeding as if their subject's history did not matter and concluding that any behavioral difference between (western) human children and these apes must be attributable to a species difference.

(ii) *Raised in captivity in peer groups because the mothers were not competent to care for them.* These are often referred to as "human-raised" apes, but to imply that they are raised by humans is tantamount to asserting that the tragically impoverished circumstances in which, for example, many human, Romanian orphans were raised (e.g. Rutter et al. 1999) constitute rearing histories within the normal range.[2] Like the Romanian orphans, these infant apes are raised in nurseries staffed by caregivers who are only responsible for the provision of food and the changing of diapers. Although often well-meaning, these caregivers are not explicitly trained or held responsible for the emotional well-being of their charges. Chimpanzees raised in these circumstances are left to fend for themselves to meet their emotional needs, displaying a range of abnormal behaviors, such as self-hugging, rocking, and other stereotypical behaviors diagnostic of sustained emotional distress (e.g. Walsh et al. 1982). As with many Romanian orphans, these chimpanzees become emotionally and cognitively handicapped. Once again, studying the communication of such socially impoverished Romanian orphans and taking that as being representative of the human species would be considered scientifically suspect.

---

[2] Rutter and colleagues (1999), incidentally, noted up to 300 times the expected incidence of autism-like behaviors in their sample of 111 Romanian orphans.

Yet, when the subjects are apes, claims that differences between them and (typically developing, western) humans are attributable to a species difference are often considered acceptable (e.g. Povinelli and Eddy 1996).

(iii) *Apes raised by their mothers in captivity.* These apes are raised by adult chimpanzees who have little or no efficacy in their environments. That is, the parents cannot control who they associate with (are caged with), when they eat, what they eat, etc. Only human children of slaves or prisoners would be a proper comparison group for these apes.

(iv) *Cross-fostered apes.* These apes are raised in close association with humans, they have rich, diversified social and physical environments and form deeply emotional bonds (i.e., attachment relationships) with their human caregivers; virtually all language-trained apes would fall into this group. As Leavens (2004a) pointed out, almost all examples of declarative pointing by apes are from this group of apes, which constitute a small fraction of captive apes. So-called declarative pointing in captive apes seems to be limited to these rare apes who, in short, seem to have the closest analog to a reasonably normal western human upbringing. Every instance of such putative declarative pointing in the captive samples of which we are aware involved pointing in communication with humans (Bonvillian and Patterson 1999; Kellogg and Kellogg 1933; Savage-Rumbaugh et al. 1998). For most of these animals, the only social partners they could, in principle, display declarative pointing with are human caregivers, because they are raised away from conspecifics. These apes are so rare that *communities* of these apes are limited to, perhaps, three or four in the world. At the Chimpanzee and Human Communication Institute, Central Washington University, USA, there are four sign-language-trained chimpanzees (Washoe,[3] Loulis, Tatu, and Dar). At the Language Research Center, Georgia State University, USA, there are three chimpanzees trained in an artificial symbol system (Lana, Sherman, and Panzee). At the Great Ape Trust of Iowa, USA, there are three bonobos raised in symbol-rich environments (Kanzi, Panbanisha, and Nyota). Thus, there are few *communities* of great apes trained in symbolic communication, and consequently few opportunities for those few apes who have had rearing histories that might foster declarative pointing to communicate in such a manner with conspecifics. Importantly, even though there are a number of symbolically trained apes, very few of these animals were cross-fostered from birth, or

---

[3] Washoe died as this chapter was going to press, aged 42 years.

even close to birth, therefore it is unclear whether an alleged paucity of declarative communication in these communities is due to species differences between humans and apes (e.g. Vauclair 1996), or due to the striking rearing history differences between these particular animals and some, especially western, human populations (Bard and Leavens in press; Leavens, Russell, and Hopkins 2005). Thus, apes raised in close association with humans do display referential behaviors that seem declarative in function. Because such communicative motivations appear to be fragile in the face of prolonged early deprivation or trauma, in both apes and humans, the number of individual apes who display this kind of behavior is relatively low.

8.5.2 *Hidden assumption #2: enriched early rearing experience of humans is irrelevant to the development of declarative pointing*

Researchers comparing apes and human infants often find behavioral differences between these groups, including a significantly greater propensity to engage in declarative communication in human children, relative to the great apes (e.g. Tomasello 1999; Tomasello and Carpenter 2005). We know that when we put apes and humans in similar ecological circumstances that they will point and engage in other referential behaviors, skillfully coordinating their communicative behavior between their social partners and distant objects, events, locations, or agents (e.g. Gómez 1996, 2004, 2005; Leavens et al. 1996; Leavens, Hopkins, and Thomas 2004; Leavens, Russell, and Hopkins 2005), yet there are exceedingly few apes that have experienced, from birth, anything like socio-emotional developmental histories that are similar to typically developing humans; perhaps four in total (Bard and Leavens in press). Thus, to the degree that the socio-emotional dynamics of the first months of life are relevant to the ontogeny of declarative communication in humans (Leavens, Hopkins, and Bard 2005; Moore and Corkum 1994; Racine and Carpendale 2007a, b), there is no adequate comparison group of great apes.

Human children are exposed to a large number of episodes in which joint attention is accompanied by intense bursts of positive emotion from their primary caregivers (Bates et al. 1975; Moore and Corkum 1994; Leavens and Todd 2005); it is therefore entirely plausible that these affective contours, which are embedded in social relationships, are relevant to children's motivations to engage in joint attention. Until a sample of apes is exposed to the same affective dynamics over the first twelve months of life, it is not possible to attribute these apparent motivational differences between humans and apes to species differences, given the obvious confounds with rearing histories. Therefore, to argue that the propensity to display declarative communication in humans is due to a species difference between humans and the other great apes is tantamount to asserting, in the absence of any compelling evidence, that the pre-experimental socio-emotional histories of human infants are irrelevant to the development of joint attention and declarative communication (cf. Tomasello 2006).

8.5.3 *Hidden assumption #3: declarative pointing is cognitively more sophisticated than imperative pointing*

Many researchers claim that pointing to share attention to distant events or objects indexes more sophisticated cognitive processing than pointing to request delivery of otherwise unattainable objects (e.g. Baron-Cohen 1995; Camaioni et al. 2004; Legerstee and Barillas 2003). We have argued, in accordance with the earlier formulations of imperative and declarative communication by Bates and her colleagues (e.g. 1975) that:

> babies exhibit protodeclarative pointing because their caregivers reliably respond with intense bursts of positive emotion to the babies' communicative efforts, such as smiling and verbalizing with very high pitch contours (motherese). This theoretical interpretation of the onset of declarative pointing concedes that babies will eventually develop representational capacities relevant to the understanding of others as mental agents, but suggests that at the onset of protodeclarative pointing, at around 12 months, babies are motivated by the expectation that their pointing will elicit appealing behavior from their social partners.
>
> (Leavens, Russell, and Hopkins 2005: 292)

Pointing is, thus, an instrumental act, fundamentally imperative in nature, whether it is used in requestive contexts or in sharing attention to distant events (Bates et al. 1975; Moore and Corkum 1994). The ontogenetic and phylogenetic emergence of pointing to share attention can and, we submit, ought to be interpreted according to the same analytical framework as pointing to request things; nothing in the empirical data requires us to appeal to young infants' capacities for the representation of invisible and abstract mental states in their social partners (notwithstanding that older children, apparently, develop this ability).

8.6   Implications for the evolution of language

The preceding considerations lead us to summarize two scenarios for the evolution of a deictic capacity. In the Representational hypothesis, our hominin ancestors faced an adaptive context in which a deep understanding of other minds conferred a selective advantage. Whether these other minds were those of fellow hominins or the hominins' prey or predators, our ancestors developed a capacity for interpreting behavior in terms of its underlying mental causes. According to this view, humans, alone among great apes, simply discovered the causal relationship between covert mental processes and overt behavior. The evolution of a theory of mind was, in this view, a prerequisite for the evolution of joint attention. Language, thus, originated in hominins who had gained the power to predict behavior in conspecifics and other organisms, and mental state linguistic terms (intentions, desires, wants, beliefs) came to label ecologically relevant psychological processes (e.g. Povinelli et al. 2003; Tomasello 1999; cf. Hauser et al. 2002). According to this view, then, joint attention—the coordination of attention between two individuals with respect to a specific, distal locus—derives from an insight into mind–body relationships that actually exist. Thus, according to this Representational hypothesis, deictic expression in the infancy period, through proto-declarative pointing, reflects the co-evolutionary interactions of mental state reasoning with the developmental sequelae of an adaptation for symbolic communication. Proponents of something like this perspective interpret ape pointing as a manifestly similar behavior to human pointing, but predicated upon rather different psychological underpinnings (e.g., esp., Povinelli et al. 2003).

We acknowledge that something like this scenario may be true in later human development. There is no question that older humans do account for the behavior of others—and even themselves—in terms of hypothetical causal agents, whether those causal agents are mental states, spirits, angels, demons, etc. (cf. Leavens 1998). Once children are old enough to believe in invisible causal agents, like deities, mental states, Santa Claus, the Easter Bunny, etc., then it is commonplace for humans to attribute behavioral consequences to these kinds of principal causes that have no physical existence (Doherty 2006; Leavens 2006; Woolley et al. 2004). But children begin to point long before they display any evidence of belief in mythical entities—because such evidence is necessarily symbolically mediated. So the Representational hypothesis lacks parsimony in accounting for the emergence of so-called proto-declaratives for two reasons: first, because it depends upon infants' representations of hypothetical entities that cannot be professed by these same children; secondly, because it attributes two separate lineages of cognitive adaptations to account for very similar pointing behavior in very closely related organisms (humans and the other apes) with very similar anatomies who point in very similar ecological circumstances; specifically, the Referential Problem Space (e.g. Leavens 2004a; Leavens, Hopkins, and Bard 2005; Leavens, Russell, and Hopkins 2005).

In the alternative scenario that we have outlined in this chapter, what we might call the Epigenetic perspective, our hominin ancestors faced epigenetically heritable *ontogenetic* contexts that were characterized by increasingly lengthy epochs of dependency of offspring upon their caregivers (Carpendale et al. 2005/2007). The importance of this extended dependency of human infants on their caregivers has been noted by others, for example, Davidson 2006. Whether this unique developmental feature (i.e., prolonged helplessness) derived from our ancestors' adaptations for Pliocene bipedalism or Plio-Pleistocene encephalization is not clear. Irrespective of its source, the Referential Problem Space has become an obligate ontogenetic context for our offspring. We would not propose the existence of a "pointing gene" or "pointing gene-complex"; rather, pointing emerges in this interdependent developmental context. Plus, importantly, when apes are placed in similar kinds of circumstances, manual pointing becomes commonplace in these populations, as well (Figure 8.2). Therefore, according to this view, the capacity to capture and redirect the attention of a social partner is predicated upon cognitive abilities shared by humans and the other great apes, which emerge in particular kinds of contexts. This is a straightforward interpretation of the fact that many captive apes point without explicit training to do so (Table 8.1, section 8.2).

That manual pointing spontaneously develops in requestive contexts in both humans and great apes suggests to us that pointing, per se, is not derived from cognitive, anatomical, or neurobiological adaptations for speech and language (e.g. Leavens 2004a; Leavens, Hopkins, and Thomas 2004). That human children will point in apparent bids to share attention with others is, in our view, not diagnostic of a precocious capacity in the infancy period for the representation of abstract, hidden, and causal mental states or processes, but is simply an instrumental act to elicit particular kinds of affective behaviors from their caregivers (e.g. section 8.3). A particular advantage of this perspective is that it easily accounts for the striking differences in propensity to point between wild and captive apes; wild apes simply do not face circumstances in which it is efficacious to point manually. Another advantage is that it integrates existing theories of cognitive development in the physical domain with development in the social domain (see e.g. Bard 1990; Leavens et al. 1996; Leavens, Hopkins, and Bard 2005; Leavens, Russell, and Hopkins 2005).

Joint attention, as evidenced by the ability to comprehend and to produce deictic behavior, is widely considered to be both an ontogenetic and a phylogenetic prerequisite for language (e.g. Bruner 1983; Butterworth 2003; Davidson 2006; Hauser et al. 2002; Werner and Kaplan 1963; reviewed by Carpenter et al. 1998). According to the evidence reviewed here, great apes easily develop deictic repertoires in the complete absence of any explicit attempt to train them. On the basis of these considerations, we conclude that deixis, the ability to direct the attention of another to a specific locus, is a shared capacity of great apes and humans. Because deixis in great apes cannot ultimately derive from adaptations for bipedalism, profligate encephalization, or neurobiological or cognitive adaptations for speech, then this suggests that our hominin ancestors were pre-adapted for joint attention, that joint attention is a faculty of "language" in a broad sense (shared by humans and other animals), as suggested by Hauser et al. (2002).

If this is correct, then the evolutionary origins of a capacity for deixis are quite ancient, probably originating in the Miocene, if not substantially earlier, simply because the last common ancestor of all living great apes is estimated to have lived in the middle Miocene, approximately 15 million years ago (Schrago and Russo 2003). This component of the faculty of language in a broad sense "thus has an ancient evolutionary history, long predating the emergence of language" (Hauser et al. 2002: 1573). If a capacity for joint attention, or deictic communication, is both ontogenetically and phylogenetically requisite to language acquisition, and if this capacity is a shared, derived cognitive trait of all existing great apes, including humans, then the early human manifestation of non-verbal deixis, through pointing, is a consequence of an interaction between hominid (Homininae and Ponginae) cognitive capacities and hominin-specific developmental circumstances, including relatively altricial births and extended infancy periods. If symbols originated in Africa (Henshilwood et al. 2002), then these symbol-using hominins already had evolutionarily ancient capacities for the capture and redirection of attention. The Referential Problem Space, which was an epiphenomenon of other human adaptations, may have been a precipitating factor in the genesis of habitually referential behavior in our species (Leavens, Hopkins, and Bard 2005, 2008). Thus, according to this view, and contrary to a widespread theoretical perspective that characterized pointing as a derivative of our adaptations for speech, non-verbal deixis does not derive phylogenetically from verbal deixis (cf. Hutto 2008).

9 The directed scratch: evidence for a referential gesture in chimpanzees?

SIMONE PIKA AND JOHN C. MITANI

9.1 Introduction

Recent genetic evidence suggests that some of the key capacities for normal speech production might have developed in our hominid ancestors probably as little as 200,000 years ago (e.g. Davidson 2003; Enard et al. 2002). Many of the neural, anatomical, and cognitive components required for language processing however must be substantially older, having evolved in the primate lineage long before the advent of speech in modern humans. One useful approach to the evolutionary roots of language therefore is the comparative approach, which investigates similarities and differences between human language and the communication systems evolved in other animal species, especially non-human primates (hereafter primates).

Until recently, most studies investigating the vocal communication of primates have focussed on three features essential for human language, the abilities to (1) learn and modify calls, (2) combine calls syntactically, (3) refer to external events or objects in the environment (e.g. Hauser 1996; Marler 1980; Owings and Morton 1998; Snowdon et al. 1982). Recent

We thank the Uganda Wildlife Authority, the Uganda National Council for Science and Technology and Makerere University for permission to work at Ngogo. Research at Ngogo has been supported by the U.S. National Science Foundation (BCS-0215622 and IOB-0516644). We are grateful to A. Tumusiime, L. Ndagizi, G. Mbabazi, and A. Magoba for invaluable assistance in the field and S. Amsler, J. Lwanga, and M. Wakefield for helpful discussion. We are indebted to Dorothee Classen, who created a beautiful drawing of the directed scratch. For comments on earlier drafts and discussion we thank Susan Goldin-Meadow, Jacques Vauclair, and one anonymous reviewer. SP was also inspired by valuable discussions with participants of the Cradle of Language Conference in Stellenbosch, South Africa.

research suggests that primates possess rudimentary abilities with respect to each of these features. For instance, chimpanzees (*Pan troglodytes*) appear to modify the acoustic structure of their calls so that they differ from those emitted by others (Crockford et al. 2004; but see also Marler 1976; Marshall et al. 1999; Mitani et al. 1992). Putty-nosed monkeys (*Cercopithecus nicitans*) combine two calls in a seemingly syntactic fashion into different sequences that are linked to specific external events, such as the presence of a predator or the imminent movement of the group (see also Zuberbühler 2002). Finally, vervet monkeys (*Cercopithecus aethiops*) produce acoustically distinct alarm calls to different predators (Struhsaker 1967). Monkeys respond to the experimental playbacks of tape recorded calls in adaptive ways, indicating that alarm calls are employed in a functionally referential manner (e.g. hiding in bushes, climbing a tree, Seyfarth et al. 1980). The use of functionally referential signals has been reported in several other monkey species (see e.g. Zuberbühler 2000, 2001), suggesting that referential communication is a widespread and perhaps universal characteristic of primate vocal behavior.

Despite these recent findings that suggest rudiments of language-like features in the vocal communication of primates, their calls are still largely hardwired and tightly tied to emotional states (Liebermann 1998; Premack 2004; Tomasello and Call 1997). Because of this, researchers have quite naturally compared speech to another mode of communication, gestures. Gestures are broadly defined as movements of the arms and hands, and their study has received a tremendous amount of recent attention (e.g. Goldin-Meadow and Mylander 1998; Iverson and Goldin-Meadow 1998; Kendon 1975; McNeill 1992; Morris et al. 1979; Pika et al. 2006). This interest has been due in part to the fact that many reconstructions of language evolution involve an initial stage in which language was carried out in gesture (e.g. Armstrong et al. 1995; Condillac 1971; Hewes 1973; Hockett 1978). Moreover, it is thought that gestures form a single, integrated system with speech (McNeill 1985) and can provide insight into an individual's mental representations and cognitive skills (e.g. Goldin-Meadow et al. 2001; Iverson and Goldin-Meadow 1998; McNeill 1992; Nicoladis et al. 1999). In addition, deaf people employ full-fledged sign languages that function without any use of speech at all (Goldin-Meadow and Mylander 1998; Klima and Bellugi 1979; Morford 1996).

Deaf individuals, who do not learn a spoken language and who are not exposed to a sign language, have been described as using gestures to communicate (for an overview see Morford 1996). These so-called homesigns exhibit many structural similarities to sign languages, but develop, contrary to sign languages, over a single generation and are used by a very limited socio-linguistic community (Morford 1996). Interestingly, to some extent gestural or ideographic communication systems have been mastered by human-reared great apes (e.g. Gardner et al. 1989; Patterson 1978a; Savage-Rumbaugh et al. 1993). This research provides evidence that apes are able to use gestures and ideograms intentionally and referentially (Gardner et al. 1989; Patterson 1978; Savage-Rumbaugh et al. 1986), and understand human speech (Savage-Rumbaugh et al. 1993). Sign language studies indicate that great apes are able to use crucial aspects of language in cases where the vocal–auditory channel can be bypassed.

Apes also routinely use gestures in their natural communication, with most attention focussed on one of our two closest living relatives, the chimpanzee (for research on other ape species see Liebal, Pika, and Tomasello 2004; Liebal et al. 2006; Pika et al. 2003; Pika et al. 2005; Tanner and Byrne 1996). Early descriptive, ethological studies showed that chimpanzees use gestures in a variety of contexts such as play, mother–infant behavior, agonistic behavior, and sex (Goodall 1986; Plooij 1978, 1979; van Hooff 1973; van Lawick-Goodall 1968a). Subsequent research on captive chimpanzees by Tomasello and his colleagues (e.g. Tomasello, George, Kruger, Farrar, and Evans 1985; Tomasello, Call, Nagell, Olguin, and Carpenter 1994; Tomasello and Camaioni 1997; Tomasello, Call, Warren, Frost, Carpenter, and Nagell 1997) followed the lead provided by studies on pre-verbal communication in human children and focussed on underlying processes of social cognition, including learning mechanisms and the flexibility of gesture use. These studies revealed that chimpanzees develop multifaceted gestural repertoires, have flexible connections between signal and function of gestures (e.g. show persistence to the goal, by using a different gesture in the same context), and adapt their gestures to various communicative circumstances such as the attentional states of recipients.

With regard to learning, Tomasello and colleagues suggested that chimpanzees acquire the majority of their gestures via an individual learning process, while social learning may be responsible for the acquisition of some gestures (for a review see Tomasello and Call 2007). Gestures such as the grooming hand clasp (McGrew and Tutin 1978), leaf clipping (Nishida 1980), and the social scratch (Nishida et al. 2004) provide further evidence for the existence of cultural variation among chimpanzee communities and social learning (Whiten et al. 2001). In the grooming hand clasp, for instance, two chimpanzees clasp hands overhead, while grooming each other with the other hand (McGrew and Tutin 1978). This gesture has been observed at some study sites, but not others (Whiten et al. 2001).

In sum, chimpanzee gestures resemble those of pre-linguistic children and just-linguistic human infants in some important ways: They are used intentionally, represent a relatively stable part of an individual's communicative repertoire, and are learned (for a recent review see, Pika 2008b; Pika et al. 2005). However, in the majority of cases, chimpanzees use gestures in dyadic interactions to request actions from others (imperatives). Very young human children also use imperative gestures (following Pika 2008b) in dyadic interactions. But they also gesture quite frequently for declarative purposes, for instance by directing the attention of others to some third entity, e.g. an event or an object, simply for the sake of sharing interest in it or commenting on it (Bates et al. 1975). These gestures are clearly triadic and referential (McNeill 1992) and have been linked with cognitive capacities such as mental state attribution (Camaioni 1993; Tomasello 1995) because the recipient must infer the signaler's intended meaning. In contrast to studies of vocal behavior, which make inferences about the referential meaning of signals based on the behavioral response of listeners, research on referential gestures examines this phenomenon from the perspective of the signaler.

To date, referential gestures such as imperative pointing (used to get another individual to help in attaining a goal, cf. Bates 1976) have been reported for captive chimpanzees interacting with their human experimenters and language-trained individuals. For example, chimpanzees use pointing gestures to direct the attention of human caretakers to food outside of their reach (Leavens et al. 1996, 2004).

Further evidence for pointing has been provided by human-raised chimpanzees who were first trained in some kind of communicative task with humans that involved close-range pointing (e.g. Gardner and Gardner 1969; Krause and Fouts 1997; Woodruff and Premack 1979). In all cases, the chimpanzees began spontaneously to point more flexibly, e.g. to locations that they wished to visit or to more distant objects they wished to obtain. In addition, anecdotal observations indicate that in the Bossou chimpanzee community, where animals use stones in a hammer and anvil fashion to crack oil-palm nuts, infant chimpanzees pointed to a stone once and to nuts nine times with their index finger (Inoue-Nakamura and Matsuzawa 1997). Considerable debate continues regarding whether chimpanzees point in a referential way, and it remains unclear whether pointing represents natural communication abilities or is a by-product of living in a human encultured environment (Tomasello and Call 1997).

In this chapter, we describe the widespread use of a gesture, the directed scratch, that appears to be used referentially by chimpanzees in the wild (Pika and Mitani 2006). The gesture occurs in the context of grooming, which consists of brushing and picking through the fur with fingers, mouth, and toes (van Lawick-Goodall 1968b). Grooming permeates virtually every aspect of chimpanzee social life and provides the opportunity for long bouts of relaxed, friendly physical contact (Goodall 1986; Muller and Mitani 2005; Nishida and Hosaka 1996; Simpson 1973). In addition to serving a hygienic function, grooming plays a crucial role in developing, maintaining, and promoting social bonds between individuals (e.g. Bygott 1979; e.g. Dunbar 1988; Watts 2000a, 2000b), but can also be self-directed to ease anxiety or frustration (Goodall 1986).

The gesture involves one chimpanzee male making a relatively loud and exaggerated scratching movement on a part of his body, which could be seen and heard by his grooming partner (see Figure 9.1). We test the following three alternative hypotheses:

- The behavior reflects behavioral conformity due to stimulus enhancement.
- The behavior represents a physical response by an individual to parasites or dirt, thereby drawing the attention of the groomer to a potential area to groom and is not used by the signaler to transfer a communicative message to the recipient.
- The gesture is used communicatively to indicate a precise spot on the body and to request a desired future action, namely grooming.

In addition, we will discuss similarities and differences to homesigns and implications for the evolutionary roots of language.

FIG. 9.1. The directed scratch

9.2 Methods

Study site

We observed chimpanzees at Ngogo, Kibale National Park, Uganda in February and March 2005. Ngogo lies at an interface between lowland and montane rainforest and is covered primarily with moist, evergreen forest interspersed with patches of *Pennisetum purpureum* grassland. Mean annual rainfall at Ngogo is 1404 mm (SD = 176 mm, n = 10 years,

1997–2006), with two dry seasons between January–February and June–July. Detailed descriptions of the Ngogo study area can be found in Struhsaker (1997) and Butynski (1990).

The Ngogo chimpanzee community

The Ngogo chimpanzee community is the largest that has been described in the wild. It contained approximately 145 individuals, including 25 adult males, 14 adolescent males, and 44 adult females, during the period considered here. Continuous observations of the Ngogo chimpanzee community have been maintained since 1995, and most animals are well habituated to the presence of human observers.

Behavioral observations

Gestures can be defined as expressive movements of the limbs or head and body postures that are directed toward a recipient, are goal-directed, mechanically ineffective, i.e., they are not designed to act as direct physical agents, and receive a voluntary response. The following behavioral criteria were used to infer goal-directedness: (1) gazing at the recipient and (2) response waiting (the signaler waits after the signal has been produced, expecting a response).

At the start of the study, we frequently saw adult males performing an exaggerated scratch which seemed to be used solicit grooming. SP subsequently focussed her observations on the use of this gesture with a special focus on gestural exchange between adult male chimpanzees (see Table 9.1).

SP noted all instances of the gesture, termed the "directed scratch," *ad libitum*, recording their occurrence in real time with a digital recorder Audioline (VR 500). SP also shot video footage of grooming bouts opportunistically using a Panasonic video camera (NV-GS 250). During each grooming bout, SP recorded the groomer, the recipient, and the number of times males performed the gesture. In addition, SP recorded two types of responses to a male who used the directed scratch: (1) the groomer stopped where he was grooming beforehand and started to groom the scratched spot, and (2) the groomer continued to groom the spot which he was grooming before the directed scratch. Analyses were based on 249 grooming bouts involving 84 dyads during a total of approximately 100 hours of observation.

The direction of pant grunts between individuals and dyadic aggressive interactions collected during February–July 2005 were used to rank males, grouping them into low-, middle-, and high-ranking categories (see Table 9.1). Pant grunts are distinctive calls given by low-ranking individuals to higher-ranking animals (Bygott 1979; Hayaki et al. 1989, see Figure 9.2).

TABLE 9.1. *Name and rank class of the*
adult males of the Ngogo community

Name	Abbreviation	Rank class
Aye-Aye	AY	Low
Bartok	BA	High
Basie	BS	High
Berg	BE	Middle
Brownface	BR	High
Brubeck	BB	Middle
Corea	CO	Middle
Dexter	DE	Low
Dizzy	DI	Low
Dolphy	DO	Middle
Garrison	GA	Middle
Getz	GE	Low
Harelip	HA	High
Hodge	HO	High
Lofty	LO	High
Miles	ML	High
Mingas	MI	Middle
Monk	MK	Middle
Morton	MO	Middle
Mweya	MW	High
Ornette	OR	Middle
Parker	PA	Middle
Pincer	PI	Middle
Stravinsky	ST	Low
Waller	WA	Low

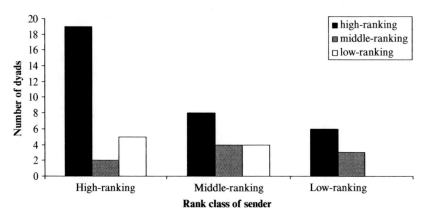

FIG. 9.2. Occurrence of the directed scratch in relation to male dominance rank. The y-axis indicates the number of observed dyads, the x-axis indicates the dominance rank of the signaler. The three different colors indicate the ranks of groomers, the recipients of signals.

9.3 Results

Directed scratching occurring between pairs of adult males was recorded 186 times in 101 (41%) of all observed grooming bouts (N = 249 bouts). It was performed on average 3.65 times/dyad and was used significantly more often in dyads consisting of high-ranking males than other possible pairings (p < 0.001; df = 6, linear-linear association, see Figure 9.2).

One hundred and nineteen times (64%), the groomer stopped grooming and groomed the scratched spot. Eight times (4%) individuals simultaneously scratched and presented a body part and were groomed there immediately. In fifty-nine cases (32%), the groomer continued to groom without touching the area scratched by the signaler. The gesture received significantly more positive than negative responses (p < 0.001; exact binominal test) and occurred in 61% (N = 51) of all observed grooming dyads (N = 84). Positive responses were observed mainly from high-ranking males to a high-ranking partner (see Figure 9.3).

9.4 Discussion

In this chapter, we describe the use of a specific gesture by adult male chimpanzees in the context of social grooming.

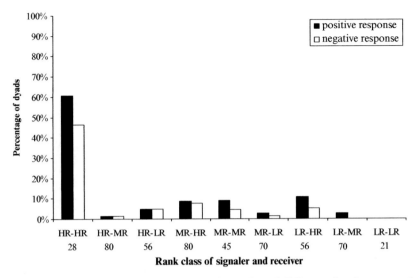

Fig. 9.3. Responses to directed scratches by males of different dominance rank. The y-axis indicates the percentage of observed dyads, the x-axis shows all possible combinations of rank dyads. The first two letters indicate the rank of the signaler, the last two letters the rank of the recipient or responder. The potential number of rank dyads is shown beneath each dyad. The two different colors indicate whether a directed scratch received a positive or a negative response. HR = high rank; MR = middle rank; LR = low rank.

The gesture, the directed scratch, involved one chimpanzee making a relatively loud and exaggerated scratching movement on a part of his body, which could be seen and heard by his grooming partner. It occurred between adult males, who responded the majority of times by grooming the indicated spot.

Three alternative hypotheses may account for these observations. First, the directed scratch may not represent a communicative signal, but instead indicate behavioral conformity due to stimulus enhancement (Whiten and Ham 1992). For example, the scratching movement may facilitate grooming with the recipient, who simply has learned the contingency rule "if he scratches, my grooming is tolerated." If this hypothesis is true, then we would expect to find a positive response mainly from low-ranking males towards high-ranking males. Our results however show that the directed scratch occurred primarily in dyads consisting of high-ranking males.

Second, directed scratching might be used during routine maintenance with no intention at all on the part of the scratching individual to communicate a specific message to nearby conspecifics. The movement and the accompanying scratching noise would draw the attention of recipients to a potential area to groom as an incidental by-product. Since all chimpanzees frequently engage in self-grooming (e.g. Goodall 1986; Watts 2000b), this hypothesis suggests that directed scratches would have been displayed uniformly across all grooming dyads, a prediction that does not accord with our observations.

Third, the gesture may be used communicatively by signalers to indicate a precise spot on their bodies. Consistent with this hypothesis is the finding that in the majority of cases the recipients responded to the gesture immediately by grooming the indicated spot. In addition, we sometimes observed the following sequence of behavior: After one male had been grooming another, the groomer started to perform the directed scratch. The recipient did not start grooming the signaler, but instead moved closer to him or used gestures such as present bodypart. The groomer then started to groom again. These observations seem to suggest that recipients understand the communicative meaning of the signal and either respond as desired (grooming the indicated spot) or request the continuation of the grooming interaction by using other gestures.

Our observations are consistent with anecdotes of other researchers. For instance, Goodall (1968: 264), who studied the Gombe chimpanzees in Tanzania, noted, "Indeed, deliberate scratching movements, during a grooming session, often served as signals since the partner normally responded by grooming the part scratched". Plooij (1978: 125), who observed the same chimpanzee community, wrote that "Two individuals are sitting together and have been engaged in self-grooming for some time. Presently one of them turns her back towards the other, scratches at a certain spot and makes a tonal grunt. At first the other continues his self-grooming. The first individual keeps her hand on the same spot, her back still turned toward the other, and waits. Finally, the other starts grooming her where she has indicated. She then takes her hand away." Van Hooff (1973: 99), who studied a group of chimpanzees in captivity, described a related behavior: "On 20 occasions it was seen that an animal gently took the hand of a fellow and brought it into contact with its own body. This occurred nine times while the actor was groom-presenting and in all cases the partner reacted by grooming."

Our results additionally suggest that the recipient of the signal possesses an understanding of the intended meaning of the gesture and that wild chimpanzees use gestures to specify an area of their body to be groomed. Directed scratches therefore qualify as referential gestures whose reference is directed to the self. In addition, they reflect greater signal specificity than related gestures such as *raise arm* and *present back* (Goodall 1986), which request grooming of larger body areas that are difficult to access. With respect to the use of the gesture, our observations show that directed scratches were mainly utilized by pairs of high-ranking males. High-ranking males form strong social bonds with each other as assayed by association frequency, proximity maintenance, and grooming behavior (Goodall 1986; Simpson 1973; Watts 2000a, 2000b). Why do high-ranking males use the directed scratch frequently? It is possible that signalers benefit by obtaining positive responses from recipients of the gesture, and they increase their chances of doing so by soliciting individuals with whom they are familiar and have formed strong social bonds.

Nearly nothing is known about the use and function of this signal in female chimpanzees. Goodall, however, noted that a chimpanzee mother, "before climbing from a tree, often pauses at a low fork and scratches, looking up at her infant. This serves as a signal; the child usually hurries to the mother and climbs aboard ready for descent" (Goodall 1986: 133). This observation therefore suggests that scratches are flexible communicative strategies which are used in different contexts and to signal different communicative messages such as "follow me" or "groom me here."

Nishida and colleagues (2004) recently described two similar, yet different, grooming behaviors employed by chimpanzees at Ngogo and in the Mahale Mountains, Tanzania. While grooming others, chimpanzees at Mahale will occasionally scratch the backs of their partners in a long and exaggerated way using flexed fingers. This method of *social scratching* (cf. Nakamura et al. 2000) differs from the method employed by Ngogo chimpanzees, who use straight fingers to "poke" the body of their grooming partners. Nishida and colleagues suggested that the differing patterns of social scratching may represent incipient cultural traditions, which were invented by individuals and socially transmitted within communities.

Here we propose that directed scratches similar to social scratches may have arisen from scratching behavior and were ritualized into communicative signals. In ontogenetic ritualization, a communicative signal is created by two individuals shaping each other's behavior during repeated interactions (Tomasello and Call 1997).

The general form of this type of learning is:

- individual A performs behavior X;
- individual B reacts consistently with behavior Y;
- subsequently B anticipates A's performance of X, on the basis of its initial step, by performing Y; and
- A anticipates B's anticipation and produces the initial step in a ritual-ized form (waiting for a response) *in order to* elicit Y.

This means that a behavior that was not at first a communicative signal becomes one as interactants anticipate each other's behavior over time (Tomasello and Call 1997). For example, touching is an important part of mother–infant interactions in chimpanzees, and many infants use a stylized *reach-arm* to indicate that they are about to touch the mother and nurse (Pika et al. 2005). Referential gestures might derive from rit-ualized exchanges between closely related individuals (mother and infant) or closely ranked individuals, such as allies or "friends." However, it is also possible that individuals have been influenced in some ways by observ-ing or grooming skilled individuals (individuals who use the directed scratch), which is called learning through social information and for some researchers represents the only kind of social learning (Galef 1988; Tomasello and Call 1997; Whiten et al. 2004).

However, further research is needed to investigate which learning process is involved and to evaluate if it is used in female–male and female–female dyads in a similar way.

Focussing on the form of the gesture, the directed scratch appears to be similar to signs used by deaf children who have never been exposed to a manual sign language (Goldin-Meadow and Feldman 1975). These so-called homesigns are structured independently of speech, have evolved over only a single generation, and are used by a very limited socio-linguistic community (i.e., the deaf individual and in some cases family members; for a review see Morford 1996). Homesigns are either deic-tic signs or "characterizing signs" (Goldin-Meadow and Feldman 1975). Deictic signs are typically pointing gestures, which effectively allow the child to make reference to any object or person in the present. Context is necessary to interpret these signs. Characterizing signs, on the other hand, are motor-iconic signs that specify actions, objects, and, less frequently, attributes (Goldin-Meadow and Feldman 1975). Their form is related to its referent by apparent physical similarity. For example, two hands flapped up and down at shoulder height can refer to a bird or the act of flying (Goldin-Meadow and Feldman 1975). Motor-iconic signs are therefore less dependent on context for interpretation than are deictic signs (Goldin-Meadow and Feldman 1975). Directed scratches seem to share components of both gesture types. They are used to make reference, but this reference does not include an outside entity or another individual. Although the directed scratch refers to a body part of the signaler himself, it seems to specify a distinct action, namely grooming a desired spot, and therefore may qualify as a characterizing sign.

In contrast to chimpanzees, who rarely combine gestures (Liebal, Call, and Tomasello 2004), homesigners appear to undergo a "lexical explosion" at the age of two and a half years (Mohay 1990). It has been argued that homesigners initially map gesture form, as a whole, on to meaning, but gradually reorganize their gestural lexicons after achieving a threshold vocabulary size such that components of gesture form map on to components of gesture meaning (Goldin-Meadow and Mylander 1990; Goldin-Meadow et al. 1995). For instance, one child initially used a C-hand shape only in combination with a twisting motion to refer to opening a jar, but later the child began combining the hand shape with different motions to refer to all wide objects that can be grasped with the hand (e.g. a toy train, a doorknob, etc.). As they develop, homesigners increase the length of their utterances and their gesture strings display recursions and exhibit simple grammatical structure (Goldin-Meadow 1982, 1987). Interestingly, the introduction of productive features such as internal structure and gesture combinations was not due to input of the hearing caretakers (Goldin-Meadow and Mylander 1983). Furthermore, homesigners use their gestures in several ways, which are crucially different from those used by chimpanzees. For example, they use gestures to talk to themselves and to refer to their own gestures (Goldin-Meadow 1993), to talk about the non-present (Butcher et al. 1991), to tell stories (Phillips et al. 2001), and to make generic statements (Goldin-Meadow et al. 2005).

Another crucial difference between the directed scratch and referential gestures in human children becomes obvious upon examining the *function* of gestures. Chimpanzees use the directed scratch to request an action from the recipient, namely grooming the indicated spot. In contrast, human children gesture for imperative purposes and declaratively to direct the attention of others to some third entity, to share interest in it, or to comment on it (Bates et al. 1975; Liszkowski et al. 2004, however see Leavens et al. this volume for a critical evaluation of the term "declarative"). This behavior is probably linked with the cognitive ability that enables humans to understand other people as intentional agents with whom they may share experience (Tomasello et al. 2005). It might have been derived from the need to create a new medium for social bonding triggered by an increase of group size in primates, superseding grooming as a servicing tool for social relationships (Dunbar 1996; Pika 2008a). While grooming mainly strengthens and services the social relationships of two individuals, referential gestures add two key features that make communication in larger groups more efficient. First, they can be used to communicate with several individuals at the same time, thereby increasing the rate at which signalers interact with recipients. Second, gesturing about third entities permits exchanging information about functionally important aspects of the world (e.g. predators, food) and the past and the future to create a wider network of individuals and relevant facts.

9.5 Conclusion

In this chapter, we present observations that suggest wild chimpanzees use a gesture, the directed scratch, in a referential fashion. Directed scratches share two crucial components with homesign systems. They involve some form of reference and may specify a distinct action, therefore qualifying as characterizing signs. Although homesign systems go a step beyond, by exhibiting simple grammatical structure and recursion (Goldin-Meadow 1982, 1987), directed scratches may constitute the first step toward symbolic gestures. Our findings are thus consistent with the hypothesis that gestures used by our closest living relatives might have been the crucial modality within which the evolutionary precursors of symbolic communication evolved (Pika 2008b; Pika et al. 2005). Additional comparative research investigating the factors triggering the development of referential gestures will be required if we are to resolve what is unique to humans and what constitutes "fossil" forms of human language or language abilities (Bickerton 1990; Jackendoff 1999; Hauser et al. 2002).

10 The origins of the lexicon: how a word-store evolved

MAGGIE TALLERMAN

10.1 Introduction

The human mental lexicon is the repository of many tens of thousands of distinct vocabulary items, and of stored information about their word classes and their selectional and subcategorization requirements. Even in its simplest form—before the syntactic capacity emerges—the lexicon requires a number of distinctive characteristics to have evolved, such as the ability to link an abstract symbol to the concept it represents, the ability to retrieve lexical items from storage quickly, and for that retrieval to be under voluntary control. Few of the capacities required to form the lexicon as we know it appear to be shared in any very obvious way with non-human primates, yet the starting point for the evolution of the lexicon must be a hominin brain with a very similar structure to that of contemporaneous primates.

This chapter has the modest goal of investigating the origins of some of the basic features of the lexicon. I concentrate on the prerequisites for the production and comprehension of a simple protolanguage, though discussion of the link between stored words and sound sequences (vital though this is) does not feature here. I propose that a word-based lexicon evolved by building on ancient conceptual categories which are likely shared by many primates. It also utilized what I will argue was a pre-existing semantic organization, and built on the hierarchical structure already in place in primate cognition. Labels themselves are shown to aid in the learning of categories both in humans and in non-human primates, and word learning is argued to be aided by a set of innate learning biases. Given these

I am extremely grateful to Andrew Carstairs-McCarthy and Fritz Newmeyer for their helpful comments on an earlier draft of this paper. Remaining problems are mine.

premises, a cognitive continuity can be established between early hominins and other primates. Evidence bearing on these issues comes from psycholinguistic studies, from work on category-specific brain deficits, and from the study of pre-linguistic infants and non-human primates.

I conclude that there are indications of a scaffolding effect in evolution: The structure of the protolexicon builds on pre-existing conceptual structure, labeling existing concepts; word learning in early hominins facilitates and structures concept learning; more structure gives rise to more categories, and also to more differentiated categories; more categories require more labels; vocabulary is then driven to increase.

10.2 What a lexicon needs

What linguists mean by the mental lexicon is the set of vocabulary items (essentially, words and idioms) of the speaker's language, with each lexical entry having a set of phonetic, semantic, syntactic, and morphological features. I start by considering some basic properties of the mental lexicon and the questions these raise for the study of language evolution. Probably the most remarkable feature of the lexicon is its sheer size, around 50,000 distinct items per speaker. Human infants learn vocabulary with ease, while in so-called ape language research, non-human primates start to learn vocabulary items only with great difficulty. Premack (1990b) reports that for chimpanzees, more than three hundred trials may be needed with the first words, though in due course a single (explicit) trial will be enough for a word to be added. Moreover, chimpanzees manage to learn perhaps a few hundred items at most, over a long period of time, vocabulary which mostly requires overt instruction rather than being acquired naturalistically (Wallman 1992; Savage-Rumbaugh et al. 1998). Compare this with children, who are estimated to learn between six and ten new lexical items per day between the ages of eighteen months and six years, by which time their vocabulary totals between 8,000 and 14,000 items, generally acquired without explicit teaching (Carey 1978; Clark 1993).

A set of questions therefore arises. How could the lexicon (or rather, the human capacity to form it) evolve, given that nothing analogous/homologous exists in other primates? How did it come to store so much information (in phylogenesis) and how could it grow so large (in ontogenesis)? How are words acquired so easily, at least by modern infants?

Although we cannot hope to fully answer all these questions, I will suggest that some useful clues can be obtained from studies of modern speakers, including infant word-learners and patients with brain lesions, and from comparative biology.

Some basic properties of a lexicon—the prerequisites needed for its operation—are shown in (1):

(1) The properties of the protolexicon

- Conceptual knowledge and representations
- Symbolic capacity and the knowledge that conspecifics use "symbolic reference" (Deacon 1997)
- Links between the stored conceptual structures and lexical-semantic representations (semantic processing)
- A sound/sign system to represent (externalize) symbols
- Links between a lexical-semantic representation and its sound or sign (phonological processing)
- A well-developed capacity for vocal (or manual) imitation
- The ability to learn an open-ended set of labels for objects and concepts via cultural transmission
- The ability to retrieve lexical items from store quickly in production and to be able to reverse the procedure in comprehension
- Retrieval to be under voluntary control

Clearly, not all of the capabilities needed to form a lexicon in modern speakers must be postulated for speakers of a protolanguage. The properties in (1) seem to cover what is needed for a protolexicon, by which I mean the earliest kind of word-store used by hominins for linguistic communication. I assume a protolanguage which was much simpler than full language, and certainly did not include a syntactic component, which is undoubtedly a much later evolutionary development. In other words, I propose a stage in which there were lexical items in a crude sense, but no word classes, and no systematic links between lexical items (in the sense of item X selects an item of class Y), nor systematic ways of combining words (cf. Bickerton 1990).

Certain parts of (1) require little justification. It is, I assume, self-evident that without a richly developed conceptual structure, we would have no lexicon. Similarly, the fact that words are symbols (Deacon 1997) needs no justification here, and so the capacity to recognize and store symbols must be a prerequisite for protolanguage. Equally important is the understanding that conspecifics are communicating intentionally, and also doing so oneself. This is not part of general primate cognition, but is essentially uniquely human, and is one aspect of the bundle of properties referred to as "theory of mind." Then, if protolanguage is to be used for communication, the symbols must also be externalized, either by sounds, signs, or both. Since protolanguage, like full language, must be culturally transmitted, then its speakers must have developed the capacity for vocal or manual imitation, and the ability to learn lexical items in this way. This capacity (learning an association between a symbol and a conventional meaning) *is* within the grasp of other primates, though it does not come naturally to them. Finally, protolanguage speakers must have control over the retrieval of lexical items from store, and this must be fast enough to make some sort of dialog possible, even if retrieval was not at the impressive rate of modern speakers (around two to four words per second; Levelt 1989).

Other aspects of (1) require more thought. I will assume that for protolanguage, three separate types of lexical information must be retrieved at once: conceptual information, lexical-semantic information, and phonological information (but of course no syntactic information). For modern speakers, it is uncontroversial that we must distinguish between semantically driven and phonologically driven lexical retrieval (Vigliocco and Hartsuiker 2002). It also seems clear that a component handling conceptual structure must be separate from its lexical representation: There is good evidence that conceptual knowledge and lexical knowledge are not co-terminous, and are separated in the brain (see also Jackendoff and Pinker 2005: 222–223). As Vigliocco and Kita (2006: 793) note, "lexico-semantic representations are conceived as intermediary representations between conceptual and other linguistic information, namely lexico-syntactic and phonological information. Specifically, [...] this level of representation is assumed to develop, during childhood, on the basis of the properties of conceptual featural representations."

Why is an intermediate level of representation required between concepts and the specifically linguistic components, syntax and phonology? Is it necessary to postulate additional structure between mental concepts and their linguistic expression? It is clear that conceptual knowledge is not mapped on to lexical structure in an identical way cross-linguistically. For instance, in Japanese a single word covers both "foot" and "leg," yet presumably Japanese speakers have no problem in conceptualizing the differences between a foot and a leg (Vigliocco and Kita 2006). Conversely, in English we talk about *putting on* clothing, headgear, footwear, gloves, jewellery, glasses, etc., whilst in Japanese, different verbs are used for distinct types of "putting on" (Clark 1993: 10). Many such examples exist (see also Hespos and Spelke 2004), even between closely related languages. Note also that in some languages, color terms are restricted to two words (black/white; light/dark), yet the perception of focal colors does not differ amongst human societies (Brown 1976). Essentially, languages differ in terms of what concepts they lexicalize and how, yet the same basic conceptual features must be common to all speakers.

There is also evidence for the separation of conceptual knowledge and lexical knowledge from the study of patients with brain lesions. It has long been observed that patients may have deficits in naming objects or persons—a lexical retrieval problem—but no corresponding deficits in recognizing the same objects or people (Humphreys and Forde 2001). Conceptual knowledge about the shape, size, function, and so on of objects can be intact, while the ability to label them is severely impaired, suggesting distinct neurological support for each process. Damasio et al. (2004) found a partial segregation of brain regions handling the two types of knowledge; for instance, the retrieval of words denoting concrete entities is handled by the left temporal lobe, whereas retrieval of conceptual knowledge concerning these same entities is located in the right hemisphere. Damasio et al. (2004: 218) also support the idea of intermediate levels of representation between concepts and words, with defects being a consequence of the breakdown in intermediary processes (see section 10.3.2 below).

Given the separation between concepts and lexicon in modern speakers, it is reasonable to assume that conceptual structure was available pre-linguistically (see also Bickerton 1990: 91), an idea I expand on in section 10.3.1.

10.3 Starting to build the protolexicon

I propose the basic steps in (2) as a possible pathway for building the protolexicon.

(2) Some basic steps towards a protolexicon

   a. A protolexicon evolved by building on pre-existing conceptual categories, likely shared by other anthropoids.

b. The protolexicon utilized a pre-existing hierarchical semantic organization, on which vocabulary was parasitic.

c. Labels for concepts are not only adaptive, they also aid categorially based word learning.

d. Constraints on word learning observed both in modern infants and in non-human primates reflect phylogenetically ancient learning biases.

There are many further, major aspects of the lexicon which I do not discuss here, including the development of a sound system (see de Boer 2001; MacNeilage and Davis 2005; Studdert-Kennedy 2005; Oudeyer 2006), the emergence of voluntary control over vocalizations, a fully developed referential symbolic capacity, compositionality, and so on. Below, I expand on the stages in (2).

10.3.1 *Conceptual categories are not dependent on language*

It is now well accepted that there is a dissociation between the possession of conceptual structure and the possession of language. Both pre-linguistic infants and non-human primates possess significant conceptual abilities, as a large literature now confirms: on infants, for instance, Spelke (1994), Pinker (1994), Carey (1997), Mareschal and Quinn (2001), Xu (2002), Hespos and Spelke (2004); on primates, for instance Premack (1983, 1990a, 1990b), Hauser and Carey (1998), Hauser (2000), Fitch, Hauser, and Chomsky (2005: 191–2), Cheney and Seyfarth (2005).

The basic step in (2a) rests on the idea that other closely related primates share much of the human perceptual organization. Most aspects of human auditory perception are shared with other primates (and indeed, other mammals); there is evidence even of categorical perception of human phonemes (Kuhl and Miller 1975). However, Johansson (2005: 88) reports that humans differ from other primates in having an enhanced ability to perceive sounds in the 2–4 kHz range, and speculates that this arose as a consequence of a selection pressure for speech perception. Turning to visual perception, trichromatic color vision (which aids animals in discovering, for instance, which fruits are ripe) is a characteristic specific to anthropoids (Ross 2000), a suborder of primates which includes monkeys, great apes, and *H. sapiens*. The visual cortex is also enlarged in anthropoids in comparison with the less closely related prosimians. It seems reasonable to assume that (in evolutionary terms) conceptual structure is based on perceptual structure, and that we therefore share a great many concepts with the more closely related non-human primates (see also Fitch et al. 2005: 191). Thus, many aspects of human conceptual organization were probably already in place before the protolexicon evolved.

Hauser and Carey investigate which aspects of what they call the "cognitive building blocks" for language (1998: 52) are species-specific, and which are part of general primate cognition, focussing in particular on the cognitive domains of number and objecthood. Using the preferential looking time paradigm (or "violation of expectancy" method), they find that both pre-linguistic infants and non-human primates become habituated to events which are "expected," but look longer at events which violate expectations in various ways. Even by three months old, infants expect an object to continue to exist when it disappears behind a barrier, and they also "know" that an object cannot be in two places at once. In fact, (contra Piaget) it seems that the sortal concept "physical object" is likely to be an innate cognitive primitive (Carey 1997; Hauser and Carey 1998). Sortal concepts enable us to individuate and identify items: We detect where one entity ends and another begins, and we detect from the physical properties of objects when we are dealing with two distinct entities. While it was previously thought that infants under about 12 months cannot use the properties or features of objects to individuate them (Xu and Carey 1996), it is now clear that this is not the case (Mareschal and Quinn 2001; Xu 2002).

What about other primates? Experiments investigating the concept of object permanence in wild rhesus monkeys and in cotton-top tamarins carried out by Hauser and Carey showed that both these groups look longer at impossible outcomes (such as an object disappearing when a screen was placed in front of it). Further tests ensured that the primates really were tracking individuated objects, and not simply an "amount of stuff" (Hauser and Carey 1998: 66). The authors conclude that non-human primates also represent the sortal object, and also (like pre-linguistic infants) the numerical concepts "one X" and "another X"; these concepts are crucial for language, but "are part of the human primate heritage and did not evolve along with the computational resources that underlie the uniquely human linguistic capacity" (Hauser and Carey 1998: 67).

It is obvious that non-human primates do make categorical distinctions between classes of objects, but are these distinctions like those of adult humans? Relatively little work has been carried out, but Hauser and Carey (1998: 81) report that although tamarins appear not to use the properties of objects for object individuation, rhesus monkeys probably *do* use perceptual differences between types of objects to establish the individuation of objects. Thus, it appears that some of the fundamental building blocks for language emerged early in primate evolution, so are not specifically linguistic.

Future research is likely to discover more cognitive primitives. The basic point, though, is that many concepts (such as object individuation, which is essential for learning discrete vocabulary items) did not emerge with language, but were already available for language to exapt.

10.3.2 *From conceptual categories to semantic organization*

Let us now narrow down the examination of what kinds of conceptual categories were most likely in place before protolanguage to focus on the categorization of objects in the material world. Animals must distinguish between categories such as edible/inedible, potable/non-potable, harmful/harmless, ally/enemy, predator/prey, light/dark, solid/liquid, etc., using the perceptual and motoric properties of objects around them. Pre-linguistic knowledge in early hominins probably revolved around the following distinctions: hierarchical knowledge (e.g. subordinate/dominant, mother/self/daughter), categorical knowledge (e.g. edible/inedible, male/female, fertile/infertile), and gradational knowledge (e.g. harmful/harmless, light/dark, ripe/unripe, near/far). These semantic categories are not necessarily mutually exclusive: For instance, something that is not normally a preferred food item might be eaten in extremis, so the category "(in)edible" is gradational too. All of these categories can be borrowed for use in the protolexicon and beyond.

Hierarchical knowledge seems to be especially important, since it potentially gives structure to the whole lexicon, and may be exapted later on in evolution for handling the hierarchies found in other areas of the grammar (syntax in particular). Semantic hierarchies occur extensively in the lexicons of modern languages; see also Bickerton (1990: 43–44), Pinker and Jackendoff (2005: 214). The modern lexicon handles highly developed semantic fields, all with hierarchical structure, involving many intersecting groups of lexical items.

How did these abilities develop? One clue is that Broca's area seems to be responsible for handling hierarchies in general, not just linguistic hierarchies (Greenfield 1991; Deacon 1997: 297; Conway and Christiansen 2001). It seems likely that brain regions which dealt with general cognitive processes in pre-linguistic primates have been co-opted for use in language. For instance, Cheney and Seyfarth (2005: 153) hypothesize that knowledge of social relationships amongst pre-linguistic primates was exapted for the representation of linguistic meaning:[1] "[The] properties of non-human primates' social knowledge [...] bear striking resemblances to the meanings we express in language, which are [...] built up by combining discrete-valued entities in a structured, hierarchical, rule-governed, and open-ended manner." Primate social knowledge is based on discrete values such as individual identity and sex, and has hierarchical structure which is not merely linear, but also nested (Cheney and Seyfarth 2005: 152), a prerequisite for linguistic hierarchies.

However, in a review of research on primate sequential learning, Conway and Christiansen (2001) report that nonhuman primates are extremely limited in their abilities to learn hierarchical behavior, compared with humans. Although there is probably a homologous substrate handling sequential learning in human and non-human primates, "apes and monkeys rarely use hierarchical routines in their spontaneous and learned actions" (Conway and Christiansen 2001: 544–545), and human infants outperform other primates in a wide variety of test situations involving hierarchical learning. Conway and Christiansen speculate that the advanced abilities of humans in this area may well reflect a species-specific evolutionary development which is related to our linguistic abilities. In the current context, the research question would then be, what drove what? Did the emerging lexicon (rather, the emerging ability to learn a lexicon) drive enhanced hierarchical abilities, or did early hominins already possess superior skills in hierarchical processing, which were then exapted for use in the protolexicon? More probably, we can postulate a scaffolding effect, with those individuals better able to handle hierarchical learning in general being in a good position to form

---

[1] The suggestion that aspects of primate social intelligence have been exapted for language use is not at all new, but now seems to be quite widely accepted; see, for instance, Burling (1993); Worden (1996, 1998); Bickerton (1998, 2000); Jackendoff (2002: 324); Snowdon (2004); Hurford (2007), amongst many other references.

a hierarchically structured lexicon, and the latter providing a basis for improved cognitive skills involving hierarchical processing.

I look next at categorization. The evidence indicates that the brain organizes information by semantic categories, and that this organization most likely pre-dates the use of such categories in language. From psycholinguistic studies, there is extensive evidence for the representation of discrete conceptual categories, which in turn are based on perceptual and functional similarity of items. It has long been observed that items with similar features come to be treated as a lexical category. Early work by Kay (1971) and Rosch (1975) showed that featural similarity is important in human categorization, and class membership is determined by the number of features shared across items in a similar category; this has now become the standard view in the field. (Though see de Almeida 1999 for a different view, and Jackendoff 2002: section 11.4 for some problems with taxonomies.)

Federmeier and Kutas (1999) discuss results from behavioral studies showing that the categorical structure of semantic memory influences language processing even when this may impede the comprehension process. They presented participants with sentences designed to set up expectations about the final word, such as "She wanted to make her eyelashes look really black and thick. So she asked to borrow her older friend's . . . ." Participants received one of three possible endings: the ending expected from the previous context, i.e. *mascara*; what is termed a within-category violation, *lipstick* (another type of cosmetic); or a between-category violation, *necklace*. The expected ending, *mascara*, is clearly processed most quickly in this context. As for the remaining two words, neither *lipstick* nor *necklace* is a very plausible ending, so it might be expected that these words would not differ in terms of processing in the given context. However, in fact, the within-category violation, *lipstick*, showed significantly facilitated processing as compared with *necklace*. Both *lipstick* and *necklace* are contextually inappropriate, but the semantic similarity between *mascara* and *lipstick* resulted in a distinct processing advantage for *lipstick*. Federmeier and Kutas also show that inherent plausibility of the different endings could not, alone, account for the results. They conclude from the study that "the experientially imposed structure of long-term memory has a significant and measurable impact on contextually driven language processes" (1999: 488–489). In other words, perceptual and functional similarity amongst items in the real world was shown to influence neural organization and also language comprehension.

Secondly, the study of category-specific brain deficits provides further evidence that words are organized in distinct brain regions according to the semantic field of the item (see, for instance, Warrington and McCarthy 1987; Caramazza and Shelton 1998; Shelton and Caramazza 1999; Humphreys and Forde 2001; Damasio et al. 2004; amongst many other references). Following brain damage, many patients have category-specific impairments for living things, while non-living things are unaffected. Conversely, there are also reports of patients with problems in word retrieval for tools and other manipulable objects, while retrieval of words for people and animals are unaffected. Damasio et al. (2004) report loss of word retrieval which is linked to highly specific brain regions handling various conceptual categories, such as fruit and vegetables, or people, or animals, or tools. The authors stress that discrete conceptual categories are indicated by the evidence.

Caramazza and Shelton (1998) and Shelton and Caramazza (1999) suggest that there are evolutionary pressures involved in the separation of stored knowledge into three basic categories, plants, animals and artefacts, and that neural structures are organized around these three major divisions. Their prediction is that *only* conceptual categories which are of evolutionary importance should give rise to category-specific deficits. This is supported in part by brain imaging data, which show that distinct brain regions are activated in the identification of living vs. non-living things (Humphreys and Forde 2001: section 5.1).

It seems plausible to propose that stored conceptual/perceptual information is organized in a very similar way in anthropoids in general, and that the lexicon is parasitic upon that organization. What had to evolve for word retrieval to be possible at all were the processes which mediate between concepts and stored words. Damasio et al. (2004: 221) describe the naming process as follows:

Naming a stimulus from a particular conceptual category is dependent on three kinds of neural structures: (i) structures which support conceptual knowledge [...]; (ii) structures which support the implementation of word-forms in eventual vocalization (the classical language areas located in the left perisylvian region, including Broca and Wernicke areas); and (iii) intermediary structures for "words", which are anatomically separable from the other two kinds of structures and from the intermediary structures for the retrieval of the concept, at least in part. In the naming process, the intermediary structures are engaged by the structures in (i) to trigger and guide the implementation process executed by the structures in (ii).

In non-human primates, I suggest, only the neural structures in (i) have evolved. With training, however, behavior which mimics the behavior produced in humans by the structures in (ii) and (iii) can to some extent be developed in other primates (though obviously not using vocalization). Thus, what language-trained apes produce is protolexical output, with no further organization at all, whereas *protolanguage itself* may well have used such pre-linguistic organizational principles as Agent First, Focus Last, and Grouping (Jackendoff 2002: ch. 8.7). This proposal differs from that of Derek Bickerton (e.g. Bickerton 1990), who suggests that language-trained apes produce something equivalent to protolanguage.

Thirdly, there is evidence concerning categorization from the ontogenetic development of normal children. Massey and Gelman (1988) showed three- and four-year-old children pictures of real but novel animals, and pictures of machines and statues with animal-like parts. When asked which of these could go up a hill by themselves, the children only chose actual animals. One initial categorial distinction may therefore be the (in)ability of an object to move on its own. In fact, even much younger infants appear capable of making similar distinctions. Rakison and Butterworth (1998) found that at fourteen and eighteen months old, infants grouped animals vs. vehicles according to whether they had legs or wheels. Given "hybrid" items, such as a cow body with wheels, they used perceptual features or parts for categorization. Mandler and McDonough (1996) also found that fourteen-month-old infants were able to distinguish between living and non-living things. If they were shown a toy dog drinking, they would make a toy rabbit drink, but not a motorcycle. Given the example of a car being started with a key, they would make a truck start with a key, but not a fish. The infants were also able to correctly generalize actions such as "drinking" and "sleeping" throughout the animal domain. Thus it appears that from the earliest linguistic stages, infants are capable of categorization.

Moreover, there is increasing evidence that even pre-linguistic infants are also entirely capable of categorization. Mareschal and Quinn (2001) report that ten-month-old infants are able to differentiate the categories of land animals vs. sea animals, provided they are given typical exemplars of land animals (such as zebras). Even three- and four-month-old infants can generalize a category of domestic cats, excluding birds, dogs, horses, and tigers. Infants of this age were also able to generalize a category "mammal" which correctly included novel instances of mammals, but excluded birds and fish. In fact, Mareschal and Quinn (2001: 443) note that "[a]lthough a previous scholarly generation considered categorization to be a developmentally late achievement, more recent research suggests that categorization has an early onset, with even newborns displaying primitive categorization abilities."

I am not, of course, suggesting that all the categories which infants and adults are capable of differentiating (and naming) are innate categories—clearly, we did not evolve to recognize vehicles or musical instruments. There may well be some innate categories (the most likely being living vs. non-living), with other categories being formed developmentally on the basis of various perceptual features. There is an ongoing debate in the literature on cognition over the route taken by infants from percept to concept (see Mareschal and Quinn 2001: 447), and, naturally, ontogeny does not necessarily recapitulate phylogeny in this regard (or any other). It is also not yet known to what extent real-world knowledge and representations stored in long-term memory affect categorization. What seems likely, though, is that primates in general, and probably anthropoid apes in particular, have evolved to recognize and distinguish very similar categories. Given such a basis, the lexicon built (or builds anew for each child) on the categories already in place.

10.3.3 *Labels aid category learning*

There is increasing evidence that the very process of labeling plays a role in the learning of distinct categories in children and adults. Evidence from comparative biology suggests that this is also the case for non-human primates. Labeling might therefore be a crucial aspect of the growth of the lexicon in evolution (or rather, the growth of the ability to commit a large word-store to long-term memory). Thus, we may begin to explain how the human lexicon comes to have such a large storage capacity: Labeling is important for categorization.

First, labels have been found to be important in the acquisition of novel categories by adults (Lupyan 2006). In Lupyan's study, participants had to learn to recognize two different classes of aliens, a "friendly" category and a "hostile" category. During a training phase, auditory feedback (a buzzer or bell) let participants know if each of their responses was correct. In training, participants were assigned either to a "label" or a "no-label" group. Once their response had been made (and whether it was correct or incorrect), participants in the "label" group saw a label bearing one of two possible nonsense words next to each alien picture. Friendly aliens were labeled *grecious*, and the hostile ones *leebish*, but participants were not given the impression at any stage that the labels were the "name" of the alien. The no-label group received auditory feedback during training, but saw no labels. As Lupyan notes (2006: 192): "Participants in the *label* group learned that aliens that look a certain way should be avoided, *and* that they are *leebish*, while participants in the *no-label* group learned only that aliens looking a certain way should be avoided." During the testing phase, no feedback and no labels were used. The results showed that participants in the "label" training group were not only more accurate in categorization, but were also better able to retain their knowledge during the testing phase, rather than decreasing in accuracy over time. The suggestion is that "learning category labels also provides for facilitated representation of the labelled concepts" (Lupyan 2006: 195). Lupyan notes that, perceptually, the difference between the two classes of aliens is (deliberately) somewhat indistinct, but having the labels provided a way for participants to represent the categorical distinction between the two categories. Moreover, many participants in the no-label condition actually reported having invented their own labels during the training phase—even though these were clearly not going to be used for communication.

Second, there is evidence that nine-month-old infants use the presence of distinct labels to establish their representations of distinct objects (Balaban and Waxman 1996; Xu 2002). Xu (2002) used the preferential looking time paradigm in a series of experiments designed to test the effects on infants of hearing distinct labels for objects. The infants saw two familiar objects coming out from and returning behind a screen, one at a time. When the screen was removed, the expected outcome was for both items to be present; in the unexpected outcome, only one was present. The presence of distinct labels for each object in a familiarization phase ("Look, [baby's name], a ball/duck") facilitated the task of object individuation for the infants; if the infants were simply told "Look, a toy", they were not able to individuate the two objects. It was also found that the facilitation effect occurred with two objects completely novel to the infants, and two accompanying nonsense words. Xu (2002: 244) suggests that words act not merely as memory aids, but as "essence placeholders":

Infants may expect that words for objects map onto distinct kinds in their environment. Given this expectation, the very fact that one object is called "a duck" and one object seen on a different occasion is called "a ball" is sufficient evidence for infants to posit two distinct kinds or essences. [...] Simply hearing and remembering words for object kinds does not give an infant or anyone else fully-fledged concepts of dog or chair, but words such as "dog" and "chair" may direct the child to set up "placeholders" for the relevant concepts and through interacting with the world, these concepts are elaborated and beliefs about these concepts are cumulated.

Third, consider the effects of providing labels for concepts in experiments with non-human primates. Premack (1990b) shows that young language-trained chimpanzees behave like young children in that they undergo the taxonomic shift (Markman and Hutchinson 1984). Initially, young children and young chimpanzees show a strong tendency to group objects together on the basis of thematic relations: When shown a picture of a dog, for instance, they select something they know to be associated with dogs, such as a bone or the dog's lead. But older children and older chimpanzees tend to sort objects on a taxonomic basis, pairing, for instance, a poodle with a labrador: Under the taxonomic assumption, labels pick out a class of objects ("dogs"), rather than an associated set of items. Younger children can, however, be prompted to undergo the taxonomic shift by the presence of a novel word (Markman and Hutchinson 1984). If they are shown a dog and given a novel label such as *dax*, then asked to find another dax, they typically pair up, say, a dog and a cat (perhaps both are "familiar pets", for instance).

In a series of tests, Premack (1990b) produced the taxonomic shift in young language-trained chimpanzees. The animals were familiar with match-to-sample tests, and already had a small vocabulary of twenty-five plastic "words," all entirely arbitrary (say, a blue triangle for an apple). When no labels were presented, the chimpanzees sorted objects thematically, for example pairing a shoe with a shoelace. When the plastic "word" that labeled the target object was presented, then the taxonomic shift occurred: For "pen," they then chose another pen. Adding a *novel* word alongside the target object (i.e. a plastic "word" which the animals had not yet learned) had the same effects, in terms of prompting the taxonomic shift. As with children, the effects appear to be prompted by the label itself. Premack confirmed this with a control test which presented foreign "words" (e.g. bottle caps, dominoes) alongside the target objects; these items are not possible words in the chimpanzees' vocabulary, and they do not prompt the taxonomic shift.

However, knowing the association between label X and item Y does not indicate that chimpanzees know that X is the *name* of Y, at least in the initial stages. Premack (1990b: 207) points out that merely presenting a consistent relationship between every instance of both X and Y is enough to produce both one-trial learning of vocabulary, and also the shift effect. In early training, plastic words are essentially used to request pieces of fruit from the trainer. Premack notes that such formative experiences (such as "X can be used to obtain Y") may be instrumental in both apes and children learning the relationship "X name of Y." Once the relationship between labels and items is established, more advanced behavior follows. For instance, when shown merely the stalk of an apple, the chimpanzees correctly chose the plastic word for "apple" rather than the word for "peach"; again, the label is shown to evoke the object. The chimpanzee Sarah was taught the word *brown* by using the instruction "brown colour of chocolate." The words for "colour of" and "chocolate" were already known, but no brown object and no chocolate were present. As Premack puts it (1990b: 210) "the animal's mental representation of the object Y is transferred to the new word X. Henceforth, Y can be evoked mentally by X." The dissociation between labels used by others and the predicate "name of" is an important point: in hominin evolution, there is no reason to expect that each speaker in initial protolinguistic exchanges understood that conspecifics had referential intentions (cf. Wray 2002: 119–124 on the concept of "what I say when I want you to ——"). The crossing of this cognitive threshold was undoubtedly a major advance in language evolution.

Finally on the importance of labeling, I noted earlier that some patients with brain lesions have a problem only with lexical retrieval (Humphreys and Forde 2001: 460). When given the name for an object, patients with category-specific deficits for living things were able to describe members of this category correctly.

I suggest that if labels facilitate category learning, then in evolutionary terms, the ability to link a concept with a label is highly adaptive. Imagine its utility for a hominin who, via labeling, could successfully distinguish between two perceptually similar mushrooms, one of which was good to eat and one of which it would be fatal to consume, or between two snakes, one harmless and one deadly. The growth of vocabulary—even if it finds little external expression at first—is thus likely to produce an organism which is fitter for its environment.

Note that there is no requirement here for the labels themselves to be externalized, just as in the case of those no-label participants in Lupyan's study who invented their own labels for the two classes of aliens. Initially (in evolution), a label might be used simply by one hominin, perhaps vocalized and perhaps not. At this stage in language evolution, Eve Clark's principle of conventionality—"for certain meanings, there is a conventional word or word-formation device that should be used in the language community" (Clark 1983: 70)—had not yet been adopted. Conventionality is an absolute requirement for the cultural transmission of language; it ensures that speakers within a community use more or less the same words to refer to the same concepts. But there is no inherent reason to suppose that the very earliest protolanguage speakers possessed this constraint. Instead, we can imagine an initial stage before any part of language was culturally transmitted, in which different speakers may have had their own, private labels, which were not used for communicative purposes at all, but which were originally merely part of "mentalese." If such labels were subsequently externalized (into protolanguage), perhaps by being vocalized unconsciously, then the labels used by the most prestigious individuals (and maybe by their offspring) might be overheard and adopted laterally, so becoming part of the community. In due course, conventionality would be adopted by the community, finally becoming fixed, perhaps by the Baldwin effect: Those speakers better able to use conventional labels to communicate may have had the best chances of survival, and so would pass on their genes to their progeny.

In full language, syntax itself helps the child to learn words; see for example Landau, Smith, and Jones (1992), Waxman (1994), among many other references on this kind of bootstrapping. We can thus assume that labels facilitate the learning of semantic categories, semantic categories are taken as the basis for establishing syntactic categories (see Carey 1997), and syntax facilitates the learning of more labels.

10.3.4 *Constraints on word learning*

The first hominins who used lexical items for communicative purposes had to solve the problem of how to map the meanings of words on to word forms (Quine's "Gavagai" problem; Quine 1960); the same problem faces modern infants, though it is likely that they have been advantaged by the genetic assimilation of a certain amount of grammatical information (i.e. they have a language faculty). However, a large literature on the mapping problem in infants proposes that word learning is guided by a small set of lexical (or conceptual) constraints, and furthermore, suggests that these are not acquired inductively, but are innate, reflecting general learning biases (e.g. Bloom 1993; Bloom 2000; Clark 1983, 1993; Markman 1989, 1990; Markman and Hutchinson 1984; Markman and Wachtel 1988; Merriman and Bowman 1989).

The whole object assumption (Carey 1978; Markman 1989, 1990) leads infants to believe that a novel word refers to the whole object, rather than a part of the object or its features or properties. And under the principle of contrast (Clark 1983, 1987, 1993), "speakers take every difference in form to mark a difference in meaning" (Clark 1993: 64); thus, every two words should have a different conventional meaning. The closely related mutual exclusivity principle (Markman 1987, 1989) leads infants to assume that each object has one and only one label (so an object cannot be both a dog and a cat).[2] Of course, in full language, all of the constraints need to be overridden to some extent in order to acquire adult-like vocabulary. For instance, whole objects do have parts, and the parts are likely to have their own label. And a single object can have several distinct labels at different hierarchical levels of specificity or generality (a corgi, a pet, a dog, a mammal, a vertebrate). However, it is reasonable to assume that the earliest hominin vocabulary did not require the innate constraints to be overridden, but simply operated under these initial assumptions, so associating one label with one whole object and one conventional meaning (see also Smith 2005 on the effects of the mutual exclusivity assumption in language evolution). In other words, the levels of sophistication found in the modern lexicon came later in evolution. If the protolexicon itself is constrained by a set of innate assumptions about the meanings of labels,

---

[2] Carstairs-McCarthy (1999: 110–112) has a useful discussion of the differences between these constraints.

then it is less difficult to envisage the earliest protolanguage speakers being able to learn vocabulary.

One possible objection here is that these constraints may be innate in modern humans, but that does not necessarily mean they were available to the earliest speakers of protolanguage. However, given evidence that non-human primates operate under the same assumptions, then we can be reasonably confident that these same general learning biases also aided hominins in the construction of the proto-lexicon; see Carey (1997), Hauser and Carey (1998). As Bickerton (1990: 107) notes, primates in ape language research consistently generalize the label applied to one token (e.g. *banana*) to all members of the class, just as children do (and indeed parrots; Pepperberg 1999). This is Clark's "type assumption" (Clark 1993: 53). And as noted earlier, language-trained chimpanzees exhibit the taxonomic shift which is characteristic of human infants' use of vocabulary.

10.4 Conclusion

The discussion above suggests a possible evolutionary pathway towards a protolexicon, which is subsequently driven to increase in size via a scaffolding effect. Pre-existing conceptual organization is available to give substance to protovocabulary, which is structured categorially and hierarchically on the basis of pre-linguistic knowledge. Having a protovocabulary is in itself adaptive, but labels also aid early hominins in the learning of categories. As more categories are learned, a finer-grained vocabulary becomes necessary, and the lexicon is driven to increase in size.

A growing body of research (which is also growing in methodological sophistication) suggests that pre-linguistic infants and non-human primates share many of the conceptual building blocks and learning biases which could contribute to the creation of a mental lexicon. Here, I have focussed on what the common aspects of primate evolution made available to pre-linguistic hominins. But the fact remains that other primates do not construct a lexicon, even after intensive training (though they clearly can store labels for concepts). Humans utilize capacities in the construction of a lexicon which are not part of the general primate heritage. For instance, vocabulary learning appears to be intricately connected with intersubjectivity (characterized by turn-taking interactions between the infant and the caregiver; see Bloom 1993: 74) and joint attention, facets of human cognition which are not shared with other primates. And in full language, human vocabulary is characterized by extensive use of functional/grammatical elements, elements which have not been reproduced in ape language research.

Many aspects of the modern human lexicon have evidently evolved solely in the hominin lineage—but that leaves plenty of time for genetic assimilation and other evolutionary processes to operate.

11   Language: symbolization and beyond

ERIC REULAND

11.1 Introduction

The study of genesis and evolution of language is one of the most intriguing and challenging endeavors we have recently embarked on, since it touches on the foundations of our humanity. Understanding the issue requires intensive interdisciplinary collaboration between archeologists, paleontologists, evolutionary biologists, linguists, and neuroscientists along the lines exemplified in the present volume. Archeologists and paleontologists access the processes underlying the evolutionary change indirectly—by studying what has been preserved in the prehistoric record. This may help establish a lower limit on the cognitive capacities of prehistoric man, but gives no direct evidence of his full capacities, including language. Evolutionary biologists—including geneticists—may access the processes underlying the evolutionary change, by studying the nature of genetic change and natural selection, but depend on an understanding of the initial and final states. Linguists and neuroscientists contribute an understanding of this final state.

As modern cosmology tells us, given a conception of *law of nature*, the present contains clues of what it must have come from. There are important limits on the rigor of evolutionary laws as we currently know them as compared to the rigor of the laws of physics. Yet, even in the absence of formally stateable laws, an informal natural logic as sketched by Oller (2007) may sufficiently constrain possible previous states in terms of a current state, to keep speculation at bay. Thus, rescinding the Linguistic

I would like to thank the organizers of the Cradle of Language conference, in particular Rudie Botha, for this important initiative and for inviting me to present my ideas. My thanks also go to the participants for many enjoyable presentations and debates. I am very grateful to Fred Coolidge for his helpful and stimulating comments on an earlier draft. Of course, all errors are my own.

Society of Paris's 1866 ban on the discussion of the origins of language does indeed appear to be justified.

Following the trail back from where we are now to where we came from requires a precise conception of language, and of the resources it draws on. Proper use of evidence from genetics and natural selection requires an understanding of the role language and the systems underlying it play in enhancing an individual's chances of survival. There is a widespread view—especially among non-linguists—that language is primarily a symbolic system to be used for communication. This view encourages us to draw far-reaching conclusions about the linguistic capacities of our ancestors from their symbolic capacities as manifested in art and technology. I will argue that such a view is too simplistic. While my approach is negative in one sense, in that it discourages a too naïve interpretation of the archeological record, my conclusions are also positive since they point the way towards a more focussed search for evidence that may be more compelling.

11.2 Linguistics and the study of language evolution

Until recently, there was very little interaction between modern linguistics and the study of language evolution. The reason is quite simple. It is only recently, with the development of the view of language reflected in the "Minimalist Program" (Chomsky 1995 and subsequent work), that fruitful interaction became possible.

The original rules of the 1950s and 1960s to express linguistic regularities—transformations—were far too crude. They differed per construction—passive versus active, question versus declarative—and also per language. The passive rule for Dutch had to differ from that for English or Russian, and although commonalities could be seen, the theory had no way to express these. In the 1970s there was intensive cooperation between linguists and psychologists about the relation between linguistic structure and processing complexity, focussing on what came to be known as the derivational theory of complexity—the more operations were carried out in deriving a sentence, the more complex it was expected to be. After some initial successes the approach failed. No simple relation between operations and complexity could be established. As we now know, given the current success of grammar-driven processing theories and theories of language impairment (see Avrutin (2001) for an overview), this failure was not a failure in principle. It just reflected the fact that the rules of that period were not sufficiently fine grained to facilitate an insightful mapping onto brain-level processes. With the development of the principles and parameters model in the 1980s (Chomsky 1981), the situation changed, but it is only over the last decade that we have been developing the necessary insight into the basic workings of the system in order to establish the connection.

Let me just briefly—for reasons of space—illustrate how the level at which a phenomenon is analyzed affects the possibility of connecting it to evolutionary processes.

11.3 Interpretive dependencies

Natural language allows different expressions to receive identical values in some actual or virtual world. For instance, in the world as we know it, English *morning star* and *evening star* both have the planet Venus as their value. That is, both *refer* to Venus. Such expressions are *co-referential*. Co-reference may hold on the basis of an empirical fact, as in the Venus case, but speakers' intentions also establish co-reference. A pronominal such as *he* can be used to refer to any object that is linguistically classified as masculine and singular, as in *John's mother thought he was guilty.* Here, *he* may refer to John but also to some other masculine individual. Co-reference as such is not encoded in the grammar.

Co-reference is not the only way to relate the interpretation of two expressions. *No one* in *no one believes he is guilty* does not refer to an individual, hence *a fortiori*, *he* cannot refer to that individual. Under the most salient reading *he* does, nevertheless, depend for its interpretation on *no one*. In this case the dependency is encoded by the grammar, and is called *binding*.

Elements with rich enough descriptive content, such as *the man*, can only bind but not be bound; pronominals such as *he, she* may but need not be bound; anaphors such as *himself* and its counterparts in other languages, on the other hand, must be bound.

Binding theory is the component of the system that is concerned with the dependencies between anaphors and pronominals and their antecedents (Chomsky 1981: 6).[1]

---

[1] In part of the literature the term *anaphor* is used for any expression that refers back to an individual previously mentioned. Under that use *the idiot* in *George decided to attack.*

It is a recurrent pattern cross-linguistically that an anaphor in the position of *himself* in (1) cannot have *Max* as its antecedent (binding indicated by italics).

(1) **Max* expected [**Mary** to admire *himself*]

The local subject *Mary* intervenes and blocks the dependency between *Max* and *himself*. This pattern has been accommodated in the theory by the "specified subject condition" (SSC), roughly saying that an anaphor cannot be bound across a subject.

Note, there is nothing "logical" about the SSC. It must reflect some property of our computational system, since nothing is wrong with the meaning of (1). Its intended meaning is adequately captured by *Max expected Mary to admire him*. So, what the SSC must reflect is how meanings are computed.

Since SSC-effects are pervasive they were taken to be part of universal grammar. Since universal grammar should reflect our genetic endowment it is only a small step to claim that the specified subject condition is innate. This is a consequence drawn by Chomsky (1980) in his contribution to the Piatelli-Palmarini volume. However, it is hard to see what type of neurocognitive structures could support a principle as specific as the SSC, and what kind of evolutionary event could have given rise to it. Moreover, it raises the question how many distinct evolutionary events would have been needed to give rise to language as we know it if events at this level of particularity are involved. Note that this does not indicate that the SSC is "wrong," since descriptively the SSC or something very close to it is simply needed. Rather, whatever is innate must be more elementary than the SSC.

Consider, then, an alternative based on a lexical property of SELF (see Reuland 2005b, in press, and forthcoming for these and related issues). SELF lexically expresses identity between two arguments of a predicate. Consequently, a structure as in (2a) is interpreted as in (2b):

(2) a. Max expected [John to admire himself]
     b. Max expected [John to SELF-admire him]

A simple combinatory procedure taking *admire* and *himself* together and computing its outcome, namely a predicate whose two arguments must be

---

The idiot thought he could fool everyone is an anaphor. Here I will follow the standard usage and reserve the term *anaphor* for "specialized" anaphors. So, *the idiot* "is" not an anaphor, although it "is used" here as anaphoric to George.

identical, gives the required result—which in the case of (1) happens to be ungrammatical since *Mary* and *him* do not match in properties and in (2) gives the local interpretation—and provides no way to link *himself* to *Max*. The SSC boils down to the prevalence of SELF-type elements cross-linguistically. No global condition is necessary. What needs to be innate is no more than the general computational procedure.

Resolving the puzzles the evolution of language poses is contingent on reductions of this type. The limited contribution to the study of the evolution of language by linguists so far need not have any deeper explanation than that, until now, any attempt was premature.

11.4 Setting the stage

In discussing the "evolution of language" it is important to observe the following distinctions:

(3) a. The evolution of the human lineage up to the emergence of language
   b. The event that gave rise to the faculty of language as we know it
   c. The subsequent evolution of humans and the emergence of language
   d. A putative evolution OF language

Does this sketch presuppose a clear-cut distinction between human and non-human in the course of our evolution? Not necessarily, and perhaps such a distinction will be hard to draw in a non-arbitrary way. At what point was some ancestor non-human and did its offspring become human? In this form, the question seems hardly sufficiently defined to warrant discussion. However, given that there happens to be a clear-cut distinction between us and our chimpanzee cousins, and there is nothing "in-between," the two lineages can be distinguished, and the distinction between (3a) and (3b) must be real, provided (3b) is real. The question is, then, is (3b) real? Does it make sense to talk about "*the event*" that gave rise to the faculty of language as we know it? As we will see, unlike in the case of (3a), it is possible to identify a trait that "clinches the matter," when added to whatever one might think of as a protolanguage and without which an ancestor could have had no "language as we know it." This trait can be present independently of whether an ancestor actually had developed the use of language. This immediately connects to (3d). As we will see, whether or not it makes sense to entertain the idea of an evolution OF in contrast to TOWARDS language very much depends on (3b): What property is constitutive of language and can it be susceptible to evolution at all?

My focus will be on *language as a computational system*. An evolutionary perspective forces us to consider:

  i. What is special about language?
  ii. Which of its properties can be understood on the basis of general principles?

Natural language embodies a systematic mapping between form and interpretation. Forms should be realized in an external physical medium; interpretations are ultimately changes in the state of certain internal sub-systems of the mind. A schematic representation of the "language system" is given in (4). In line with the usage in Chomsky (1995), C_{HL} stands for the *Computational system of Human Language*. The terms *PF-interface* (Phonetic Form) and *C-I-interface* (Conceptual-Intentional) stand for the interfaces with the sound (or gesture) system and the interpretation system respectively. These systems are embedded in what we may broadly call the *human cognitive system* (HCS), better known as the human *mind*.

(4)

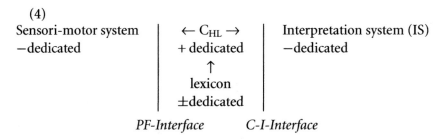

I present this schema here since it enables us to formulate the issues sharply, and properly considered it should not be controversial. Our capacity for language obviously relies on many processes that are not dedicated to language (expressed as −*dedicated* in (4)). Our articulatory system is used for functions varying from eating to respiration. Our auditory system can process sounds irrespective of whether or not they are specific to language. Our thought system can process a variety of information types that reach us through the different channels provided by our senses.

Our lexicon is closely related to our conceptual system, the system that allows us to organize our internal representation of the world around us.[2] The concepts of elephant, sloth, trout, poison ivy, fear, running, hunting are independently important for any being. Hence, they are not dedicated to language. Having them is presumably not even specific to man. Hence, in so far as a concept is part of the lexical entry, such as *sloth, running*, etc., which represents the mapping between these concepts and the arbitrary sound sequence indicated by the italics, such an entry cannot be completely dedicated either.[3] However, the fact that word forms are combinable, that they contain properties that are just there to drive to computation, indicates that certain formal aspects of the lexicon are dedicated to language, hence the characterization ± *dedicated*.

Syntax (C_{HL}) is just the computational system effecting the form—meaning mapping. As we saw in section 11.2, one of the most important questions in the study of the evolution of language is how rich the syntactic system is. The minimalist program seriously explores the idea that the syntactic system is intrinsically very simple, with the following principles:

i. Merge:
  • Combine two expressions into a composite expression
  • Indicate which of the two determines the further combinatorial properties of the result (the "head")
ii. Agree:
  • Check whether two expressions match in features
  • Share feature values[4]

Merge goes only little beyond an operation that any computational system must have by necessity. *Check* does not go beyond the power that any computational system must have that contains an identity predicate. Sharing feature values can in principle be reduced to Merge (overwrite a

---

[2] This schema does not prejudge the "size" of lexical elements: minimal size morphemes, or constructions in the sense of Jackendoff (2002).

[3] In section 11.7 we will discuss some semantic properties of lexical items that cannot be readily understood in conceptual terms.

[4] Often also iii. *Delete* (Don't realize (part of) a certain expression) is give as an item on this list. Discussing it would lead too far afield; properly considered, *delete* reflects a relation between expressions and the form system, rather than that it is part of the computational system itself.

value with a value that was already there).[5] The next section explores some consequences such a simple system would have for our general aim.

11.5 Is there a "clincher" in the evolution towards language?

My discussion of this issue is against the background of the current more general debate about what is special about language, as in Hauser, Chomsky, and Fitch (2002), Pinker and Jackendoff (2005), Fitch, Hauser, and Chomsky (2005), Jackendoff and Pinker (2005). I will not recap this discussion; some of the issues will come up as we proceed. The main issue is what sets us apart in our linguistic abilities from even our most closely related non-human primate family members.

As schematized in (4), the computational system of human language enables a mapping between forms and interpretations. The mapping is based on an inventory of lexical elements representing elementary form–meaning pairs, and a combinatory system. The lexical elements allow access to a conceptual system. Further requirements for language include memory systems (Baddeley 2000, 2001, 2003; Ullman 2004; Coolidge and Wynn 2005, 2006c). Their structure must be such that they allow planning (not just needed for language), and planning in turn involves imagination: the ability to construct models of the world that reflect how it should be—in view of some goals—and compare these with a model reflecting how it is (see Reuland 2005a). Having planning and imagination entails having at least a rudimentary theory of mind (imagining how it would look if I were you, etc.). Summarizing:

(5) Cognitive faculties underlying language
     Realization system

   • Elementary form/meaning combinations
   • Conceptual system
   • Combinatory system

---

[5] If the essence of the linguistic combinatorics does indeed need no more than this, a close relation between the language faculty and mathematics, as suggested by Chomsky—most recently in Chomsky (2005a)—looks quite plausible indeed. Note that a system ensuing from very simple operations need not be "simple" in expressive power, as just a moment's reflection on the basic operations of mathematics and its expressive power shows (Kleene 1952/1971).

Interpretation system
Memory systems
Imagination
  • Planning
  • Theory of Mind (ToM)

This system can be compared to what is found in non-human primates. They have a realization system that is not incompatible with language (either gestures or sound—see Fitch 2006b for an overview of arguments that the import of anatomy should not be overrated). They have a conceptual system, memory systems, and at least rudimentary planning, and some form of ToM (see Bischof-Koehler 2006 for discussion). But, even if they have all these in at least some rudimentary form, they don't have language. Given this, there is an asymmetry. Whereas chimpanzees show some planning capacity under natural conditions, and some ToM under experimental conditions—both rudimentary as compared to humans— their language is not just rudimentary under natural conditions, but absent. Their language under experimental conditions stays far behind given what one would expect if planning and ToM were the decisive factors. The situation is summarized in (6):

(6) Non-humans may have functional homologs of:
  • Expression system
  • Inventory of elements representing elementary form/meaning combinations (under experimental conditions)
  • Conceptual system
  • Interpretation system
  • Memory systems
  • Planning
  • Theory of Mind (rudimentary, under experimental conditions)
  But no rudimentary form of a language in the relevant sense.

The crucial question is then: Why? Hauser, Chomsky, and Fitch (2002), and Fitch, Hauser, and Chomsky (2005) explore the idea that the core of the issue resides in the combinatorics of the syntactic system. To put it simply: Humans have *recursion*, non-humans don't. It is the property of recursion that gives rise to the discrete infinity characteristic of human language. Within the conception of Chomsky (2005) the property of recursion requires no more than Merge in the sense introduced above, concatenation, such that *object*$_1$ + *object*$_2$ → *a composite object of the same type*, hence in turn amenable to concatenation, yielding composite objects in unlimited numbers.

Pinker and Jackendoff (2005) and Jackendoff and Pinker (2005), by contrast, argue that the differences between human and non-human functional homologs in cognitive functions are pervasive. There is no reason to single out recursion and the human *syntactic* combinatory system.

This debate touches on a further fundamental issue: What type or types of evolutionary event could have given rise to language? Take a proto-human in the "final stage" before language: What is language the result of?

- Gradual changes in what was already there?
  - Adaptive, continuous, quantitative, the property has proven its worth, more is obviously better, hence selected for, ... [6]
- Discontinuity
  - A newly emerged property, a qualitative difference, has yet to prove its worth, has not been selected for—although it can be after the event, ...

It is important to see that there can be no evolutionary pressure on a trait without that trait already being there as a "target." Hence, at each turning point in the evolution of a species there must have been an evolutionary event that cannot be understood in adaptive terms. Hence, in our endeavor to understand the origins of language we must focus on those changes that (i) are constitutive of language, and (ii) cannot be gradual; and then look for possible concomitant genetic changes.

Comparing the cognitive faculties underlying language and their functional homologs in non-humans, there is an important asymmetry. With all the caveats about adaptive value, one can imagine a gradual increase in working memory,[7] accuracy of articulation, suppression of breathing, vocal range, speed in lexical access, etc., that could be selected for. But one cannot imagine a gradual increase in *recursivity*: Recursivity is a yes–no

---

[6] There is an important caveat about adaptive value. From the primordial soup evolved species as diverse as: squids, E-Coli, jacaranda trees, lichens, sloths, us, ants, bonobos, cats, corn, ... This relativizes any story about adaptive values. The crucial notion is a niche, a particular type of environment. Any explanation of an evolutionary development in terms of adaptive value must be relativized to a particular niche, which may not be easy to reconstruct.

[7] Much of my discussion of working memory here and in other places in this contribution has been inspired by the intriguing work by Coolidge and Wynn (2005, 2006).

property. There isn't such a thing as a bit of recursivity. This implies that the transition from a system without recursion to a system that has it is necessarily discontinuous.

Therefore, also if Pinker and Jackendoff are right in that recursivity is not the only property that is special to language, there is still a reason to single it out: It is the one property that is non-gradual by necessity.

11.6 The effect of adding recursion to a system without it

As I will show, adding recursion to a system implies a discontinuity in more than one respect. Given the properties of the linguistic space, recursion necessarily alters the nature of signs. To put it a bit provocatively, recursion effectively turns language into a formal system. In order to see why and how, let us take a not uncommon view as a starting point: a protolanguage as a collection of *Saussurean signs*.

Saussure's (1916) conception of a sign is a simple one. A sign is an arbitrary conventional pairing between a form in some medium—a *signifiant*– and a meaning/concept—a *signifié*–as in the venerable example in (7):

(7)

So, a Saussurean sign is a pair:

(8) a. <signifiant, signifié>, or
     b. <f,i>, where *f* is a form in a medium (sound, gesture), and *i* its interpretation as a concept.

Such signs appear to be not incompatible with non-human primate cognitive systems. Yet it is this idea of a sign as the basic linguistic unit which is prevalent in the popular conception of man's linguistic ability as essentially an ability to use symbols, as in Deacon's (1997). It also shows up in the discussion about how to relate archeological findings to the evolution of language, where indications of symbolic behavior are taken as clues for the presence of language, or even the presence of *fully developed syntactic language*. Note, however, that this conception of a sign does not yet accommodate recursion. Recursion minimally requires concatenation, combining two objects into an object of the same type, which is in turn available for concatenation. This entails that linguistic signs must be triples of the general form in (9), rather than pairs as in (8).

(9) $\langle f, g, i \rangle$
     with f and i as above, and g a formal instruction driving the computation

The addition is g, as a formal instruction representing combinability, perhaps a simple "edge feature" in the sense of Chomsky (2005). The addition of g leads us beyond the Saussurean sign. It is a minimal change, *prima facie* trivial perhaps, but it is *qualitative* in nature. Adding this property to the sign opens the door for purely grammatical "machinery."

Discussing recursion and its consequences for the system, the following distinction should be observed:

A. Peripheral recursion: a string of vocabulary items is expanded by adding material at its (right) periphery (this type of grammar is also called a finite state grammar). Using the model of "phrase structure rules" (Chomsky 1959), a very simple set of instructions of this type may have the form:

(10) $S \rightarrow xS; S \rightarrow x$
     x ranges over vocabulary items. If the vocabulary consists of the items a and b, this grammar produces all strings consisting of a's and b's.

There is an important limitation on this type of grammar, namely that it is unable to represent unbounded dependencies. A simple example is given in (11).

B. Embedded recursion. Here, material is not necessarily added at the periphery.

So, suppose one wishes to generate the set of strings over the vocabulary a,b in which each occurrence of a is paired with exactly one b, the following instructions will do:

(11) $S \rightarrow aSb; S \rightarrow ab$
     Write down *ab* and put in the middle another pair *ab*, etc., and stop at some point. This yields the set of strings ab;aabb;aaabbb, ... $a^n b^n$

(11) is a typical instance of recursion: calling an instruction, while carrying out that same instruction. Note that (11) allows one to match *a*'s and *b*'s without an upper bound on the number of paired elements.

The rules in (11) exemplify a *Context Free phrase structure grammar*. The one given here is a very simple one. More complicated patterns may be generated by allowing recursion over more than one category, as in (12), which reflects a simple sentential structure, with S standing for sentence, NP for noun phrase and VP for verb phrase:

(12) S → NP VP, NP → ...; VP →....

In the expansion of VP one may encounter NP's, for instance when the sentence has a direct object; in the expansion of NP one may encounter S's and VP's, for instance when the NP has a relative clause, etc. (13) illustrates this pattern:

(13)

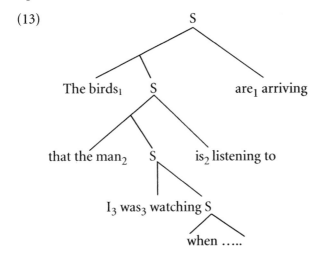

(13) shows a dependency between *the birds* and *are*, separated by a dependency between *the man* and *is*, in turn separated by the dependency between *I* and *was*. Note that at many points there can be further expansion. Adjectives can be added to *man* and *birds*, adverbial modifiers to *arriving, listening, watching*, both as single adverbs, and in the form of full clauses like the *when*-clause indicated. When the structure is put on paper it may seem that little changes in principle by a "transition" from peripheral to embedded recursion. But a moment's reflection shows that appearances are deceptive.

Language is realized along a temporal-spatial dimension. Hence, an instruction such as "write down *ab* and put in the middle another pair *ab*, etc.," cannot be carried out. What is possible goes as follows. While carrying out an instruction it may be temporarily halted, another instruction or instance of the first one may be started, and the system will only return to the initial instruction after completing the second one, etc. So, in the case of $a^n b^n$, the procedure starts the instruction of writing a pair $<a,b>$, but temporarily halts this instruction after writing *a*, retains in memory that at some point a *b* has to follow, starts writing the next pair, writes *a*, halts, etc., and after writing the last *a* and the first *b*, returns to the pre-final instruction, carries it out, returns to the next instruction waiting in line, etc. until the store is empty.

Thus, given the properties of the medium, embedded recursion requires that you internally represent material before and after you realize it. You must keep track of what you have done in order to carry out what you have to do. That is, the process involves planning, and sufficient working memory to be able to do the planning.

This has a further non-trivial consequence. While peripheral recursion affects the sign required by a grammatical feature to be added, embedded recursion disrupts the unity of the sign. Planning puts demands on the elements it operates on. These elements can no longer have the form in (9), repeated in (14a), rather they must have the form in (14b):

(14) a. $<f, g, i>$, with f a representation in a medium and i a concept.
    b. $<c_f, g, c_i>$, where c_f and c_i are formal mental encodings of relations with the language external systems of realization and interpretation.

Thus, what must be stored is not the sign, but the instruction to create a sign. What the combinatorial system operates on, are therefore not the signs, but the instructions to form signs. Effectively, this is a further qualitative change. It turns language into a formal system. So, in the case of Saussurean signs "handover" to realization and interpretation systems must take place sequentially:

(15) I_1 I_2 I_3 I_4
    ↑ ↑ ↑ ↑
    S_1 S_2 S_3 S_4
    ↓ ↓ ↓ ↓
    F_1 F_2 F_3 F_4

In the case of embedded recursion, handover takes place in packages, where LI stands for *lexical item*, and I and F for *interpretation* and *form* as earlier:

(16)

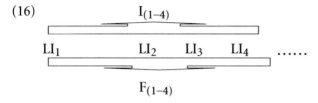

The counterpart in this system to the original notion of a sign—if one would look for it—is the complexes, rather than individual lexical items. The complexes in (16) get interpreted not just on the basis of the individual lexical items but also on the basis of their relations, reflected in the way in which the complex has been put together. A trivial illustration of the role of structure is the contrast between *mice chase cats*, and *cats chase mice*, *mice cats chase*. Same words, different structures, different interpretations. Hence, a more appropriate rendering of (16) can be given as in (17):

(17)

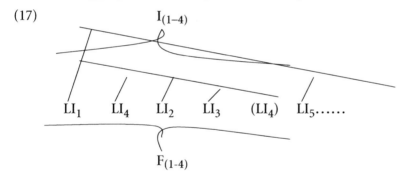

(17) expresses that what is handed over to the realization and interpretation systems are structured packages. The contribution lexical items make to interpretation is determined in part by their own internal properties, in part by their position in the structure, as was illustrated by the mice chasing cats. Because interpretability is a condition on the package as a whole, elements with minimal direct contribution to the interpretation can arise: "LIs" marking relations between expressions.

Consider, for instance, the sentence in (18):

(18) The Vandals *will* depend <u>on</u> the destruction <u>of</u> Rome for their place in history.

It is clear than one can associate with *the Vandals* an entity in the external world, a particular tribe, and with *Rome* a particular city. The nouns *destruction, place, history* are all associated with concepts, as is the verb *depend*. However, upon just a little reflection it will be clear that no concept is associated with the prepositions *on* and *of* in this sentence. There is simply no answer to the question of what they *mean* in this sentence. They do contribute to the interpretation, however. *On* formally marks the relation between the verb *depend* and its complement the *destruction of Rome*, and *of* marks the relation between the noun *destruction* and its complement *Rome*. While *on* and *of* are purely formal markers here, the prepositions *for* and *in* can be argued to carry an independent meaning, in addition to marking a formal relation. What about determiners such as *the*? Again, it is impossible to find a concept they express. What they do is link the utterance to the discourse. For *the* to be used felicitously, there must be a uniquely identifiable element in the discourse as a value for the expression that is headed by *the*. To use a venerable example, the sentence *The present king of France is bald* is infelicitous since there is no present king of France. In the verbal domain something similar can be said about *will*. It places the proposition expressed by the sentence in the future— that is, links it to discourse—but is not itself associated with a lexical concept.

Sometimes expressions play a dual role, as is illustrated in (19):

(19) Which city did the Vandals destroy?

Which city has, on the one hand, the role of the object of *destroy*. On the other hand, it marks the sentence as a question. Such a dual use of expressions is a hallmark of natural language. A standard way of expressing it is by a copying operation, as in (20):

(20) <u>Which city</u> did the Vandals destroy (which city)

The copy in brackets is in the canonical object position, hence reflects its role as an object; the fronted copy is in the position where canonically the force of a sentence (question, assertion) is expressed, hence marks the sentence as a question. The lower copy is put in brackets to indicate that it is not sent off to the realization system. Note that the claim that *which city* performs a dual role is independent of one's pet theory of natural language. There is a number of theoretical proposals as to how precisely the relation between the fronted element and the verb is computed. (20)

just sketches one—parsimonious—proposal as it has been developed in Chomsky (1995) and subsequent literature.

The lower copy in (20) is an instance of an element that does play a role in the computations the language system has to perform, but is not independently realized in the linguistic form. Just as on the form side we find elements such as *on* and *of* that only make their contribution to interpretation indirectly, there are elements that play a role in interpretation but are only indirectly realized at the form side. (21) illustrates the role of so-called null subjects in languages such as Italian. As (21a) shows, in Italian the form *odia* can be combined with a third person subject, *Gianni*. Here the direct object is the anaphor, *se stesso* "himself". Just like English *himself*, *se stesso* must have an antecedent. In (21b) the subject is omitted. This Italian sentence is equivalent to its English counterpart with a pronominal.

(21) a. Gianni odia se stesso
        Gianni hates himself
    b. Odia se stesso
       He hates himself

So, whereas in English the pronominal is obligatory, in Italian it may be absent, and is in fact preferred to be absent. Yet, the anaphor *se stesso* is interpreted as if it has a normal antecedent. The simplest story is then that Italian allows a pronominal element not to be directly expressed. The computational system operates with a pronominal element just like *he* in English. A property of Italian—which it shares with a great many languages—is that it allows this element not to be directly expressed. Why the phrasing "directly"? Irrespective of the details, the basic mechanism is that it is the rich inflectional system of Italian which—unlike English—allows the presence of this pronominal to be reconstructed. And, coming back to the discussion in section 11.3, it is interpretation by binding itself—instead of reference to objects—which depends on language as a formal system.

Because realization and interpretation take place in packages, and realizability and interpretability are conditions on whole packages, both null elements (lacking an independent instruction for realization) and purely grammatical elements (lacking an independent instruction for interpretation) can arise and be used.

Thus, severing the direct connection between form and interpretation, as necessitated by embedded recursion realized in a linear medium, leads to what may well be the most characteristic property of language:

(22) Desymbolization

11.7 Desymbolization and beyond

Having LI's as purely mental objects severed from direct realization and interpretation opens the door for core properties of language as we know it:

(23) Core properties of language:
- "Abstract" functional categories
  - Articles, auxiliaries, complementizers
- Formal encoding of dependencies by markers such as Case and Agreement
  - Der Verkaüfer gibt dem Mann den Schein
    The sales man gives the man the ticket
- Null-elements
  - *pro* odia se stesso
  - Bill will love his cat and Charles will <del>love his cat</del> too
- Quantificational structures
  - The man who gives his paycheck to his wife is wiser than the man who gives it to his mistress
- Dual use of expressions
  - What did John think Mary asked Peter to do (<del>what</del>)

Due to desymbolization, language allows operations to apply blindly, irrespective of meaning. If the linguistic combinatory system operates without regard to meaning this has two important consequences. On the one hand it enables unconstrained creativity; on the other it enables an efficient use of limited processing resources.

Creativity is unleashed if anaphors are assigned their antecedents with complete disregard for what are possible states of affairs, as in *the magician put himself under himself*, or if morphology and configuration govern the assignment of arguments to predicates equally blindly. *John worries his fate* is not interpreted as *his fate worries John*, despite the fact that only the latter appears to make sense. The formal rules of language allow us to talk about square circles, colorless green ideas, parallel lines intersecting at infinity, black or white holes—and why they can or cannot exist— curved spaces, quantum leaps, Schroedinger's cat, etc. Desymbolization of language allows us to ignore common sense, play with expectations, say the impossible, model what is not the case, express the inconceivable, escape from the here and now, and create poetry. In the end desymbolization feeds into imagination and gives rise to the richness and diversity of human culture as we know it.

The effectiveness of desymbolization of language clearly depends on working memory. Working memory should be able to hold interpretable (proposition-sized) chunks. Such chunks in principle correspond with "phases" in current versions of generative grammar (Chomsky 1995 and related work). But on the other hand, desymbolization reduces the load on working memory if the complexity of the task is held constant.

It is independently known from the study of individuals with reduced processing resources (children, agrammatic aphasics) that such reduction substantially influences linguistic behavior (specifically the ability to handle pronominals and anaphors, functional structure, quantification) (see Avrutin 2001 for an overview). Recent experimental work (Koornneef et al. 2006) has shown that in determining anaphoric dependencies the human processor initially takes the quick and dirty route, while incorporating discourse information later. This indicates that the capacity of the human processor just about meets the requirements of the language system, but does not have substantial "free space." There is a measurable cost associated with dragging meaning and discourse information along, while carrying out linguistic computations. If so, this also puts a bonus on purely formal operations.

Again, the necessary evolutionary event need have been no more than the event enabling manipulations of instructions rather than full signs. But restrictions on processing capacity favor making the computations as efficient as possible—that is, making use of functional elements to encode relations that will be interpreted in the end where available. But still, a minimal processing capacity would have been needed to get the process going at all. What is crucial from our present perspective is that this leads to the thesis in (24):

(24)   A qualitative change may depend for its effectiveness on a quantitative change

Consequently it is important to distinguish between stages (3b) and (3c) in the evolution of humanity. It is logically possible that the genetic event responsible for the discontinuity required for embedded recursion, i.e. the event enabling the emergence of combinability—which we might equate with the option to hold an LI in working memory, postponing its realization and interpretation—occurred at a stage when working memory was not yet able to hold proposition-size chunks. This could then have been followed by gradual increase in working memory driven by language-independent factors. This entails that on this model there could have been a time lag—perhaps substantial—between the emergence of the language faculty, that is the moment that language became *possible*, and the time the language faculty became fully *usable*. This provides an interesting perspective on the monogenesis of language, again, exploring logical possibilities.

Clearly, the event allowing embedded recursion is constitutive of language, and must be shared by all humans. Similarly, an event *allowing* the expansion of working memory must also be shared. However, what cannot be excluded is that the actual—gradual—expansion of working memory was driven by an evolutionary process within a sufficiently similar niche as determined by a common evolutionary path, but completed in different populations after migration had set in, for instance after the exodus from Africa. If so, it is possible for language as we know it to have started in different places. But, note, this is only a logical possibility. It is equally well possible that a substantial enough working memory was already in place at the moment the conditions for recursion came to be met. If so, language may well have arisen without much time lag, and monogenesis is reasonable.

Interestingly, only the first option is compatible with speculations about protolanguage as an impoverished system, and various restricted language systems as providing windows into the genesis of language (Arbib 2004; Botha 2006; Jackendoff 1999, 2002).

Many (or even all) functional elements derive from full lexical items by *grammaticalization*, a process by which lexical elements become semantically bleached, and in the end lose their lexical semantics entirely. From the current perspective the pervasive role of grammaticalization processes in natural language has a deeper cause than just "wear and tear," but derives from computational optimization—kept in check by the fact that not every lexical element can become grammaticalized, assuming some content has to be expressed in the end.

What does this tell us about the first stage of natural language after it emerged? Clearly, grammaticalization must have been an important factor right from the start, and it should not have taken much more than a generation after the event for functional elements to develop. What if processing capacity of early humans was still limited as compared to ours? If so, the need to opt for content may have affected the use of functional elements, just like it does in agrammatic aphasics. Therefore, here too, it is of the utmost importance to separate claims about a system from claims about its use.

Desymbolization turns language into a formal system, and therefore can be viewed as a biological precursor of our recent electronic revolution. In a nutshell we can summarize the following stages in the development from concept to imagination:

(25) Stages of development

- Forming an internal model of the external world, evaluating its possible subsequent states, selecting one, selecting actions to make that one true-goal directed behavior
- Forming an internal model of the external/internal world including the—presumed—mental state of (one of) its actants, evaluating its possible subsequent states, selecting one and selecting actions to make that one true—manipulation/deception
- ... ...
- Forming an internal model of the external/internal world including the—presumed—mental state of (one of) its actants and including one's own mental state, evaluating its possible subsequent states and changing it
- Imagining the future: escaping the limits of the material world (Bischof-Koehler 2006)

Representing what the other is representing (including what the other is representing about what others are representing about...including oneself) is facilitated by the ability to manipulate elements in which form and interpretation are severed: Create, interpret later. This, for one thing, also leads to a recursive ToM, another hallmark of humanity.

11.8 By way of conclusion: language and the archeological record

It should be clear from the discussion so far, that evidence of symbolic activity by itself is not a proper diagnostic of the presence of language. Symbolic behavior is a precondition for language, not sufficient. So, shells with holes, use of ochre, etc. are insufficient to show the presence of "fully syntactic language." (see also *The Cradle*: chapter 5.) This leaves open the possibility that certain types of symbolic behavior would turn out to be sufficient.

Consider, for instance, a figurine such as the lion man from Hohlenstein-Stadel,[8] crucially depicting an impossible object. One may certainly argue that a figurine depicting an impossible object can only have been conceived of by an ancestor able to manipulate concepts independently from their literal interpretation. That is, put two concepts together and then see what the result means—and make it. However, the oldest finds of such impossible objects date from relatively recent times—around 30,000 years BP.

If the cradle of humanity lies in Africa and the exodus of modern humans from Africa took place as early as around 85,000 years BP (Oppenheimer 2004), the crucial evolutionary event must have taken place before that, hence far before 30,000 BP. Hence one should look for other—older—types of evidence.[9] A possible source is the occurrence of recursive decorations on artifacts. One could argue that the ability to produce recursive

---

[8] On display in the archeological collection of the Museum in Ulm.
[9] The absence of older impossible figurines must then be attributed to other factors, such as chance of discovery or decay of material. Or even the fact that even now the occurrence of people who really transcend the bounds of their time (da Vinci, Galilei, Newton, Einstein) is extremely rare.

patterns in one domain is a reasonable indication for recursive capabilities in another. And given our discussion so far, recursion is a constitutive property of language. However, in order to really serve as an indication the pattern should be more complex than mere iteration, as in the standard repetitive designs. It would be highly interesting to know whether such more complex patterns have actually been found.[10]

A last potential source of evidence is the complexity of collaborative tasks.[11] One could argue that certain tasks, such as building rafts to travel significant distances at sea, as had to be done for humans to reach Australia via the islands of the Indonesian archipelago, require a substantial degree of division of labor and subsequent coordination. A crucial factor is that the tasks involved cannot be shared and coordinated by mere inspection— you watch what I do and imitate it. If they cannot, one could argue that the requisite division of labor must involve explicit instruction. Even so, this need not entail a "fully syntactic language." For the latter, one would require instructions going beyond the here and now, involving temporal reference, perspective, as in *I order you to...*, *I think that you...*, and quantification (*every x, all x, most x, a few x, 1,2,3, ... x*, etc.). Interestingly, this is an issue where one need not be satisfied with indirect evidence and speculation: A realistic experiment can be set up. One could devise a task as complex as mounting an expedition by raft—taking into account that the first endeavor of this type must have been the more daunting for the lack of any precedent—and determine how much linguistic information-sharing it would require to be successfully completed. In a nutshell: Could it be completed by a group of humans deprived of other ways of communicating than imitation-intention reading? If not, this would be a strong indication that the groups of humans successfully completing such an enterprise had language. Moreover, this could serve as a more general model, since seafaring is not the only feat early humans had to accomplish.

---

[10] Of course, since a decorative pattern is always finite, formally it could always be captured by a finite state machine. Yet, it is conceivable that one could find patterns showing self-embedding in such a way that a generalization of that pattern would lead to a system beyond finite state.

[11] This issue came up in a discussion with Chris Knight during the Cradle of Language conference.

Thus, to answer the question of how one can correlate the emergence of language with independent findings, we should systematically identify complex tasks that we can establish our ancestors have carried out[12] and then show that their completion requires desymbolized language as we know it.

---

[12] Fred Coolidge (personal communication) drew my attention to a particular endeavor by Stiner and Kuhn (2007). They argue that around 50,000 BP a significant change in the nature of collaborative tasks occurred in the Mediterranean area, together with a shift in diet toward smaller animals. This time period also contains the first evidence of art and small-tools activities like sewing. They suggest a connection between how much cooperation labor requires, and how it is divided among the group members. They further link it to a broad cultural shift that led to increasingly different roles for prehistoric men and women. This is then a further example of a type of collaborative task that could be formally modeled and put to a test as indicated in the text. Of course, as in other cases of changes dated after the human exodus from Africa this hypothesis raises many further issues about the time frame and the relation of these changes to human cognitive development in general. Addressing these issues would lead me far beyond the scope of this article.

12 Grammaticalization from a biolinguistic perspective

ELLY VAN GELDEREN

12.1 Introduction

Estimates about the origin of modern human language range from 50,000 to 150,000 years ago. These estimates are based on archeological findings, the presence of tools and beads in e.g. the Blombos cave at 70,000 years ago, and mutations in a gene connected to speech (FOXP2) at about 120,000 years ago. Genetics and archeology work well together and suggest a homeland for modern humans in Africa. What can linguistics contribute to this picture? In this chapter, I show that a biolinguistic approach (e.g. Chomsky 2005b, 2007) has much to offer. In this introduction, I first briefly mention some other linguistic approaches that geneticists and others have often turned to, namely genetic and areal linguistics. In the remainder of the chapter, I argue for a biolinguistic approach.

Genetic linguistics provides insights into linguistic relationships, and areal linguistics can show which features are typical for the areas where language is supposed to have started. Genetic groupings such as the four families in Africa and the three in the Americas are much contested (see the criticism Greenberg received throughout his life). Areal linguistics (e.g. Nichols 1992; Haspelmath et al. 2006) shows us more about recent trends than about original features. For instance, since Dryer's (1999) maps of Object–Verb and Verb–Object distributions show both orders in Central Africa and we know that these orders can change quickly, this approach cannot be used to give us insight into an earlier state.

Thanks to audiences in Oslo, Stellenbosch, and Montreal and especially to Harry Bracken, Terje Lohndal, and Eric Reuland for very useful discussion and comments on an earlier version.

In this chapter, I will therefore examine what (historical) syntax has to say when couched within a biolinguistic framework. Hauser, Chomsky, and Fitch (2002) argue that recursion sets human language apart from animal communication and Chomsky (2005b: 11) specifies this further by saying that Merge, linking two elements, was the " 'Great Leap Forward' in the evolution of humans." Likewise, Piattelli-Palmarini and Uriagereka (2005) emphasize the role of recursion and Merge. Some principles follow for free from Merge and some from general cognitive principles. The emergence of a binary merge brings with it certain relations, such as heads and elements merged with heads into phrases, and c-command, as will be explained below. Heads and phrases, merged in binary fashion, in turn define argument structure or thematic structure. Organizing the thematic layer through Merge is one aspect relevant to the evolution of language. I will argue that grammaticalization was the other step, though not a mutation, responsible for markings in the grammatical layer. Typical grammaticalizations are prepositions starting to function as case markers, verbs as auxiliaries and affixes, and pronouns as agreement morphemes. These changes are cyclical and continue to occur in contemporary languages. These changes, I argue, can be seen in terms of cognitive economy of the syntactic derivation, e.g. semantically "lighter" elements are preferred over "heavier" ones. The evidence for these claims, and also for the nature of early language, comes from observable linguistic changes.

The outline is as follows. In section 12.2, I present a very general picture of the Minimalist Program, and in particular its biolinguistic focus. This framework is elaborated on in section 12.3, especially where the operation Merge is concerned. In sections 12.4 and 12.5, grammaticalization is the focus. I discuss how it follows from economy and how it is relevant to language evolution. Section 12.6 is a conclusion.

12.2 A Minimalist sketch of the language organ

Starting in the 1950s, Chomsky and the generative model he develops present an alternative to then current behaviorist and structuralist frameworks. Chomsky focusses not on the structures present in the language/outside world but on the mind of a language learner/user. The input to language learning is seen as poor (the "poverty of the stimulus" argument) since speakers know so much more than what they have evidence for in their input. How do we know so much on the basis of such impoverished data? The answer to this problem, "Plato's Problem" in Chomsky (1986), is universal grammar (henceforth UG), the initial state of the faculty of language, a biologically innate organ. UG helps the learner make sense of the data and build up an internal grammar.

Initially, many principles were attributed to UG, but currently (e.g. Chomsky 2004, 2005b, 2007) there is an emphasis on principles not specific to the faculty of language, i.e. UG, but to "general properties of organic systems" (Chomsky 2004: 105), also called "third factor principles" in Chomsky (2005b). Merge is one such operation that can be seen as a UG principle but also as one possibly "appropriated from other systems" (Chomsky 2007: 7) and relevant to other systems. In this chapter, I argue that economy principles are such general cognitive principles.

The biolinguistic angle also makes us ask (a) what the structure of the language organ is and (b) why it is this way. The answer to the first question may be that it uses Merge or recursion and the answer to the second question would lie in the relation between the Narrow Syntax and demands of other organs, e.g. the sensory motor one. Thus, there is a Narrow Syntax (with Merge) and mappings to two interfaces, the sensory-motor interface, PHON, and the conceptual-intentional one, SEM. As mentioned, Chomsky has suggested that some rewiring of the brain, a small mutation or the result of one, brought about Merge. Merge, linking two elements, was the "great leap forward" in the evolution of humans. "The individual so endowed [with Merge] would have the ability to think, plan, interpret, and so on." Then, "[a]t some stage modes of externalization were contrived" (Chomsky 2007: 14). Phonology and morphology are involved in the externalization and are highly varied since there are no universal principles involved, unlike with Merge.

Work on animal communication has shown that animals use symbols. Bickerton (1990, 2000) has argued that animal communication probably uses thematic structure, i.e. SEM, but no recursion of structures, i.e. Merge. We know that some animals have an impressive set of sounds, so PHON, but not a large vocabulary. Chomsky entertains both the possibility that syntax was "inserted into already existing external systems," namely the sensory-motor system, PHON, and system of thought, SEM (Chomsky 2002: 108), as well as the one where the externalization develops after Merge (Chomsky 2007: 14). Figure 12.1 shows the three components of human language. I will assume that Merge appears after SEM and PHON

symbolic	
thematic	=SEM
sounds	
vocabulary	=PHON
Merge/recursion	
grammaticalization	=Narrow Syntax

FIG. 12.1. Three separate systems

are already developed, but for the purpose of this chapter nothing hinges on this.

The vocabulary develops after sounds are abundant enough (see Carstairs-McCarthy 1999). One could see this as a result of Merge as well.

Merge comes in two kinds, Internal and External Merge. Chomsky (2005b: 14) suggests that External Merge is relevant to the argument structure, whereas Internal Merge is relevant for scope and discourse phenomena, as in Figure 12.2. This means External Merge may have been an early feature of language. The longest utterance of Nim, a chimpanzee trained by Terrace in the 1970s, is apparently (1).

(1) Give orange me give eat orange me eat orange give me eat orange give me you.

This sentence obviously has thematic structure, but this is not expressed in the hierarchical way that human language is. (External) Merge helped organize the thematic structure in human language. In many languages, marking the thematic positions is done through pure Merge (e.g. Chinese, English), but in some languages, inherent Case and adpositions mark thematic roles (e.g. Sanskrit, Latin, Malayalam, Japanese, Tagalog). This special marking has come about through grammaticalization of location and instrument markers to case markers. Definiteness and specificity are the second semantic aspect that needs to be marked. The differences between the two kinds of Merge are listed in Figure 12.2.

Austronesian languages that mark topic show a difference in morphology for the two systems of Merge. As is well known, Tagalog marks its topic through *ang*, as shown in (2). This topic marker is a definiteness

Merge:	External Merge	-	Internal Merge
	=		=
	Theta		Discourse/Quantification
Grammaticalized through:			
	adpositions/inherent Case		definiteness/displacement

FIG. 12.2. The two kinds of Merge

marker as well (technically, only *a-* is and *-ng* is a ligature linking the article to the noun, according to Frawley 1976). The other markers *ng* (for Actor, Patient, and Instrument) and *sa* (for Goal, Source, Location, and Benefactive) mark the theta-roles of the non-topics, and derive from location markers (Finney 1999):

(2) b-um-ili   ng kotse ang lalake
    AF-PF-buy P car   TP man
    "The man bought a car" (Tagalog; Frawley 1976: 106)

This picture suggests that syntax and morphology evolved independently. Some have argued that they are therefore separate systems, e.g. Jackendoff (2002: 260). Bobaljik (2006) too has agreement adding features after Narrow Syntax. I will make plausible that External Merge emerged first, followed by Internal Merge. Grammaticalization affected both, however.

12.3 How does Merge work?

I will now turn to an abstract model of how a sentence is produced using a Minimalist approach. There is a lexicon from which lexical items are selected, after which Merge combines two items, e.g. *know* and *it* in (3), and one of the two heads projects, in this case V, to a higher VP:

(3)

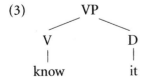

The items that merge are not arbitrarily selected. The head is searching to satisfy a feature, e.g. a thematic one in (3). The head is also the one projecting up, and this projection can then in its turn be selected. The VP domain is the thematic layer, i.e. where the argument structure is determined.

Apart from Merge, there are "atomic elements, lexical items LI, each a structured array of properties (*features*)" (Chomsky 2007: 6). Each language learner selects the features compatible with the input. Thus, the features are parameterized; not the syntax. Features come in two kinds. Interpretable ones include number on nouns and are interpreted by the conceptual-intentional interface, i.e. are relevant to the meaning of a sentence. Uninterpretable features are grammatical in nature, and include agreement features (also known as phi-features) on verbs and Case features on nouns. These uninterpretable features need to be valued and deleted since they are not relevant to the meaning. In Figure 12.1, the SEM level would have only interpretable features, whereas Narrow Syntax would work with both.

I will suggest that the uninterpretable features were not present during the stage at which Merge appeared originally. They were added through language change prompted by economy principles, grammaticalization, and ended up incorporating distinctions having to do with specificity, topicality, and quantification. Continuing the derivation in (3) will hopefully make the function of features clearer.

A sentence consists of three layers: a VP with basic information about the arguments; a TP where tense, mood, and aspect are expressed; and a CP where the sentence type is indicated, e.g. a question or assertion. In a language such as Modern English, T has interpretable tense features but uninterpretable phi-features. It probes ("looks down the tree") for a nominal to agree with. It finds this nominal ("goal") in *they* and each element values its uninterpretable features: the noun's Case as nominative and the verb's phi-features as third person plural. The final structure will look like (4), where the features that are not "struck through" are interpretable. The subject moves to Spec TP for language-specific reasons:[1]

---

[1] The derivation in (4) uses early lexical insertion, i.e. a lexicalist approach, as in Chomsky (1995, 2004). For the purposes of this paper, nothing hinges on this. Note that Merge is neutral as to where lexical insertion takes place; I will add lexical items in the tree for convenience.

(4)

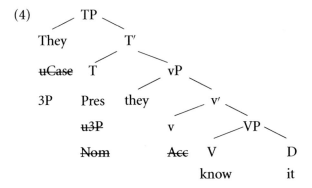

The reason the effects of Merge are so far-reaching is that structures made by Merge involve heads, complements (or first-merged), and specifiers (or second-merged). Merge, thus, automatically brings with it the structural relations shown in Figure 12.3.

A lot can of course be said about each of these. For instance, it has been argued that all languages are right-branching as in (i) in Figure 12.3. This would mean there are no headedness parameters. Pidgins and creoles are typically SVO, however, i.e. (bi), and this may also be the proto-order, though e.g. Newmeyer (2000) argues that the protolanguage was SOV, i.e. (ii).

Turning to language evolution, languages closer to the protolanguage will have Merge but there is no reason they would have Move (Internal Merge) and Agree/Probing as in (4) (though Newmeyer 2000: 385, n. 4 suggests that protolanguages may have been inflectional). My focus on grammaticalization as a process responsible for morphology assumes that agreement and Case arise later (see Reuland, this volume, for another view).

---

a. Merge involves projection, hence headedness, specifiers, and complements.

b. The binary character of Merge results in either:

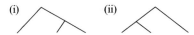

c. There is c-command of the specifier over (the head and) the complement, resulting in the special nature of the specifier.

Fig. 12.3. Relations connected with Merge

So, the first step in the evolution of syntax is Merge. It brings with it notions of headedness (once you merge two elements, one determines the resulting label) and structural hierarchy. These notions also determine possible argument structures. The next step is for grammatical heads, such as auxiliaries and prepositions, to appear, as we will discuss in section 12.4.

12.4 Grammaticalization

As is well known, grammaticalization is a process whereby lexical items lose phonological weight and semantic specificity and gain grammatical functions.

Grammaticalization has frequently been investigated in a functionalist framework. Recently, however, structural accounts have started to appear (e.g. Abraham 1993; Roberts and Roussou 2003; van Gelderen 2004) accounting for the cyclicity of the changes involved. Van Gelderen, for instance, uses economy principles that help the learner acquire a grammar that is more economical, and as a side effect more grammaticalized.

Two economy principles, provided as (5) and (8) below, are formulated in van Gelderen (2004). They are part of the cognitive system and help learners construct a grammar. Principle (5) is at work in the internalized grammar and holds for Merge (projection) as well as Move (checking). It is most likely not a principle specific to language but a property of organic systems, such as if you want to carry an object, you don't also carry the table on which the object is situated:

(5) **Head Preference Principle (HPP)**
　　　Be a head, rather than a phrase.

This means that a speaker will prefer to build structures such as (6a) rather than (6b). The pronoun is merged in the head position in (6a), and in the specifier position in (6b). Specifier positions can accommodate entire phrases but require an additional merge:

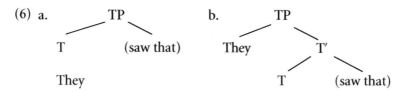

The speaker will only use (6b) for structures where a phrase is necessary, e.g. coordinates such as *you and I*. In some languages, there are prescriptive rules stopping this change (as there are in French; see Lambrecht 1981).

Under a Minimalist view of change, syntax is inert and doesn't change; it is the lexical items that are reanalyzed.[2] Pronouns are reanalyzed from emphatic full phrases to clitic pronouns to agreement markers, and negatives from full DPs to negative adverb phrases to heads. This change is slow, however, since a child learning the language will continue to have input of, for instance, a pronoun as both a phrase and a head. Lightfoot (1999) develops an approach as to how much input a child needs before it resets a parameter. In the case of pronouns changing to agreement markers, there will have to be a large input of structures that provide evidence to the child that the full phrase is no longer analyzed as that. This is already the case in French since the pronoun is always adjacent to the finite verb in spoken French. The child, therefore, always produces the pronoun in that position, even though regular subjects can precede or follow the verb (see Pierce 1992). However, rather than blame the change on a changed input (a cue), I blame it on factors internal to language and cognition.

Another instance of the HPP is the well-known fact that native speakers of English (and other languages) producing relative clauses prefer to use the head of the CP (the complementizer *that*) rather than the specifier (the relative pronoun *who*) by a ratio of 9:1 in speech. In addition, speakers strand prepositions in speech. For instance, children acquiring their language obey this same economy principle. Thus, according to Diessel (2004), young children produce only stranded constructions in English, as in (7a), using the head *that*, and not the version where the entire Preposition Phrase is fronted, as in (7b):

(7) a. those little things **that** you play **with**
        (Adam 4:10, from Diessel 2004: 137)
    b. those little things **with which** you play

Once they become (young) adults, they are taught to take the preposition along and to disobey the HPP.

The Head Preference Principle is relevant to a number of historical changes: Whenever possible, a word is seen as a head rather than a phrase. Examples of changes predicted by the HPP are given in Table 12.1.

---

[2] The word "reanalysis" is used to emphasize that the language changes; of course the child analyzes.

TABLE 12.1. *Examples of reanalysis due to the Head Preference Principle*

Relative pronoun *that* to complementizer	Demonstrative to article
Negative adverb to negation marker	Adverb to aspect marker
Adverb to complementizer	Full pronoun to agreement

Within Minimalism, there is a second economy principle that is relevant to grammaticalization. Combining lexical items to construct a sentence, i.e. merging them, "comes 'free' in that it is required in some form for any recursive system" (Chomsky 2004: 108) and is "inescapable" (Chomsky 1995: 316, 378). Initially, a distinction was made between Merge and Move and it was less economical to merge early and then move than to wait as long as possible before merging. In van Gelderen (2004), this is formulated as in (8):

(8) **Late Merge Principle (LMP)**
       Merge as late as possible

In later Minimalism, Merge is reformulated as External Merge and Move as Internal Merge, with no distinction in status. One could argue that (8) is still valid since the special Merge, i.e. Internal Merge, requires steps additional to those that Merge, i.e. External Merge, requires. The extra step is the inclusion in the numeration of copies in the case of Internal Merge. Traces are not allowed, since they would introduce new material into the derivation after the initial selection, and therefore copies of elements to be moved have to be included in the lexical selection. Move/Internal Merge is not just Move but "Copy, Merge, and Delete." Since the numeration has to contain more copies of the lexical item to be internally merged, and since those copies have to be deleted in the case of traditional Move, (8) could still hold as an economy principle.

As mentioned, Chomsky (2005b: 14) suggests a real difference between the two kinds: External Merge is relevant to the argument structure, whereas Internal Merge is relevant for scope and discourse phenomena. This indicates a crucial difference between the two kinds of operations, and nicely expresses the intuition that External Merge is the Merge that made possible "the great leap" and that Internal Merge was brought about by the workings of the cognitive system. In section 12.6, I provide a way of reformulating the LMP: If the set of lexical items taken from the lexicon contains elements whose properties are less relevant to the thematic structure (External Merge), they can be used with fewer thematic, i.e. interpretable, features.

The Late Merge Principle works most clearly in the case of heads. Their grammaticalization path is always to higher functional categories. The history of *after* presents an interesting example. The preposition and adverb in Old English, according to the OED, indicate place (or order) or time, as in (9), and manner, where *according to* would be the modern equivalent:

(9) Fand þa ðær inn æþelinga gedriht swefan **æfter**
found then there in noble company sleeping after
symble
feast
"He found therein a company of nobles sleeping after their feast".

(Beowulf 118-119)[3]

Of the forty-one instances of *after* in the relatively early *Beowulf*, only one occurs inside a fronted PP and in the *Christ* from the *Exeter Book*, again an early text, there is none out of fifteen. The objects of these prepositions are full nouns or personal pronouns. None of these introduces a subordinate sentence.

This changes in later texts in that the PPs are fronted more often and the object of *after* is a demonstrative. The version of the *Anglo-Saxon Chronicle* known as *Chronicle A* contains entries that up to 891 are copied by Hand I but after 892 are entered for each year. Before 892, *after* is followed by a noun or pronoun and rarely (8%) by a demonstrative; the PP is preposed in 27% of the cases. In the later parts (i.e. entered after 892), many of the objects of *after* are demonstratives, as in (10), namely 17 out of 22 (= 77%). That the demonstrative preference starts so clearly with the entries of 892 might indicate that the language is closer to that which might have been spoken around 900:

(10) Her forðferde Wulfstan diacon...7 **æfter þon** forðferde Gyric mæsse preost.
"In this year died Wulfstan ... and after that died Gyric the priest".

(*Chronicle A*, entry for the year 963)

---

[3] References to *Beowulf* are from the Klaeber edition, to the *Anglo-Saxon Chronicle* from Thorpe, to the Old English Gospel from Skeat, and to the *Paston Letters* from Davis. Others are taken from the OED.

TABLE 12.2. *Percentages of demonstrative (Dem) objects with* after *and fronting of the PP*

	Beowulf	< 892 Chron A	> 892 Chron A
Dem object	0	2/26 = 8%	17/22 = 77%
Fronting	1/41 = 2%	7/26 = 27%	12/22 = 55%

The use of the demonstrative object in (10) indicates that the PP *æfter þon* is starting to be analyzed as an adverb linking the sentence to another. This is confirmed by the frequent fronting of the PP (12 out of 22 = 55%), as also shown by (10). The fronting can be seen as a consequence of Late Merge. In Table 12.2, the differences for *Beowulf*, the early part of *Chronicle A*, and the later part are summarized, with percentages rounded off.

The first instances of conjunctive use of *after* that the OED mentions involve sentences such as (11) to (13), with the dates given as in the OED. These are not conjunctions, i.e. heads, but full phrases (PPs) in the specifier of the CP. They indicate time so could be derived from a structure such as (14) and are different from (10) in that a complementizer follows the PP:

(11) Witodlice **æfter þam þe ic of deaþe arise** ic cume to eow on galilee
      Surely after that that I of death arise I come to you in Galilee

                          (c. 1000 *West Saxon* Matthew 26. 32 Hatton Ms)

(12) **Efter þan þet þe mon bið dead**
      After that that the man is dead

                                          (c. 1175 *Lamb. Hom.* 51)

(13) **Affterr þatt tatt** he wass dæd
      After that that he was dead
      "After he was dead"

                                          (c. 1200 *Ormulum* 7667)

The tree for (11) to (13) would be as in (14):

(14)

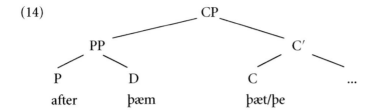

Interestingly, the much earlier Lindisfarne glosses render the relevant part of (11) as (15), without the complementizer. The complementizer-less stage represents an earlier variety. This is confirmed by data in Rissanen (2006), who examines the Helsinki Corpus Old English parts and finds an increase in complementizer following the PP:

(15) **æfter ðon** uutedlice ic eft-ariso ic forlioro l iowih in galileam
"after that surely I arise-again I come before you in Galilee"

(Lindisfarne Matthew 26. 32)

The development explained so far has been that the PP with *after* gets fronted and that its object increasingly often is a demonstrative, not a full noun. The demonstratives are still inflected and cannot be "mistaken" for complementizers. This means the PP is still adverbial. The second stage is for a complementizer to follow the PP. The third stage is for the demonstrative to disappear and then for the preposition to be reanalyzed as a complementizer, as in (16) and (17):

(16) Aftir he hadde take þe hooli Goost

(c. 1360 Wyclif *De Dot. Eccl.* 22)

(17) After thei han slayn them

(1366 Mandeville 174)

The changes are indicated in (18):

(18) a. PP ~~PP~~ 900 (Chronicle A) – present
     b. PP C 1000 (West Saxon Gospel) – 1600
     c. P C 1220 (Lambeth) – 1600 (OED 1611)
     d. C 1360 (Wycliff) – present

This accounts for the change from lexical to functional **head** or from functional to higher functional head so frequently described in the grammaticalization literature (e.g. Heine and Kuteva 2002). Late Merge also accounts for lexical **phrases** becoming base generated in the functional domain. An example is *fortunately* (which replaces Old English CP-adverbs such as *witodlice* and *soþlice*). When it is first introduced into the English language from French in 1386, it is as adjective, as in (19), meaning "happy, successful, favored by fortune." It then changes to a higher adverb, as in (20) and (21), initially by moving:

(19) Whan a man ... clymbeth vp and wexeth **fortunat**

(OED, 1386, Chaucer)

(20) **Most fortunately:** he hath atchieu'd a Maid That paragons description, and wilde Fame: One that excels the quirkes of Blazoning pens

(Shakespeare, *Othello* II. i. 61–63)

(21) **Fortunately,** Lord De la War ... met them the day after they had sailed

(OED, 1796)

Structure (22a) shows the more recent structural representation and (22b) the earlier one. The preferred one under the LMP is (22a):

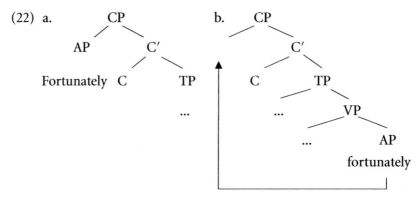

Other examples of the LMP are given in Table 12.3.

How exactly does Late Merge account for language change? If non-thematically marked elements can wait to merge outside the VP (Chomsky 1995: 314–315), they will do so. I will therefore argue that if, for instance, a preposition can be analyzed as having fewer semantic features and is less relevant to the argument structure (e.g. *to*, *after*, and *of* in ModE), it will

TABLE 12.3. *Examples of reanalysis due to the Late Merge Principle*

for, from P > C	negative objects to negative markers
modals: V > T	*to*: P > M(ood)

tend to merge higher (in TP or CP) rather than merge early (in VP) and then move. Like the Head Preference Principle, Late Merge is argued to be a motivating force of linguistic change, accounting for the change from specifier to higher specifier and head to higher head. Roberts and Roussou (2003), Wu (2004), and Simpson and Wu (2002) also rely on some version of Late Merge.

Concluding section 12.4, under the LMP as under the HPP, syntax is inert; it is the lexical items that are reanalyzed by the language learner. Two principles, the HPP and the LMP, provide an insight into what speakers do when they construct a sentence. In the next section, I will apply these to a scenario for language evolution.

12.5 Grammaticalization and language evolution

As argued above, Merge could have been the first step in creating syntax from a stage that consisted of either words or gestures (e.g. Corballis 2002), and as Traugott (2004: 134) puts it, as "an exaptation of thematic role structure." The current section provides a scenario for the use of Merge and subsequent steps.

Once External Merge applies, certain structural and thematic relationships crystalize, unlike those in (1), uttered by Nim. Chomsky (2007: 11) talks about edge features as determining what merges externally, and at the VP level this is probably determined by thematic features. Thus a V selects a DP to merge and a (light verb) v merges with a VP (in which a DP with a specific theta role occurs). The vP, or VP-shell, represents the thematic level, and one that adult native speakers employ when they speak or write in "fragments", as in (23a). Children first reach this thematic stage, as (23b) shows from Abe, before producing sentences with grammatical categories (though they understand grammatical categories before they produce them):

(23) a. Gone for lunch
      b. like a cookie   (Abe, 3.7)

In many languages, thematic relations are additionally marked, namely by inherent case (Chomsky 1986: 193), e.g. dative to mark a Goal theta role in (24):

(24) þæt he **sæ-mannum** onsacan   mihte
      that he sailors-DAT   strive-against might
      "that he might strive against the sailors"

                                                          (*Beowulf* 2954)

This inherent Case can be argued to be derived through grammaticalization of adpositions (e.g. Tauli 1958).

The next step, which is an automatic result of Merge and economy (Narrow Syntax), is when Internal Merge (movement) arises, as well as grammatical elements relevant to specificity, definiteness, and quantification. Tense and aspect are relevant to specificity as well. A language where definiteness is expressed by preposing is Chinese, as well known from the work by Li and Thompson (1978). Cf. (25):

(25) Chinese
      a. chi le   fan
          eat PF rice
          "I ate some rice"
      b. fan chi le
          rice eat PF
          "I ate the rice"

                                                   (Yi Ting Chen p.c.)

Definite time adverbials also precede the verb whereas durative ones follow in Chinese. There are other languages, however, in which such grammatical functions are not purely done through movement but through grammatical elements. They develop when one feature of a lexical element is emphasized over others (hence the slight semantic loss). Similar data exist for other complementizers as well as sentence-adverbs and auxiliaries.

The two principles used above (HPP and LMP) make learners analyze lexical material that is already part of the structure and change the position of it. There are also a number of changes where a new element comes from outside of the sentence, e.g. a special pronoun being incorporated into the

CP to indicate subordination, and an emphatic topic pronoun becoming the subject (in Spec TP). This can be expressed by means of a principle that incorporates (innovative) topics and adverbials in the syntactic tree:

(26) **Specifier Incorporation Principle (SIP)**
      When possible, be a specifier rather than an adjunct.

Sometimes, these "renewals" are innovations from inside the language, as in the case of the Old English negative nominal *na wiht* "no creature" (the root of *not*) to mark negation; but other times, these renewals are borrowed through contact with other languages. One such possible case is the introduction into English of the *wh*-relative. In Old English, there are a number of relative strategies, but by Early Middle English, the complementizers *þat* and *þe* are typical. This is predicted under the HPP since those forms are heads (see van Gelderen 2004: 83–87). By later Middle English, this form is competing with the *wh*-pronoun still present in present-day English (be it mainly in written English). Mustanoja cites Latin influence for the introduction of the *wh*-pronoun. Romaine (1982) shows that the introduction of the *wh*-pronouns was stylistically influenced, and Rydén (1983) shows both Latin and French influence. The first instances of *who* occur in epistolary idioms that are very similar to those in French letters of the same period. For instance, in many of the collections of letters from the fifteenth century, the same English and French formulaic constructions occur, such as in (27a) from Bekynton and (27b) from the *Paston Letters*:

(27) a. a laide de Dieu notre Seigneur, **Qui** vous douit bonne vie et
         longue
         "With the help of God, our Lord, who gives us a good and long
         life"
                                             (Bekynton, from Rydén 1983: 131)
      b. be the grace of God, **who** haue yow in kepyng
         "by the grace of God, who keeps you"
                                             (*Paston Letters* 410)

The *wh*-pronoun is in the specifier position (since it can pied pipe a preposition and is inflected). This shows that, for creative reasons, speakers can start to use the specifier again.

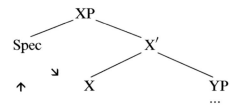

FIG. 12.4. The Linguistic Cycle

How are the three principles mentioned so far responsible for cyclical change? Let's see what happens when we combine the effects of the HPP and the LMP, as in Figure 12.4. The HPP will be responsible for the reanalysis, as a head, of the element in the specifier position; the LMP will ensure that new elements appear in the specifier position or in the head.

This scenario works perfectly for changes where a negative object such as Old English *na wiht* "no creature" becomes a spec(ifier) and subsequently a head *not* of a NegP, and for a locative adverb being reanalyzed as part of the higher CP. The SIP would enable the specifier position to be filled from outside of the clause, e.g. by a pronoun.

Givón (1979) and others have talked about topics that are later reanalyzed as subjects, and call this a shift from the pragmatic to the syntactic. What this means is that speakers tend to use the Phrase Structure rules, rather than loosely adjoined structures. With (25) added, typical changes can therefore be seen as (28):

(28) a. Head   → higher Head   → 0 (= LMP)
     b. Adjunct → Spec → Head → 0 (= SIP/LMP and HPP)
        Phrase   →

The change in (28a) is the one from lower head (either lexical or grammatical) to higher head, via LMP. The change in (28b) shows that either an adjunct (via SIP) or a lower phrase (via LMP) can be reanalyzed as specifiers, after which the specifier is reanalyzed as head (via HPP).

In this section, I have suggested that the emergence of syntax could have followed the path that current grammaticalization also follows. In particular, Merge brings with it a set of relations and a set of economy principles. These economy principles are responsible for what is traditionally called grammaticalization.

12.6 Conclusion and feature economy

I have examined two steps that are required in the change from pre-syntactic language to language as we currently know it. The evolutionary change is Merge and the structural and thematic relations it entails to build a basic lexical layer (the VP). The others are the economy principles that enable learners to choose between different analyses. These two principles result in what is known as grammaticalization and build the non-lexical layers (the TP and CP). Lexical material is also incorporated into the syntax through a third principle, the SIP. This principle allows the speaker to creatively include new material, e.g. as negative reinforcement in special stylistic circumstances.

It is possible to formulate economy in terms of features: The computational load (in the Narrow Syntax) is less when semantic or interpretable features are not included in the derivation. Uninterpretable features keep the derivation going as it were. Full phrases have more features (to check) and they are more likely to be interpretable. Apart from the preference for heads, there is also a preference for positions higher in the tree, i.e., merged later in the derivation. For instance, a PP base generated in the VP can come to be used as a sentence connector. These changes too can be accounted for through computational economy: The lower (externally merged) element in the tree has more semantic features whereas the grammatical/functional element has uninterpretable features (uF). Thus, this approach eliminates the "imperfection" of uF.

What does this tell us about the shape of the original language? The emergence of syntax followed the path that current change also follows, i.e. one that children take acquiring the language. Chomsky (2002: 113) sees the semantic component as expressing thematic as well as discourse information. If thematic structure was already present in protolanguage (Bickerton 1990), the evolutionary change of Merge made them linguistic. What was added through grammaticalization is the morphology, the second layer of necessary information.

13 Recursion, phonological storage capacity, and the evolution of modern speech

FREDERICK L. COOLIDGE AND
THOMAS WYNN

13.1 Introduction

It has been proposed that the faculty of language in the narrow sense (FLN) generates internal representations and maps them into instructions to a sensory-motor system by a phonological interface and into instructions to an interpretation system by a semantic interface (e.g., Hauser, Chomsky, and Fitch 2002). It has also been claimed that a core property of FLN, and unique only to human language, is recursion, that is, embedding a phrase within a phrase, e.g., *Hermione said that Hagrid wants to see you*. Modern speech and thought is replete with recursive phrases, and theoretically, modern language, like natural numbers, is capable of infinite generative recursion, e.g., *Ron said that Hermione said that Hagrid wants to see you*. However, those who advance recursion as the key to modern language, and consequently modern thinking, fail to conjecture exactly how recursion accomplishes its magic. Hauser et al. did not specifically address the natural selection advantages of human recursion, other than noting that it may have evolved for reasons other than language and offering a vague statement that recursion has "limitless expressive power." It is possible that in their thinking, recursion is simply the property of combinability. Thus, combinability gave rise to recursion and its selective advantage over time would have been the ability to make more complex computations. Aboitiz, García, Bosman, and Brunetti (2006), who have also posited that recursion is highly dependent upon phonological storage capacity (PSC), also neglected to explicate the specific advantages and mechanisms of recursion other than noting that it limits "syntactical processing."

To our minds, the question becomes what is the relationship of recursion to modern language and thinking? And what might be the mechanism or subspecies of recursion that bestows its advantages to cognition?

13.2 Working memory, its executive functions, and phonological storage capacity

We think one key to unlocking this mystery is PSC. PSC has been proposed to be a subsystem of the working memory (WM) model, originally proposed by Baddeley and Hitch (1974). An important component of PSC is an articulatory processor or phonological loop. The articulatory processor, which can be employed vocally or subvocally, is a rehearsal mechanism for maintaining sounds or words in active attention. As currently conceived (Baddeley 2000, 2001; Baddeley and Logie 1999), WM is a multi-component cognitive system reflecting a capacity to hold and manipulate information in active attention consistent with short- and long-term goals, in spite of task-irrelevant interference. WM consists of a central executive, which manipulates three subsystems: the aforementioned (a) phonological storage system with a vocal and subvocal articulation processor; (b) a visuospatial sketchpad (VSSP), which temporarily stores and manipulates visual and spatial information and is critical to solving visual and spatial problems and spatial orientation; and (c) an episodic buffer that integrates information from the other two subsystems and serves as a temporary store for this information and other material to be acted upon by the central executive. In the past three decades, the central executive and its subsystems have received strong empirical support (e.g., Miyake and Shah 1999; Shah and Miyake 2005).

Interestingly, however, Baddeley's central executive has older theoretical roots. As we have previously noted (Coolidge and Wynn 2001, 2005), the concept of executive functions is often traced to Luria (1966), who noted that patients with frontal lobe damage frequently have their speech, motor abilities, and sensations intact, yet are often unable to carry out complex, purposive, and goal-directed actions. He also found that they could not accurately evaluate the success or failure of their behaviors and were unconcerned with their failures, hesitant, indecisive, and indifferent to the loss of their critical self-awareness. Lezak (1982) also noted that frontal lobe damaged patients frequently lost their ability to be independent, constructive, creative, and socially productive and appropriate despite their intact perceptual, language, and long-term memory abilities. We find executive function models particularly useful because they allow us to articulate with the archeological record; for example, the reliance upon long-range contingency planning.

From a neuropsychological perspective, Pennington and Ozonoff (1996) defined executive functions as a unique domain of abilities that involves organization in space and time, selective inhibition, response preparation, goal-attainment, planning, and flexibility. They viewed the domain of executive functions as partially distinct yet overlapping with other cognitive domains such as sensation, perception, language, and long-term memory. Current neuropsychological assessment of executive functions invariably includes measures of planning, sequential memory, and temporal order memory (e.g., Lezak 1995). We have recently proposed that these classic concepts of executive functions are identical to Baddeley's central executive (Coolidge and Wynn 2005). Based upon empirical studies of contemporary WM tasks, Oberauer, Suss, Wilhelm, and Wittman (2003) found that working memory could be differentiated into two facets: one, its cognitive functions (Baddeley's central executive) and the other related to its content domains (akin to Baddeley's phonological store and the visuospatial sketchpad).

Neuropsychological and brain imaging research indicates that WM is largely a frontal lobe neural network, with significant links to parietal and temporal lobes. The dorsolateral prefrontal circuit is generally associated with the executive functions mentioned previously. The orbitofrontal prefrontal region is more closely connected to the limbic system and has been shown to be associated with the processing of emotions and the regulation and decision-making associated with social behavior and social interactions. Both systems are closely connected, and the prefrontal cortex has extensive projections to almost all regions of the temporal and parietal lobes, some projections to the occipital lobe, and to subcortical structures such as the basal ganglia, the cerebellum, and many brainstem nuclei. The gist of these interrelationships appears to be that the prefrontal cortex coordinates the processing of broad regions of the central nervous system. A third region of the prefrontal cortex is the anterior cingulate gyrus, and it is thought to mediate motivational systems and action selection (Pennington 2002).

Although difficult to measure precisely, in part because of its highly transitory nature, the neurological substrate for phonological storage appears to be the left inferior parietal lobe and the posterior portion of the superior gyrus of the temporal lobe. Also implicated, within the inferior portions of the left parietal lobe, are the angular gyrus, which is important for subvocal articulation and the conversion of written words to internal monolog, and the supramarginal gyrus, which is involved in the processing of novel words and has additional phonological functions (e.g., Gernsbacher and Kaschak 2003).

In modern thinking, phonological representations of words or sounds associated with the visual images become available to vocal or subvocal articulation for further rehearsal and storage. The neurological substrate of the VSSP includes the primary visual cortex in the occipital lobes with a ventral stream of information to the temporal lobes for object identity (what), and a dorsal stream of information to the parietal lobes for object location (where) and object motion (Gernsbacher and Kaschak 2003). As will be seen later in this chapter, the role of the VSSP as a representational system for objects and locations, which allows successful interactions with the environment, cannot be overstated. Indeed, Konrad Lorenz (1973) saw spatial orientation and the potential to create an "imagined space" within the central nervous system as the basis for all conceptual thinking and language.

13.3 Heritability of working memory and its subsystems

There is increasing evidence that WM's various components have a highly heritable basis. In a behavioral genetic study of child and adolescent twins, core functions of the central executive (e.g., planning, organizing, and goal attainment) were found to be exceptionally heritable (77%) and attributable to an additive genetic (or polygenic) influence (Coolidge et al. 2000). The phonological storage component of working memory has also been shown to be strongly heritable, e.g., 35% to 56%, and polygenic (Rijsdijk, Vernon, and Boomsma 2002; Ando, Ono, and Wright 2002). Ando et al. found that their measures of the central executive and VSSP were also strongly heritable (37% to 57%). Hansell et al. (2001), using event-related potential slow-wave measures of WM within a VSSP-related task, also found a similar polygenic heritability (35% to 52%).

13.4 Recursion and phonological storage capacity

Baddeley and his colleagues (Baddeley and Logie 1999; Baddeley, Gathercole, and Papagno 1998) have tentatively proposed that phonological storage capacity "might reasonably be considered" to form a bottleneck for language production and comprehension, and indeed recent empirical studies support this contention (Gathercole, Pickering, Ambridge, and Wearing 2004). Furthermore and highly provocative are the findings that WM capacity and to a lesser extent phonological storage capacity are significantly related to general intelligence and fluid intelligence (i.e., novel problem solving; Kane and Engle 2002; Engle and Kane 2004). Adults who have "greater" PSC have also been found to score higher on verbal tests of intelligence (indeed, it is a subtest of the Wechsler Adult Intelligence Scale) and higher on measures of verbal fluency; they also do better on retroactive and proactive interference tasks (Kane and Engle 2002). In children who are matched on non-verbal intelligence measures, those with greater PSC had a larger vocabulary, produced longer utterances, and demonstrated a greater range of syntactic construction (Adams and Gathercole 2000). Taken on the whole, these findings tend to support Baddeley's tentative contention that PSC may have evolved primarily for the acquisition of language, and this evidence lends supports for his bottleneck hypothesis.

The crux of the first part of our present argument is that the use of recursion required greater PSC. Recursion may, theoretically at least, be infinitely generative but it is obviously limited by PSC. Aboitiz et al. (2006) have noted that PSC represents a short-term memory ensemble that can be phylogenetically tracked to earlier homologs in hominid evolution and to current primate brain systems. Further, they postulate that language has evolved primarily through the expansion of short-term memory capacity, "which has allowed the processing of sounds, conveying elaborate meanings and eventually participating in syntactic processes" (p. 41). They believed that an expanding memory system allowed more complex memories representing multiple items to be combinatorially manipulated, which they believed to the equivalent of Hauser et al.'s syntactic recursion. However, such linguistic recursion would demand significant working memory resources.

Aboitiz et al.'s (2006) neurological epicenter for this expanded working memory capacity and generation of the phonological loop is the evolutionary development of the posterior superior temporal lobe gyrus and the inferior parietal lobes areas. They also agreed with Furster (1997), who noted that the dorsolateral prefrontal cortex plays an important role with reconciling short-term past and short-term future and cross-temporal contingencies. Thus, keeping track of what was said a few moments ago, minutes ago, and insuring that one's present speech is in accord with previous utterances is a function of the complex inter-actions of the prefrontal cortex, temporal, and parietal areas as well as their interconnectivity with other cortical areas and subcortical structures as well.

Aboitiz et al. (2006) also noted that empirical studies of short and long sentences appear to reveal that short sentences do not impose an inordinate load on WM capacity or short-term memory systems. They further argued that longer canonical sentences, particularly those that present objects of the action first rather than subjects of the action, do impose a significantly greater load upon general WM capacity and its phonological subsystem than non-recursive and subject-first sentences. Furthermore, we have already noted empirical evidence in children and adults that found that those with greater PSC produce longer utterances containing more complex syntax.

13.5 Recursion, phonological storage capacity, and speech acts

In our present hypothesis, we recognize an alternative possibility: that it may not necessarily be recursion or the length of an utterance, per se, that were evolutionarily advantageous. Thus, if recursion is defined as calling an instruction into working memory, and the instruction is presented first, then no great burden on working memory is required. However, if the instruction occurs at the end of a phrase, then there is an added burden on working memory.

There is also the possibility that recursion may have affected the range of speech acts or the pragmatics of speech. A speech act refers to the act which is done or performed by speaking (e.g., Adams 2002). There is far from a general consensus on a single taxonomy assessing the intent of communication, although speech act analyses typically measure excla-matives (shouts of pain, pleasure, or surprise), imperatives (commands), declaratives (statements of fact, greetings, denials), interrogatives (questions or requests), and subjunctives (expresses subjective statements, such as wishes, possibilities, and statements that are contrary to facts). It should also be noted that numerous subsequent and rival systems have emerged for the analysis of speech acts (see Adams 2002; Cruse 2000; Levinson 2000). Interestingly, the first four of these speech acts can be expressed by simple or even single morphemic structures: exclamations (ouch!), imperatives (move!), declaratives (nice!), and interrogatives (where?), and thus, recursion does not appear to be a necessary condition for those speech acts. However, the subjunctive mode of speech, "what if" thinking, does appear to require recursion or longer canonical utterances. Thus, recursion may have allowed the formation and release of subjunctive thinking but recursion, in turn, required expanded PSC and greater WM capacity. Interesting support for this latter idea comes from a study (and we recognize that the study is controversial) by Everett (2005) of an Amazonian tribe that appears to lack recursion in their language, Pirahã. Everett noted that the Pirahã language did not make references to refer to the ancient past, or the distant future, and it lacked creation myths, references to non-living relatives, abstract concepts, or references to distant places. Although Everett did not think it was an inability of their language to make such references, despite a lack of recursion (he thought it was due to a cultural prohibition), it is provocative to think that recursive embedding may foster or allow such thinking.

13.6 The enhanced working memory hypothesis

We have previously proposed (Coolidge and Wynn 2001, 2005, 2006a) that it may have been a genetic neural mutation or epigenetic phenomenon that affected WM capacity sometime between 150,000 years ago and 30,000 years ago, and we labeled this change *Enhanced Working Memory* (EWM). We also have proposed that EWM accounted for the apparent explosion of culture complexity that appeared in various parts of the world after 40,000 years ago. The exact timing plays itself out in several scenarios but is tangential to the current discussion (for further details see Coolidge and Wynn 2005). A genetic mutation, as a stimulus for complex culture, has previously been proposed by Mithen (1996b) and Klein and Edgar (2002), although neither provided a cognitive model or a neurological basis.

How would EWM, by way of recursion, have enabled modern thinking? One mechanism might have been that the speaker can "hold in mind" a much greater number of options, and as such, can give the speaker a greater range of behavioral flexibility and even creativity. We previously hypothesized (Coolidge and Wynn 2005) that reflection upon a greater number of options allows the organism not only a choice among those options, perhaps based on previous successes or failures of each option, but also to choose a future option or actively create an alternative plan of action.

Another mechanism may have been that EWM may have aided the rapid evolution of culture through "thought experiments." Shepard (1997) thought that the mere accumulation of facts (as in Baddeley's semantic memory or Mithen's natural history intelligence or technical intelligence) would not result in advances in scientific human knowledge but its advancement would require thought experiments. He postulated that every real experiment might have been preceded by thought experiments that increased the probability of the success of the real experiment. Dawkins (1989) also proposed that natural selection would have favored the reproductive success of those organisms capable of simulation. He described systems highly similar to those of a central executive and replete with the executive function metaphors. For example, he viewed consciousness as the culmination of an evolutionary trend where consciousness served as an executive decision-maker with the acquired "ability to predict the future and act accordingly."

EWM might also have been required for fully symbolic thought, as reflected in therianthropic art such as the *Löwenmensch* of Hohlenstein-Stadel and Hohle Fels cave, the latter of which is characteristic of the Aurignacian culture of the Upper Paleolithic at about 32,000 years ago. Certainly, monsters and therianthropes would have lurked in dreams of early *Homo* (see Coolidge and Wynn 2006b for further details). However, it may have taken truly modern minds, with expanded attention capacity and recursive iteration, to turn those monsters into tangible icons and systems of meaning. Do the shell beads at Blombos necessarily represent fully modern speech and thinking? We do not think so. We do believe they represent *something*, but we do not believe their making and wearing necessarily implies fully modern syntactic speech. Many contemporary primates can distinguish between members and non-members of their group. Shell beads almost certainly did mark social identity, and an identity that was more elaborate than a simple "us–them" distinction. This may well have implications for human concept formation, but it does not seem to us that such a category distinction requires syntactical language.

There is also another line of reasoning to lend weight to increased phonological storage capacity and EWM as critical to modern thinking. The anthropological literature is replete with the effects of oral language, oral social records as characteristics of mythic culture, folk-telling, and myth-sharing on the evolution of modern thinking (e.g. Arsuaga 2002; Donald 1997; Dunbar 1996; Hodgson and Helvenston 2006; Sugiyama 2001). Perhaps the simplest interpretation of the effect EWM may have had on linguistic communication is to conclude that it enhanced narrative capacity. There might be an increase in the length and complexity of sentences, thus accounting for the claims of those who emphasize oral language and oral traditions as characteristic of modern culture. Arsuaga has argued that modern culture was made very effective by the ability to share myths that linked people both to the natural world and their ancestors. Sugiyama has speculated that narratives are excellent substitutes for time-consuming and sometimes dangerous first-hand experience. She also posits that fitness in varying habitats may have particularly aided foraging knowledge by transmitting information about geography, plants, fauna, weather, and other aspects through narratives.

13.7 Genetic evidence for the Upper Paleolithic revolution

The genetic hypothesis for the change in culture in the Upper Paleolithic was recently strengthened in a genetic haploid typing study by Evans et al. (2005). By sequencing a gene *Microcephalin* (MCPH1) that regulates brain size, where mutations in this gene are known to cause microcephaly, they found that a genetic variant of MCPH1 increased rapidly in modern humans about 37,000 years ago (with a 95% confidence interval from 14,000 years ago to 60,000 years ago). They also concluded that the gene variant appeared quickly, making it unlikely that the gene appeared through simple neutral drift. Interestingly, they could not conclude that the gene was necessarily selected for because of its direct effect upon neural substrate, although that remains an intriguing possibility. Equally intriguing, however, is the possibility that there was some extraordinarily advantageous phenotypic consequence of the gene upon cognition, language, or personality. Indeed, as previously noted, we believe that a genetic mutation or some epigenetic phenomenon did have a phenotypic effect upon working memory capacity and that the change was naturally selected for and spread rapidly because of its extraordinary consequence of EWM for cognition and language.

13.8 Parietal lobe hypertrophy and modern thinking

One other recent piece of evidence helps supports this tentative coalition of EWM, increased phonological storage, the development of recursive thinking and speech, and the use of the subjunctive pragmatic of speech. Despite what has been historically assumed, there is some suggestion that the frontal lobes have undergone evolutionary inertia within *Hominoidea* based on allometric analyses (Semendeferi, Lu, Schenker, and Damasio 2002). Bruner's (2004) recent allometric analyses also support this frontal lobe stasis, particularly between Neanderthals and modern *Homo sapiens*. Certainly, the evolution of the genus *Homo* has been associated with greater cranial capacity, increasing encephalization, and frontal widening. However, Bruner proposed two different allometric trajectories in the evolution of human brains. One trajectory suggests that as cranial capacity increased, the parietal areas underwent a shortening and flattening. Occipital lobes, in general, have shown a steady reduction in the evolution of humans, and a change from a posterior location behind the parietal lobes to a more advanced location inferior to the parietal lobes. The allometric trajectory that best distinguished anatomically modern *Homo sapiens* and Neanderthals was a tendency towards klinorhynchy or globularity in modern humans (Bruner, Manzi, and Arsuaga 2003). Bruner (2004) speculated that the sequela of globularity might have been greater interconnectivity between the major lobes of the brain, and an expansion of the parietal lobes. And as we previously have noted, the supramarginal and angular gyri of the inferior parietal lobes play major roles in subvocal articulatory processing (inner speech). Furthermore, Carruthers (2002) noted the important role that inner speech plays in intermodular thinking, i.e., making visual and spatial representations more accessible to cognitive processing. Bruner further speculated that considering the role of the parietal lobes in visuospatial integration and the role that the inferior parietal lobes play in making this information accessible to language, and thus, to the recognition and communication of the external environment, these parietal lobe structures may be directly related to the evolution of an accurate internal representation of the external world.

In summary, recursion is said to be the hallmark of modern language. There is empirical evidence that recursion not only requires greater working memory capacity but also greater phonological storage capacity. We believe that a genetic neural mutation that occurred sometime between 150,000 and 30,000 years ago enhanced working memory capacity and/or phonological storage capacity. The sequela of the latter change allowed longer recursive and canonical utterances, and a consequent increase in the complexity and information content of utterances.

14 Why women speak better than men (and its significance for evolution)

BART DE BOER

14.1 Introduction

One of the many striking differences between humans and our closest primate relatives is the shape of the vocal tract. Whereas orangutans, bonobos, chimpanzees, and gorillas all have similar vocal tracts with low flat tongues and high larynges, humans have a round tongue and a larynx that is positioned low in the throat (Fitch 2000; Negus 1949). The combination of a low larynx and a wide gap between the larynx and the velum makes it impossible for (adult) humans to swallow and breathe simultaneously. It is generally assumed (e.g. Fitch and Giedd 1999, section III C) that this increases the probability of choking on one's food. Even if the resulting reduction of fitness is not enormous, it must nevertheless be explained evolutionarily why the difference between humans and other higher primates has evolved.

One explanation that is sometimes mentioned (e.g. Pollick and de Waal 2007) is that the lowered larynx does not have an adaptive function, but that it is a direct side effect of bipedalism. This explanation is not really supported by evidence, and there is in fact some evidence that indicates that bipedalism does not influence the position of the larynx. As for the lack of positive evidence, the original sources that are usually referred to in this context (Aiello 1996; DuBrul 1958) do not really make a direct link between bipedalism and the anatomy of the human vocal tract. They only state that bipedalism removed some constraints on the function of the mouth and the larynx. The disappearance of these constraints allowed different functions of the larynx and vocal tract to evolve. However, these sources do not propose that the development of the human larynx did not serve an adaptive purpose.

When looking at other animals, one also does not find a clear correlation between bipedalism and the position of the larynx or the shape of the vocal tract. Kangaroos can be considered bipedal animals, but do not have a lowered larynx, whereas there are quite a few animals with lowered larynges (Fitch and Reby 2001) that are quadrupedal. Although this is still an underexplored area of research, it does indicate that bipedalism does not have much to do with the position of the larynx.

An explanation that does involve an adaptive function of the lowered larynx is that of size exaggeration (Fitch and Hauser 2002; Fitch and Reby 2001; Ohala 1984). Fitch and colleagues have found that in many animal species males have larynges that are much lower than those of the females of the species. He has also found that the signals that can be produced with these lowered larynges tend to impress other members of the species (or predators) and thus confer an evolutionary advantage. However, most mammals with lowered larynges still have a flat tongue, and can also still directly connect the larynx with the nasal cavity such that they can breathe and swallow simultaneously. Although it is therefore quite possible that size exaggeration played a role in the evolution of (especially the male) human vocal tract, I would argue that the size exaggeration hypothesis does not completely explain the unique shape of the human vocal tract.

The classical functional hypothesis about the shape of the human vocal tract is that it is an adaptation for speech (Negus 1938, 1949). The round shape of the tongue, and the extra space in the pharyngeal (throat) cavity that is created by the lowered larynx and the high velum, make it possible to control two independent cavities and thus create the largest possible set of distinctive speech sounds. Given the advantage of being able to produce distinctive signals efficiently, the disadvantages of the human vocal tract shape were offset evolutionarily.

This final hypothesis has been used as the basis of research into the vocal abilities and by extension the linguistic abilities of Neanderthals. It has first been investigated by Lieberman, Crelin, Wilson, and Klatt (Lieberman and Crelin 1971; Lieberman et al. 1972; Lieberman et al. 1969) and followed up by other researchers (e.g. Boë et al. 2002; Carré et al. 1995). This work has made effective use of computer modeling of the acoustic properties of different hypothetical vocal tracts. The results of this work have been rather controversial and contradictory, however. Even though all researchers have used very similar models and methods, they draw different conclusions.

Simplifying the discussion somewhat, it can be said that Lieberman et al. find that the position of the larynx does matter, and that Neanderthals did not have a lowered larynx. Carré et al. (1995) find that the position of the larynx does matter, and that Neanderthals probably had a lowered larynx; while Boë et al. (2002) find that a lowered larynx does not matter, and that Neanderthals were therefore capable of complex speech. Part of the controversy is due to the different anatomical reconstructions that are used, but an important part of the controversy is also caused by the different views of the authors about the role of articulatory constraints. It appears that Lieberman et al. and Carré et al. think that articulatory constraints are crucial, whereas Boë et al. appear to be of the opinion that controlling articulators differently can compensate for different anatomical constraints.

This discussion cannot really be resolved if one works with hypothetical reconstructions of (Neanderthal) vocal tracts. There are just too many unknowns. This chapter therefore proposes to investigate the role of a descended larynx with vocal tracts that we do have data about: those of human males and human females. There exist reliable data both about the anatomy of the human vocal tract (e.g. Fitch and Giedd 1999) and about corpora of utterances (e.g. Peterson and Barney 1952). However, as I want to exclude linguistic influence, and as I want to be able to extend the research to hypothetical ancestral vocal tracts, a computer model will also be used for this research.

In this chapter, the areas of acoustic space that are accessible by models of the male and female vocal tract are compared. The notion of accessible acoustic area is similar to the maximum vowel space (Boë et al. 1989). As there are other differences between the male and female vocal tracts than the position of the larynx, an artificial model that has a larynx with a female shape at the male position will also be included in the comparison.

The results of the simulation will be compared with data from male and female speakers, and finally the implications for (modeling) the evolution of speech are discussed.

14.2 Method

Two things are needed for the modeling part of this chapter. First, an articulatory model is needed that can easily be modified to model both the male and the female vocal tracts. Second, a method is needed to calculate the area of acoustic space that can be reached by each variant of the model.

14.2.1 *Articulatory model*

The articulatory model is based on Mermelstein's geometric articulatory model (Mermelstein 1973). A geometric model explicitly models the physical parts (larynx, pharynx, tongue, velum, palate, etc.). As the aim of the research is to investigate the influence of (subtle) anatomical variation, a geometrical model was preferred over models that use a statistical approximation to vocal tract shapes that have been traced from X-ray or MRI images, such as Maeda's model (Maeda 1989). Another geometric model is the one developed by Goldstein (Goldstein 1980), but in this model the shape of the upper and lower vocal tracts cannot be controlled independently, something which is needed if one wants to investigate the effect of larynx lowering in isolation.

The Mermelstein model consists of two parts. The first part is a geometrical model that can calculate the mid-sagital section of the vocal tract for different settings of articulatory parameters. There are eight articulatory parameters: the horizontal and vertical displacement of the hyoid bone which indirectly influences the height of the larynx, the jaw angle, the angle and displacement of the tongue with respect to the jaw, the angle of the tongue blade, and finally the protrusion and the spread of the lips. For values of these parameters that fall within a realistic range, outlines of the vocal tract can be calculated.

Using a model of the mid-sagital section only results in a two-dimensional projection of the vocal tract and this is insufficient for calculating the acoustic properties of the vocal tract. For this, the cross-sectional area of the vocal tract along its length is needed. Therefore, the Mermelstein model has a second part, which is a set of formulae to convert the mid-sagital section into the cross-sectional areas along the length of the vocal tract. Both are described in Mermelstein's original paper(Mermelstein 1973). The geometric part of the model was modified for the different articulatory models. The conversion from the mid-sagital section to the cross-sectional areas was kept unchanged for all models used in this chapter.

The Mermelstein model is a model of the male vocal tract, and was used directly as the model of the male vocal tract in this chapter. Two other

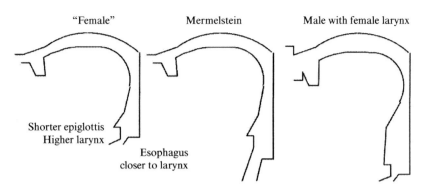

Fig. 14.1. Comparison of the three vocal tract models used in the paper. The middle (male) model is a direct reimplementation of the Mermelstein (1973) model. The left model is the female version of this model, with the changes indicated in the figure. The right model is one with male dimensions and female larynx shape.

models were derived from the original model. The female vocal tract was derived from the male vocal tract by raising the larynx by 22 mm. However, this does not result in a very realistic model of the female vocal tract, as the male epiglottis is larger than the female one, and the distance between the esophagus and the larynx is also larger in the male vocal tract than in the female vocal tract. Therefore, in the female model the epiglottis was reduced, as well as the distance between the esophagus and the larynx. These modifications are illustrated in Figure 14.1.

Because of the differences in anatomy in the region of the larynx, the comparison of the male and female models involves more than the effect of a lowered larynx. Therefore a comparison between two models that only differ in the position of the larynx is desirable, even though this involves a model that does not correspond to a real human vocal tract. It was decided to create a model with a female larynx at the position of the male larynx, instead of a model with a male larynx at the female position, because the larger male larynx at the higher female position impedes the movement of the tongue. The model is illustrated in the right frame of Figure 14.1.

14.2.2 *Area of acoustic space*

In order to calculate the articulatory abilities of a given model, an estimate must be made of what part of the available acoustic space can be reached by the model. In the case of the experiments presented here, the acoustic space was considered to be determined by the first and second formant, formants being resonances of the vocal tract, numbered by increasing frequency. Although this space is insufficient to describe consonants, most vowels can be described in it, and it is therefore used by all researchers who investigate models of the descended larynx.

Human perception is logarithmic. This means that humans perceive a doubling of frequency as sounding the same at every frequency. Therefore the logarithm (base 10) of the frequency of the formants was used. In this way every articulation can be characterized as a point in a two-dimensional acoustic space.

For estimating the area that each model can cover in acoustic space, a measure is calculated that is closely related to the Maximal Vowel Space (Boë et al. 1989). The measure used here is perhaps slightly less accurate, but easier to calculate automatically. A large number (10,000 in the experiments presented here) of random settings of the articulatory parameters are generated. The acoustic signal is calculated for each setting that results in an articulation for which the vocal tract is open. The vocal tract is considered open whenever the minimal cross-sectional area anywhere is greater than or equal to 0.1 cm². Smaller areas would result in frication noise, and therefore not in a clear vowel that can be described by formants alone. Finally, the acoustic signal corresponding to this vocal tract configuration is calculated using a lossless tube approximation (Kelly and Lochbaum 1973; Rabiner and Schafer 1978). This procedure results in a cloud of points in acoustic space.

The approximate area occupied by this point cloud is estimated by calculating the convex hull. The convex hull of a set of points is the volume or area that is determined by all linear interpolations between all points in the set. In a two-dimensional data set, the edge of the convex hull can be imagined as a rubber band tightly wrapped around the point cloud. The procedure of determining a convex hull is illustrated in Figure 14.2.

When a sufficiently large number of random articulations is used, this procedure results in a reliable estimate of the acoustic space that can be reached by a given articulator. Random articulations are used because, given the complexity of the mapping between articulations and their acoustic result, a systematic exploration of the available space is impossible. Also, when using a random scheme instead of a deterministic scheme,

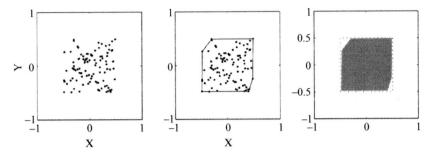

FIG. 14.2. Calculation of a convex hull. The original point cloud, consisting of 100 random points in an arbitrary 2-D space (not to be confused with acoustic space), is illustrated on the left. The edge of the corresponding convex hull is added in the middle, and the grey polygon in the right frame is the actual convex hull. The extent of the space from which the random points were sampled is indicated by the dotted line in the right figure. Note how corners are rounded, and edges are only approximated.

repeated measurements can give an idea of the spread of the areas calculated by the method.

The use of a convex hull is justified when a sufficiently large number of points are used, because when articulations are close together, it can be assumed that intermediate articulations would also have acoustic signals that are intermediate between the acoustic signals corresponding to the articulation. This approximates the assumption of linearity in the calculation of the convex hull. Because of the random sampling procedure, the convex hull will usually not completely cover the reachable space. This tends to underestimate the area. On the other hand, if the original area is not really convex, the procedure tends to overestimate the area. As these biases are similar for all vocal tract configurations tested, and as sizes are compared (not measured absolutely), this is not a problem.

14.3 Results

In order to investigate the effect of a lowered larynx, the different computer models were simulated and compared. Furthermore, confirmation of the results was sought in an existing data set of human vowel articulations.

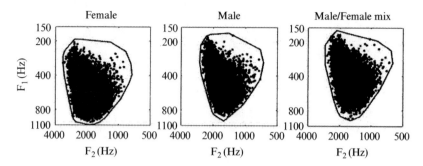

Fɪɢ. 14.3. Examples of 10,000 point data sets generated for the female, male, and mixed models (black dots) as well as the convex hull of all 100,000 data points combined (black lines). As the axes are logarithmic, areas can be compared visually. Note that the female model's area is largest, while the male model's area is smallest.

14.3.1 *Simulation*

With each articulatory model, ten data sets were generated, each consisting of 10,000 articulations. For each of these data sets, the area in acoustic space was calculated. Three sample data sets are presented in Figure 14.3 as well as the convex hull around all 100,000 articulations per articulator (which gives the best idea of the extent of the acoustic space).

The exact areas are given in Table 14.1. The significance of the differences in area was calculated using the Wilcoxon rank sum test, and it was found that the difference between the male and female models was significant with $p < 0.01$, while the difference between the female and mixed models was significant with $p = 0.014$. Given that the female areas tend to be the largest, it can be concluded that the models with the lower larynx cover a smaller area of acoustic space than the model with the higher larynx. It must be stressed that the difference is small, but that it is significant.

14.3.2 *Human data*

The articulatory abilities of male and female speakers can also be compared using human data. Although human utterances are usually influenced in some way by the speaker's native language, an idea of the available acoustic space can nevertheless be gained when working with carefully articulated

TABLE 14.1. *Areas of convex hulls of 10 times 10,000 randomly generated articulations with the female, male, and male position with female shape vocal tract models*

Female	Male	Mixed
0.3023	0.2587	0.297
0.3066	0.2687	0.3004
0.3089	0.2692	0.3029
0.3092	0.2704	0.304
0.3111	0.2709	0.3059
0.3173	0.2789	0.3061
0.3225	0.2822	0.3072
0.3311	0.283	0.308
0.3347	0.2841	0.3086
0.3395	0.285	0.3282
$\mu = 0.318$	$\mu = 0.275$	$\mu = 0.307$
$\sigma = 0.013$	$\sigma = 0.0088$	$\sigma = 0.0083$

words or isolated vowels. As the study presented here was mostly concerned with constructing a model, an existing data set was used. Using an existing data set also prevents unconscious observer bias and makes for easier verification of results. Here Peterson and Barney's (1952) classic data set was used, as reconstructed and made available on the web by Watrous (1991).

For all male and female speakers the area of the convex hull of their twenty vowel utterances was calculated. As in the simulation experiments, the convex hull was calculated in the acoustic space of the logarithm of the first and second formant. The results did only become more significant when the comparison was performed with formants in Mel or Bark. Using the Wilcoxon rank sum test, it was found that the female vowels covered a larger area than the male vowels, with $p = 0.0352$. The average size of the female vowel space was 0.1782 $(\log_{10}$ Hz$)^2$ with standard deviation 0.04. The male vowel space had on average an area of 0.157 with standard deviation 0.035.

14.4 Conclusion and discussion

The results show that the female vocal tract is able to produce a larger range of acoustic signals than the male vocal tract, given the same articulatory constraints. This was found both in computational simulations of the two types of vocal tracts and in the Peterson and Barney (1952) data set of vowels recorded from human subjects. The conclusion to be drawn from this is that a lower larynx does not necessarily mean better articulatory capabilities.

A different explanation for the lower position of the (adult) male larynx is therefore needed, and a likely candidate is the theory of size exaggeration as proposed most recently by Fitch and colleagues (Fitch 2000; Fitch and Hauser 2002; Fitch and Reby 2001). This does not mean that the human vocal tract did not evolve for speech, or that any vocal tract configuration would be equally well suited to vocal communication. On the contrary, I still consider it likely that the unique shape of the human vocal tract is due to selection for the ability to produce distinctive speech. The research presented in this chapter does not really shed light on this issue, though.

In order to investigate the adaptive value for speech of the human vocal tract further, models with higher larynges than the female model are needed. Owing to articulatory constraints, however, this is hard to realize with the present model. Future work could focus on building accurate models of vocal tracts of monkeys and apes.

There are two more conclusions relevant to the evolution of speech that can be drawn from this work. The first is that the differences in acoustic abilities for the models with different larynx shapes and positions are not very large. This makes it plausible that usable complex vocal communication systems would also be possible with vocal tracts of monkeys and apes, and possibly with any mammal vocal tract. Although this does not mean that the human vocal tract was not influenced by selection for speech, it makes it likely that the descent of the larynx, and probably other modifications for speech, were not the crucial factors that they are sometimes made out to be.

Finally, given that the female vocal tract is better for speech than the male vocal tract, it is better to base hypotheses about the vocal abilities of Neanderthal and other ancestral vocal tracts on the female vocal tract, rather than on the male vocal tract. The modern human male vocal tract has apparently undergone other evolutionary pressures than those for distinctive speech. Any investigation into articulatory abilities based on the male vocal tract would therefore confuse these pressures with the pressures for better speech. Although many questions still remain unanswered, and a number of different variations of the model still need to be investigated, the research described in this chapter has at least illustrated the use of realistic geometric articulatory models in investigating the acoustic abilities of different vocal tracts.

15 Mosaic neurobiology and anatomical plausibility

WENDY K. WILKINS

15.1 Introduction

Language is a species characteristic of humans. This species-specific feature is biologically based, requiring a particularly human neuroanatomy due, ultimately, to a particularly human genetic endowment and its expression. Yet, no non-human, not even our closest primate relative, has a system, communicative or otherwise, that even approaches language in the particulars of its organizational features and its expressive complexity. Further, no non-human primate relative would seem to possess a system that convincingly shows evidence of a shared evolutionary precursor to human language—thus language's reputation for being a longstanding unsolvable evolutionary puzzle.

The most productive current theoretical model of language assumes language to be a (more or less) autonomous and modular aspect of cognition. This leads to the notion of something like a "language organ" (see, for example, Anderson and Lightfoot 2002) and it is this language organ that would seem to be lacking in our primate relatives.[1] Yet there is little if any evidence of a language organ—in the sense of a single, autonomous, neurobiological language module—in human neurobiology. Language presents a good demonstration of the fact that there need be no

I am indebted to Jennie Wakefield for a decade-long conversation about matters involving the evolutionary biology of language. Her influence on the ideas expressed here is most gratefully acknowledged, whether or not she would agree with me on certain of the details as I have developed them for this chapter.

[1] Note, though, the distinction here between language and speech. There may well be evidence of evolutionary precursors to human speech in extant primate species, and therefore comparative work can yield evidence about potential ancestral features. But speech is not language; the two must be considered separately (see Fitch 2000).

one-to-one correspondence between constructs in the cognitive model of human cognition and anatomical parts of the biological model.

A better understanding of the biology of language can be achieved by recognizing that underlying language in the brain is a system of neuro-anatomical structures with a high level of interconnectivity, a language system rather than an organ in the most usual understanding of that term. Language requires a mosaic of functionally interconnected anatomical parts which, in and of themselves, may not be specialized for language. It is only in the entirety of the system, with all pieces of the mosaic in place, that linguistic cognition emerges.[2]

But this sort of understanding of the biology of language, which I would take to be the common sense view, is too readily lost in work on the evolution of language. In work on this topic, we tend to discuss the evolution of language as though it were an indivisible whole, instead of the evolution of linguistic features or specific aspects of linguistic cognition. We treat language as though it were, indeed, a single biological organ, or an indivisible single behavior.

Additionally, there is often discussion, more or less directly, of what the key evolutionary development was. It might have been symbols, recursion, theory of mind, shared goals, cooperative problem solving, or some single feature of the vocal tract or the neocortex. Whatever the favorite key ingredient at any particular moment or for any particular researcher, such speculation obscures the fact that language actually requires all the parts. A system with recursion also needs a vocabulary. Symbols are not linguistic until they form words that occur in hierarchically structured phrases and clauses. Highly structured sentences do not serve most linguistic purposes with no connection, somehow, to semantics/meaning/concepts. And we have no way of knowing whether language even exists unless there is some sort of output mechanism: a phonology, a morphology. Plus, all the perceptual pieces must be in place. Language actually, ultimately, requires all the parts.

Further, as likely as not, discussion of the evolution of language leaves out biology entirely. Claims are made about linguistic precursors, or innovations, or adaptations, or pre-adaptations, or spandrels, or exap-tations with no attention paid to requisite biological bases. Researchers

---

[2] Hurford (2003) also relies on the term "mosaic," the language mosaic, but not in the neurobiological context.

are apparently free to make hypotheses about stages in the evolutionary development of language with little or no attention to whether such stages could, even in principle, be sustained by a primate-type brain. We do all know, of course, that evolution must work on biology—in fact, it must work at the level of DNA—but we nevertheless rarely consider the real biological plausibility of proposed evolutionary scenarios when it comes to language. The lack of attention to biology in the study of language evolution is manifest in at least two distinct ways.

Someone might propose that language was evolutionarily shaped, adapted, from some particular behavior found in a related species (for example, differentiated alarm calls in monkeys; communal grooming behavior in apes; teaching and learning of innovations in tool use, etc.). Yet no evidence is provided that the neuroanatomical structures underlying the proposed precursor in fact have anything to do with neuroanatomical structures involved in language in humans. But, evolution leaves homologs in its wake. A scenario is considerably less convincing in the absence of homologous structures found in closely related species (or in the fossil record itself).

Alternatively, someone might propose that there were earlier (proto) forms of language, and that these earlier forms are plausible, or maybe even logically necessary, in light of what is known about language acquisition, or languages in contact situations, or what would be culturally necessary given the known archeological record. It is apparently, however, not incumbent on those who propose such theories to suggest what sort of anatomical structure—what sort of brain—would yield linguistic systems of the proposed sort, and how they would then be shaped (presumably by natural selection) into the neuroanatomical structures in contemporary *Homo sapiens*.

In this chapter I discuss a research strategy intended to overcome these shortcomings. I provide a recommendation for how work on the evolution, or at least the evolutionary biology, of language ought to proceed.

15.2 Overview of the research strategy—mosaic neurobiology

Progress on the evolutionary biology of language requires that we work interdisciplinarily. We need to recognize what is special about language, but we also need to understand something of the real neurobiology and functioning of the brain. Wilkins and Wakefield (1995: 161) suggest that it is necessary to "weav[e] together threads provided by paleoneurology, comparative neuroanatomy, and evolutionary theory, as well as linguistic theory." That same article cautions, however, that in order for the discussion of the evolution of language "to reach an adequate level of sophistication, the linguist's voice must be heard ... As linguists are all too aware, even the best and most sophisticated researchers in allied disciplines underestimate the difficulties and complexities of language. Nowhere is this more evident than in questions of evolution" (Wilkins and Wakefield 1995: 180). Yet it is only relatively recently that linguists are taking questions of evolution seriously and are making the effort to do the interdisciplinary work necessary for progress in this area. Hauser, Chomsky, and Fitch (2002: 1570) observe that answering important questions about language evolution "requires a collaborative effort among linguists, biologists, psychologists, and anthropologists." Their article is intended to "promote a stronger connection between biology and linguistics by identifying points of contact and agreement between the fields."

This stronger connection to the facts of biology should lead us to understand that the emergence of a complicated cognitive capacity like language requires the examination of the shaping of each of the individual pieces of an anatomical mosaic—the system of neuroanatomical parts that function together to subserve language. In doing this, we have no reason to believe, certainly even less reason to expect, that all of the pieces in the mosaic will have similar evolutionary histories. Each piece may have been, in fact most probably was, evolutionarily shaped to serve some non-linguistic function. Then at the propitious evolutionary moment, the pieces were all available for use in a neurobiological system sufficient for language, by means of "specialization-through-reconfiguration" (Marcus 2004: 134). Importantly, on this view, we might well expect many (probably most, maybe even all) of the individual mosaic pieces to have identifiable precursors with evident reflexes in extant primates or even other mammals (if a particular feature is sufficiently ancient).

In order to understand the emergence of linguistic capacity, this innovation in the hominid line, we must necessarily work backwards, so to speak, from the language-relevant neuroanatomy. Each piece of the mosaic will have a different evolutionary story, more or less evident in ancestral species, depending on the prospects for biological evidence in the fossil record. But most often the only way to work on these issues is via comparative neuroanatomy—especially comparative primate neuroanatomy (in the search for homologs), but also with respect to other species in the search for relevant analogs.

Of course this working backwards from the language-relevant neuroanatomy would depend on our knowing what the language-relevant neuroanatomy actually is. And we really do not, or not fully—yet we do know more than we used to. Additionally, to really work backwards from the known facts of contemporary biology, we would need to know much more about how the genome influences brain morphology, and this remains largely unknown. But again, as important cross-fertilizing connections between development research and work on evolution mature, we can expect to know increasingly more.

15.3 The earliest evidence and African origins, the POT and Broca's area

Among the things that are known about language-relevant neuroanatomy is the importance of the periSylvian region of the left hemisphere. We know that Broca's area and the parietal-occipital-temporal junction (POT), plus Wernicke's area (especially for auditory linguistic processing) are necessary, if not sufficient, for language. So we can begin by working backwards from here, investigating the evolutionary biology of these particular brain regions. The most convincing analysis of the evolutionary development of these areas, the one that is most anatomically plausible, necessarily involves consideration of evolutionary changes involving control of the hand and arm. It is here that we see the relevant continuity between humans and non-human primate relatives, and it is here that the case is made for an "out of Africa" view of language origins.

The investigation of the earliest evidence of the relevant neocortical features (Wilkins and Wakefield 1995) involved the claim that in ancestral populations (*Homo habilis*) there were precursors to known language-involved neuroanatomical structures. A good case can be made that the emergence of these features (arguably visible on endocasts[3]) was related

---

[3] Endocasts are molds made from the interior surface of the skull. Often they are made of latex, but some rare, naturally occurring endocasts have been found. Because of

to neural control of the thumb. This case is made stronger by recent work on the posterior parietal cortex, involved in the execution of a grasping action, that underlies spatial structure as relevant for language. A brief review of the discussion of the findings relevant for *Homo habilis* leads into the discussion of spatial structure; in turn, the recent work on spatial structure supports the earlier analysis of the evolutionary biology of the POT.

During the *H. habilis* period there is evidence of important changes in the hand with respect to the thumb, as well as early evidence of tool making and predation at a distance (e.g. the felling of small game by the apparently overhand throwing of stones). The proposed evolutionary scenario in this regard derives from the observation that humans, but not present-day monkeys or apes, have a POT (inclusive of Brodmann's area 39 and adjacent portions of 40 and 22) all close to the terminus of the Sylvian fissure. In non-human primates, an overt feature of the left lateral surface of the brain is the lunate sulcus, which is indicative of the lack of a human-like posterior expansion in this area. The POT region is responsible, in humans, for modality-neutral or amodal representations. In other words, this is the most highly developed association area, and it is the farthest removed from direct connectivity with sensory inputs. No equally sensory-remote association cortex, like the POT, has been found in non-human primates. And the POT region is intimately connected to linguistic cognition and behavior, both receptive and productive.[4]

It is very difficult, and controversial, to interpret endocast, and hence fossil skull, evidence. Thus, it is highly controversial to suggest that *H. habilis* was the first species to show evidence of the disappearance of the lunate sulcus on the lateral surface of the cortex. Some researchers suggest that this feature was also characteristic of the earlier *Australopithecus*, or that the endocast evidence is sufficiently poor (few specimens, poorly

calcification on the inside surface of the skull, endocasts can reveal certain features of gross neuroanatomical structure.

[4] The recent tractography work by Catani and ffytche (2005) provides support for the scenario developed by Wilkins and Wakefield (1995). Their work, in corroboration of much earlier work by Geschwind, clearly shows the involvement of the POT region in language, i.e. a posterior region larger and more inclusive than just Wernicke's area. The expansion of the posterior region is primarily what caused the disappearance on the lateral cortical surface of the lunate sulcus in hominids, creating what some researchers now call Geschwind's territory, and what was called by Geschwind himself, the association area of association areas (Geschwind 1965). See also footnote 7.

preserved skulls, etc.) that no claims can be justified (Holloway 1995 and references therein). So perhaps the dating of this modification of the posterior anatomy in the hominid lineage cannot be precisely determined. But the additional evidence of the hand morphology and the lithic remains (tools, stones evidently for throwing) appearing in the evolutionary record contemporaneously helps make the case.[5]

Whenever the change in posterior neuroanatomy happened, it is generally accepted that it was closer to the present than the last common ancestor of the hominids and pongids, and therefore, as far as is currently known, sometime in the last 5 or 6 million years. No researcher has suggested that the pongid, rather than the hominid, neuroanatomical configuration is the innovation, and in fact it would seem that the disappearance of the lunate sulcus on the lateral surface of the cerebral hemisphere, which leads to the creation of the POT, might well be an inevitable result of the increasing size of the posterior parietal cortex in the hominid line.

There is an important methodological point here: A claim about neuroanatomy leads to a position on the interpretation of endocasts from fossil skulls (essentially supporting the work of Falk (1980, 1983) rather than Holloway (e.g. 1978)). The case is made convincing not through the adjudication of a disagreement among paleontologists, but because of the other corroborating evidence, such as changes in the hand morphology. In terms of the current brain morphology and anatomy, the uniqueness of the POT in human posterior brain anatomy is established via comparative primate neuroanatomy, regardless of the situation for *H. habilis*. "The ... indirect method for studying brain evolution is through comparative primate neuroanatomy. Brains from extant primates can be examined at the macro- and microscopic levels to resolve questions of structural and functional relationships" (Wilkins and Wakefield 1995: 166).

This, again, anticipates an important point made by Hauser, Chomsky, and Fitch (2002). They, too, advocate a research program that involves comparative work. We do not know, *a priori*, which aspects of the

---

[5] This work, relying evolutionarily on what is known about the development of the thumb and neural control of the hand, has been interpreted as supporting gestural origins of language. I take no particular stand on whether gesture or speech was the expressive basis for the first (proto)language. I do note a quite intimate connection between the neuroanatomy relevant for the hand and that relevant for aspects of the vocal tract. Further investigation of this matter is certainly warranted.

neuroanatomy are unique to humans (if any). Further, and importantly, we do not know whether a similar behavioral characteristic across species is biologically supported in the same way (i.e. by the same anatomical structure) until we look. If we find behaviors supported by the same anatomical substrates in related species, we can be pretty sure that they are really shared traits. If, however, we find an apparently similar behavior but supported by radically different anatomical structures, there is reason to be skeptical about presumed evolutionary connections. This is, in fact, why it is difficult, if not impossible, to motivate accounts of language evolution that involve adaptation from some primate communication system or other. The behaviors may seem similar on some level, but the anatomy underlying the behaviors is not.

Importantly, evidence of structures that are indeed similar, potential homologs, may give clues to ancestral developments. Comparative work has revealed, for example, possible evidence of an incipient Wernicke's area in the great apes. There is evidence of a lateral asymmetry of the planum temporale, which on some accounts is a feature of Wernicke's area. The planum in the great apes appears to be larger on the left (Gannon et al. 1998). This is consistent with the claim that the planum evolved about 15 million years ago (Hopkins et al. 1998). This similarity between humans and apes with respect to the asymmetry of the planum temporale is a feature of the gross neuroanatomy. There is also evidence of important differences between humans and apes at the cytoarchitectonic (microscopic) level (Buxhoeveden et al. 2001a, 2001b). "This pattern of similarities and differences is exactly what we would expect to find when investigating the evolutionary development of an apparently species-specific characteristic" (Wilkins 2005: 283). "Nothing about the brain was built overnight; evolution proceeds, in general, not by starting over but by tinkering with what is already in place" (Marcus 2004: 131).

To the extent that the planum temporale is part of Wernicke's area, and to the extent that Wernicke's area is necessary for language, the evolutionary development of the planum temporale is important for language. If the planum is a linguistically relevant piece of the neuroanatomical mosaic, we can trace its evolutionary origin by the study of comparative primate neuroanatomy, as the above-mentioned researchers have been doing. We will not find a protolanguage organ per se in the great apes, but we should expect to find homologous mosaic pieces, such as precursors to Wernicke's area.

Just as there is disagreement about the dating of the disappearance of the lunate sulcus on the lateral cortical surface in hominids, there is also some level of controversy about the appearance of Broca's area in the fossil record (that is, its appearance on endocasts) and with respect to the prospects for homologs in extant primates. There is even considerable disagreement about what role Broca's area plays with respect to language functioning. Work on this anatomical feature has suggested that the classical symptoms of Broca's aphasia are not always associated with lesions or other focal damage to Broca's area, and further, damage known to be affecting Broca's area does not necessarily lead to the classical characteristics of agrammatism (Grodzinsky 2000 and associated commentary; Embick et al. 2000).

Wilkins and Wakefield (1995) claimed that Broca's area is evolutionarily derived from motor association cortex, and a very good case can be made for its role in temporal sequencing and hierarchical structure—which need not be language-specific (as originally demonstrated by Greenfield 1991). More recent findings suggest that an incipient Broca's area, or at least a left-hemisphere asymmetry of the inferior frontal gyrus, may be evident in the pongid brain (Cantalupo and Hopkins 2001). "The existence of a Broca's area homologue in the great apes, if it were to be supported by studies at the microarchitectonic level, would lend support to a theory of the very early emergence of neurolinguistic preconditions in the hominid line" (Wilkins 2005: 278–279).

While many details remain to be discovered, it is undeniable that in the course of human evolution, human brains developed in such a way as to feature both a POT and a Broca's area, and it is therefore relevant to investigate not only when this occurred, but what the anatomical precursors of these areas might have been in older and related species. We can do this in part by a study of comparative primate anatomy, and importantly, by recognizing that in evolutionary biology, we need to consider more than simple adaptation. In very early human evolutionary history, a motor-related frontal area co-evolved with a somatosensory posterior area due to adaptations related to control of the hand, especially the thumb. These adaptations were shaped by selection for better tool making and use and better predation at a distance. This resulted in Brodmann's areas 44 and 45 (roughly, but not simply, so-called Broca's area) and Brodmann's areas 39 and 40, the POT, connected via the major fiber tract, including the superior longitudinal fasciculus and the arcuate fasciculus. These features, so important for language, did not evolve originally in support of linguistic cognition or behavior. Once in place, however, they were available for exaptation, and in modern humans are critically important pieces of the language system. Homologs, and therefore evidence of ancestral precursors, can be found in non-human primates. Importantly, however, these homologs are not features that support communication systems in related ape or monkey species.

In summary thus far, we have a scenario that involves adaptation or adaptations specifically for better neural control of the hand. Improvements in hand control made for better toolmakers and hunters, and such related behaviors and systems. The resulting neuroanatomical structures were then available for exaptation (or reappropriation) for other purposes (a relatively normal and unremarkable process). Evolutionary development of the posterior parietal cortex created the neuroanatomical basis for amodal representations—that is, representations with no single modality-relevant signature. This POT region is connected to Broca's area, which is derived from motor cortex and involves hierarchical structuring. By virtue of its connections to the POT, it can impart order and structure, specifically hierarchical structure, on the amodal representations, hence human-specific conceptual structure, as necessary for language.

15.4 Language—narrow versus broad construals

Human-specific conceptual structure is necessary, but not sufficient for language. This connects directly, then, to a lengthy contemporary discussion in the scientific literature about the evolution of language: the exchange among Hauser, Chomsky, and Fitch (2002), Pinker and Jackendoff (2005), Fitch, Hauser, and Chomsky (2005a), and Jackendoff and Pinker (2005). Much of this debate back and forth involves which aspects of human cognition are uniquely human and which aspects of uniquely human cognition are unique to the language faculty. The discussion is frequently couched in terms of the distinction between the faculty of language narrowly construed, or FLN, and the faculty of language broadly construed, or FLB. FLN contains aspects of language that are both uniquely human and unique to language; FLB contains organism-internal features of language that may be shared with other human cognitive systems and/or with other species. For Hauser, Chomsky, and Fitch, FLN contains only recursion.[6]

Surely conceptual structure, relevant for language, but also for other sorts of non-linguistic cognition, falls into the FLB realm. However, it may well be that hierarchically structured, modality-neutral representations are uniquely human.[7]

> Most, if not all, of FLB is based on mechanisms shared with nonhuman animals. . . . FLB as a whole thus has an ancient evolutionary history, long predating the emergence of language, and a comparative analysis is necessary to understand this system. The available comparative data on animal communication systems suggest that the faculty of language as a whole relies on some uniquely human capacities that have evolved recently . . . only FLN falls into this category. . . . FLB contains a wide variety of cognitive and perceptual mechanisms shared with other species, but only those mechanisms underlying FLN—particularly its capacity for discrete infinity—are uniquely human.
>
> (Hauser, Chomsky, and Fitch 2002: 1573)

This FLN–FLB dichotomy, as here described, would not seem to countenance human-specific aspects of conceptual structure that are necessary for language. Because these would be shared with other aspects of cognition, they would not fall within FLN; but because they are not shared with other species, they would not fall within FLB.

Because of expansion and exaptation within the biological system relevant to FLB (specifically within the frontal-parietal system involving Broca's area and the POT), there is at least one uniquely human aspect of conceptual-intentional FLB: hierarchically structured modality-neutral representation. The claim here is that this aspect of conceptual structure

---

[6] What exactly is meant by recursion in this context is the subject of much contemporary discussion, most notoriously perhaps, in the context of the language Pirahã, claimed to have no recursive grammatical structures (see, for example, Everett 2005; Nevins et al. 2007; Everett 2007). Particularly relevant in this discussion, and as highlighted by Pinker and Jackendoff, is the potential distinction between recursion and discrete infinity. Further review of this, while important, lies beyond the scope of this chapter.

[7] This is, of course, an empirical issue. Evidence to date suggests that the sort of highly processed information characteristic of the POT is unique to humans. Barsalou et al. (2003) take issue with the notion of amodal, or modality neutral, representations, recasting the relevant findings in terms of what they call modality-specific re-enactments. While there is much in their work with which I would take issue, the important point for current purposes is that however the human capacity is to be characterized, it is not shared with other primates.

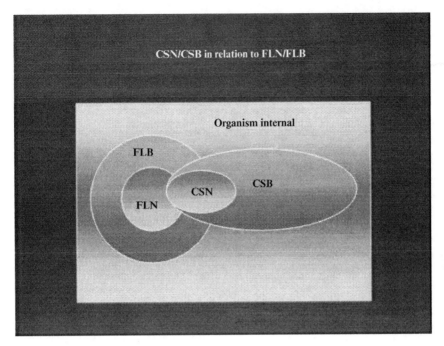

Fig. 15.1. CSN/CSB in relation to FLN/FLB

connects very directly to FLN, and may, in fact, have served to influence its evolutionary development.

Following Chomsky's example in developing the notion of FLN versus FLB, it is equally relevant to distinguish between conceptual structure broadly construed and narrowly construed, and hence between CSN and CSB. Without directly addressing here the issue of whether recursion is a/the feature of FLN, I suggest the representation of the interaction between FLN and CSN as depicted in Figure 15.1.

The features of conceptual structure provided for by the Broca's area–POT complex are those that are contained in CSN. Those aspects of CSN that are then unique to language intersect and overlap with FLN. As indicated, there are features of CSB not unique to language and presumably also not unique to humans. There is credible evidence supporting the idea that the nature of CSN is responsible, in large part, for the nature of linguistic meaning as represented in the lexicon, made up (as suggested by Jackendoff 2002 and many references therein) of relevant pieces of conceptual structure. This would fit well also with suggestions in Hauser,

Chomsky, and Fitch (2002) about a potentially uniquely human aspect of what is currently, in their model, part of FLB, namely the acquisition of words.[8]

15.5 Spatial concepts and spatial structure

Returning to the neuroanatomical mosaic relevant to language, let us consider next the fact that conceptual structure, especially as revealed in language, is intimately connected with spatial structure. Many linguists have made this point, often in conjunction with discussions of thematic relations, and it is explicitly discussed in detail in Jackendoff (2002, and earlier work cited therein). Language is permeated with spatial concepts of motion and location, a fact captured in linguistic theory by some version of spatial function representation like that given in example (1).

$$(1) \quad \text{a.} \quad [_{\text{Event}} \text{ GO } ([\alpha], \begin{bmatrix} \text{FROM } ([\beta]) \\ \text{TO } ([\gamma]) \end{bmatrix}_{\text{Path}})]$$

$$\text{b.} \quad [_{\text{State}} \text{ BE } ([\alpha], [_{\text{Place}} \beta])]$$

$$\text{c.} \quad [_{\text{Event}} \text{ STAY } ([\alpha], [_{\text{Place}} \beta])]$$

(1a), for example, would be a partial meaning representation for an event predicate that involves an entity going along a path. The variables in square brackets would be co-indexed with particular syntactic formatives (e.g. NPs or PPs bearing particular grammatical relations) in a given sentence. So, (1a) would be relevant for a sentence in which entity α goes along a path from β to γ, such as *The horse trotted from the stall to the arena*. (1b) involves an entity, α, in a state of being at place β, such as in *Sonny is in the pasture*, and (1c) is the partial meaning representation for a staying-type event, such as in *The mare waited at the gate*. Sentential meanings can involve spatial predicates in more or less concrete fashion, as indicated in (2), all of which involve GO-type events as in (1a).

(2) a. The ball rolled to Bill.   (spatial motion)
    b. Susan inherited the estate from her mother.   (possession)

---

[8] CSN as conceived of here certainly constitutes a considerable part of conceptual-intentional FLB, and is likely also, as a matter of fact, to touch on aspects of sensory-motor FLB. Thus, as we learn more, the diagram may become increasingly complicated.

    c. She abruptly went from happy to sad. (ascription of properties)
    d. The meeting lasted from noon to dusk.   (temporal duration)
    e. The road goes from Phoenix to Tucson.

(geographical extension)

Further, individual verbal predicates can lexicalize multiple components of the spatial function representation, as in (3).

(3) a. He pocketed the proceeds.
      (pocket = go from some location to in-a-pocket)
    b. She pastured the horses.
      (pasture = go along a path from not-in-a-pasture to in-a-pasture)
    c. The sky darkened.
      (darken = go from less-dark to more-dark)

Much more can be, and has been, said about spatial predicate representation (see, again, Jackendoff 2002 and many references therein). The spatial functions involving GO, BE, and STAY result in the thematic relations of theme (an entity GOing, BEing, or STAYing), location (the Place of the theme), source (the beginning point of a Path), and goal (the end point of a Path). Conceptual structures for predicates include thematic information of this sort, and this information is included in the lexicon, where word meanings are stored or created.

Also available to the lexicon is information about objects. Jackendoff, for instance, has suggested that lexical entries involve 3D model representations much like those proposed by Marr (see Landau and Jackendoff 1993, in addition to Jackendoff 2002), and that therefore conceptual structures per se need not include all spatial information, only what is relevant for the syntax. Such syntactically relevant features would include, for example, indications of shape or orientation that might affect morphology in languages with classifier systems. The lexicon would also include features that can specifically affect word meanings, like the way the shape of the hand distinguishes between "slap" and "punch," etc.

Without taking the time to rehearse all the reasons, it is evident that spatial structure is relevant to conceptual structure, and that this is an aspect of conceptual structure that is relevant to language (in the sense of conceptual-intentional FLB, because spatial structure is certainly relevant to non-linguistic conceptual structure as well). Thus, it is appropriate to investigate the neuroanatomy underlying spatial structure and to consider the manner in which it becomes incorporated into the linguistic system, or in other words, to consider the anatomical basis of aspects of spatial structure as part of the neurobiological language mosaic.

15.6 Conceptual Space

As it turns out, it is neither accidental nor surprising that language incorporates aspects of spatial structure. In fact, conceptual structure, because of its basic underlying biology, necessarily includes aspects of spatial cognition (Wakefield and Wilkins 2007). Spatial cognition involves portions of posterior parietal cortex (PPC) that lie adjacent to the POT, specifically Brodmann's areas 5 and 7, which lie along the intraparietal sulcus.

There has been a great deal of work on the neuroanatomical basis of spatial cognition, and it is well accepted that spatial information is based on quite broadly distributed structures. The aspects of spatial representation that the PPC is responsible for involve information about either the location of an object or its geometrical configuration and orientation. It is also responsible for information concerning an intended action associated with a specific object, especially the reaching for or grasping of an object with a particular shape and at a particular location.

The comparative areas in the monkey brain are 7a, 7b, and 5, again lying along the intraparietal sulcus. Especially relevant are areas within the intraparietal sulcus. Four of these areas are dedicated to functions that involve the hand and forearm, and specifically the shape of the hand and the extension of the arm that are needed to execute a successful grasp (Andersen 1997; Andersen et al. 1997; Andersen and Buneo 2002; Binkofski et al. 1998; Colby and Duhamel 1996; Culham and Kanwisher 2001; Freund 2001; Matelli and Luppino 2001; Murata et al. 2000; Rushworth et al. 2001; Shikata et al. 2003). Other varieties of spatial cognition are handled elsewhere in the brain. Thus, the aspects of spatial cognition for which PPC anatomy is responsible are specifically somatosensory in nature (Freund 2001). "PPC neurons specialize in the conversion of spatially-defined object representations—built from sensory input—to spatially-defined, body-part end state representations such that real-time execution of an intended action brings the object and the body part in question into spatial and/or geometric congruity" (Wakefield and Wilkins 2007: 374–375).

Recall, however, that the parietal lobe is not responsible for motor programs (actions). The PPC representations relevant for spatially defined object representation and body-part end states (i.e. grasping) cannot contain any information about real-time execution. Therefore they themselves do not actually result in any action. Importantly, however, these PPC areas are directly and reciprocally connected to premotor areas of the frontal lobe (for discussion of neuroanatomy relevant to the real-time execution of a spatio-temporally configured plan, see Andersen et al. 1997; Cerri et al. 2003; Graziano and Gross 1998; Hoshi and Tanji 2000; Kakei et al. 2003; Matsumoto et al. 2003). Each of the four relevant areas of the intraparietal sulcus of the PPC is connected to a specific premotor area. Only because the PPC and frontal lobe structures work together can a successful object-oriented action (a successful grasp) be executed. These frontal-parietal circuits are basic to the primate cortical motor system, and homologous in humans and non-human primates.

This particular PPC-frontal circuit is actually only one part of the story about spatial representations, the one involving limb-related peripersonal space. As far as spatial structure reflected in conceptual structure, and ultimately in language, is concerned, there must be an explanatory story as well about objects in motion and at a distance, and an account of the linguistically salient egocentric–allocentric distinction. These are also addressed in Wakefield and Wilkins (2007), in which it is demonstrated that they all have a close and important connection to the PPC-frontal circuitry.

Returning to the matter of the thematic relations (theme, source, goal, location) exemplified in (1)–(3), the idea is that these relations are derivable from, actually based in, the anatomy of the PPC-frontal system just discussed. A limb executing a grasp necessarily involves a theme moving along a path from an initial location to a goal.[9] A grasp is literally the archetypal path-involved event.[10]

---

[9] In connection to interesting recent work, such as by Arbib 2005 and Rizzolatti and Arbib 1998, on mirror neurons, it is relevant to note that for primates visual information becomes readily integrated into this somatosensory-based spatial representation because limb movements are easily visible to the individual executing the movement. This visual integration is critically important, also, to the mosaic neurobiology relevant for language.

[10] An anonymous referee for this volume has mentioned that the "mapping of space (or tracking of objects) does seem to be relevant for reference, at least of a deictic kind." This is not an area that I have pursued, but it would seem to be of potential interest. Deictic reference, of the most concrete sort (keeping track linguistically of objects salient in the

What is particularly relevant here, for conceptual structure and therefore language, is the evolutionary relationship between spatial structure-related, non-POT areas of the PPC and the POT itself, as well as between frontal lobe areas F5 and F4 and Broca's area. Given the evolutionary development and expansion of the parietal lobe, and its direct and reciprocal connections to the frontal lobe, and the evolutionary adaptations involving the hand, it is neither accident nor coincidence that representations resulting from the POT (that is, conceptual structure in humans) intimately involve spatial information of precisely this action-related sort. Somatosensory spatial representations concerning the hand and arm, and how the limb connects with objects external to the body, all involve objects, their body-external locations, and the paths that the limb must traverse to connect with the objects. Given what is known about human PPC, much from the study of homologous areas in the non-human primates, and given how the PPC is connected to the uniquely human POT (see detail in Wakefield and Wilkins 2007 and references therein), human conceptual structure necessarily involves somatosensory-based spatial structure. Serious consideration of the anatomy of PPC and its connectivity with the POT leads to the conclusion that it could be no other way.

In summary then with respect to these particular sorts of spatial constructs and their evident involvement in human conceptual structure and language, there is reason to consider PPC (and connected frontal areas) part of the mosaic neurobiology of language. The PPC is responsible for the fact that object place and path-related thematic relations are so salient in human linguistic expression. Evidence for the spatial basis of these aspects of conceptual structure is clearly evident in the non-human primates. The basic research has been done in monkeys and involves single electrode mapping, and is thus extremely precise. The discussed regions of PPC (areas 7 and 5), with their indisputable homologs in the non-human primates, were certainly features of the neuroanatomy of the last common ancestor of the pongids and hominids.

The human POT derived from primate precursors in the PPC; human [spatial structure], therefore, is derived from primate spatial cognition. And basic aspects

spatial context) would certainly seem within the cognitive capacity of many non-human species. It would be more abstract aspects of reference, such as are typically accounted for by constraints on pronouns and anaphors, that would most likely require human-specific capacity. Whether any of this is due to anatomical structures in the PPC remains to be determined.

of human [conceptual structure] derive from the connectivity that developed between the POT (amodal, action-related spatial representation) and Broca's area (imparting hierarchical structure to the POT-derived spatial tier primitives).

(Wakefield and Wilkins 2007: 390)

These recent discoveries about homologous primate posterior parietal neuroanatomy, plus what is known about neocortical expansion in the hominid line, underscore support for the research strategy developed in Wilkins and Wakefield (1995) plus the particulars of the analysis of the evolutionary creation of the POT and its connections to Broca's area.

15.7 Anatomical plausibility

As far as we know, the details of the spatial features of conceptual structure are human-specific, especially the generalization of space-related thematic relations across semantic fields (as illustrated in (2) and (3)). The anatomical basis of these spatial thematic relations, however, is shared with the non-human primates. In all likelihood, the basic facts of spatial structure in its more concrete form would also be shared. This is just what is to be expected if we insist, as I believe we should, that each and every claim about the evolution of language be biologically, specifically anatomically, plausible. Language neuroanatomy is comprised of a biological system of highly interconnected pieces put together in uniquely human fashion. The PPC-frontal circuitry underlying these thematic relations is shared with all primates, but the PPC evolutionary development yielding the POT is uniquely human. Hence an account of a piece of human linguistic uniqueness.

Clearly, this sort of account does not mean that linguistic precursors are non-existent in other species. Importantly, however, it also does not provide evidence that such precursors are to be found in the communication systems of other species. A thorough examination of the anatomical basis of the neurobiology of language does not motivate an evolutionary account of language involving simply the adaptation of primate communication systems. The story is much more subtle and complicated.

The various pieces of the human neuroanatomical mosaic that we have considered here include Broca's area, the POT, PPC areas 7 and 5, and peripherally, Wernicke's area and the planum temporale. All of these would appear to be language-relevant neuroanatomy, without which language would be either impossible, or minimally, would have a markedly different character. There are other parts of the brain that are also involved in linguistic cognition, including certain subcortical structures, especially the major parietal-frontal fiber tracts, and maybe others.[11] Wilkins (2007) suggests, based most proximately on work by Cheney and Seyfarth (2005), that certain non-spatial aspects of conceptual structure may derive from other prefrontal areas (also connected to the POT).

Thematic relations involving the structure of actions (such as agent, patient, benefactee, etc.) would seem to be most closely related to aspects of the "social calculus" (Bickerton 2000). These are arguably most directly derivable from the same sorts of prefrontal processes involved in social relations, many of which are characteristic of non-human primates. Thus, another anatomical mosaic piece becomes potentially relevant to the over-all story of the evolutionary biology of language, and would seem to call out for further investigation. If it turns out to be the case that the underly-ing anatomy relevant for action-event structure can be definitively located, and if it turns out to be the case that this anatomy is shared between humans and other primates, it is fair to claim that it would be a feature of the last common ancestor of both. It would thus be a feature of the more modern *H. habilis* neuroanatomy.

Further, if the anatomical basis of action-event structure can be found, including the basis (as in a social calculus) of the critical distinction between an agent (doer of an action) and a patient (one who undergoes an action), this would allow for an account of the most basic of syn-tactic (phrase structure) configurations: the external–internal argument distinction. Universal grammar of human language would seem to need to distinguish between the grammatical subject (the prototypical external argument) and the predicate (the verb phrase or other constituent con-taining non-subject arguments). Recent work on alarm calls of monkeys and gestures of apes is providing insight into complicated systems of social relations in which it is necessary for members of groups to keep track of, for instance, who has done what to whom. Surely the anatomical structures that allow this tracking will be shown to be shared across primate species.

---

[11] Lieberman (2007, and elsewhere) has written extensively in support of the involve-ment of the basil ganglia in language.

Such anatomical structure would then be ripe for evolutionary exaptation into the biological system underlying language.

15.8 Conclusion

The primary point to be made here is that, whatever else we may require of research on the origins of language, we must insist that the hypotheses made be anatomically (and, ultimately, genetically) plausible. One way to assure such biological plausibility is to be mindful of work on the neurobiology of language in the only language-possessing species, *H sapiens*, and to consider the evolutionary trajectory of each aspect of the language faculty. To do this requires that attention be paid to comparative primate neuroanatomy and recognition that the biology of language involves a mosaic of many functionally interconnecting anatomical mosaic pieces.

To the extent that the specific features of primate neuroanatomy discussed above remain well supported (considerable further support is provided in Wakefield and Wilkins 2007), there is good reason to believe that the first language-ready (or, minimally, protolanguage-ready) hominid was *H. habilis*, fossil remains of whom have been located only in Africa. While not the original focus of the research program, this does provide a basis for the claim not only that the roots of the language-capable brain are as ancient as the original bifurcation of the hominid and pongid lines, but also that language ability originated on the African continent and spread outward from there as other, more modern, species developed.

References

Aboitiz, F., García, R. R., Bosman, C., and Brunetti, E. (2006). Cortical memory mechanisms and language origins. *Brain and Language* 98: 40–56.

Abraham, W. (1993). Grammatikalisierung und Reanalyse: einander ausschließende oder ergänzende Begriffe. *Folia Linguistica Historica* 13: 7–26.

Adams, A.-M. and Gathercole, S. E. (2000). Limitations in working memory: implications for language development. *International Journal of Language and Communication Disorders* 35: 95–116.

Adams, C. (2002). Practitioner review: the assessment of language pragmatics. *Journal of Child Psychology and Psychiatry* 43: 973–987. http://clt.sagepub.com/cgi/external_ref?access_num=10.1111/1469-7610.00226&link_type=DOI

Adams, P. R. (1997). Hebb and Darwin. *Journal of Theoretical Biology* 195: 419–498.

—— (2000). To sleep, perchance to dream: the neocortical basis of mind, sleep and dreams. *Science Spectra* 23: 46–55.

—— and Cox, K. (2002). A new interpretation of thalamocortical circuitry. *Philosophical Transactions of the Royal Society of London Sciences. Series B: Biological Sciences* 357: 1767–1779.

Adamson, L. R. (1996). *Communication development during infancy*. Boulder, CO: Westview Press.

Aiello, L. C. (1996). Terrestriality, bipedalism and the origin of language. In W. G. Runciman, J. Maynard-Smith, and R. I. M. Dunbar (eds.), *Evolution of social behaviour patterns in primates and man*. Oxford: Oxford University Press, 269–290.

—— and Dunbar, R. I. M. (1993). Neocortex size, group size, and the evolution of language. *Current Anthropology* 34: 184–193.

—— and Wheeler, P. (1995). The expensive-tissue hypothesis. *Current Anthropology* 36: 199–221.

Albersnagel, F. A. (1988). Velten and musical mood induction procedures: a comparison with accessibility of thought associations. *Behaviour Research and Theory* 26(1): 79–96.

Andersen, R. A. (1997). Multimodal integration for the representation of space in the posterior parietal cortex. *Philosophical Transactions of the Royal Society of London. Series B: Biological Sciences* 352(1360): 1421–1428.

—— and Buneo, C. A. (2002). Intentional maps in posterior parietal cortex. *Annual Review of Neuroscience* 25: 189–220.

Andersen, R. A., Snyder, L. H., Bradley, D. C., and Xing, J. (1997). Multimodal representation of space in the posterior parietal cortex and its use in planning movements. *Annual Review of Neuroscience* 20: 303–330.

Anderson, S. R. and Lightfoot, D. W. (2002). *The language organ: linguistics as cognitive physiology*. Cambridge: Cambridge University Press.

Ando, J., Ono, Y., and Wright, M. J. (2002). Genetic structure of spatial and verbal working memory. *Behavior Genetics* 31: 615–624.

Aoki, K. and Feldman, M. W. (1987). Toward a theory for the evolution of cultural communication. Coevolution of signal transmission and reception. *PNAS USA* 84: 7164–7168.

Arbib, M. A. (2003). The evolving mirror system: a neural basis for language readiness. In M. H. Christiansen and S. Kirby (eds.), *Language evolution*. Oxford: Oxford University Press, 182–200.

——(2004). From monkey-like action recognition to human language: an evolutionary framework for neurolinguistics. *Behavioral and Brain Sciences*. Text distributed by BBS for peer commentary.

——(2005). From monkey-like action recognition to human language: an evolutionary framework for neurolinguistics. *Behavioral and Brain Sciences* 28(2): 105–124.

Arensburg, B., Schepartz, L. A., Tillier, A. M., Vandermeersch, B., and Rak, Y. (1990). A reappraisal of the anatomical basis for speech in Middle Palaeolithic hominids. *American Journal of Physical Anthropology* 83: 137–156.

——Tillier, A. M., Duday, H., Schepartz, L. A., and Rak, Y. (1989). A Middle Palaeolithic human hyoid bone. *Nature* 338: 758–760.

Armstrong, D. F., Stokoe, W. C., and Wilcox, S. E. (1995). *Gesture and the nature of language*. Cambridge: Cambridge University Press.

Arsuaga, J. L. (2002). *The Neanderthal's necklace*. New York: Four Walls Eight Windows.

Ashton, N. M. and McNabb, J. (1994). Bifaces in perspective. In N. M. Ashton and A. David (eds.), *Stories in stone. Lithics studies society* (Occasional Paper) 4: 182–191.

Auer, P., Couper-Kuhlen, E., and Müller, F. (1999). *Language in time: the rhythm and tempo of spoken interaction*. New York: Oxford University Press.

Avrutin, S. (2001). Linguistics and agrammatism. *GLOT International* 5(3): 1–11.

Axelrod, R. (2005). Agent-based modeling as a bridge between disciplines. In L. Kenneth and L. Tesfatsion (eds.), *Handbook of computational economics*, Vol. 2. Amsterdam: Agent-Based Computational Economics.

Baddeley, A. D. (2000). The episodic buffer: A new component of working memory? *Trends in Cognitive Sciences* 4: 417–423.

——(2001). Is working memory still working? *American Psychologist* 11: 851–864.

——(2003). Working memory and language: an overview. *Journal of Communication Disorders* 36(3): 189–208.

Baddeley, A. D. and Hitch, G. J. (1974). Working memory. In G. A. Bower (ed.), *Recent advances in learning and motivation*. New York: Academic Press, 47–90.

—— and Logie, R. H. (1999). Working memory: the multiple-component model. In A. Miyake and P. Shah (eds.), *Models of working memory: mechanisms of active maintenance and executive control*. New York: Cambridge University Press, 28–61.

—— Gathercole, S., and Papagno, C. (1998). The phonological loop as a language learning device. *Psychological Review* 105: 158–173.

Bak, P. (1996). *How nature works: the science of self-organized criticality*. New York: Copernicus.

Bakeman, R. and Adamson, L. B. (1986). Infants' conventionalized acts: gestures and words with mothers and peers. *Infant Behavior and Development* 9: 215–230.

Balaban, M. and Waxman, S. (1996). Words may facilitate categorization in 9-month-old infants. *Journal of Experimental Child Psychology* 64: 3–26.

Baldwin, D. A. and Moses, L. J. (1996). The ontogeny of social information gathering. *Child Development* 67: 1915–1939.

Balter, M. (2005). Are humans still evolving? *Science* 309: 234–237.

Bard, K. A. (1990). "Social tool use" by free-ranging orangutans: a Piagetian and developmental perspective on the manipulation of an animate object. In S. T. Parker and K. R. Gibson (eds.), *"Language" and intelligence in monkeys and apes: comparative developmental perspectives*. Cambridge: Cambridge University Press, 356–378.

—— (1992). Intentional behavior and intentional communication in young free-ranging orangutans. *Child Development* 62: 1186–1197.

—— and Leavens, D. A. (in press). Socio-emotional factors in the development of joint attention in human and ape infants. In L. Roska-Hardy and E. M. Neumann-Held (eds.), *Learning from animals?* London: Psychology Press.

—— and Vauclair, J. (1984). The communicative context of object manipulation in ape and human adult–infant pairs. *Journal of Human Evolution* 13: 181–190.

Baronchelli, A., Felici, M., Caglioti, E., Loreto, V., and Steels, L. (2006). Sharp transition towards shared vocabularies in multi-agent systems. *Journal of Statistical Mechanics: Theory and Experiment* P06014.

Baron-Cohen, S. (1989). Perceptual role-taking and protodeclarative pointing in autism. *British Journal of Developmental Psychology* 7: 113–127.

—— (1995). *Mindblindness: an essay on autism and theory of mind*. Cambridge, MA: MIT Press.

—— (1999). The evolution of a theory of mind. In M. C. Corballis and S. E. G. Lea (eds.), *The descent of mind: psychological perspectives on Hominid Evolution*. Oxford: Oxford University Press, 261–277.

Barot, S., Ugolini, A., and Brikci, F. B. (2007). Nutrient cycling efficiency explains the long-term effect of ecosystem engineers on primary production. *Functional Ecology* 21: 1–10.

Barrett, L. and Henzi, P. (2005). The social nature of primate cognition. *Proceedings of the Royal Society* B 272: 1865–1875.

Barsalou, L. W., Simmons, W. K., Barbey, A. K., and Wilson, C. D. (2003). Grounding conceptual knowledge in modality-specific systems. *Trends in Cognitive Sciences* 7(2): 84–91.

Barton, R. A. and Dunbar, R. I. M. (1997). Evolution of the social brain. In A. Whiten and R. Byrne (eds.), *Machiavellian intelligence II*. Cambridge: Cambridge University Press, 240–263.

Basso, E. (1985). *A musical view of the universe*. Philadelphia: University of Pennsylvania Press.

Batali, J. (2002). The negotiation and acquisition of recursive grammars as a result of competition among exemplars. In E. Briscoe (ed.), *Linguistic evolution through language acquisition: formal and computational models*. Cambridge: Cambridge University Press, 111–172.

Bates, E. (1976). Language and context: the acquisition of pragmatics. New York: Academic Press.

——Camaioni, L., and Volterra, V. (1975). The acquisition of performatives prior to speech. *Merrill-Palmer Quarterly* 21: 205–226.

Bateson, G. (1950/1973). A theory of play and fantasy. In G. Bateson, *Steps to an ecology of mind*. London: Paladin, 150–166.

Bednarik, R. (1995). Concept-mediated marking in the Lower Palaeolithic. *Current Anthropology* 36: 605–632.

Bekoff, M. (2001). Social play behavior: cooperation, fairness, trust, and the evolution of morality. *Journal of Consciousness Studies* 8(2): 81–90.

——and Allen, C. (1998). Intentional communication and social play: how and why animals negotiate and agree to play. In M. Bekoff and J. A. Byers (eds.), *Animal play: evolutionary, comparative, and ecological perspectives*. Cambridge: Cambridge University Press, 97–114.

Bennett, M. R. and Hacker, P. M. S. (2003). *Philosophical Foundations of Neuroscience*. Oxford: Blackwell.

Benson, J. D. and Greaves, W. S. (2005). *Functional dimensions of ape-human discourse*. London: Equinox.

Benzon, W. L. (2001). *Beethoven's Anvil: music in mind and culture*. Oxford: Oxford University Press.

Bergstrom, C. T. and Lachmann, M. (2004). Shannon information and biological fitness. Information theory workshop. *IEEE* 50–54.

Berlin, B. (2005). "Just another fish story?" Size-symbolic properties of fish names. In A. Minelli, G. Ortalli, and G. Sanga (eds.), *Animal names*. Venice: Instituto Veneto di Scienze, Lettre ed Arti, 9–21.

Bickerton, D. (1984). The language bioprogram hypothesis. *Behavioral and Brain Sciences* 7: 173–188.

—— (1990). *Language and species.* Chicago: Chicago University Press.

—— (1995). *Language and human behaviour.* Seattle: University of Washington Press.

—— (1998) Catastrophic evolution: the case for a single step from protolanguage to full human language. In J. R. Hurford, M. Studdert-Kennedy, and C. Knight (eds.), *Approaches to the evolution of language: social and cognitive bases.* Cambridge: Cambridge University Press, 341–358.

—— (2000). How protolanguage became language. In C. Knight, M. Studdert-Kennedy, and J. Hurford (eds.), *The evolutionary emergence of language: social function and the origins of linguistic form.* Cambridge: Cambridge University Press, 264–284.

—— (in press) *Adam's tongue: how humans made language and how language made humans.* New York: Farrar Straus and Giroux.

Binkofski, F., Dohle, C., Posse, S., Stephan, K. M., Hefter, H., Seitz, R. J., and Freund, H. J. (1998). Human anterior parietal area subserves prehension: a combined lesion and functional MRI Activation Study. *Neurology* 50: 1253–1259.

Bischof-Koehler, D. (2006). Theory of mind and mental time travel: specifically human abilities. Paper presented at the Second Biennial Conference on Cognitive Science, 9–13 June, St. Petersburg.

Bispham, J. (2006). Rhythm in music: what is it? who has it? and why? *Music Perception* 24(2): 125–134.

Bjorklund, D. F. and Green, B. (1992). The adaptive nature of cognitive immaturity. *American Psychologist* 47: 46–54.

Blacking, J. (1973, 1976). *How musical is man?* Seattle: University of Washington Press. London: Faber.

—— (1995). *Music, culture and experience.* London: University of Chicago Press.

Blood, A. J. and Zatorre, R. J. (2001). Intensely pleasurable responses to music correlate with activity in brain regions implicated in reward and emotion. *Proceedings of the National Academy of Sciences* 98(20): 11818–11823.

Bloom, L. (1993). *The transition from infancy to language: acquiring the power of expression.* Cambridge: Cambridge University Press.

Bloom, P. (2000). *How children learn the meanings of words.* Cambridge, MA: MIT Press.

Bobaljik, J. (2006). Where's phi? Agreement as a post-syntactic operation. http://web.uconn.edu/bobaljik/papers/Phi.pdf.

Bodamer, M. D. and Gardner, R. A. (2002). How cross-fostered chimpanzees (*Pan troglodytes*) initiate and maintain conversations. *Journal of Comparative Psychology* 116: 12–26.

Boë, L.-J., Heim, J.-L., Honda, K., and Maeda, S. (2002). The potential Neandertal vowel space was as large as that of modern humans. *Journal of Phonetics* 30(3): 465–484.

——Perrier, P., Guerin, B., and Schwartz, J.-L. (1989). Maximal vowel space. Paper presented at the Eurospeech, Paris.

Bolinger, D. (1978). Intonation across languages. In J. H. Greenberg (ed.), *Universals of human language. Volume 2: Phonology.* Stanford: Stanford University Press, 471–524.

Boltz, M. G. (2001). Musical soundtracks as a schematic influence on the cognitive processing of filmed events. *Music Perception* 18: 427–454.

——(2004). The cognitive processing of film and musical soundtracks. *Memory and Cognition* 32(7): 1194–1205.

Bonvillian, J. D. and Patterson, F. G. P. (1999). Early sign-language acquisition: comparisons between children and gorillas. In S. T. Parker, R. W. Mitchell, and H. Lyn Miles (eds.), *The mentalities of gorillas and orangutans: comparative perspectives.* Cambridge: Cambridge University Press, 240–264.

Borenstein, E., Kendal, J., and Feldman, M. (2006). Cultural niche construction in a metapopulation. *Theoretical Population Biology* 70: 92–104.

Botha, R. (2003). *Unravelling the evolution of language.* Amsterdam: Elsevier.

——(2006). On the Windows Approach to language evolution. *Language and Communication* 26: 129–143.

Boyd, R. and Richerson, P. (1985). *Culture and the evolutionary process.* Chicago: Chicago University Press.

Boysen, S. T. and Berntson, G. G. (1989). Numerical competence in a chimpanzee (*Pan troglodytes*). *Journal of Comparative Psychology* 103: 23–31.

Bramble, D. M. and Lieberman, D. E. (2004). Endurance running and the evolution of *Homo. Nature* 432: 345–352.

Brown, R. (1976). Reference. In memorial tribute to Eric Lenneberg. *Cognition* 4: 125–153.

Brown, S. (1998). Play as an organizing principle: evidence and personal observations. In M. Bekoff and J. A. Byers (eds.), *Animal play: evolutionary, comparative, and ecological perspectives.* Cambridge: Cambridge University Press, 243–259.

Brown, S. (2000). The "musilanguage" model of human evolution. In N. L. Wallin, B. Merker, and S. Brown (eds.), *The origins of music.* Cambridge, MA: MIT Press, 271–300.

Bruner, E. (2004). Geometric morphometrics and paleoneurology: brain shape evolution in the genus *Homo. Journal of Human Evolution* 47: 279–303.

——Manzi, G., and Arsuaga, J. L. (2003). Encephalization and allometric trajectories in the genus *Homo*: evidence from the Neanderthal and modern lineages. *Proceedings of the National Academy of Sciences* 100: 15335–15340.

Bruner J. S. (1976). The nature and uses of immaturity. In J. S. Bruner, A. Jolly, and K. Sylva (eds.), *Play: its role in development and evolution*. Harmondsworth: Penguin, 28–61.

—— (1983). *Child's talk: learning to use language*. New York: Norton.

Bryson, J. J., Bilovich, A., and Cace, I. (in preparation). Adaptive altruistic cooperation in unstructured populations.

Burghardt, G. M. (2005). *The genesis of animal play: testing the limits*. Cambridge, MA: MIT Press.

Burling, R. (1993). Primate calls, human language, and nonverbal communication. *Current Anthropology* 34: 25–53.

Butcher, C., Mylander, C., and Goldin-Meadow, S. (1991). Displaced communication in a self-styled gesture system: pointing at the nonpresent. *Cognitive Development* 6: 315–342.

Butterworth, G. (2003). Pointing is the royal road to language for babies. In S. Kita (ed.), *Pointing: where language, culture, and cognition meet*. Mahwah, NJ: Erlbaum, 9–33.

—— and Grover, L. (1988). The origins of referential communication in human infancy. In L. Weiskrantz (ed.), *Thought without language*. Oxford: Clarendon Press, 5–24.

Butynski, T. M. (1990). Comparative ecology of blue monkeys (Cercopithecus Mitis) in high- and low-density subpopulations. *Ecological Monographs* 60: 1–26.

Buxhoeveden, D. P., Switala, A. E., Litaker, M., Roy, E., and Casanova, M. F. (2001a). Lateralization of minicolumns in human planum temporale is absent in non-human primate cortex. *Brain, Behavior, and Evolution* 57(6): 349–358.

—————————— (2001b). Morphological differences between minicolumns in human and nonhuman primate cortex. *American Journal of Physical Anthropology* 115: 361–371.

Byers, J. A. (1998). Biological effects of locomotor play: getting into shape, or something more specific? In M. Bekoff and J. A. Byers (eds.), *Animal play: evolutionary, comparative, and ecological perspectives*. Cambridge: Cambridge University Press, 205–220.

Bygott, D. (1979). Agonistic behavior and dominance among wild chimpanzees. In D. Hamburg and E. McCown (eds.), *The great apes*. Menlo Park, CA: B. Cummings, 405–427.

Calhim, S., Shi, J., and Dunbar, R. I. M. (2006). Sexual segregation among feral goats: testing between alternative hypotheses. *Animal Behaviour* 72: 31–41.

Call, J. and Tomasello, M. (1994). Production and comprehension of referential pointing by orangutans (*Pongo pygmaeus*). *Journal of Comparative Psychology* 108: 307–317.

Call, J. and Tomasello, M. (1996). The effect of humans on the cognitive development of apes. In A. E. Russon, K. A. Bard, and S. T. Parker (eds.), *Reaching into thought: the minds of the great apes*. Cambridge: Cambridge University Press, 371–403.

—— (2005). What chimpanzees know about seeing revisited: an explanation of the third kind. In N. Eilan, C. Hoerl, T. McCormack, and J. Roessler (eds.), *Joint attention: communication and other minds*. Oxford: Oxford University Press, 45–64.

Calvin, W. H. (1983). A stone's throw and its launch window: timing precision and its implications for language and hominid brains. *Journal of Theoretical Biology* 104: 121–135.

Camaioni, L. (1993). The development of intentional communication: a re-analysis. In J. Nadel and L. Camaioni (eds.), *New perspectives in early communicative development*. London: Routledge, 82–96.

—— Perucchini, P., Bellagamba, F., and Colonnesi, C. (2004). The role of declarative pointing in developing a theory of mind. *Infancy* 5: 291–308.

Cangelosi, A., Smith, A. D. M., and Smith, K. (eds.) (2006). *The evolution of language*. London: World Scientific Co.

Cantalupo, C. and Hopkins, W. D. (2001). Asymmetric Broca's area in great apes. *Nature* 414(6863): 505.

Caramazza, A. and Shelton, J. R. (1998). Domain specific knowledge systems in the brain: the animate–inanimate distinction. *Journal of Cognitive Neuroscience* 10: 1–34.

Carey, S. (1978). The child as word-learner. In M. Halle, J. Bresnan, and G. A. Miller (eds.), *Linguistic theory and psychological reality*. Cambridge, MA: MIT Press, 264–293.

—— (1997). Do constraints on word meanings reflect prelinguistic cognitive architecture? *The Japanese Journal of Cognitive Science* 4: 35–58.

Carpendale, J. I. M., Lewis, C., Müller, U., and Racine, T. P. (2005). Constructing perspectives in the social making of minds. *Interaction Studies* 6: 341–358. (Repr. in P. Hauf and F. Fosterling (eds.) (2007). *Making Minds: The Shaping of Human Minds through Social Contexts*. Amsterdam: Benjamins, 163–178.)

Carpenter, M., Nagell, K., and Tomasello, M. (1998). Social cognition, joint attention, and communicative competence from 9 to 15 months of age. *Monographs of the Society for Research in Child Development* 65(4): Serial No. 255.

Carré, R., Lindblom, B., and MacNeilage, P. F. (1995). Rôle de l'acoustique dans l'évolution du conduit vocal humain. *Comptes rendus de l'Académie des Sciences* Série II 320(série IIb): 471–476.

Carruthers, P. (2002). The cognitive functions of language. *Behavioral and Brain Sciences* 25: 657–674.

—— (2006). *The architecture of the mind: massive modularity and the flexibility of thought*. Oxford: Oxford University Press.

Carstairs-McCarthy, A. (1999). *The origins of complex language: an inquiry into the evolutionary beginnings of sentences, syllables and truth.* Oxford: Oxford University Press.

Cartmill, E. A. and Byrne, R. W. (2007). Orangutans modify their gestural signaling according to their audience's comprehension. *Current Biology* 17: 1345–1348.

Catani, M. and ffytche, D. H. (2005). The rises and falls of disconnection syndromes. *Brain* 128: 2224–2239.

Cavalli-Sforza, L. L. and Feldman, M. W. (1981). *Cultural transmission and evolution: a quantitative approach.* Princeton, NJ: Princeton University Press.

Cerri, G., Shimazu, H., Maier, M. A., and Lemon, R. N. (2003). Facilitation from ventral premotor cortex of primary motor cortex outputs to macaque hand muscles. *Journal of Neurophysiology* 90(2): 832–842.

Chase, J. M. and Leibold, M. A. (2003). *Ecological niches. Linking classical and contemporary approaches.* Chicago: University of Chicago Press.

Cheney, D. L. and Seyfarth, R. M. (1990). *How monkeys see the world.* Chicago: Chicago University Press.

————(2005). Constraints and preadaptations in the earliest stages of language evolution. *The Linguistic Review* 22: 135–159.

Chomsky, N. (1959). On certain formal properties of grammars. *Information and Control* (2): 137–167.

——(1980). On cognitive structures and their development: a reply to Piaget. In M. Piatelli-Palmarini (ed.), *Language and learning: the debate between Jean Piaget and Noam Chomsky.* Cambridge, MA: Harvard University Press.

——(1981). *Lectures on government and binding.* Dordrecht: Foris.

——(1986). *Knowledge of language.* New York: Praeger.

——(1995). *The minimalist program.* Cambridge, MA: MIT Press.

——(2002). *On nature and language.* Cambridge: Cambridge University Press.

——(2004). Beyond explanatory adequacy. In A. Belletti (ed.), *Structures and beyond.* Oxford: Oxford University Press, 104–131.

——(2005a). On phases. Ms. Cambridge, MA: MIT.

——(2005b). Three factors in language design. *Linguistic Inquiry* 36(1): 1–22.

——(2007). Approaching UG from below. In U. Sauerland et al. (eds.), *Interfaces + Recursion = Language?* Berlin: Mouton de Gruyter, 1–29.

Christiansen, M. H. and Kirby, S. (eds.) (2003). *Language evolution.* Oxford: Oxford University Press.

Clark, A. (2005). Language, embodiment, and the cognitive niche. *Trends in Cognitive Science* 10(8): 370–374.

Clark, E. V. (1983). Convention and contrast in acquiring the lexicon. In T. B. Seiler and W. Wannenmacher (eds.), *Cognitive development and the development of word meaning.* Berlin: Springer-Verlag, 67–89.

Clark, E. V. (1987). The principle of contrast: a constraint on language acquisition. In B. MacWhinney (ed.), *Mechanisms of language acquisition*. Hillsdale, NJ: Lawrence Erlbaum, 1–33.

—— (1993). *The lexicon in acquisition*. Cambridge: Cambridge University Press.

Clegg, M. (2001). The comparative anatomy and evolution of the human vocal tract. Unpub. thesis, University of London.

Clendinnen, I. (2005). *Dancing with strangers: Europeans and Australians at first contact*. Cambridge: Cambridge University Press.

Cohen, D. H. (2001). "The imperfect seeks its perfection": harmonic progression, directed motion, and Aristotelian physics. *Music Theory Spectrum* 23(2): 139–169.

Colby, C. L. and Duhamel, J.-R. (1996). Spatial representation for action in parietal cortex. *Cognitive Brain Research* 5(1–2): 105–115.

Combes, C. (2001). *Parasitism: the ecology and evolution of intimate interactions*. Chicago: University of Chicago Press.

Conard, N. J. and Bolus, M. (2003). Radiocarbon dating the appearance of modern humans and timing of cultural innovations in Europe: new results and new challenges. *Journal of Human Evolution* 44: 331–371.

Condillac, E. B. (1971). An essay on the origin of human knowledge; being a supplement to Mr. Locke's Essay on the human understanding. A facimile, reproduction of the translation of Thomas Nugent. Gainesville, FL: Scholars' Facsimile and Reprints.

Condon, W. S. (1986). Communication: rhythm and structure. In J. R. Evans and M. Clynes (eds.), *Rhythm in psychological, linguistic, and musical processes*. Springfield, IL: Charles C. Thomas, 55–78.

Conway, C. M. and Christiansen, M. H. (2001). Sequential learning in non-human primates. *Trends in Cognitive Sciences* 5: 539–546.

Cook, N. (1998). *Music: a very short introduction*. Oxford: Oxford University Press.

Coolidge, F. L. and Wynn, T. (2001). Executive functions of the frontal lobes and the evolutionary ascendancy of *Homo sapiens*. *Cambridge Archaeological Journal* 11: 255–260.

—— —— (2005). Working memory, its executive functions, and the emergence of modern thinking. *Cambridge Archaeological Journal* 15: 5–26.

—— —— (2006a). The role of enhanced working memory in the production of animal and therianthropic art in the Upper Paleolithic. XVth meeting of the International Union for Prehistoric and Protohistoric Sciences, Lisbon.

—— —— (2006b). The effects of the tree-to-ground sleep transition in the evolution of cognition in early *Homo*. *Before Farming: The Archaeology and Anthropology of Hunter-Gatherers* 4: 1–18.

—— —— (2006c). Recursion, pragmatics, and the evolution of modern speech. Paper presented at the Cradle of Language Conference, 6–10 November 2006, Stellenbosch, South Africa.

Coolidge, F. L., Thede, L. L., and Young, S. E. (2000). Heritability and the comorbidity of ADHD with behavioral disorders and executive function deficits: a preliminary investigation. *Developmental Neuropsychology* 17: 273–287.

Corballis, M. C. (1991). *The lopsided ape: evolution of the generative mind.* New York: Oxford University Press.

——(1992). On the evolution of language and generativity. *Cognition* 44: 197–226.

——(2002). Did language evolve from manual gestures? In A. Wray (ed.), *The transition to language.* Oxford: Oxford University Press, 163–180.

Couper-Kuhlen, E. (1993). *English speech rhythm: form and function in everyday verbal interaction.* Amsterdam: J. Benjamins.

Cox, A. W. (2001). The mimetic hypothesis and embodied musical meaning. *Musicae Scientiae* 5: 95–209.

Crawford, V. P. and Sobel, J. (1982). Strategic information transmission. *Econometrica* 50(6): 1431–1451.

Crockford, C., Herbinger, I., Vigilant, L., and Boesch, C. (2004). Wild chimpanzees produce group-specific calls: a case for vocal learning? *Ethology* 110: 221–243.

Croft, W. (2000). *Explaining language change: an evolutionary approach.* London: Longman.

——(2001). *Radical construction grammar: syntactic theory in typological perspective.* Oxford: Oxford University Press.

Cross, I. (1999). Is music the most important thing we ever did? Music, development and evolution. In Suk Won Yi (ed.), *Music, mind and science.* Seoul: Seoul National University Press, 10–39.

——(2001). Music, mind and evolution. *Psychology of Music* 29: 95–102.

——(2003). Music and evolution: causes and consequences. *Contemporary Music Review* 22(3): 79–89.

——(2005). Music and meaning, ambiguity and evolution. In D. Miell, R. MacDonald, and D. Hargreaves (eds.), *Musical communication.* Oxford: Oxford University Press, 27–43.

——(2006). Music and social being. *Musicology Australia* 28: 114–126.

Cruse, D. A. (2000). *Meaning in language: an introduction to semantics and pragmatics.* New York: Oxford University Press.

Culham, J. C. and Kanwisher, N. G. (2001). Neuroimaging of cognitive functions in human parietal cortex. *Current Opinion in Neurobiology* 11(2): 157–163.

Damasio, A. (1994). *Descartes' error: emotion, reason and the human brain.* New York: Putnam.

Damasio, H., Tranel, D., Grabowski, T. J., Adolphs, R., and Damasio, A. R. (2004). Neural systems behind word and concept retrieval. *Cognition* 92: 179–229.

Darwin, C. (1871). *The descent of man, and selection in relation to sex* (2 vols.). London: Murray.

Darwin, C. (1881). *The formation of vegetable mold through the action of worms, with observations on their habits.* London: Murray.

—— (1872/1998). *The expression of the emotions in man and animals* 3rd edn. London: HarperCollins.

Davidson, I. (1997). Conference report. *Evolution of Communication* 1: 157–179.

—— (2003). The archaeological evidence of language origins: states of the art. In M. H. Christiansen and S. Kirby (eds.), *Language evolution.* Oxford: Oxford University Press, 140–157.

—— (2006). The importance of archaeological evidence for investigating the evolutionary emergence of language. Keynote address presented at the Cradle of Language Conference, 7–10 November 2006, Stellenbosch, South Africa.

Davies, J. B. (1978). *The psychology of music.* London: Hutchinson.

Davies, N. B., Kilner, R. M., and Noble, D. G. (1998). Nestling cuckoos, *cuculus canorus,* exploit hosts with begging calls that mimic a brood. *Proceedings of the Royal Society of London. Series B: Biological Sciences* 265: 673–678.

Davis, N. (1971). *Paston letters and chapters of the fifteenth century.* Part I. Oxford: Clarendon.

Dawes, C. T., Fowler, J. H., Johnson, T., McElreath, R., and Smirnov, O. (2007). Egalitarian motives in humans. *Nature* 446: 794–796.

Dawkins, R. (1982). *The extended phenotype.* Freeman: Oxford.

—— (1989). *The selfish gene.* New York: Oxford University Press.

de Almeida, R. G. (1999). What do category-specific semantic deficits tell us about the representation of lexical concepts? *Brain and Language* 68: 241–248.

de Beule, J. and Bergen, B. K. (2006). On the emergence of compositionality. In A. Cangelosi, A. Smith, and K. Smith (eds.), *Proceedings of the 6th evolution of language conference.* London: World Scientific, 107–115.

de Boer, B. (2001). *The origins of vowel systems.* Oxford: Oxford University Press.

de Miguel, C. and Heneberg, M. (2001). Variation in hominin brain size: how much is due to method? *Homo* 52: 3–58.

de Waal, F. B. M. (1982). *Chimpanzee politics: power and sex among apes.* New York: Harper and Row.

Deacon, T. W. (1997). *The symbolic species: the co-evolution of language and the brain.* London: Penguin Press and New York: Norton.

Deliège, I. and Sloboda, J. A. (eds.) (1996). *Musical beginnings.* Oxford: Oxford University Press.

d'Errico, F. and Nowell, A. (2000). A new look at the Berekhat Ram figurine: implications for the origins of symbolism. *Cambridge Archaeological Journal* 10: 123–167.

—— and Villa, P. (1997). Holes and grooves: the contribution of microscopy and taphonomy to the problem of art origins. *Journal of Human Evolution* 33(1): 1–31.

d'Errico, F., Henshilwood, C., Lawson, G., Vanhaeren, M., Tillier, A.-M., Soressi, M., Bresson, F., Maureille, B., Nowell, A., Lakarra, J., Backwell, L., and Julien, M. (2003). Archaeological evidence for the emergence of language, symbolism, and music—an alternative multidisciplinary perspective. *Journal of World Prehistory* 17(1): 1–70.

Dibble, H. (1989). The implications of stone tool types for the presence of language during the Lower and Middle Palaeolithic. In P. Mellars and C. Stringer (eds.), *The human revolution.* Edinburgh: Edinburgh University Press, 415–432.

Diessel, H. (2004). *The acquisition of complex sentences.* Cambridge: Cambridge University Press.

Dilley, L. C. and McAuley, J. D. (2007 in revision). Distal prosodic effects on word segmentation and lexical processing. *Journal of Memory and Language.*

Dissanayke, E. (2000). Antecedents of the temporal arts in early mother–infant interaction. In N. L. Wallin, B. Merker, and S. Brown (eds.), *The origins of music.* Cambridge, MA: MIT Press, 389–410.

Doherty, M. (2006). The development of mentalistic gaze understanding. *Infant and Child Development* 15: 179–186.

Donald, M. (1991). *Origins of the modern mind: three stages in the evolution of culture and cognition.* Cambridge, MA: Harvard University Press.

——(1997). Précis of origins of the modern mind: three stages in the evolution of culture and cognition. *Behavioral and Brain Sciences* 16: 737–791.

Douglas, J. (2006). Play between adult and juvenile male bonobos (*Pan Paniscus*), MA thesis, Department of Psychology, Hunter College, City University of New York.

Drake, C. and Bertrand, D. (2001). The quest for universals in temporal processing in music. *Annals of the New York Academy of Sciences* 930: 17–27.

Dryer, M. (1999). Typological maps. http://linguistics.buffalo.edu/people/faculty/dryer/dryer/typological.maps.

DuBrul, E. L. (1958). *Evolution of the speech apparatus.* Springfield, IL: Charles C. Thomas.

Dugatkin, L. A. and Bekoff, M. (2003). The evolution of fairness: a game theory model, *Behavioral Processes* 60: 209–214.

Dunbar, R. I. M. (1988). *Primate social systems.* New York: Cornell University Press.

——(1991). Functional significance of social grooming in primates. *Folia Primatologica* 57: 121–131.

——(1992). Neocortex size as a constraint on group size in primates. *Journal of Human Evolution* 22: 469–493.

——(1993). Coevolution of neocortex size, group size and language in humans. *Behavioral and Brain Sciences* 16: 681–735.

——(1996). *Grooming, gossip and the evolution of language.* London: Faber and Faber and Cambridge, MA: Harvard University Press.

Dunbar, R. I. M. (1998). Theory of mind and the evolution of language. In J. Hurford, M. Studdert-Kennedy, and C. Knight (eds.), *Approaches to the evolution of language*. Cambridge: Cambridge University Press, 92–110.

—— (2003). Why are apes so smart? In P. Kappeler and M. Pereira (eds.), *Primate life histories and socioecology*. Chicago: Chicago University Press, 285–298.

—— (2004, 2006). *The human story*. London: Faber and Faber.

—— (2007). Mind the bonding gap: constraints on the evolution of hominin societies. In S. Shennan (ed.), *Pattern and process in cultural evolution*. Berkeley: University of California Press.

—— and Shultz, S. (2007). Understanding primate brain evolution. *Philosophical Transactions of the Royal Society, London* 362B: 649–658.

—— Cornah, L., Daly, F., and Bowyer, K. (2002). Vigilance in humans: a test of alternative hypotheses. *Behaviour* 139: 695–711.

—— Duncan, N., and Marriot, A. (1997). Human conversational behaviour. *Human Nature* 8: 231–246.

Durham, W. H. (1991). *Coevolution: genes, culture and human diversity*. Stanford: Stanford University Press.

Dwyer, G., Levin, S. A., and Buttel, L. (1990). A simulation of the population dynamics and evolution of myxomatosis. *Ecological Monographs* 60: 423–447.

Edelman, G. (1987). *Neuronal Darwinism: the theory of neuronal group selection*. New York: Basic Books.

Ekman, P. (2003). *Emotions revealed*. London: Weidenfeld and Nicolson.

Elman, J. L., Bates, E. A., Johnson, M. H., Karmiloff-Smith, A., Parisi, D., and Pluckett, K. (1996). *Rethinking innateness: a connectionist perspective on development*. Cambridge, MA: MIT Press.

Embick, D., Marantz, A., Miyashita, Y., O'Neill, W., and Sakai, K. (2000). A syntactic specialization for Broca's area. *Proceedings of the National Academy of Sciences* 97(11): 6150–6154.

Emlen, S. T. (1984). Cooperative breeding in birds and mammals. In J. R. Krebs and N. B. Davies (eds.), *Behavioural ecology* (2nd edn.). Oxford: Blackwell, 305–339.

Enard, W., Przeworski, M., Fisher, S. E., Lai, C. S., Wiebe, V., Kitano, T., Monaco, A. P., and Pääbo, S. (2002). Molecular evolution of FOXP2, a gene involved in speech and language. *Nature* 418: 869–872.

Engle, R. W. and Kane, M. J. (2004). Executive attention, working memory capacity, and a two-factor theory of cognitive control. *The Psychology of Learning and Motivation* 44: 145–199.

Evans, P. D., Gilbert, S. L., Mekel-Bobrov, N., Vallender, E. J., Anderson, J. R., Vaez-Azizi, L. M., Tishkoff, S. A., Hudson, R. R., and Lahn, B. T. (2005). *Microcephalin*, a gene regulating brain size, continues to evolve adaptively in humans. *Science* 309: 1717–1720.

Everett, D. L. (2005). Cultural constraints on grammar and cognition in Pirahã: another look at the design features of human language. *Current Anthropology* 46(4): 621–646.

——(2007). Cultural constraints on grammar in Pirahã: a reply to Nevins, Pesetsky, and Rodrigues. http://ling. auf. net/lingBuzz/000427.

Evers, S. and Suhr, B. (2000). Changes of the neurotransmitter serotonin but not of hormones during short time music perception. *European Archives of Psychiatry and Clinical Neuroscience* 250(3): 144–147.

Fairbanks, L. A. (2000). The developmental timing of primate play: a neural selection model. In S. T. Parker, J. Langer, and M. L. McKinney (eds.), *Biology, brains, and behavior: the evolution of human development.* Santa Fe: School of American Research Press, 131–158.

Falk, D. (1980). A re-analysis of the South African Australopithecine natural endocasts. *American Journal of Physical Anthropology* 53: 525–539.

——(1983). The Taung endocast: a reply to Holloway. *American Journal of Physical Anthropology* 60: 479–480.

——(2004). Prelinguistic evolution in early hominins: whence motherese? *Behavioral and Brain Sciences* 27: 491–503.

Federmeier, K. and Kutas, M. (1999). A rose by any other name: long-term memory structure and sentence processing. *Journal of Memory and Language* 41: 469–495.

Feld, S. (1982). *Sound and sentiment: birds, weeping, poetics and song in Kaluli expression.* Philadelphia: Publications of the American Folklore Society NS 5. BZVDW.

——(1996). Pygmy POP. A genealogy of schizophonic mimesis. *Yearbook for Traditional Music* 28: 1–35.

——and Fox, A. A. (1994). Music and language. *Annual Review of Anthropology* 23: 25–53.

Feldman, M. W., Aoki, K., and Kumm, J. (1996). Individual versus social learning: evolutionary analysis in a fluctuating environment. *Anthropological Science* 104: 209–232.

Fernald, A. (1989). Intonation and communicative intent in mother's speech to infants: is the melody the message? *Child Development* 60: 1497–1510.

——(1991). Prosody in speech to children: prelinguistic and linguistic functions. *Annals of Child Development* 8: 43–80.

——(1992). Meaningful melodies in mothers' speech. In H. Papoušek, U. Jürgens, and M. Papoušek (eds.), *Nonverbal vocal communication: comparative and developmental perspectives.* Cambridge: Cambridge University Press, 262–282.

Finney, J. (1999). *General diachronic course of proto-Austronesian casemarkers.* SEALS 9. Tempe: Arizona State University Monograph Series.

Fitch, W. T. (2000). The evolution of speech: a comparative review. *Trends in Cognitive Sciences* 4(7): 258–267.

Fitch, W. T. (2004). Kin selection and "mother tongues": a neglected component in language evolution. In D. K. Oller and U. Griebel (eds.), *Evolution of communication systems: a comparative approach*. Cambridge, MA: MIT, 275–296.

——(2005). The evolution of language: a comparative review. *Biology and Philosophy* 20: 193–230.

——(2006a). The biology and evolution of music: a comparative perspective. *Cognition* 100(1): 173–215.

——(2006b). Comparative data and fossil cues to speech. Paper presented at the Cradle of Language Conference, 7–10 November 2006, Stellenbosch, South Africa.

——and Giedd, J. (1999). Morphology and development of the human vocal tract: a study using magnetic resonance imaging. *Journal of the Acoustical Society of America* 106(3.1): 1511–1522.

——and Hauser, M. D. (2002). Unpacking "honesty": vertebrate vocal production and the evolution of acoustic signals. In A. M. Simmons, R. R. Fay, and A. N. Popper (eds.), *Acoustic communication*. New York: Springer, 65–137.

——and Reby, D. (2001). The descended larynx is not uniquely human. *Proceedings of the Royal Society of London. Series B: Biological Sciences* 268: 1669–1675.

——Hauser, M. D., and Chomsky, N. (2005). The evolution of the language faculty: clarifications and implications. *Cognition* 97: 179–210.

Flack, J. C., Girvan, M., de Waal, F. B. M., and Krakauer, D. C. (2006). Policing stabilizes construction of social niches in primates. *Nature* 439: 426–429.

——Jeannotte, L. A., and de Waal, F. B. M. (2004). Play signaling and the perception of social rules by juvenile chimpanzees. *Journal of Comparative Psychology* 118(2): 149–159.

Foley, R. A. (1995). *Humans before humanity.* Oxford: Blackwell.

Fouts, R. S., Hirsch, A. D., and Fouts, D. H. (1982). Cultural transmission of a human language in a chimpanzee mother–infant relationship. In H. E. Fitzgerald, J. A. Mullins, and P. Gage (eds.), *Child nurturance: studies of development in primates*. New York: Plenum Press, 159–193.

Fragaszy, D. M. and Perry, S. (2003). *The biology of traditions.* Cambridge: Cambridge University Press.

Francis, E. J. and Michaelis, L. A. (2002). *Mismatch: form–function incongruity and the architecture of grammar.* Stanford: CSLI Publications.

Franco, F. and Butterworth, G. (1996). Pointing and social awareness: declaring and requesting in the second year. *Journal of Child Language* 23: 307–336.

Frank, R. H. (1988). *Passions within reason: the strategic role of the emotions.* New York: W. W. Norton and Co.

Frawley, W. (1976). Comparative syntax in Austronesian. Unpub. PhD thesis, University of California at Berkeley.

Freeberg, T. M. (2006). Social complexity can drive vocal complexity. *Psychological Science* 17: 557–561.

Freeman, W. (2000). A neurobiological role for music in social bonding. In N. L. Wallin, B. Merker, and S. Brown (eds.), *The origins of music.* Cambridge, MA: MIT Press, 411–424.

Freund, H.-J. (2001). The parietal lobe as a sensorimotor interface: a perspective from clinical and neuroimaging data. *Neuroimage* 14(1.2): S142–S146.

Furness, W. H. (1916). Observations on the mentality of chimpanzees and orang-utans. *Proceedings of the American Philosophical Society* 55: 281–290.

Furster, J. M. (1997). *The prefrontal cortex: anatomy, physiology, and neuropsychology of the frontal lobe.* New York: Raven Press.

Futuyma, D. J. (1998). *Evolutionary biology* (3rd edn.). Sunderland, MA: Sinauer.

Galef, B. G., Jr. (1988). Imitation in animals: history, definition, and interpretation of data from the psychological laboratory. In T. R. Zentall and B. G. Galef, Jr. (eds.), *Social learning: psychological and biological perspectives.* Hillsdale, NJ: Erlbaum, 3–28.

Gamble, C. (1999). *The palaeolithic societies of Europe.* Cambridge: Cambridge University Press.

——(2007). *Origins and revolutions: human identity in earliest prehistory.* Cambridge: Cambridge University Press.

Gannon, P. J., Holloway, R. L., Broadfield, D. C., and Braun, A. R. (1998). Asymmetry of chimpanzee planum temporale: humanlike pattern of Wernicke's brain language area homolog. *Science* 279(5348): 220–222.

Gardner, B. T. and Gardner, R. A. (1971). Two-way communication with an infant chimpanzee. In A. M. Schrier and F. Stollnitz (eds.), *Behavior of nonhuman primates: modern research trends* (Vol. 4). New York: Academic Press, 117–183.

Gardner, R. A. and Gardner, B. (1969). Teaching sign language to a chimpanzee. *Science* 165: 664–672.

—— —— and Van Cantford, T. E. (1989). *Teaching sign language to chimpanzees.* Albany: State University of New York Press.

Gathercole, S. E., Pickering, S. J., Ambridge, B., and Wearing, H. (2004). The structure of working memory from 4 to 15 years of age. *Developmental Psychology* 40: 177–190.

Geissmann, T. (2000). Gibbon songs and human music from an evolutionary perspective. In N. L. Wallin, B. Merker, and S. Brown (eds.), *The origins of music.* Cambridge, MA: MIT Press, 103–124.

Gernsbacher, M. A. and Kaschak, M. P. (2003). Neuroimaging studies of language production and comprehension. *Annual Review of Psychology* 54: 91–114.

Geschwind, N. (1965). Disconnexion syndromes in animal and man. *Brain* 88(3): 585–644.

Ghirlanda, S. and Enquist, M. (in press). Cumulative culture and explosive demographic transitions. *Quality & Quantity* 41: 581–600.

Givón, T. (1979). From discourse to syntax: grammar as a processing strategy. In T. Givón (ed.), *Syntax and semantics: discourse and syntax.* New York: Academic Press, 81–112.

Givón, T. (1998). On the co-evolution of language, mind and brain. *Evolution of Communication* 2: 45–116.

Godfrey-Smith, P. (1996). *Complexity and the function of mind in nature.* Cambridge: Cambridge University Press.

Goldberg, A. (2006). *Constructions at work: the nature of generalization in language.* Oxford: Oxford University Press.

Goldin-Meadow, S. (1982). The resilience of recursion: a study of a communication system developed without a conventional language model. In E. Wanner and L. Gleitmann (eds.), *Language acquisition: the state of the art.* New York: Cambridge University Press.

—— (1987). Underlying redundancy and its reduction in a language developed without a language model: constraints imposed by conventional linguistic input. In B. Lust (ed.), *Studies in the acquisition of anaphora.* Boston, MA: D. Reidel Company, 105–133.

—— (1993). When does gesture become language? A study of gesture used as a primary communication system by deaf children of hearing parents. In K. R. Gibson and T. Ingold (eds.), *Tools, language and cognition in human evolution.* New York: Cambridge University Press, 63–85.

—— and Feldman, H. (1975). The creation of a communication system: a study of deaf children of hearing parents. *Sign Language Studies* 8: 225–234.

—— and Mylander, C. (1983). Gestural communication in deaf children: non-effect of parental input on language development. *Science* 221: 372–374.

———— (1990). The role of parental input in the development of a morphological system. *Journal of Child Language* 17: 527–563.

———— (1998). Spontaneous sign systems created by deaf children in two cultures. *Nature* 391: 279–281.

—— Butcher, C., and Mylander, C. (1995). The resilience of combinatorial structure at the word level: morphology in self-styled gesture systems. *Cognition* 56: 195–262.

—— Gelman, S., and Mylander, C. (2005). Expressing generic concepts with and without a language model. *Cognition* 96: 109–126.

—— Nussbaum, H., Kelly, S. D., and Wagner, S. (2001). Explaining math: gesturing lightens the load. *Psychological Science* 12: 516–522.

Goldstein, U. G. (1980). An articulatory model for the vocal tracts of growing children. Unpub. PhD thesis, Massachusetts Institute of Technology, Cambridge, MA.

Golinkoff, R. M. (1986). "I beg your pardon?": the preverbal negotiation of failed messages. *Journal of Child Language* 13: 455–476.

Gómez, J. C. (1996). Ostensive behavior in great apes: the role of eye contact. In A. E. Russon, K. A. Bard, and S. T. Parker (eds.), *Reaching into thought: the minds of the great apes.* Cambridge: Cambridge University Press, 131–151.

—— (2004). *Apes, monkeys, children and the growth of mind.* Cambridge, MA: Harvard University Press.

——(2005). Requesting gestures in captive monkeys and apes: conditioned responses or referential behaviours? *Gesture* 5: 91–105.

Goodall, J. (1968). A preliminary report on expressive movements and communication in the Gombe Stream chimpanzees. In P. C. Jay (ed.), *Primate studies in adaptation and variability.* New York: Holt, Rinehart and Winston, 313–382.

——(1986). *The chimpanzees of Gombe: patterns of behaviour.* Cambridge, MA: The Belknap Press of Harvard University Press.

Gopnik, A. (1999). Theory of mind. In R. A. Wilson and F. C. Keil (eds.), *MIT encyclopedia of cognitive sciences.* Cambridge, MA: MIT Press, 838–841.

Gorbman, C. (1987). *Unheard melodies.* Bloomington: Indiana University Press.

Grant, P. R. and Grant, B. R. (1995). Predicting micoroevolutionary responses to directional selection on heritable variation. *Evolution* 49: 241–251.

Gray, S. M. and McKinnon, J. S. (2007). Linking color polymorphism maintenance and speciation. *TREE* 22: 71–79.

Graziano, M. S. and Gross, C. G. (1998). Spatial maps for the control of movement. *Current Opinion in Neurobiology* 8(2): 195–210.

Greenfield, P. M. (1991). Language, tools and brain: the ontogeny and phylogeny of hierarchically organized sequential behavior. *Behavioral and Brain Sciences* 14: 531–595.

Grodzinsky, Y. (2000). The neurology of syntax: language use without Broca's area. *Behavioral and Brain Sciences* 23(1): 1–55.

Gussenhoven, C. (2002). Intonation and interpretation: phonetics and phonology. Speech Prosody 2002: An International Conference. Aix-en-Provence.

——(2005). *The phonology of tone and intonation.* Cambridge: Cambridge University Press.

Haiman, J. (1994). Ritualization and the development of language. In W. Pagliuca (ed.), *Perspectives on grammaticalization.* Amsterdam: John Benjamins, 3–28.

Hammerstein, P. (ed.) (2003). *Genetic and cultural evolution of cooperation.* Cambridge, MA: MIT Press.

Hansell, N. K., Wright, M. J., Smith, G. A., Geffen, G. M., Geffen, L. B., and Martin, N. G. (2001). Genetic influence on ERP slow wave measures of working memory. *Behavior Genetics* 31: 603–614.

Hanski, I. and Singer, M. C. (2001). Extinction-colonization and host-plant choice in butterfly metapopulations. *American Naturalist* 158: 341–353.

Haspelmath, M. (2007). Pre-established categories don't exist–consequences for language description and typology. *Linguistic Typology* 11(1): 119–132.

——Dryer, M. S., Gil, D., and Comrie, B. (eds.) (2006). *The world atlas of language structures.* Oxford: Oxford University Press.

Hauser, M. D. (1996). *The evolution of communication.* Cambridge, MA: Cambridge University Press.

——(2000). *Wild minds: what animals really think.* New York: Henry Holt.

Hauser, M. D. and Carey, S. (1998). Building a cognitive creature from a set of primitives: evolutionary and developmental insights. In C. Allen and D. Cummings (eds.), *The evolution of mind.* Oxford: Oxford University Press, 51–106.

—— Chomsky, N. and Fitch, W. T. (2002). The faculty of language: what is it, who has it, and how did it evolve? *Science* 28: 1569–1579.

Hayaki, H., Huffman, M. A., and Nishida, T. (1989). Dominance among male chimpanzees in the Mahale Mountains National Park, Tanzania–a preliminary study. *Primates* 30: 187–197.

Hayes, K. J. and Hayes, C. (1954). The cultural capacity of chimpanzee. *Human Biology* 26: 288–303.

Heine, B. and Kuteva, T. (2002). *World lexicon of grammaticalization.* Cambridge: Cambridge University Press.

Henshilwood, C. S. and Sealy, J. (1997). Bone artifacts from the Middle Stone Age at Blombos Cave, Southern Cape, South Africa. *Current Anthropology* 38: 890–5.

—— d'Errico, F., Vanhaeren, M., van Niekerk, K., and Jacobs, Z. (2004). Middle stone age shell beads from South Africa. *Science* 304: 404.

—— —— Yates, R., Jacobs, Z., Tribolo, C., Duller, G. A. T., Mercier, N., Sealy, J. C., Valladas, H., Watts, I., and Wintle, A. G. (2002). Emergence of modern human behaviour: Middle Stone age engravings from South Africa. *Science* 295: 1278–1280.

Henzi, P., de Sousa Pereira, L., Hawker-Bond, D., Stiller, J., Dunbar, R. I. M., and Barrett, L. (2007). Look who's talking: developmental trends in the size of conversational cliques. *Evolution and Human Behaviour* 28: 66–74.

Hespos, S. J. and Spelke, E. S. (2004). Conceptual precursors to language. *Nature* 430: 453–456.

Hewes, G. W. (1973). Primate communication and the gestural origin of language. *Current Anthropology* 12: 5–24.

Heyes, C. M. and Galef, B. G. (1996). *Social learning in animals: the roots of culture.* London: Academic Press.

—— and Huber, L. (2000). *The evolution of cognition.* Cambridge, MA: MIT Press.

Hill, R. A. and Dunbar, R. I. M. (2003). Social network size in humans. *Human Nature* 14: 53–72.

Hockett, C. F. (1960). Logical considerations in the study of animal communication. In W. E. Lanyon and W. N. Tavolga (eds.), *Animal sounds and communication.* Washington, DC: American Institute of Biological Sciences, 392–430.

—— (1978). In search of Jove's brow. *American Speech* 53: 243–313.

Hodgson, D. and Helvenston, P. A. (2006). The emergence of the representation of animals in palaeoart: insights from evolution and the cognitive, limbic and visual systems of the human brain. *Rock Art Research* 23: 3–40.

Holloway, R. L. (1978). Problems of brain endocast interpretation and African hominid evolution. In C. Jolly (ed.), *Early hominids of Africa.* New York: St. Martin's Press.

—— (1995). Evidence for POT expansion in early *Homo*: a pretty theory with ugly (or no) paleoneurological facts. *Behavioral and Brain Sciences* 18(1): 191–193.

Hopkins, W. D., Marino, L., Rilling, J. K., and MacGregor, L. A. (1998). Planum temporale asymmetries in great apes as revealed by magnetic resonance imaging. *Neuroreport* 9(12): 2913–2918.

—— Tagliatela, J., and Leavens, D. A. (2007). Chimpanzees differentially produce novel vocalizations to capture the attention of a human. *Animal Behaviour* 73: 281–286.

Hopper, P. (1987). Emergent grammar. Berkeley Linguistics Conference (BLS), 13: 139–157.

Hoshi, E. and Tanji, J. (2000). Integration of target and body-part information in the premotor cortex when planning action. *Nature* 408(6811): 466–470.

Hostetter, A. B., Cantero, M., and Hopkins, W. D. (2001). Differential use of vocal and gestural communication by chimpanzees (*Pan Troglodytes*) in response to the attentional status of a human (*Homo Sapiens*). *Journal of Comparative Psychology* 115: 337–343.

Houghton, P. (1993). Neanderthal supralaryngeal vocal tract. *American Journal of Physical Anthropology* 90: 139–146.

House, J. (2006). Constructing a context with intonation. *Journal of Pragmatics* 38(10): 1542–1558.

Hughes, D. (1991). Grammars in non-Western musics: a selective survey. In P. Howell, R. West, and I. Cross (eds.), *Representing musical structure*. London: Academic Press, 327–362.

Hui, C., Li, Z. Z., and Yue, D. X. (2004). Metapopulation dynamics and distribution, and environmental heterogeneity induced by niche construction. *Ecological Modelling* 177: 107–118.

Humphreys, G. W. and Forde, E. M. E. (2001). Hierarchies, similarity, and interactivity in object recognition: "category-specific" neuropsychological deficits. *Behavioral and Brain Sciences* 24: 453–509.

Hurford, J. R. (2003). The language mosaic and its evolution. In M. Christiansen and S. Kirby (eds.), *Language evolution*. Oxford: Oxford University Press.

—— (2007). *Language in the light of evolution. Volume 1: foundations of meaning.* Oxford: Oxford University Press.

—— Studdert-Kennedy, M., and Knight, C. (eds.) (1998). *Approaches to the evolution of language: social and cognitive bases.* Cambridge: Cambridge University Press.

Huron, D. (1996). The melodic arch in western folksongs. *Computing in Musicology* 10: 3–23.

—— (2006). *Sweet anticipation: music and the psychology of expectation.* Cambridge, MA: MIT Press.

—— Kinney, D., and Precoda, K. (2006). Influence of pitch height on the perception of submissiveness and threat in musical passages. *Empirical Musicology Review* 1(3): 170–177.

Husain, G., Thompson, W. F., and Schellenberg, E. G. (2002). Effects of musical tempo and mode on arousal, mood, and spatial abilities. *Music Perception* 20(2): 151–171.

Hutto, D. D. (2008). First communions: mimetic sharing without theory of mind. In J. Zlatev, T. Racine, C. Sinha, and E. Itkonen (eds.), *The shared mind: perspectives on intersubjectivity*. Amsterdam: John Benjamins, 245–276.

Ihara, Y. and Feldman, M. W. (2004). Cultural niche construction and the evolution of small family size. *Theoretical Population Biology* 65: 105–111.

Inoue-Nakamura, N. and Matsuzawa, T. (1997). Development of stone tool use by wild chimpanzees (*Pan Troglodytes*). *Journal of Comparative Psychology* 111: 159–173.

Iverson, J. M. and Goldin-Meadow, S. (1998). Why people gesture when they speak. *Nature* 396: 228.

Jackendoff, R. (1999). Possible stages in the evolution of the language faculty. *Trends in Cognitive Sciences* 3: 272–279.

——(2002). *Foundations of language: brain, meaning, grammar, evolution*. Oxford: Oxford University Press.

——and Pinker, S. (2005). The nature of the language faculty and its implications for evolution of language (Reply to Fitch, Hauser, and Chomsky). *Cognition* 97: 211–225.

Janik, J. M. and Slater, P. J. B. (1997). Vocal learning in mammals. *Advances in the Study of Behavior* 26: 59–99.

Jespersen, O. (1895/1983). *Progress in language. Amsterdam Classics in Linguistics 17*. Amsterdam: John Benjamins.

Johansson, S. (2005). *Origins of language: constraints on hypotheses*. Amsterdam: John Benjamins.

Johnson, C. M. (2001). Distributed primate cognition: a review. *Animal Cognition* 4: 167–183.

Johnstone, R. A. and Grafen, A. (1992). The continuous Sir Philip Sidney game: a simple model of biological signalling. *Journal of Theoretical Biology* 156: 215–234.

Jones, C. G., Lawton, J. H., and Shachak, M. (1994). Organisms as ecosystem engineers. *Oikos* 69: 373–386.

——————(1997). Positive and negative effects of organisms as physical ecosystem engineers. *Ecology* 78: 1946–1957.

Jones, M. R. and Boltz, M. (1989). Dynamic attending and responses to time. *Psychological Review* 96: 459–491.

Jungers, W. L., Pokempner, A., Kay, R. F., and Cartmill, M. (2003). Hypoglossal canal size in living hominoids and the evolution of human speech. *Human Biology* 75: 473–484.

Juslin, P. and Sloboda, J. A. (eds.) (2001). *Music and emotion: theory and research*. Oxford: Oxford University Press.

Kaczmarek L. (2000). Gene expression in learning processes. *Acta Neurobiologiae Experimentalis* 60: 419–424.

Kakei, S., Hoffman, D. S., and Strick, P. L. (2003). Sensorimotor transformation in cortical motor areas. *Neuroscience Research* 46: 1–10.

Kane, M. J. and Engle, R. W. (2002). The role of the prefrontal cortex in working memory capacity, executive attention, and general fluid intelligence: an individual-differences perspective. *Psychonomic Bulletin and Review* 9: 637–671.

Kassabian, A. (2001). *Hearing film: tracking identifications in contemporary Hollywood film music.* London: Routledge.

Kay, P. (1971). Taxonomy and semantic contrast. *Language* 47: 866–887.

Kay, R. F., Cartmill, M., and Balow, M. (1998). The hypoglossal canal and the origin of human vocal behaviour. *Proceedings of the National Academy of Sciences, USA* 95: 5417–5419.

Kellogg, W. N. and Kellogg, L. A. (1933). *The ape and the child: a study of early environmental influence upon early behavior.* New York: McGraw-Hill.

Kelly, J. L. Jr., and Lochbaum, C. C. (1973). Speech synthesis. In J. L. Flanagan and L. R. Rabiner (eds.), *Speech synthesis.* Stroudsburg, PA: Dowden, Hutchison and Ross, Inc., 127–130.

Kendon, A. (1975). Gesticulation, speech and the gesture theory of language origin. *Sign Language Studies* 9: 349–373.

—— (2004). *Gesture: visible action as utterance.* Cambridge: Cambridge University Press.

Kerr, N., Dunbar, R. I. M., and Bentall, R. (2003). Theory of mind deficits in bipolar affective disorder. *Journal of Affective Disorders* 73: 253–259.

Key, C. A. and Aiello, L. C. (1999). The evolution of social organization. In R. Dunbar, C. Knight, and C. Power (eds.), *The evolution of culture.* Edinburgh: Edinburgh University Press, 15–33.

Kinderman, P., Dunbar, R. I. M., and Bentall, R. P. (1998). Theory-of-mind deficits and causal attributions. *British Journal of Psychology* 89: 191–204.

King, B. J. (2004). *The dynamic dance: nonvocal communication in African great apes.* Cambridge, MA: Harvard University Press.

—— and Shanker, S. (2003). How can we know the dancer from the dance: the co-regulated nature of ape communication. *Anthropological Theory* 3(1): 5–26.

Kingsolver, J. G., Hoekstra, H. E., Hoekstra, J. M., Berrigan, D., Vignieri, S. N., Hill, C. E., Hoang, A., Gilbert, P., and Beerli, P. (2001). The strength of phenotypic selection in natural populations. *American Naturalist* 157: 245–261.

Kirby, S. (1999). *Function, selection, and innateness: the emergence of language universal.* Oxford: Oxford University Press.

—— (2000). Syntax without natural selection: how compositionality emerges from vocabulary in a population of learners. In C. Knight, M. Studdert-Kennedy, and J. R. Hurford (eds.), *The evolutionary emergence of language:*

social function and the origins of linguistic form. Cambridge: Cambridge University Press, 303–323.

—— (2001). Spontaneous evolution of linguistic structure: an iterated learning model of the emergence of regularity and irregularity. *IEEE Journal of Evolutionary Computation* 5: 101–110.

—— (2003). Learning, bottlenecks and the evolution of recursive syntax. In E. Briscoe (ed.), *Linguistic evolution through language acquisition.* Cambridge: Cambridge University Press, 173–204.

—— and Hurford, J. (2002). The emergence of linguistic structure: an overview of the iterated learning model. In A. Cangelosi and D. Parisi (eds.), *Simulating the evolution of language.* London: Springer Verlag, 121–148.

Kirkpatrick, M. and R. Lande, (1989). The evolution of maternal characters. *Evolution* 43: 485–503.

Klaeber, F. (1922/1941). *Beowulf.* Boston: Heath and Co.

Kleene, S. C. (1952/1971). *Introduction to metamathematics.* Groningen: Wolters-Noordhoff.

Klein, R. G. and Edgar, B. (2002). *The dawn of human culture.* New York: John Wiley and Sons.

Klima, E. and Bellugi, U. (1979). *The signs of language.* Cambridge, MA: Harvard University Press.

Knight, C. (1991). *Blood relations: Menstruation and the origins of culture.* London and New Haven: Yale University Press.

—— (2000). Play as precursor of phonology and syntax. In C. Knight, M. Studdert-Kennedy, and J. R. Hurford (eds.), *The evolutionary emergence of language: social function and the origins of linguistic form.* Cambridge: Cambridge University Press, 99–119.

—— (2008). Language, co-evolved with the rule of law. *Mind and Society* 7: 109–128.

—— Power, C., and Watts, I. (1995). The human symbolic revolution: a Darwinian account. *Cambridge Archaeological Journal* 5: 75–114.

—— Studdert-Kennedy, M., and Hurford, J. (eds.) (2000). *The evolutionary emergence of language.* Cambridge: Cambridge University Press.

Knösche, T. R., Neuhaus, C., Haueisen, J., Alter, K., Maess, B., Witte, O. W., and Friederici, A. D. (2005). Perception of phrase structure in music. *Human Brain Mapping* 24: 259–273.

Koornneef, A. W., Wijnen, F., and Reuland, E. (2006). Towards a modular approach to anaphor resolution. In R. Artstein and M. Poesio (eds.), *Ambiguity in Anaphora workshop proceedings.* Malaga, Spain: ESSLI, 65–72.

Kortmulder, K. (1998). *Play and evolution: second thoughts on the behaviour of animals.* Utrecht: International Books.

Krahmer, E. and Swerts, M. (2007). The effects of visual beats on prosodic prominence: acoustic analyses, auditory perception and visual perception. *Journal of Memory and Language* 57(3): 396–414.

Krause, J. and Ruxton, G. D. (2002). *Living in groups*. Oxford: Oxford University Press.

Krause, M. A. and Fouts, R. S. (1997). Chimpanzee (*Pan troglodytes*) pointing: hand shapes, accuracy, and the role of eye gaze. *Journal of Comparative Psychology* 111: 330–336.

Kuhl, P. and Miller, J. D. (1975). Speech perception by the chinchilla: voiced–voiceless distinction in alveolar plosive consonants. *Science* 190: 69–72.

Labov, W. (1986). *Principles of linguistic change*. Oxford: Blackwell.

Ladd, D. R. (1984). Declination: a review and some hypothesis. *Phonology Yearbook* 1: 53–74.

Laland, K. N. and Sterelny, K. (2006). Seven reasons (not) to neglect niche construction. *Evolution* 60: 1751–1762.

——Odling-Smee, F. J., and Feldman, M. W. (1996). On the evolutionary consequences of niche construction. *Journal of Evolutionary Biology* 9: 293–316.

——————(1999). Evolutionary consequences of niche construction and their implications for ecology. *Proceedings of the National Academy of Sciences. USA* 96: 10242–10247.

——————(2000). Niche construction, biological evolution, and cultural change. *Behavioral Brain Sciences* 23: 131–175.

——————(2001). Cultural niche construction and human evolution. *Evolutionary Biology* 14: 22–23.

——————and Kendal, J. (in press). Conceptual barriers to progress within evolutionary biology. *Biological Journal of the Linnean Society*.

——Richerson, P. J., and Boyd, R. (1993). Animal social learning: towards a new theoretical approach. In P. P. G. Bateson (ed.), *Perspectives in Ethology. Vol. 10. Behavior and Evolution*. New York: Plenum Press, 249–277.

Lambrecht, K. (1981). *Topic, antitopic, and verb agreement in non standard French*. Amsterdam: John Benjamins.

Landau, B. and Jackendoff, R. S. (1993). "What" and "where" in spatial language and spatial cognition. *Behavioral and Brain Sciences* 16: 217–265.

——Smith, L. B., and Jones, S. (1992). Syntactic context and the shape bias in children's and adults' lexical learning. *Journal of Memory and Language* 31: 807–825.

LeDoux, J. (1996). *The emotional brain*. New York: Simon and Schuster.

Leavens, D. A. (1998). Having a concept "see" does not imply attribution of knowledge: some general considerations in measuring "theory of mind". *Behavioral and Brain Sciences* 21: 123–124.

——(2002). On the public nature of communication. *Behavioral and Brain Sciences* 25: 630–631.

——(2004a). Manual deixis in apes and humans. *Interaction Studies* 5: 387–408.

——(2004b). Book review of S. Kita (ed.), *Pointing: where language, culture and cognition meet. Cognitive Systems Research* 5: 157–165.

Leavens, D. A. (2006). It takes time and experience to learn how to interpret gaze in mentalistic terms. *Infant and Child Development* 15: 187–190.

—— and Hopkins, W. D. (1998). Intentional communication by chimpanzees: a cross-sectional study of the use of referential gestures. *Developmental Psychology* 34: 813–822.

—— —— (1999). The whole hand point: the structure and function of pointing from a comparative perspective. *Journal of Comparative Psychology* 113: 417–425.

—— —— (2005). Multimodal concomitants of manual gesture by chimpanzees: influence of food size and distance. *Gesture* 5: 73–88.

—— and Todd, B. K. (2005). The affective envelope of joint attention. Invited symposium paper presented at the Biennial Meeting of the Society for Research in Child Development, 7–10 April, Atlanta, GA.

—— Hopkins, W. D., and Bard, K. A. (1996). Indexical and referential pointing in chimpanzees (*Pan Troglodytes*). *Journal of Comparative Psychology* 110: 346–353.

—— —— —— (2005). Understanding the point of chimpanzee pointing: epigenesis and ecological validity. *Current Directions in Psychological Science* 14: 185–189.

—— —— —— (2008). The heterochronic origins of explicit reference. In J. Zlatev, T. Racine, C. Sinha, and E. Itkonen (eds.), *The shared mind: perspectives on intersubjectivity*. Amsterdam: John Benjamins, 187–214.

—— —— and Thomas, R. K. (2004). Referential communication by chimpanzees (*Pan Troglodytes*). *Journal of Comparative Psychology* 118: 48–57.

—— Russell, J. L., and Hopkins, W. D. (2005). Intentionality as measured in the persistence and elaboration of communication by chimpanzees (*Pan Troglodytes*). *Child Development* 76: 291–306.

—— Hostetter, A. B., Wesley, M. J., and Hopkins, W. D. (2004). Tactical use of unimodal and bimodal communication by chimpanzees, *Pan troglodytes*. *Animal Behaviour* 67: 467–476.

Lee, K. E. (1985). *Earthworms: Their ecology and relation with soil and land use*. London: Academic.

Legerstee, M. and Barillas, Y. (2003). Sharing attention and pointing to objects at 12 months: is the intentional stance implied? *Cognitive Development* 18: 91–110.

Lehmann, J., Korstjens, A. K., and Dunbar, R. I. M. (2007). Group size, grooming and social cohesion in primates. *Animal Behaviour* 74: 1617–1629.

Lerdahl, F. and Jackendoff, R. (1983). *A generative theory of tonal music*. Cambridge, MA: MIT Press.

Leroi, A. and Swire, J. (2006). The recovery of the past. *The World of Music* 48(3): 43–54.

Levelt, W. J. M. (1989). *Speaking: from intention to articulation*. Cambridge, MA: MIT Press.

Levinson, S. C. (2000). *Pragmatics*. Cambridge: Cambridge University Press.

Lewontin, R. C. (1983). Gene, organism, and environment. In D. S. Bendall (ed.), *Evolution from molecules to men*. Cambridge: Cambridge University Press.

Lezak, M. D. (1982). The problem of assessing executive functions. *International Journal of Psychology* 17: 281–297.

——(1995). *Neuropsychological assessment* (3rd edn.). New York: Oxford University Press.

Li, C. and Thompson, S. (1978). An exploration of Mandarin Chinese. In W. A. Lehmann (ed.), *Syntactic typology*. Austin: University of Texas Press, 223–265.

Liebal, K., Call, J., and Tomasello, M. (2004). Chimpanzee gesture sequences. *Primates* 64: 377–396.

——Pika, S., and Tomasello, M. (2004). Social communication in siamangs (Symphalangus Syndactulus): use of gestures and facial expression. *Primates* 45: 41–57.

——————(2006). Gestural communication of orangutans (Pongo pygmaeus). *Gesture* 6: 1–38.

——————Call, J., and Tomasello, M. (2004). To move or not to move: how apes adjust to the attentional state of others. *Interaction Studies* 5: 199–219.

Lieberman, P. (1979). Hominid evolution, supralaryngeal vocal tract physiology and the fossil evidence for reconstructions. *Brain and Language* 7: 101–126.

——(1990). Hyoid bone position and speech: reply to Dr Arensberg. *American Journal of Physical Anthropology* 94: 275–278.

——(1998). *Eve spoke: human language and human evolution*. New York: W. W. Norton and Co.

——(2007). The evolution of human speech: its anatomical and neural bases. *Current Anthropology* 48: 39–66.

——and Crelin, E. S. (1971). On the speech of Neanderthal man. *Linguistic Inquiry* 2: 203–222.

————and Klatt, D. H. (1972). Phonetic ability and related anatomy of the newborn and adult human, Neanderthal man, and the chimpanzee. *American Anthropologist* 74: 287–307.

——Klatt, D. H., and Wilson, W. H. (1969). Vocal tract limitations on the vowel repertoires of rhesus monkey and other nonhuman primates. *Science* 164: 1185–1187.

Lightfoot, D. (1999). *The development of language*. Malden: Blackwell.

Lindtvedt, K., Ragir, S., Takach, S., and Rice, D. (2005). Fair play in Bonobo chimpanzees (*Pan Paniscus*): observations of gender differences. American Association of Physical Anthropology Meetings, 6–9 April, Milwaukee, WI.

Liszkowski, U., Carpenter, M., Henning, A., Striano, T., and Tomasello, M. (2004). Twelve-month-olds point share attention and interest. *Developmental Science* 7: 297–307.

Lomax, A., Rudd, R., Grauer, V. A., Berkowitz, N., Hawes, B. L., and Kulig, C. (1978). *Cantometrics: an approach to the anthropology of music: audiocassettes and a handbook*. Berkeley: University of California Extension Media Center.

Lorenz, K. (1973). *Die Rückseite des Spiegels*. München: R. Piper and Co.

Lovejoy, O. (1981). The origin of man. *Science* 211: 341–350.

Lupyan, G. (2006). Labels facilitate learning of novel categories. In A. Cangelosi, A. D. M. Smith, and K. Smith (eds.), *Evolution of language. Proceedings of the 6th International Conference (Evolang)*. Singapore: World Scientific, 190–197.

Luria, A. R. (1966). *Higher cortical function in man*. New York: Basic Books.

——Tsvetkova, L. S., and Futer, D. S. (1965). Aphasia in a composer. *Journal of Neurological Science* 2: 288–292.

MacDonald, R., Hargreaves, D., and Miell, D. (eds.) (2002). *Musical identities*. Oxford: Oxford University Press.

MacLarnon, A. and Hewitt, G. (1995). The hominid vertebral canal and the evolution of speech. *American Journal of Physical Anthropology. Supplement* 20: 139.

——— (1999). The evolution of human speech: the role of enhanced breathing control. *American Journal of Physical Anthropology* 109: 341–363.

MacNeilage, P. and Davis, B. (2005). Functional organization of speech across the life span: a critique of generative phonology. *The Linguistic Review* 22: 161–181.

Maeda, S. (1989). Compensatory articulation during speech: evidence from the analysis and synthesis of vocal tract shapes using an articulatory model. In W. J. Hardcastle and A. Marchal (eds.), *Speech production and speech modelling*. Dordrecht: Kluwer, 131–149.

Maess, B., Koelsch, S., Gunter, T. C., and Friederici, A. D. (2001). Musical syntax is processed in Broca's area: an MEG study. *Nature Neuroscience* 4: 540–545.

Malinowski, B. (1974). *Magic, science, and religion, and other essays*. London: Souvenir Press.

Mandler, J. M. and McDonough, L. (1996). Drinking and driving don't mix: inductive generalisation in infancy. *Cognition* 59: 307–335.

Mania, D. and Mania, U. (1988). Deliberate engravings on bone artefacts of *Homo erectus*. *Rock Art Research* 5: 91–107.

Marcus, G. (2004). *The birth of the mind: how a tiny number of genes creates the complexities of human thought*. New York: Basic Books.

Marean, C. W. and thirteen others (2007). Early human use of marine resources and pigment in South Africa during the Middle Pleistocene. *Nature* 449: 905–908.

Mareschal, D. and Quinn, P. C. (2001). Categorization in infancy. *Trends in Cognitive Sciences* 5: 443–450.

Markman, E. M. (1987). How children constrain the possible meanings of words. In U. Neisser (ed.), *Concepts and conceptual development: ecological and intellectual factors in categorization.* Cambridge: Cambridge University Press, 255–287.

—— (1989). *Categorization and naming in children: problems of induction.* Cambridge, MA: MIT Press.

—— (1990). Constraints children place on word meanings. *Cognitive Science* 14: 154–173.

—— and Hutchinson, J. E. (1984). Children's sensitivity to constraints on word meaning: taxonomic vs. thematic relations. *Cognitive Psychology* 16: 1–27.

—— and Wachtel, G. F. (1988). Children's use of mutual exclusivity to constrain the meanings of words. *Cognitive Psychology* 20: 121–157.

Marler, P. (1976). An ethological theory of the origin of vocal learning. In S. R. Harnad, H. D. Steklis, and J. Lancaster (eds.), *Origins and evolution of language and speech.* New York: The New York Academy of Sciences, 386–395.

—— (1980). *Primate vocalization: affective or symbolic? In T. A. Sebeok and J. Umiker-Sebeok (eds.), speaking of apes.* New York: Plenum Press.

Marrett, A. (2005). *Songs, dreamings, and ghosts: the Wangga of North Australia.* Hanover, CT: Wesleyan University Press.

Marshall, A. J., Wrangham, R. W., and Arcadi, A. C. (1976). *The !Kung of Nyae Nyae.* Cambridge: Cambridge University Press.

—————— (1999). Does learning affect the structure of vocalisations in chimpanzees? *Animal Behaviour* 58: 825–830.

Martin, R. D. (1989). *Primate origins and evolution.* London: Chapman and Hall.

Martínez, I., Rosa, M., Arsuaga, J.-L., Jarabo, P., Quam, R., Lorenzo, C., Gracia, A., Carretero, J.-M., Bermúdez de Castro, J.-M., and Carbonell, E. (2004). Auditory capacities in Middle Pleistocene humans from the Sierra de Atapuerca in Spain. *Proceedings of the National Academy of Sciences* 101: 9976–9981.

Massey, C. and Gelman, R. (1988) Preschoolers' ability to decide whether pictured unfamiliar objects can move themselves. *Developmental Psychology* 24: 307–317.

Matelli, M. and Luppino, G. (2001). Parietofrontal circuits for action and space perception in the Macaque monkey. *Neuroimage* 14(1.2): S27–S32.

Matsumoto, R., Ikeda, A., Ohara, S., Matsihashi, M., Baba, K., Yamane, F., Hori, T., Mihara, T., Nagamine, T., and Shibasaki, H. (2003). Motor-related functional subdivisions of human lateral premotor cortex: epicortical recording in conditional visuomotor task. *Clinical Neurophysiology* 114(6): 1102–1115.

Maynard-Smith, J. and Harper, D. (2003). *Animal signals.* Oxford: Oxford University Press.

McBrearty, S. and Brooks, A. (2000). The revolution that wasn't: a new interpretation of the origin of modern human behavior. *Journal of Human Evolution* 38: 453–563.

McComb, K. and Semple, S. (2005). Coevolution of vocal communication and sociality in primates. *Biology Letters* 1: 381–385.

McGrew, W. C. and Tutin, C. E. G. (1978). Evidence for a social custom in wild chimpanzees? *Man* 13: 234–251.

McNeill, D. (1985). So you think gestures are nonverbal? *Psychological Review* 92: 350–371.

—— (1992). *Hand and mind*. Chicago: The University of Chicago Press.

McNeill, W. H. (1995). *Keeping together in time: dance and drill in human history*. Cambridge, MA: Harvard University Press.

Mellars, P. (1996). *The Neanderthal legacy*. Princeton: Princeton University Press.

—— Gravina, B., and Bronk Ramsey, C. (2007). Confirmation of Neanderthal/ modern human interstratification at the Chatelperronian type-site. *Proceedings of the National Academy of Sciences* 104: 3657–3662.

Mendez, M. F. (2001). Generalized auditory agnosia with spared music recognition in a left-hander. Analysis of a case with a right temporal stroke. *Cortex* 37: 139–150.

Menzel, C. R. (1999). Unprompted recall and reporting of hidden objects by a chimpanzee (*Pan Troglodytes*) after extended delays. *Journal of Comparative Psychology* 113: 426–434.

Merker, B. (2000). Synchronous chorusing and human origins. In N. L. Wallin, B. Merker, and S. Brown (eds.), *The origins of music*. Cambridge, MA: MIT Press.

Mermelstein, P. (1973). Articulatory model for the study of speech production. *Journal of the Acoustical Society of America* 53(4): 1070–1082.

Merriman, W. E. and Bowman, L. L. (1989). The mutual exclusivity bias in children's word learning. *Monographs of the Society for Research in Child Development* 54.

Metz-Lutz, M.-N. and Dahl, E. (1984). Analysis of word comprehension in a case of pure word deafness. *Brain and Language* 23: 13–25.

Meysman, F. J. R., Middleburg, J. J., and Heip, C. H. R. (2006). Bioturbation: a fresh look at Darwin's last idea. *TREE* 21: 688–695.

Miell, D., MacDonald, R., and Hargreaves, D. (eds.) (2005). *Musical communication*. Oxford: Oxford University Press.

Miles, H. L. (1990). The cognitive foundations for reference in a signing orang-utan. In S. T. Parker and K. R. Gibson (eds.), *"Language" and intelligence in monkeys and apes: comparative developmental perspectives*. Cambridge: Cambridge University Press, 511–539.

Miller, G. (1999). Sexual selection for cultural displays. In R. Dunbar, C. Knight, and C. Power (eds.), *The evolution of culture*. Edinburgh: Edinburgh University Press, 71–91.

—— (2000). Evolution of human music through sexual selection. In N. L. Wallin, B. Merker, and S. Brown (eds.), *The origins of music*. Cambridge, MA: MIT Press, 329–360.

Miller, L. K. (1989). *Musical savants: exceptional skill in the mentally retarded*. Hillsdale, NJ: Lawrence Erlbaum.

Miller, M. N. and Byers, J. A. (1998). Sparring as play in young pronghorn males. In M. Bekoff and J. A. Byers (eds.), *Animal play: evolutionary, comparative, and ecological perspectives.* Cambridge: Cambridge University Press, 141–160.

Mitani, J. C. (1985). Gibbon song duets and intergroup spacing. *Behaviour* 92: 59–96.

——(1996). Comparative studies of African ape vocal behavior. In W. C. McGrew, L. F. Marchant, and T. Nishida (eds.), *Great ape societies.* Cambridge: Cambridge University Press.

——and Gros-Louis, J. (1995). Species and sex differences in the screams of chimpanzees and bonobos. *International Journal of Primatology* 16: 393–411.

——Hasegawa, T., Gros-Louis, J., Marler, P., and Byrne, R. W. (1992). Dialects in wild chimpanzees? *American Journal of Primatology* 27: 233–243.

Mithen, S. (1996a). On early Palaeolithic concept mediated marks, mental modularity and the origins of art. *Current Anthropology* 37: 666–670.

——(1996b). *The prehistory of the mind.* London: Thames and Hudson.

——(2000). Comment on F. d'Errico and A. Nowell. A new look at the Berekhat Ram figurine: implications for the origins of symbolism. *Cambridge Archaeological Journal* 10: 123–167.

——(2005). *The singing Neanderthals: the origins of music, language, mind and body.* London: Weidenfeld and Nicolson.

Miyake, A. and Shah, P. (eds.) (1999). *Models of working memory: mechanisms of active maintenance and executive control.* New York: Cambridge University Press.

Mohay, H. (1990). The interaction of gesture and speech in the language development of two profoundly deaf children. In V. Volterra and C. Erting (eds.), *From gesture to language in hearing and deaf children.* Heidelberg: Springer Verlag, 187–204.

Moll, H. and Tomasello, M. (2007). Co-operation and human cognition: the Vygotskian intelligence hypothesis. *Philosophical Transactions of the Royal Society* 362: 639–648.

Monnot, M. (1999). Function of infant-directed speech. *Human Nature* 10: 415–443.

Montague, R. (1974) *Formal philosophy: selected chapters.* New Haven: Yale University Press.

Moore, C. (1998). Social cognition in infancy (commentary on M. Carpenter, K. Nagell, and M. Tomasello, Social cognition, joint attention and communicative competence from 9 to 15 months of age). *Monographs of the Society for Research in Child Development* 63 (Serial No. 255): 167–174.

——and Corkum, V. (1994). Social understanding at the end of the first year of life. *Developmental Review* 14: 349–372.

Morford, J. P. (1996). Insights to language from the study of gesture: a review of research on the gestural communication of non-signing deaf people. *Language and Communication* 16: 165–178.

Morgan, J. I. and Curran, T. (1991). Stimulus transcription coupling in the nervous system: involvement of the inducible pro-onocogenes *fos* and *jun*. *Annual Review of Neuroscience* 14: 421–451.

Morley, I. (2003). The evolutionary origins and archaeology of music: an investigation into the prehistory of human musical capacities and behaviours. Unpub. PhD thesis, University of Cambridge.

Morris, D., Collett, P., Marsh, P., and O'Shaughnessy, M. (1979). *Gestures, their origins and distribution.* New York: Stein and Day.

Morton, E. S. (1977). On the occurrence and significance of motivation-structural rules in some bird and mammal sounds. *The American Naturalist* 111(981): 855–869.

Mufwene, S. S. (2001). *The ecology of language evolution.* Cambridge: Cambridge University Press.

—— (2002). Competition and selection in language evolution. *Selection* 3(1): 45–56.

Muller, M. and Mitani, J. C. (2005). Conflict and cooperation in wild chimpanzees. *Advances in the Study of Behavior* 35: 275–331.

Murata, A., Gallese, V., Luppino, G., Kaseda, M., and Sakata, H. (2000). Selectivity for the shape, size, and orientation of objects for grasping in neurons of monkey parietal area AIP. *Journal of Neurophysiology* 83(5): 2580–2601.

Mustanoja, T. (1960). *A middle English syntax.* Helsinki: Société Neophilologique.

Nakamura, M., McGrew, C., Marchandt, L. F., and Nishida, T. (2000). Social scratch: another custom in wild chimpanzees? *Primates* 41: 237–248.

Negus, V. E. (1938). Evolution of the speech organs of man. *Archives of Otolaryngology* 28: 313–328.

—— (1949). *The comparative anatomy and physiology of the larynx.* London: William Heinemann Medical Books Ltd.

Nettl, B. (2005). *The study of ethnomusicology: thirty-one issues and concepts* (2nd edn.). Urbana and Chicago: University of Illinois Press.

Nevins, A., Pesetsky, D., and Rodrigues, C. (2007). Pirahã exceptionality: a reassessment. http://ling. auf. net//lingBuzz/000411.

Newmeyer, F. (2000). On the reconstruction of "proto-world" word order. In C. Knight, M. Studdert-Kennedy, and J. Hurford (eds.), *The evolutionary emergence of language: social function and the origins of linguistic form.* Cambridge: Cambridge University Press, 372–388.

Nichols, J. (1992). *Linguistic diversity in space and time.* Chicago: University of Chicago Press.

Nicoladis, E., Mayberry, R. I., and Genesee, F. (1999). Gesture and early bilingual development. *Developmental Psychology* 35: 514–526.

Nishida, T. (1980). The leaf-clipping display: a newly-discovered expressive gesture in wild chimpanzees. *Journal of Human Evolution* 9: 117–128.

—— and Hosaka, K. (1996). Coalition strategies among adult male chimpanzees of the Mahale Mountains, Tanzania. In W. C. McGrew, T. Nishida, and L. F. Marchandt (eds.), *Great ape societies.* Cambridge: Cambridge University Press, 114–134.

—— and Turner, L. (1996). Food transfer between mother and infant chimpanzees of the Mahale Mountains National Park, Tanzania. *International Journal of Primatology* 17: 947–968.

—— Mitani, J. C., and Watts, D. P. (2004). Variable grooming behaviours in wild chimpanzees. *Folia Primatologica* 75: 31–36.

Oately, K. and Jenkins, J. J. (1996). *Understanding emotions.* Oxford: Blackwell.

Oberauer, K., Suss, H.-M., Wilhelm, O., and Wittman, W. W. (2003). The multiple faces of working memory: storage, processing, supervision, and coordination. *Intelligence* 31: 167–193.

Odling-Smee, F. J. (1988). Niche constructing phenotypes. In H. C. Plotkin (ed.) *The role of behavior in evolution.* Cambridge, MA: MIT Press, 73–132.

—— (2006). How niche construction contributes to human gene-culture coevolution. In J. C. K. Wells, S. Strickland, and K. Laland (eds.), *Social information transmission and human biology.* Boca Raton, FL: Taylor and Francis.

—— Laland, K. N., and Feldman, M. W. (2003). *Niche construction: the neglected process in evolution.* Monographs in Population Biology 37. Princeton, NJ: Princeton University Press.

Ohala, J. J. (1984). An ethological perspective on common cross-language utilization of F0 of voice. *Phonetica* 41(1): 1–16.

—— (1994). The frequency code underlies the sound-symbolic use of voice pitch. In L. Hinton, J. Nichols, and J. J. Ohala (eds.), *Sound symbolism.* Cambridge: Cambridge University Press, 325–347.

Oller, D. K. (2007). Natural logic of vocal capabilities and the evolution of language. Paper presented at the ILA conference, 29 March–1 April. Hunter College, New York.

O'Neill, D. K. (1996). Two-year-old children's sensitivity to a parent's knowledge state when making requests. *Child Development* 67: 659–677.

Oppenheimer, S. (2004). *Out of Africa's Eden.* Johannesburg: Jonathan Ball.

Oudeyer, P.-Y. (2006). *Self-organization in the evolution of speech.* Oxford: Oxford University Press.

—— and Kaplan, F. (2007). Language evolution as a Darwinian process: computational studies. *Cognitive Processing* 8(1): 21–35.

Owings, D. H. and Morton, E. S. (1998). *Animal vocal communication: a new approach.* Cambridge: Cambridge University Press.

Owren, M. J. and Rendall, D. (2001). Sound on the rebound: bringing form and function back to the forefront in understanding nonhuman primate vocal signaling. *Evolutionary Anthropology* 10: 58–71.

Palmer, C. and Hutchins, S. (2006). What is musical prosody? *The Psychology of Learning and Motivation* 46: 245–278.

Panksepp, J. (1998). *Affective neuroscience: the foundations of human and animal emotions*. New York: Oxford University Press.

Papousek, M., Papousek, H., and Symmes, D. (1991). The meanings of melodies in motherese in tone and stress languages. *Infant Behavior and Development* 14: 415–440.

Parsons, L. (2003). Exploring the functional neuroanatomy of music performance, perception and comprehension. In I. Peretz and Robert Zatorre (eds.), *The cognitive neuroscience of music*. Oxford: Oxford University Press, 247–268.

Patel, A. D. (2003). Language, music, syntax and the brain. *Nature Neuroscience* 6: 674–681.

Patterson, F. (1978a). Conversations with a gorilla. *National Geographic* 134: 438–465.

——(1978b). Linguistic capabilities of a lowland gorilla. In F. C. C. Peng (ed.), *Sign language and language acquisition in man and ape: new dimensions in comparative pedolinguistics*. Boulder, CO: Westview Press, 161–201.

Pelegrin, J. (1993). A framework for analysing prehistoric stone tool manufacture and a tentative application to some early stone industries. In A. Berthelet and J. Chavaillon (eds.), *The use of tools by human and non-human primates*. Oxford: Clarendon Press, 302–314.

Pennington, B. F. (2002). *The development of psychopathology*. New York: Guilford Press.

——and Ozonoff, S. (1996). Executive functions and developmental psychopathology. *Journal of Child Psychology and Psychiatry* 37: 51–87.

Pepperberg, I. M. (1999). *The Alex studies*. Cambridge, MA: Harvard University Press.

Peretz, I. (1993). Auditory atonalia for melodies. *Cognitive Neuropsychology* 10: 21–56.

——and Zatorre, R. (eds.) (2003). *The cognitive neuroscience of music*. Oxford: Oxford University Press.

——Ayotte, J., Zatorre, R. J., Mehler, J., Ahad, P., Penhune, B., and Jutras, B. (2002). Congenital amusia: a disorder of fine-grained pitch discrimination. *Neuron* 33: 185–191.

Peterson, G. E. and Barney, H. L. (1952). Control methods used in a study of the vowels. *Journal of the Acoustical Society of America* 24(2): 175–184.

Petitto, L. (1988). "Language" in the prelinguistic child. In F. Kessel (ed.), *Development of language and language researchers*. Hillsdale, NJ: Lawrence Erlbaum Associates, 187–222.

Phillips, S. B. V. D., Goldin-Meadow, S., and Miller, P. J. (2001). Enacting stories, seeing worlds: similarities and differences in the cross-cultural narrative development of linguistically isolated deaf children. *Human Development* 44: 311–336.

Piattelli-Palmarini, M. and Uriagereka, J. (2005). The evolution of the narrow faculty of language. *Lingue e Linguaggio* 1–52.

Pickering, M. J. and Garrod, S. (2004). Toward a mechanistic psychology of dialogue. *Behavioral and Brain Sciences* 274: 169–225.

Pierce, A. (1992). *Language acquisition and syntactic theory*. Dordrecht: Kluwer.

Pika, S. (2008a). What is the nature of the gestural communication of great apes? In J. Zlatev, T. Racine, C. Sinha, and E. Itkonen (eds.), *The shared mind*. Amsterdam: John Benjamins.

——(2008b). Gestures of apes and pre-linguistic human children: similar or different? *First Language* 28: 116–140.

——and Mitani, J. C. (2006). Referential gesturing in wild chimpanzees (*Pan Troglodytes*). *Current Biology* 16: 191–192.

——Liebal, K., and Tomasello, M. (2003). Gestural communication in young gorillas (*Gorilla gorilla*): gestural repertoire, learning, and use. *American Journal of Primatology* 60: 95–111.

——————(2005). The gestural repertoire of bonobos (*Pan Paniscus*): flexibility and use. *American Journal of Primatology* 65: 39–61.

————Call, J., and Tomasello, M. (2005). The gestural communication of apes. *Gesture* 5: 41–56.

——Nicoladis, M., and Marentette, P. F. (2006). A cross-cultural study on the use of gestures: evidence for cross-linguistic transfer? *Bilingualism: Language and Cognition* 9: 319–327.

Pinker, S. (1994). *The language instinct: how the mind creates language*. New York: Morrow.

——(1997). *How the mind works*. New York: Norton.

——and Bloom, P. (1990). Natural language and natural selection. *Behavioral and Brain Sciences* 13: 707–784.

——and Jackendoff, R. (2005). The faculty of language: what's special about it? *Cognition* 95: 201–236.

Pitt, M. A. and Samuel, A. G. (1990). The use of rhythm in attending to speech. *Journal of Experimental Psychology: Human Perception and Performance* 16: 564–573.

Plooij, F. X. (1978). Some basic traits of language in wild chimpanzees? In A. Lock (ed.), *Action, gesture and symbol*. London: Academic Press, 111–131.

——(1979). How wild chimpanzee babies trigger the onset of mother–infant play. In M. Bullowa (ed.), *Before speech*. Cambridge: University Press, 223–243.

Pollick, A. S. and de Waal, F. B. M. (2007). Ape gestures and language evolution. *Proceedings of the National Academy of Sciences* 104(19): 8184–8189.

Poss, S. R., Kuhar, C., Stoinski, T. S., and Hopkins, W. D. (2006). Differential use of attentional and visual communicative signaling by orangutans (*Pongo pygmaeus*) and gorillas (*Gorilla gorilla*) in response to the attentional status of a human. *American Journal of Primatology* 68: 978–992.

Povinelli, D. J. and Davis, D. R. (1994). Differences between chimpanzees (*Pan Troglodytes*) and humans (*Homo Sapiens*) in the resting state of the index finger: implications for pointing. *Journal of Comparative Psychology* 108: 134–139.

——and Eddy, T. J. (1996). What young chimpanzees know about seeing. *Monographs of the Society for Research in Child Development* 61(3, Serial No. 247).

——and Vonk, J. (2003). Chimpanzee minds: suspiciously human? *Trends in Cognitive Sciences* 7: 157–160.

——Bering, J. M., and Giambrone, S. (2003). Chimpanzee "pointing": another error of the argument by analogy? In S. Kita (ed.), *Pointing: where language, culture, and cognition meet*. Hillsdale, NJ: Erlbaum, 35–68.

Premack, D. (1983). The codes of man and beasts. *Behavioral and Brain Sciences* 6: 125–167.

——(1990a). The infant's theory of self-propelled objects. *Cognition* 36: 1–16.

——(1990b). Words: what are they, and do animals have them? *Cognition* 37: 197–212.

——(2004). Is language the key to human intelligence? *Science* 303: 318–320.

Putnam, H. (1988). *Representation and reality*. Cambridge, MA: MIT Press.

Quine, W. v. O. (1960). *Word and object*. Cambridge, MA: MIT Press.

Rabiner, L. R. and Schafer, R. W. (1978). *Digital processing of speech signals*. Englewood Cliffs, NJ: Prentice-Hall.

Racine, T. P. (2004). Wittgenstein's internalistic logic and children's theories of mind. In J. I. M. Carpendale and U. Müller (eds.), *Social interaction and the development of knowledge*. Mahwah, NJ: Lawrence Erlbaum Associates, 257–276.

——(2005). The role of shared practice in the origins of joint attention and pointing. Unpub. PhD thesis: Simon Fraser University.

——and Carpendale, J. I. M. (2007a). The embodiment of mental states. In W. F. Overton, U. Mueller, and J. Newman (eds.), *Body in mind, mind in body: developmental perspectives on embodiment and consciousness*. Mahwah, NJ: Erlbaum, 159–190.

————(2007b). Shared practices, understanding, language and joint attention. *British Journal of Developmental Psychology* 25: 45–54.

————(2007c). The role of shared practice in joint attention. *British Journal of Developmental Psychology* 25: 3–25.

——Leavens, D. A., Susswein, N., and Wereha, T. (2008). Conceptual and methodological issues in the investigation of primate intersubjectivity. In F. Morganti, A. Carassa, and G. Riva (eds.), *Enacting intersubjectivity: a cognitive and social perspective to the study of interactions*. Amsterdam: IOS Press, 65–79.

Ragir, S. (1994). Vocal/auditory cognitive mapping, shared meaning and consciousness. In J. Wind, A. Jonker, R. Allott, and L. Rolfe (eds.), *Studies in language origins* (Vol. 3). Amsterdam: John Benjamins, 205–219.

—— (2002). Constraints on communities with indigenous sign languages: clues to the dynamics of language genesis. In A. Wray (ed.), *The transitions to language*. Cambridge: Cambridge University Press, 272–294.

—— Dividze, N., Levine, A., Rice, D., and Savage-Rumbaugh, E. S. (2005). Playing with meaning: the development of play in infant bonobo chimpanzees (18–48 months old) in a human-bonobo colony. Association of Physical Anthropology Meetings, 6–9 April, Hilton Hotel, Milwaukee Wisconsin.

Rakison, D. H. and Butterworth, G. E. (1998) Infants' use of object parts in early categorization. *Developmental Psychology* 34: 49–62.

Repp, B. H. (2006). Musical synchronization. In E. Altenmuller, M. Wiesendanger, and J. Kesserling (eds.), *Music, motor control, and the brain*. Oxford: Oxford University Press, 55–76.

Reuland, E. (2005a). On the evolution and genesis of language: the force of imagination. *Lingue e Linguaggio* 1: 81–110.

—— (2005b.) Binding conditions: how are they derived? In S. Müller (ed.), *Proceedings of the HPSG05 Conference Department of Informatics, University of Lisbon*. Stanford: CSLI Publications http://cslipublications. stanford. edu/

—— (forthcoming). *Anaphora and language design*. Cambridge, MA: MIT Press.

—— (in press). Anaphoric dependencies: how are they encoded? Towards a derivation-based typology. In E. König and V. Gast (eds.), *Reciprocals and reflexives–cross-linguistic and theoretical explorations*. Berlin: Mouton de Gruyter.

Reynolds, Peter C. (1981). *On the evolution of human behavior: the argument from animals to man*. Berkeley: University of California Press.

Richards, P. (2007). The emotions at war: a musicological approach to understanding atrocity in Sierra Leone. In P. 6, S. Radstone, C. Squire, and A. Treacher (eds.), *Public emotions*. Basingstoke: Palgrave-Macmillan, 62–84.

Richardson, D. C., Dale, R., and Kirkham, N. Z. (2006). The art of conversation is coordination: common ground and the coupling of eye movements during dialogue. *Psychological Science* 18(5): 407–413.

Richerson, P. and Boyd, R. (1997). The evolution of human ultra-sociality. In I. Eibl-Eibisfeldt and F. Salter (eds.), *Ideology, warfare, and indoctrinability*. Oxford: Berghahn Books, 71–95.

—— —— (2005). *Not by genes alone*. Chicago: Chicago University Press.

Richman, B. (1987). Rhythm and melody in gelada vocal exchanges. *Primates* 28: 199–223.

Rickard, N. S., Toukhsati, S. R., and Field, S. E. (2005). The effect of music on cognitive performance: insight from neurobiological and animal studies. *Behavioral and Cognitive Neuroscience Review* 4(4): 235–261.

Rijsdijk, F. V., Vernon, P. A., and Boomsma, D. I. (2002). Application of hierarchical genetic models to raven and WAIS subtests: a Dutch twin study. *Behavior Genetics* 32: 199–210.

Rissanen, M. (2006). Talk given at International Conference on English Historical Linguistics, Madison, WI, August 2006.

Rizzolatti, G. and Arbib, M. A. (1998) Language within our grasp. *Trends in Neuroscience* 21: 188–194.

Roberts, I. and Roussou, A. (2003). *Syntactic change*. Cambridge: Cambridge University Press.

Roberts, M. B. and Parfitt, S. A. (1999). *Boxgrove, A Middle Pleistocene Hominid Site at Eartham Quarry, Boxgrove, West Sussex*. London: English Heritage Archaeological Report no. 17.

Robertson, H. A. (1992). Immediate-early genes, neuronal plasticity, and memory. *Biochemistry and Cell Biology* 70: 729–737.

Rolfe, L. (1996). Theoretical stages in the prehistory of grammar. In A. Lock and C. R. Peters (eds.), *Handbook of human symbolic evolution*. Hove: Blackwell, 776–792.

Romaine, S. (1982). *Socio-historical linguistics*. Cambridge: Cambridge University Press.

Rosch, E. (1975). Cognitive representations of semantic categories. *Journal of Experimental Psychology: General* 104: 192–233.

Ross, C. F. (2000). Into the light: the origin of Anthropoidea. *Annual Review of Anthropology* 29: 147–194.

Rumbaugh, D. M. (ed.) (1977). *Language learning by a chimpanzee: the Lana Project*. New York: Academic Press.

Rushworth, M. F. S., Paus, T., and Sipila, P. K. (2001). Attentional systems and the organization of the human parietal cortex. *Journal of Neuroscience* 21(14): 5262–5371.

Rutter, M., Anderson-Wood, L., Beckett, C., Bredenkamp, D., Castle, J., Groothues, C., Kreppner, J., Keaveney, L., Lord, C., O'Connor, T. G., and the English and Romanian Adoptees (ERA) Study Team. (1999). Quasi-Autistic Patterns following Severe Early Global Privation. *Journal of Child Psychology* 40: 537–549.

Rydén, M. (1983). The emergence of *who* as relativizer. *Studia Linguistica* 37: 126–134.

Satchell, J. E. (1983). *Earthworm ecology: from Darwin to vermiculture*. London: Chapman and Hall.

Saussure, F. de (1916). *Cours de linguistique générale*, ed. Charles Bally and Albert Sechehaye with Albert Riedlinger. Paris and Lausanne: Payot.

Savage-Rumbaugh, E. S. (1984). *Pan Paniscus* and *Pan Troglodytes*: contrast in preverbal communicative competence. In R. L. Susman (ed.), *The pygmy chimpanzee: evolutionary biology and behavior*. New York: Plenum Press, 395–413.

Savage-Rumbaugh, E. S. (1986). *Ape language: from conditioned response to symbol.* New York: Columbia University Press.

—— Shanker, S. G., and Taylor, T. J. (1998). *Apes, language and the human mind.* New York: Oxford University Press.

—— Wilkerson, B., and Bakeman, R. (1977). Spontaneous gestural communication among conspecifics in the pygmy chimpanzee (*Pan paniscus*). In G. Bourne (ed.), *Progress in ape research.* New York: Academic Press, 97–116.

—— McDonald, K., Sevcic, R. A., Hopkins, W. D., and Rupert, E. (1986). Spontaneous symbol acquisition and communicative use by pygmy chimpanzees (*Pan Paniscus*). *Journal of Experimental Psychology: General* 115: 211–235.

—— Murphy, J., Sevcic, R. A., Brakke, K. E., Williams, S. L., and Rumbaugh, D. M. (1993). Language comprehension in ape and child. *Monographs of the Society for Research in Child Development* 58: 1–256.

Schrago, C. G. and Russo, C. A. M. (2003). Timing the origin of New World monkeys. *Molecular Biology and Evolution* 20: 1620–1625.

Schwilk, D. W. and Ackerly, D. D. (2001). Flammability and serotiny as strategies: correlated evolution in pines. *Oikos*, 94: 326–336.

Semendeferi, K., Lu, A., Schenker, N., and Damasio, H. (2002). Humans and great apes share a large frontal cortex. *Nature Neuroscience* 5: 272–276.

Seyfarth, R. M. (2004). Continuities in vocal communication argue against a gestural origin of language (comment on "From monkey-like action recognition to human language: an evolutionary framework for neurolinguistics" by M. Arbib). *Behavioral and Brain Sciences* 24: 104–124.

—— and Cheney, D. L. (2003). Signalers and receivers in animal communication. *Annual Review of Psychology* 54: 145–173.

—— —— and Marler, P. (1980). Vervet monkey alarm calls: semantic communication in a free-ranging primate. *Animal Behaviour* 28: 1070–1094.

Shah, P. and Miyake, A. (eds.) (2005). *The Cambridge handbook of visuospatial thinking.* New York: Cambridge University Press.

Shelton, J. R. and Caramazza, A. (1999). Deficits in lexical and semantic processing: implications for models of normal language. *Psychonomic Bulletin and Review* 6: 5–27.

Shennan, S. (2002). *Genes, memes and human history.* London: Thames and Hudson.

Shepard, R. N. (1997). The genetic basis of human scientific knowledge. In G. R. Bock and G. Cardew (eds.), *Characterizing human psychological adaptations.* London: Wiley and Sons, 4–13.

Shikata, E., Hamzei, F., Glauche, V., Koch, M., Weiller, C., Binkofski, F., and Büchel, C. (2003). Functional properties and interaction of the anterior and posterior intraparietal areas in humans. *European Journal of Neuroscience* 17(5): 1105–1110.

Shockley, K., Santana, M.-V., and Fowler, C. A. (2003). Mutual interpersonal postural constraints are involved in cooperative conversation. *Journal of Experimental Psychology: Human Perception and Performance* 29(2): 326–332.

Silver, M. and Di Paolo, E. (2006). Spatial effects favour the evolution of niche construction. *Theoretical Population Biology* 20: 387–400.

Simpson, A. and Wu, X.-Z. Z. (2002). From D to T—determiner incorporation and the creation of tense. *Journal of East Asian Linguistics* 11: 169–202.

Simpson, M. (1973). Social grooming of male chimpanzees. In J. Crook and R. P. Michael (eds.), *Comparative ecology and behaviour of primates*. London: Academic Press, 411–505.

Sinha, C. (1999). Grounding, mapping and acts of meaning. In T. Janssen and G. Redeker (eds.), *Cognitive linguistics: foundations, scope and methodology*. New York: De Gruyter, 223–255.

——(2005). Biology, culture and the emergence and elaboration of symbolization. In A. P. Saleemi, B. Ocke-Schwen, and A. Gjedde (eds.), *In search of a language for the mind-brain: can the multiple perspectives be unified?* Aarhus: Aarhus University Press, 311–335.

Siviy, S. M. (1998). Neurobiological substrates of play behavior: glimpses into the structure and function of mammalian playfulness. In M. Bekoff and J. A. Byers (eds.), *Animal play: evolutionary, comparative, and ecological perspectives*. Cambridge: Cambridge University Press, 272–294.

Skeat, W. (ed.) (1881–7). *The Gospel according to St. Matthew, St. Mark, St. Luke and St. John*. Cambridge. Repr. Darmstadt: Wissenschaftliche Buchgesellschaft.

Slobin, M. (1993). *Subcultural sounds: micromusics of the West*. Hanover, CT: Wesleyan University Press.

Sloboda, J. A., O Neill, S. A., and Ivaldi, A. (2001). Functions of music in everyday life: an exploratory study using the Experience Sampling Method. *Musicae Scientiae* 5(1): 9–32.

Small, C. (1998). *Musicking*. London: Wesleyan University Press.

Smith, A. D. M. (2005). Mutual exclusivity: communicative success despite conceptual divergence. In M. O. Tallerman (ed.), *Language origins: perspectives on evolution*. Oxford: Oxford University Press, 372–388.

Snowdon, C. T. (2004). Social processes in the evolution of complex cognition and communication. In D. K. Oller and U. Griebel (eds.), *Evolution of communication systems: a comparative approach*. Cambridge, MA: MIT Press, 131–150.

——Brown, C. H., and Petersen, M. R. (1982). *Primate communication*. Cambridge: Cambridge University Press.

Sole, R. and Goodwin, B. (2000). *Signs of life: how complexity pervades biology*. New York: Basic Books.

Spelke, E. S. (1994). Initial knowledge: six suggestions. *Cognition* 50: 431–445.

Sperber, D. and Wilson, D. (1995). *Relevance: communication and cognition*. Oxford: Blackwell.

Stanford, C. B. (1999). *The hunting apes: meat eating and the origins of human behavior.* Princeton: Princeton University Press.

Steels, L. (1995). A self-organizing spatial vocabulary. *Artificial Life* 2(3): 319–332.

—— (2005). The emergence and evolution of linguistic structure: from lexical to grammatical communication systems. *Connection Science* 17(3–4): 213–230.

—— and de Beule, J. (2006). Unify and merge in fluid construction grammar. In C. Lyon, L. Nehaniv, and A. Cangelosi (eds.), *Emergence and evolution of linguistic communication. Lecture notes in Computer Science.* Berlin: Springer-Verlag, 197–223.

—— and Kaplan, F. (2001). AIBO's first words: the social learning of language and meaning. *Evolution of Communication* 4(1): 3–32.

—— and Loetzsch, M. (2008). Perspective alignment in spatial language. In K. Coventry, T. Tenbrink, and A. Bateman (eds.), *Spatial language and dialogue.* Oxford: Oxford University Press.

Stevens, C. (2004). Cross-cultural studies of musical pitch and time. *Acoustics, Science and Technology* 25(6): 433–438.

Stiller, J. and Dunbar, R. I. M. (2007). Perspective-taking and social network size in humans. *Social Networks* 29: 93–104.

—— Nettle, D., and Dunbar, R. I. M. (2004). The small world of Shakespeare's plays. *Human Nature* 14: 397–408.

Stinchcombe, J. R. and Schmitt, J. (2006). Ecosystem engineers as selective agents: the effects of leaf litter on the emergence time and early growth in *Impatiens Capensis. Ecosystem letters* 9: 258–270.

Stiner, M. and Kuhn, S. (2007). What's a mother to do? A hypothesis about the division of labor and modern human origins. *Current Anthropology* 47: 6.

Stringer, C. B. and Gamble, C. (1993). *In search of the Neanderthals.* London: Thames and Hudson.

Struhsaker, T. T. (1967). Auditory communication among vervet monkeys (Cercopithecus aethiops). In S. A. Altmann (ed.), *Social communication among primates.* Chicago: Chicago University Press, 281–324.

—— (1997). *Ecology of an African rain forest.* Gainesville, FL: University Presses of Florida.

Studdert-Kennedy, M. (2005). How did language go discrete? In M. Tallerman (ed.), *Language origins: perspectives on evolution.* Oxford: Oxford University Press, 48–67.

Stylianou, M. (2007). Does executive function training improve mentalising ability? Unpub. PhD thesis, University of Liverpool.

Sugarman, S. (1984). The development of preverbal communication: its contribution and limits in promoting the development of language. In R. L. Scheifelbush and J. Pickar (eds.),*The acquisition of communicative competence.* Baltimore: University Park Press, 23–67.

Sugiyama, M. S. (2001). Food, foragers, and folklore: the role of narrative in human subsistence. *Evolution and Human Behavior* 22: 221–240.

Susswein, N. and Racine, T. P. (2008). Sharing mental states: causal and definitional issues in intersubjectivity. In J. Zlatev, T. P. Racine, C. Sinha, and E. Itkonen (eds.), *The shared mind: perspectives on intersubjectivity.* Amsterdam: John Benjamins, 141–162.

————— (in presss). Wittgenstein and not-just-in-the-head cognition. *New Ideas in Psychology.*

Swarbrick, R. (2000). A social cognitive model of paranoid delusions. Unpub. PhD thesis, University of Manchester.

Számadó, S. and Szathmáry, E. (2006). Selective scenarios for the emergence of natural language. *Trends in Ecology and Evolution* 21(10): 555–561.

Takach, S. G. and Lindtvedt, K. (2005). *TakLin subtrak video coding program* (Version 1. 92) [Computer Software]. New York: Staten Island.

Tallerman, M. O. (ed.) (2005). *Language origins: perspectives on evolution.* Oxford: Oxford University Press.

Tanner, J. E. (2004). Gestural phrases and exchanges by a pair of zoo-living lowland gorillas. *Gesture* 4: 1–24.

—— and Byrne, R. (1996). Representation of action through iconic gesture in a captive lowland gorilla. *Current Anthropology* 37: 162–173.

—— Patterson, F. G., and Byrne, R. W. (2006). The development of spontaneous gestures in zoo-living gorillas and sign-taught gorillas: from action and location to object representation. *Journal of Developmental Processes* 1: 69–102.

Tauli, V. (1958). *The structural tendencies of languages.* Helsinki.

Taylor, T. J. (1997). *Theorizing language.* Amsterdam: Pergamon.

Terrace, H. S. (1979). *Nim.* New York: Washington Square Press.

Thibault, P. J. (2005). *Agency and consciousness in discourse: self–other dynamics as a complex system.* London: Continuum International.

Thieme, H. (1997). Lower Palaeolithic hunting spears from Germany. *Nature* 385: 807–810.

Thomas, D. A. (1995). *Music and the origins of language: theories from the French enlightenment.* Cambridge: Cambridge University Press.

Thompson, J. L., Krovitz, G. E., and Nelson, A. J. (eds.) (2003). *Patterns of growth and development in the Genus Homo.* Cambridge: Cambridge University Press.

Thompson, J. N. (1994). *The coevolutionary process.* Chicago: University of Chicago Press.

Thorpe, B. (1861). *Anglo-Saxon Chronicle I and II.* London: Longman.

Thorpe, W. H. (1958). The learning of song patterns by birds, with special reference to the Chaffinch, *Fringilla coelebs. Ibis* 100: 535–570.

Titon, J. T. (ed.) (1996). *Worlds of music: an introduction to the music of the world's peoples.* New York: Schirmer Books.

Titze, I. R. (1994). *Principles of voice production.* Englewood Cliffs, NJ: Prentice Hall.

Tomasello, M. (1994). The question of chimpanzee culture. In R. W. Wrangham, W. C. McGrew, F. B. M. de Waal, and P. G. Heltne (eds.), *Chimpanzee cultures.* Cambridge, MA: Harvard University Press, 301–317.

——(1995). Joint attention as social cognition. In C. Moore and P. J. Dunham (eds.), *Joint attention: its origins and role in development.* Hillsdale, NJ: Lawrence Erlbaum Associates, 103–130.

——(1999). *The cultural origins of human cognition.* Cambridge, MA: Harvard University Press.

——(2003). *Constructing a language.* Cambridge, MA: Harvard University Press.

——(2006). Why don't apes point? In N. Enfield and S. C. Levinson (eds.), *Roots of human sociality: culture, cognition and interaction.* Oxford: Berg, 506–524.

——and Call, J. (1997). *Primate cognition.* New York: Oxford University Press.

————(2007). *The gestural communication of monkeys and apes.* Mahwah, NJ: Lawrence Erlbaum Associates.

——and Camaioni, L. (1997). A comparison of the gestural communication of apes and human infants. *Human Development* 40: 7–24.

——and Carpenter, M. (2005). The emergence of social cognition in three young chimpanzees. *Monographs of the Society for Research in Child Development* 70: Serial No. 279.

——Call, J., and Hare, B. (2003a). Chimpanzees understand psychological states–the question is which ones and to what extent. *Trends in Cognitive Sciences* 7: 153–156.

————(2003b). Chimpanzees versus humans: it's not that simple. *Trends in Cognitive Sciences* 7: 239–240.

——Call, J., Nagell, K., Olguin, K., and Carpenter, M. (1994). The learning and use of gestural signals by young chimpanzees: a trans-generational study. *Primates* 35: 137–154.

——Carpenter, M., Call, J., Behne, T., and Moll, H. (2005). Understanding and sharing intentions: the origins of cultural cognition. *Behavioral and Brain Sciences* 28(5): 675–691.

——George, B. L., Kruger, A. C., Farrar, M. J., and Evans, A. (1985). The development of gestural communication in young chimpanzees. *Journal of Human Evolution* 14: 175–186.

——Call, J., Warren, J., Frost, T., Carpenter, M., and Nagell, K. (1997). The ontogeny of chimpanzee gestural signals. In S. Wilcox, B. King, and L. Steels (eds.), *Evolution of communication.* Amsterdam/Philadelphia: John Benjamins, 224–259.

Toth, N. and Schick, K. (1993). Early stone industries and inferences regarding language and cognition. In K. R. Gibson and T. Ingold (eds.), *Tools, language and cognition in human evolution.* Cambridge: Cambridge University Press, 346–362.

Traugott, E. (2004). Exaptation and grammaticalization. In M. Akimoto (ed.), *Linguistic studies based on Corpora.* Tokyo: Hituzi Syobo, 133–56.

—— and Heine, B. (1991). *Approaches to grammaticalization. Volumes I and II.* Amsterdam: John Benjamins.

Trehub, S. E. (2003). Musical predispositions in infancy: an update. In I. Peretz and R. Zatorre (eds.), *The cognitive neuroscience of music.* Oxford: Oxford University Press, 3–20.

Trevarthen, C. (1999/2000). Musicality and the intrinsic motive pulse: evidence from human psychobiology and infant communication. *Musicae Scientiae*, special issue: *Rhythm, musical narrative, and the origins of human communication*: 155–215.

Trinkaus, E. (1995). Neanderthal mortality patterns. *Journal of Archaeological Science* 22: 121–142.

Trivers, R. L. (1971). The evolution of reciprocal altruism. *Quarterly Review of Biology* 46: 35–57.

Turnbull, C. M. (1965). *Wayward servants: the two worlds of the African pygmies.* New York: Natural History Press.

Turner, J. S. (2000). *The extended organism: the physiology of animal-built structures.* Cambridge, MA: Harvard University Press.

—— (2007). *The tinkerer's accomplice: how design emerges from life itself.* Cambridge, MA: Harvard University Press.

Turq, A. (1992). Raw material and technological studies of the Quina Mousterian in the Perigord. In H. Dibble and P. Mellars (eds.), *The Middle Palaeolithic: adaptation, behaviour and variability.* Philadelphia: The University Museum, University of Pennsylvania, 75–85.

Ueno, A. (2006). Food sharing and referencing behavior in chimpanzee mother and infant. In T. Matsuzawa, M. Tomonaga, and M. Tanaka (eds.), *Cognitive development in chimpanzees.* Tokyo: Springer-Verlag, 172–181.

Ullman, M. (2004). Contributions of neural memory circuits to language: the declarative/procedural model. *Cognition* 92: 231–270.

van Gelderen, E. (2004). *Grammaticalization as economy.* Amsterdam: John Benjamins.

van Hooff, J. A. R. A. M. (1973). A structural analysis of the social behaviour of a semi-captive group of chimpanzees. In M. von Cranach and I. Vine (eds.), *Social communication and movement, studies of interaction and expression in man and chimpanzee.* London and New York: Academic Press, 75–162.

van Lawick-Goodall, J. (1968a). A preliminary report on expressive movements and communication in the Gombe stream chimpanzees. In P. C. Jay (ed.), *Primates: studies in adaptation and variability.* New York: Holt, Rinehart, and Winston, 313–374.

van Lawick-Goodall, J. (1968b). The behavior of free-ranging chimpanzees in the Gombe Stream Reserve. *Animal Behaviour Monographs* 1: 161–311.

van Schaik, C. P. and Dunbar, R. I. M. (1990). The evolution of monogamy in large primates: a new hypothesis and some critical tests. *Behaviour* 115: 30–62.

—— Ancrenaz, M., Borgen, G., Galdikas, B., Knott, C., Singleton, I., Suzuki, A., Utami, S. S., and Merrill, M. (2003). Orangutan cultures and the evolution of material culture. *Science* 299: 102–105.

Vanderschuren, L. J., Niesink, R., and Van Ree, J. M. (1997). The neurobiology of social play behavior in rats. *Neuroscience and Biobehavioral Reviews* 21: 309–326.

Vauclair, J. (1996). *Animal cognition*. Cambridge, MA: Harvard University Press.

Veà, J. J. and Sabater-Pi, J. (1998). Spontaneous pointing behaviour in the wild pygmy chimpanzee (*Pan paniscus*). *Folia Primatologica* 69: 289–290.

Vigliocco, G. and Hartsuiker, R. (2002). The interplay of meaning, sound, and syntax in sentence production. *Psychological Bulletin* 128: 442–472.

—— and Kita, S. (2006). Language-specific properties of the lexicon: implications for learning and processing. *Language and Cognitive Processes* 21: 790–816.

Voight, B. F., Kudaravalli, S., Wen, X., and Pritchard, J. K. (2006) A map of recent position selection in the human genome. *PLoS Biology* 4(3): e72.

Waddington, C. H. (1969). Paradigm for an evolutionary process. In C. H. Waddington (ed.), *Towards a theoretical biology*. Edinburgh: Edinburgh University Press, 106–128.

Wakefield, J. L. and Wilkins, W. K. (2007) Conceptual space. In S. Karimi, V. Samiian, and W. K. Wilkins (eds.), *Phrasal and clausal architecture: syntactic derivation and interpretation*. Amsterdam: John Benjamins.

Wallman, J. (1992). *Aping language*. Cambridge: Cambridge University Press.

Walsh, S., Bramblett, C. A., and Alford. P. L. (1982). A vocabulary of abnormal behaviors in restrictively reared chimpanzees. *American Journal of Primatology* 3: 315–319.

Wang, E. and Steels, L. (2008). Self-interested agents can bootstrap symbolic communication if they can punish cheaters. Proceedings of the 7th Evolution of Language Conference, Barcelona.

—— Kodama, G., Baldi, P., and Moyzis, R. K. (2006). Global landscape of recent inferred Darwinian selection for *Homo sapiens*. *Proceedings of the National Academy of Sciences* 103: 135–140.

Warrington, E. K. and McCarthy, R. (1987). Categories of knowledge: further fractionations and an attempted integration. *Brain* 110: 1273–1296.

Watrous, R. L. (1991). Current status of Peterson-Barney vowel formant data. *Journal of the Acoustical Society of America* 89(5): 2459–2460.

Watt, R. J. and Ash, R. L. (1998). A psychological investigation of meaning in music. *Musicae Scientiae* 2(1): 33–54.

Watts, D. P. (2000a). Grooming between male chimpanzees at Ngogo, Kibale National Park, Uganda. II. Male rank and priority of access to partners. *International Journal of Primatology* 21: 211–238.

—— (2000b). Grooming between male chimpanzees at Ngogo, Kibale National Park, Uganda. I. Partner number and diversity and reciprocity. *International Journal of Primatology* 21: 189–210.

Waxman, S. R. (1994). The development of an appreciation of specific linkages between linguistic and conceptual organization. *Lingua* 92: 229–257.

Wennerstrom, A. (2001). *The music of everyday speech: prosody and discourse analysis.* Oxford: Oxford University Press.

Werner, H. and Kaplan, B. (1963). *Symbol formation: an organismic-developmental approach to language and the expression of thought.* New York: Wiley and Sons.

Whiten, A. (1998). Imitation of the sequential structure of actions by chimpanzees (*Pan troglodytes*). *Journal of Comparative Psychology* 112: 270–281.

—— (2000). Chimpanzee cognition and the question of mental re-representation. In D. Sperber (ed.), *Metarepresentation: a multidisciplinary perspective.* Oxford: Oxford University Press, 139–167.

—— and Ham, R. (1992). On the nature and evolution of imitation in the animal kingdom: reappraisal of a century of research. *Advances in the Study of Behaviour* 21: 239–283.

—— Horner, V., Litchfield, C., and Marshall-Pescini, S. (2004). How do apes ape? *Learning and Behaviour* 32: 36–52.

—— Custance, D. M., Gomez, J., Teixidor, P., and Bard, K. (1996). Imitative learning of artificial fruit processing in children (*Homo sapiens*) and chimpanzees (*Pan troglodytes*). *Journal of Comparative Psychology* 110: 3–14.

—— Goodall, A. G., McGrew, W. C., Nishida, T., Reynolds, V., Sugiyama, Y., Tutin, C. E. G., Wrangham, R. W., and Boesch, C. (2001). Charting cultural variation in chimpanzees. *Behaviour* 138: 1489–1525.

—— Goodall, J., McGrew, W. C., Nishida, T., Reynolds, V., Sugiyama, Y., Tutin, C. E. G., Wrangham, R. W., and Boesch, C. (1999). Cultures in chimpanzees. *Nature* 399: 682–685.

Wilkins, W. K. (2005). Anatomy matters. *The Linguistic Review* 22(2–4): 271–288.

—— (2007). Layers, mosaic pieces, and tiers. *The Linguistic Review* 24(4): 475–484.

—— and Wakefield, J. L. (1995). Brain evolution and neurolinguistic preconditions. *Behavioral and Brain Sciences* 18(1): 161–182.

Wilson, D. and Wharton, T. (2006). Relevance and prosody. *Journal of Pragmatics* 38(10): 1559–1579.

Wilson, M. and Wilson, T. (2005). An oscillator model of turn-taking. *Psychonomic Bulletin and Review* 12(6): 957–968.

Wilson, S. J. and Pressing, J. (1999). Neuropsychological assessment and modeling of musical deficits. *MusicMedicine* 3: 47–74.

Wittgenstein, L. (1958). *Philosophical investigations* (3rd edn.). Englewood Cliffs, NJ: Prentice-Hall.

Woodburn, J. (1980). Hunters and gatherers today and reconstruction of the past. In E. Gellner (ed.), *Soviet and Western Anthropology.* London: Duckworth, 95–117.

Woodruff, G. and Premack, D. (1979). Intentional communication in the chimpanzee: the development of deception. *Cognition* 7: 333–362.

Woolley, J. D., Boerger, E. A., and Markman, A. B. (2004). A visit from the candy witch: factors influencing children's belief in a novel fantastical being. *Developmental Science* 7: 456–464.

Worden, R. (1996). Primate social intelligence. *Cognitive Science* 20: 579–616.

—— (1998). The evolution of language from social intelligence. In J. R. Hurford, M. Studdert-Kennedy, and C. Knight (eds.), *Approaches to the evolution of language: social and cognitive bases.* Cambridge: Cambridge University Press, 148–166.

Wrangham, R. W., Jones, J. H., Laden, G., Pilbeam, D., and Conklin-Brittain, N. L. (1999). The raw and the stolen. Cooking and the ecology of human origins. *Current Anthropology* 40: 567–594.

Wray, A. (1998). Protolanguage as a holistic system for social interaction. *Language and Communication* 18: 47–67.

—— (2000). Holistic utterances in protolanguage: the link from primates to humans. In C. Knight, M. Studdert-Kennedy, and J. R. Hurford (eds.), *The evolutionary emergence of language: social function and the origins of linguistic form.* Cambridge: Cambridge University Press, 285–302.

—— (2002). Dual processing in protolanguage: performance without competence. In A. Wray (ed.), *The transition to language.* Oxford: Oxford University Press, 113–137.

Wright, J. P. and Jones, C. G. (2006). The concept of organisms as ecosystem engineers ten years on: progress, limitations and challenges. *BioScience* 3: 203–209.

Wu, Z. (2004). *Grammaticalization and language change in Chinese.* London: RoutledgeCurzon.

Wynn, T. (1995). Handaxe enigmas. *World Archaeology* 27: 10–23.

Xu, F. (2002). The role of language in acquiring object kind concepts in infancy. *Cognition* 85: 223–250.

—— and Carey, S. (1996). Infants' metaphysics: the case of numerical identity. *Cognitive Psychology* 30: 111–153.

Yallop, C. and Clark, J. (1990). *An introduction to phonetics and phonology.* Oxford: Basil Blackwell.

Yerkes, R. M. (1943). *Chimpanzees: a laboratory colony.* New Haven: Yale University Press.

Zhang, J., Harbottle, G., Wang, C., and Kong, Z. (1999). Oldest playable musical instruments found at Jiahu early Neolithic site in China. *Nature* 401: 366–368.

Zhou, W.-X., Sornette, D., Hill, R. A., and Dunbar, R. I. M. (2005). Discrete hierarchical organization of social group sizes. *Proceedings of the Royal Society, London* 272B: 439–444.

Zlatev, J., Racine, T. P., Sinha, C., and Itkonen, E. (2008). Intersubjectivity: what makes us human? In J. Zlatev, T. P Racine, C. Sinha, and E. Itkonen (eds.), *The shared mind: perspectives on intersubjectivity*. Amsterdam: Benjamins, 1–14.

Zuberbühler, K. (2000). Referential labelling in Diana monkeys. *Animal Behaviour* 59: 917–927.

—— (2001). Predator-specific alarm calls in Campbell's monkeys, *Cercopithecus campbelli*. *Behavioral Ecology and Sociobiology* 50: 414–422.

—— (2002). A syntactic rule in forest monkey communication. *Animal Behaviour* 63: 293–299.

—— (2005). The phylogenetic roots of language—evidence from primate communication and cognition. *Current Directions in Psychological Science* 14: 126–130.

Index

Page numbers in **bold** indicate a whole chapter on the subject

Contents: *The Cradle of Language*

STUDIES IN THE EVOLUTION OF LANGUAGE

General Editors
Kathleen R. Gibson, *University of Texas at Houston,*
and James R. Hurford, *University of Edinburgh*

IN PREPARATION

Darwinian Linguistics
Evolution and the Logic of Linguistic Theory
Stephen R. Anderson

The Evolution of Morphology
Andrew Carstairs McCarthy

The Evolution of Linguistic Form
Language in the Light of Evolution 2
James R. Hurford

Biolinguistic Approaches to Language Evolution
Edited by Anna Maria di Sciullo and Cedtric Boeckx

TO BE PUBLISHED IN ASSOCIATION WITH THE SERIES

The Oxford Handbook of Language Evolution
edited by Maggie Tallerman and Kathleen R. Gibson

PUBLISHED IN ASSOCIATION WITH THE SERIES

Language Diversity
Daniel Nettle

Function, Selection, and Innateness
The Emergence of Language Universals
Simon Kirby

The Origins of Complex Language
An Inquiry into the Evolutionary Beginnings of Sentences, Syllables, and Truth
Andrew Carstairs McCarthy